DATE DUE

PRINTED IN U.S.A.

THE JUSTICES
OF THE
UNITED STATES
SUPREME COURT

•

THEIR LIVES
AND MAJOR OPINIONS

THE JUSTICES
OF THE
UNITED STATES
SUPREME COURT

•

THEIR LIVES
AND MAJOR OPINIONS

Volume
V

Edited by Leon Friedman & Fred L. Israel

CHELSEA HOUSE PUBLISHERS

New York • Philadelphia

CHELSEA HOUSE PUBLISHERS

EDITORIAL DIRECTOR: Richard Rennert
EXECUTIVE MANAGING EDITOR: Karyn Gullen Browne
COPY CHIEF: Robin James
PICTURE EDITOR: Adrian G. Allen
CREATIVE DIRECTOR: Robert Mitchell
ART DIRECTOR: Joan Ferrigno
PRODUCTION MANAGER: Sallye Scott

The Justices of the United States Supreme Court: Their Lives and Major Opinions

SENIOR EDITOR: Jake Goldberg
COPY EDITORS: Amy Handy, Apple Kover, William Kravitz
EDITORIAL ASSISTANT: Scott D. Briggs
PRODUCTION ASSISTANT: Laura Morelli
PICTURE RESEARCHER: Sandy Jones

1 3 5 7 9 8 6 4 2

Library of Congress Cataloging-in-Publication Data
    The Justices of the United States Supreme Court: Their Lives and Major
    Opinions / Leon Friedman & Fred L. Israel, editors.
    Rev. ed. of: The Justices of the United States Supreme Court, 1789–1978. 1st.
    pbk. ed. 1980.
    p. cm.—
    Includes bibliographical references and index.
    ISBN 0-7910-1377-4.
    1. United States Supreme Court—Biography. 2. Judges—United States—
    Biography. I. Friedman, Leon. II. Israel, Fred L. III. Justices of the United
    States Supreme Court.
KF8744.F75 1995   94-41711
347.73'2634—dc20   CIP
                                                                  [B]
[347.3073534]   [B]

All photographs from the collection of the Supreme Court of the United States.

Contents

Volume V

About the Editors and Contributors

<u>Volume V</u>

LEON FRIEDMAN is professor of law at Hofstra University Law School. He is the author of numerous books and articles on legal subjects and is the editor of *United States vs. Nixon: The President Before the Supreme Court*.

FRED L. ISRAEL is professor of American history at City College of New York. He is the editor of *Major American Peace Treaties of Modern History* and, with Arthur Schlesinger, Jr., is the editor of *History of American Presidential Elections*. For many years, Professor Israel has compiled the Gallup Polls into annual reference volumes.

ROY M. MERSKY is Hyder Centennial Professor of Law and director of research at the University of Texas at Austin Law School. He is the author of many articles on law and library science.

LOUIS H. POLLAK was Dean of the Yale Law School from 1965 to 1970 and from 1978 on served as a United States judge for the Eastern District. He is the author of *The Constitution and the Supreme Court: A Documentary History*.

•

ALBERT P. BLAUSTEIN was professor of law at Rutgers University Law School at Camden. He is the author of *Civil Rights and the American Negro* and editor of *Constitutions of the World*.

THEODORE EISENBERG is professor of law at the Cornell University Law School and is the author of *Civil Rights Legislation* and *Bankruptcy and Debtor-Creditor Law*.

EDWARD DE GRAZIA is professor of law at the Benjamin N. Cardozo School of Law of Yeshiva University. He is the author most recently of *Girls Lean Back Everywhere: The Law of Obscenity and the Assault of Genius*. (The author wishes to thank Yale Law School student Elizabeth de Grazia for the major contributions she made to the researching, drafting, and editing on David Hackett Souter.)

CHRISTOPHER HENRY practices law in New York City and is the author of two books on immigration law.

SUSAN N. HERMAN is professor of law at the Brooklyn Law School. She is the author of *Hiring Rights: A Practical Guide*.

ELIZABETH MENSCH and ALAN FREEMAN are professors of law at the School of Law of the State University of New York at Buffalo. They have collaborated on a number of works, including *The Politics of Virtue: Is Abortion Debatable?* (The authors would like to thank Jeff Powell and Michael McConnell for their help in preparing the essay on Sandra Day O'Connor.)

LEONARD ORLAND is professor of law at the University of Connecticut Law School. He is the author of numerous books on criminal law and correctional practice.

JEFFREY ROSEN is legal affairs editor of the *New Republic*.

William H. Rehnquist

☆ 1924–　　☆

APPOINTED BY RICHARD M. NIXON

YEARS ON COURT
1972–
APPOINTED CHIEF JUSTICE 1986

by
CHRIS HENRY

Villiam Hubbs Rehnquist joined the Supreme Court as an Associate Justice in 1972 and became its Chief Justice in 1986. Surviving bitter and prolonged confirmation battles in the Senate after both of his nominations, Rehnquist became arguably the most controversial person to have served on the Supreme Court during the twentieth century.

From the time his college studies were interrupted by World War II through his long and successful career as an attorney in private practice and until he joined the Nixon administration in 1969 as a senior official in the Justice Department, Rehnquist stayed, by inclination and choice, at the conservative end of the American political spectrum. Throughout his professional life he remained far removed, both ideologically and circumstantially, from the evolving liberal center of American political thought and judicial practice.

Rehnquist was one of a very few survivors of the debacle that Richard M. Nixon's presidency became; many of Rehnquist's peers and closest associates in that administration found themselves disgraced, disbarred, or even imprisoned as a result of acts committed, presumably, on behalf of the president. Senate liberals fought Nixon's nomination of Rehnquist to the Supreme Court with every established fact, rumor, and innuendo available to them in the autumn of 1971, but the president's popularity and power were such that Rehnquist could not be stopped. The political landscape was altered inexorably by the Watergate scandal in the next three years; in fact Rehnquist would be Nixon's last successful appointment to the Supreme Court.

In 1986 the same liberal forces in the Senate, joined by many moderates, waged a similar battle when President Ronald Reagan gambled on a Rehnquist nomination to replace retiring Chief Justice Warren Earl Burger. Most of the same arguments that had been used against Rehnquist a decade and a half before were resurrected. The confirmation battle was protracted, venomous, and clearly political. Once again, Rehnquist was victorious.

In the years that followed his confirmation as the nation's sixteenth Chief Justice, Rehnquist would redefine the role of the Supreme Court and reshape its identity. He would, without perceptibly altering his own ideological beliefs, move from being a lone dissenter in many instances to being at the intellectual center of a new Court, which he would forcefully lead to innumerable reversals and modifications of its most liberal decisions of the 1960's and 1970's.

William H. Rehnquist would prove to be one of the most tenacious and resilient Justices in the Court's history. Reviled by his detractors, his opinions often misinterpreted and eviscerated by the popular media, Rehnquist's new Supreme Court would, ironically, become as powerful and prominent in its quest for judicial minimalism as it had been in its activist heyday during the enthusiastic liberal leadership of Chief Justice Earl Warren and the tenure of such legendary liberal Justices as William O. Douglas. Clearly, it would be more effective and reliable in the eyes of Republican conservatives than it had been during the uninspired and unsuccessful attempt at conservative leadership by Rehnquist's predecessor, Chief Justice Burger.

According to his own statements and to the recollections of many longtime friends and associates, Justice Rehnquist's personality, political philosophy, and most crucially, his opinion of the role of the Supreme Court within the framework of the American political system have remained virtually unchanged since his days as a student at Stanford Law School, which he attended with classmates such as Associate Justice Sandra Day O'Connor in the early 1950's. Rehnquist stated often throughout his career that he did not equate personal growth with ideological change; it was this consistency of outlook which subjected him to the greatest challenges in his public life, but which also enabled him eventually to gain a firm control of the Supreme Court and alter its direction entirely in the late 1980's and early 1990's. Rehnquist himself never "evolved," nor did he desire to do so; rather, the Supreme Court evolved into an institution of his creation. At one time Rehnquist's opinions were dismissed as eccentric by many of his colleagues who formed the liberal center of the Supreme Court. Rehnquist's views were often so far removed from mainstream judicial thinking as to be relegated to a sort of juridical black hole comprised of Rehnquist and a handful of other conservative judges. From this position as an outsider Rehnquist maneuvered until the Court was his, and as his philosophies became those of the Court, he became its gravitational center.

William H. Rehnquist was born into an upper-middle-class family in Milwaukee, Wisconsin, on October 1, 1924. His parents raised him in an affluent suburb of Milwaukee called Shorewood. When he was nine years old, Rehnquist became seriously ill with pneumonia and whooping cough and had to remain at home from school for about three months. His physical activities were extremely limited during that time, but he was allowed to read as much as he liked. After going through all of the *Hardy Boys* books that were available at the local library, the precocious nine-year-old developed a taste for murder mysteries.

During his formative years Rehnquist had little contact with members of the racial and ethnic minority groups who tended to reside in the inner-city neighborhoods of Milwaukee. Rehnquist's mother was a skilled linguist, fluent in several languages, and a graduate of the University of Wisconsin; his father was a businessman who did well as a paper wholesaler. Both were staunch Republicans who believed in self-sufficiency and hard work. They encouraged their children to adopt these values, and young William Rehnquist did so with relish.

Rehnquist was, even as a high school student, a political activist of the most conservative persuasion. When Pearl Harbor was destroyed by the Japanese bombing attack on the Sunday morning of December 7, 1941, Rehnquist had just turned seventeen. Days after Congress declared war on Japan Rehnquist began to make his own contributions to the American war effort, helping to organize rallies at his high school and volunteering his services to the local civil defense authorities.

Rehnquist graduated from high school in 1942 but did not immediately enlist in the armed services, as did many of his male classmates. He had received a scholarship to attend Kenyon College in Gambier, Ohio, a medium-sized liberal arts college. Rehnquist quit Kenyon after one year and enlisted in the U.S. Army; shortly afterward he found himself stationed in North Africa, observing weather patterns and passing the information along to superiors who might accelerate or delay battle plans based on that knowledge.

The army had recognized Rehnquist's high intelligence shortly after he enlisted, and during the time he spent in the hot, dry African climate, he recognized something about himself. He did not really care for Wisconsin's cold winter weather. During his time in the army, Justice Rehnquist recently recalled in a speech at the dedication of the Arlington (Virginia) Central Library Facility, books were scarce and his chief reading materials were newspapers and comic books.

After World War II ended, Rehnquist returned to the United States, but not to Kenyon College. He headed for the warmth of southern California and completed his bachelor of arts degree at Stanford University in 1948. Rehnquist decided to leave California for two years to pursue postgraduate studies at Harvard University, where in 1950 he earned a masters degree in political science. But, complaining to friends about Harvard's liberalism, he returned to Stanford later that year to begin work on his law degree, which he completed in 1952. During the previous seven years Rehnquist's intellectual abilities had been sharpened and his focus had narrowed; the young man who had quit Kenyon College after one year was now graduating from one of the finest law schools in the country at the top of his class.

In late 1951 Supreme Court Justice Robert H. Jackson visited Stanford and, at the request of one of Rehnquist's professors, met with Rehnquist briefly. This was to be perhaps the most crucial meeting of Rehnquist's life, but despite Rehnquist's outstanding academic credentials, a coincidence proved just as important to the outcome of this meeting. Justice Jackson happened to have immediate need of a clerk, and Rehnquist happened to be graduating from Stanford in January, 1953, in the middle of the normal school year.

Rehnquist impressed Justice Jackson during their brief, informal meeting; nevertheless, no job was offered. Although Rehnquist left the meeting believing that he had botched his one great opportunity, Justice Jackson's office conveyed a job offer several weeks later. Rehnquist accepted without hesitation, joining Jackson's staff in 1952. Even as a clerk fresh out of law school, Rehnquist quickly gained a reputation among other clerks as somewhat of a maverick, and his rock-ribbed conservatism and acerbic tongue had not yet been tempered by the diplomacy and sense of humor that would come in later years.

One of Rehnquist's most important assignments when he worked for Justice Jackson would almost prove to be his undoing decades later during his confirmation hearings for both Associate Justice and Chief Justice. The language that he used and the sentiments that he expressed in a memorandum he prepared for Justice Jackson regarding *Brown* v. *Board of Education*, 347 U.S. 483 (1954), would cause some senators to question his interpretation of the Fourteenth Amendment. Although he would never retract the statements in question, Rehnquist would make several attempts to put the memorandum in a proper historical context.

Rehnquist, supporting his premise that the Supreme Court should not rule in favor of the plaintiff in *Brown* and attempt to force integration in schools nationwide, expressed the opinion that the Supreme Court was powerless to enforce such integration or, in fact, any other remedy that was greatly at variance with the will of the local population. To most observers this seemed to mean that Rehnquist was voicing the opinion that although bigotry might be wrong, it was neither within the Court's power or domain to protect the rights of the minority if the bigotry was pervasive enough to avoid enforcement.

Essentially, Rehnquist seemed to be opining that the Court's powers were limited and that the Court should realize that limitation. Rehnquist took a narrow view of individual rights, as evidenced by his writings during his tenure as one of Justice Jackson's clerks. Although he served the Justice for only a little more than a year, Rehnquist's memos during that brief period proved to be invaluable to his opponents in 1971, when he was first nominated to serve on the Court, and then again in 1986, when President Reagan sought, successfully, to elevate him to the office of Chief Justice.

Chief Justice Rehnquist has throughout his legal career consistently held an extremely conservative view of the proper role of the Supreme Court within the American governmental system. Although he has over the years moderately expanded this narrow vision, Rehnquist still remains convinced that the Court cannot act as a sort of superlegislature, constantly adjudicating disputes between aggrieved individuals and various branches of government. Rehnquist's writings while when he was Justice Jackson's clerk seemed to suggest that the Court had virtually no role in enforcing individual rights but should serve primarily or solely as an arbiter of disputes between the various branches of government.

In 1953 Rehnquist returned to Arizona, and several months later he married Natalie Cornell. In the years that followed they had two daughters and a son. Rehnquist, apparently unmotivated or unimpressed by the splendid assortment of career positions that have always been available to former Supreme Court clerks, instead joined a small Phoenix law firm and set about pursuing the day-to-day drudgery of wills, estates, real estate closings, and property disputes that are the bread and butter of any small law firm involved in a general practice.

On at least one occasion Rehnquist departed from his duties as a private practitioner. In 1957 he dissolved the two-man partnership that he had formed with another lawyer only the previous year and became a partner in the law firm of Cunningham, Carson, and Messenger. A year later, in 1958, Rehnquist was made a special prosecutor for the state of Arizona. His law enforcement work led to criminal indictments against a handful of public officials in the state who were accused of white-collar crimes, such as extortion and bribery, in relation to state-controlled transportation funds.

Arizona was the home state of the archconservative United States senator Barry Goldwater, who would later capture the Republican party's nomination for president in 1964. It was in this milieu that Rehnquist's already rigid conservative beliefs were nurtured and refined. Rehnquist became active in Arizona politics and vocally denounced political and judicial liberalism at virtually every opportunity. He did so with intelligence, charm, and dispassion, and even some of his staunchest opponents admired his logic and persuasiveness.

In a speech to a local bar association he criticized the liberal wing of the United States Supreme Court, saving his harshest criticism for Justices Hugo Black and William O. Douglas. (Douglas, more than a decade later, would become a personal friend and mentor to the newly confirmed Justice Rehnquist. Twenty-six years Rehnquist's senior, Justice Douglas warned Rehnquist that he would be miserable if he let the Court dominate his life.)

Rehnquist also volunteered to serve as a Republican challenger during various elections. His chief responsibilities were to challenge the voting credentials of any voter not likely to be a Republican party voter, i.e., blacks, Hispanics, poor whites, migrant workers, etc. As usual, Rehnquist joined the task with vigor; during his confirmation hearings he would be questioned about allegations that he and others engaged in shoving matches in confrontations with potential voters. The charges, while repeated by several persons who claimed to witness the events, were not substantiated and were eventually discounted by most members of the Senate.

Also, Rehnquist publicly opposed a proposed local law, under consideration by the Phoenix city council, which sought to prohibit racial and religious discrimination in sundry areas of public accommodation. Rehnquist, speaking on behalf of individual liberties and the rights of property owners, told the city council that he believed owners of businesses had a right to discriminate and to choose their own customers as they saw fit. Rehnquist's view was in the minority, even for Phoenix, Arizona, in the summer of 1964, and the measure became law.

Although Barry Goldwater was destroyed at the polls in November, 1964, when running for president, Rehnquist remained a committed as ever to his firm conservative beliefs. He befriended Richard Kleindienst, who was himself a crony of Richard Nixon. They joined a virtual army of understated but powerful political activists who shored up mainstream Republican support for Nixon and enabled him to recapture the party's presidential nomination in 1968. After Nixon's victory, both Rehnquist and Kleindienst were rewarded with Justice Department appointments that were important enough to warrant confirmation proceedings in the Senate. Kleindienst was named deputy attorney general, and Rehnquist was designated assistant attorney general and chief legal counsel.

These midlevel appointments required only cursory Senate investigations. Rehnquist was an unknown and did not merit close scrutiny. That, however, would be the last time that the Senate displayed a laissez-faire posture toward a Rehnquist nomination. Almost immediately after his confirmation Rehnquist became the Nixon administration's chief "hit man," seeking out and destroying liberal targets with lethal accuracy. Unlike other top Nixon aides, who were often thuglike and humorless, Rehnquist was known even to his liberal adversaries as being charming, gracious, and intelligent. Rehnquist's usefulness to Nixon increased daily. Completely unknown to the American public at the time of his appointment, William H. Rehnquist soon became a household name.

In a speech that he delivered on May 1, 1969, typical of many that he gave between 1969 and the early 1970's, Rehnquist, referring to student demonstrations and building takeovers fueled by the antiwar and civil rights movements that were exploding on the nation's campuses, said, "I suggest to you that this attack of the new barbarians constitutes a threat to the notion of a government of law which is every bit as serious as the crime wave in our cities. . . . [T]he barbarians of the New Left have taken full advantage of their minority right to urge and advocate their views as to what substantive changes should be made in the laws and policies of this country."

The antiwar protests, largely student-dominated and virtually endemic in all of the country's major non-Southern cities by the end of 1969, posed a great threat to the Nixon presidency. Indeed, Nixon was virtually obsessed by the antiwar movement and used the United States Justice Department to carry out his personal campaign against it. Rehnquist was one of a handful of men responsible for formulating a federal policy designed to monitor and control the ever-expanding antiwar movement. In 1969 Assistant Attorney General Rehnquist wrote a memorandum in which he endorsed continued army surveillance of civilian antiwar protestors.

In the autumn of 1971 Nixon was overjoyed by the prospect of being able to nominate not just one, but two Supreme Court Justices. The incumbents who held those seats, John Harlan and Hugo Black, were two of the most famous Justices to have served the Court in the twentieth century. Harlan was a reliable conservative, and Black, a onetime member of the Ku Klux Klan, had been transformed in later life into one of the most libertarian justices to have ever served on the Supreme Court.

Nixon envisioned this unique set of circumstances as his opportunity to reconstruct the Court, by appointing two extremely conservative lawyers. Nixon cared little about judicial experience or academic credentials; his goal was to find two reliable conservatives and get them past the confirmation proceedings. In fact Nixon had presented six prospective nominees' credentials to the American Bar Association (ABA) for that group's comments, but neither of his eventual nominees had been included in the list. In reality, the ABA list was just a smokescreen; Nixon didn't care what the ABA thought of Rehnquist or anyone else. The two top names on the list were so undistinguished that the legal profession, various political figures, and many senators objected. President Nixon, bruised by the Haynsworth-Carswell fiasco, looked around for two other candidates with better credentials. He selected Lewis Powell, a leading lawyer from Virginia, and William Rehnquist.

Lewis Powell was Nixon's first pick, although he would prove to be a wild card in the Court's deck; Powell was not one bit an ideologue and not easily swayed by the other Justices. Powell would be confirmed by the Senate easily; Rehnquist's confirmation, however, would turn into a political bloodbath that would presage the ferocity of the Watergate hearings that would end Nixon's political career less than three years later.

Although Powell, who was sixty-four years old when nominated by Nixon, had outstanding credentials (including thirty-nine years in private practice as well as being a former president of the American Bar Association, the American Bar Foundation, and the American College of Trial Lawyers), Rehnquist by comparison had relatively minor qualifications. Rehnquist had severe liabilities as well, which quickly became evident during the confirmation proceedings. Vigorous questioning from Democratic and liberal Republican senators failed to distract Rehnquist; his answers were polite, but always minimal. Rehnquist volunteered no information that wasn't specifically requested and often replied that he could not recall specific events.

Even many liberal senators, however, were reluctant to deny Rehnquist a position on the Supreme Court because of his political leanings alone. Two traditionally liberal Democratic senators, Adlai Stevenson III of Illinois and Thomas Eagleton of Missouri, proclaimed their support for Rehnquist and praised his intellect, if not his ideology. Finally, almost two months after he had been nominated, Rehnquist was confirmed by the United States Senate on December 11, 1971. The vote was 68 to 26, and more Democrats supported Rehnquist's nomination than opposed it. In addition, every Republican senator but three backed the nomination. The three Republicans were from New York, New Jersey, and Massachusetts, and included the Senate's only black member, Edward Brooke of Massachusetts.

William Hubbs Rehnquist was sworn in as the nation's 100th Associate Justice on January 7, 1972, about five months before the burglary of a Washington, D.C., office building that would change the course of American history. The office building was part of a complex called Watergate, and the five men arrested at the scene of the burglary, who were all connected with President Nixon's campaign organization, the Committee to Reelect the President, proved to be the proverbial tip of the iceberg. By the time the affair was over the Nixon presidency would be destroyed. Richard M. Nixon and his second-in-command, Spiro T. Agnew, would become the first president and vice president to resign their offices, Agnew in October, 1973, and Nixon in August, 1974. Numerous other top aides to the president lost not only their positions and prestige but their freedom as well, including a handful from the Justice Department. Rehnquist's old friend and mentor Richard Kleindienst, then attorney general, resigned in April of 1973.

Rehnquist escaped any entanglement with the Watergate scandal by dint of his elevation to the Supreme Court, but surely, had that not happened, his career too might well have ended in ignominy, as very few of Nixon's top aides were able to avoid the cloud of corruption that eventually swallowed up the Nixon presidency. In fact Rehnquist was the last of four Supreme Court Justices to be appointed by President Nixon. Although he was safely confirmed and removed at least somewhat from the political firestorm that consumed the nation for more than two years, Rehnquist's intimate connection with the Nixon presidency would continue to hamper him for fifteen years and nearly cost him the Senate's confirmation as Chief Justice in 1986.

Other political forces, much stronger and more lasting than those resulting from the Watergate scandal, would align themselves squarely against Rehnquist. One of the great political and social debates of the time, and one which was not hypothetical but would touch the lives of nearly every American family, was that which concerned the procreative rights of American citizens. This was a conflict in the making which loomed ever larger as the social mores of the country were transformed during the 1960's. Chief Justice Warren's liberal court had decided in *Griswold* v. *Connecticut*, 381 U.S. 479 (1965), that a state could not proscribe the use of contraceptives, regardless of the marital status of the users. But to arrive at this decision, Justice Douglas, its author, first articulated the "right to privacy," which had not before been recognized by the Court.

It was *Griswold's* establishment of the previously unknown right to privacy that set the stage for *Roe* v. *Wade*, 410 U.S. 113 (1973), which expanded the horizons of the right to privacy while at the same time making determinations as to the viability of a fetus at various stages of development. Partly because the Court was venturing into unfamiliar territory, attempting to draw clear legal lines in an area that by its very nature was subject to the uncertainties of medical science, and partly because fetal viability outside the womb is greatly dependent upon evolving medical technology, *Roe* v. *Wade's* scientific basis has been on rocky ground since the day of the decision. The very language of the decision itself, which attempted to balance the right of privacy against legitimate state interests by determining fetal viability, was a technological mess in the making. As medical science evolved, previous assumptions about fetal viability would be challenged. Added to that, the debate over abortion took on much greater proportions, and public recognition of a woman's right to an abortion became a key litmus test used by liberal and feminist organizations to determine which judges or politicians were fit to serve in public office.

Justice Rehnquist, one of two dissenters in *Roe* v. *Wade* in 1973, sealed his fate of thirteen years later, when he would face perhaps the most arduous confirmation proceedings of any Chief Justice in the history of the Court. More than any other factor, it was clearly Rehnquist's views on abortion rights that triggered the massive outpouring of public opposition to his nomination. This part of Rehnquist's dissent summarized his views:

> *I have difficulty in concluding, as the Court does, that the right of privacy is involved in this case. Texas, by the statute here challenged, bars the performance of a medical abortion by a licensed physician on a plaintiff such as Roe. A transaction resulting in an operation such as this is not private in the ordinary usage of that word. Nor is the privacy that the Court finds here even a distant relative of the freedom from searches and seizures protected by the Fourth Amendment to the Constitution, which the Court has referred to as embodying a right to privacy. . . . The decision here to break pregnancy into three distinct terms and to outline the permissible restrictions the State may impose in each one, for example, partakes more of judicial legislation than it does of a determination of the intent of the drafters of the Fourteenth Amendment.*

It was not unusual for Justice Rehnquist to be the lone dissenter during the Court's liberal era; occasionally he would find himself allied with one or two other Justices, but quite often Rehnquist's single voice provided the only counterpoint to an otherwise unified Court. Even Chief Justice Burger, whose job it was to bring the Court around to a more conservative, or even more centrist posture (at least that was what President Nixon had envisioned when he appointed Burger), often voted with the Court's liberals.

Rehnquist, an unadulterated and unrepentant conservative, remained mired in a juridical limbo for most of the 1970's and some of the 1980's, with the sole consolation that, as the Court's lone dissenter, he had the opportunity to write as many dissenting opinions as he chose and did not have to tailor his views to suit those Justices who would be joining in his opinions, since there usually were none!

Among his single-vote dissents were a number involving the First Amendment. Thus he dissented by himself when the Court extended First Amendment protection to commercial speech in *Virginia Board of Pharmacy* v. *Virginia Citizens Council*, 425 U.S. 748 (1976). He was the sole dissenter in a later commercial free speech case, where the Court established the basic standards for evaluating these cases (*Central Hudson Gas and Electric* v. *Public Service Commission*, 447 U.S. 597 [1980]). He also voted to uphold various state and local laws restricting door-to-door solicitation, even though all the other members of the Court found the laws unconstitutional (*Hynes* v. *Mayor and Council of Borough of Oradell*, 425 U.S. 610 [1976], and *Village of Schaumburg* v. *Citizens for a Better Environment*, 444 U.S. 620 [1980]). He also dissented by himself in *Richmond Newspapers* v. *Virginia*, 448 U.S. 555 (1978), where the Court struck down an order closing a courtroom to the press.

Among his other single dissents in other cases were his votes in *Sugarman* v. *Dougall*, 413 U.S. 634 (1973), where the Court struck down restrictions on aliens; *Bob Jones University* v. *United States*, 461 U.S. 574 (1983), where the Court upheld the removal of tax-exempt status from a private religious college that had a racially discriminatory admission policy; *Larkin* v. *Grendel's Inn*, 459 U.S. 1 (1982), where the Court invalidated a Massachusetts law that gave a religious body veto power over the approval of a liquor license within 500 feet of the church; *In re Primus*, 436 U.S. 412 (1978), where the Court overturned professional discipline imposed on a civil liberties lawyer who solicited a client by mail for a public interest lawsuit; *Zablocki* v. *Redhail*, 434 U.S. 374 (1978), where the Court struck down a Wisconsin law that required a judge's permission before a man could get married if he had outstanding support obligations to a prior family; *Supreme Court of New Hampshire* v. *Pipes*, 470 U.S. 274 (1985), where the Court struck down a restrictive rule prohibiting out-of-state lawyers from practicing law within the state; *Thomas* v. *Review Board of Indiana*, 450 U.S. 707 (1981), where the Court reversed a determination of a state unemployment board that refused benefits to a person who left his job in an armament factory because of religious scruples; *Miller* v. *Fenton*, 474 U.S. 104 (1985), where the Court held that a federal court may, on federal habeas corpus, exercise plenary review over a state court determination that a confession was voluntary; *Cruz* v. *Beto*, 405 U.S. 319 (1972), where the Court upheld a complaint filed by a state prisoner that his religous rights were violated when the prison officials would not let him practice his Buddhist religion.

As a private individual and as a judge, Rehnquist would undoubtedly be categorized by most observers as a conservative, although by classical definition Rehnquist is something more complex. The essential tenet of conservatism, individual responsibility coupled with economic opportunity unfettered by governmental regulation, is not one shared by Rehnquist. His decisions clearly indicate a belief that the government should have nearly unlimited discretion in regulating all of its citizens' activities, even those which are entirely private, unless specifically prohibited from doing so by the actual words of the United States Constitution. But whenever the words of the Constitution do articulate the rights of individuals, Rehnquist guards and enforces those rights as zealously and impartially as do the most liberal of his Court brethren. A doctrinaire conservative, seeking to tailor the Constitution to his own ends, would never have decided as Rehnquist did on numerous occasions. Thus, although the conservative label might fit Rehnquist as an individual, it does not accurately portray him as a Justice.

Even in areas where a traditional conservative could be expected to decide otherwise, such as in cases regarding economic regulations, Justice Rehnquist has usually supported governmental restrictions rather than individual liberties. Although definitions have changed during the last century, Rehnquist has never fit the description of a doctrinaire conservative. Rather, he would be better described as a "judicial minimalist," a Justice with an exceedingly limited view of the role of the Supreme Court, a Justice who believes that the Court exists only for a very narrowly defined purpose and, as the only branch of government that is not democratically elected, certainly not as a superlegislative body. Rehnquist's dissent in *Roe* v. *Wade*, wherein he alluded to the Court partaking of "judicial legislation," supports this premise, as do numerous excerpts from his speeches and writings.

Although Rehnquist was often without allies inside the chambers of the Supreme Court, he was not alone in the milieu of public opinion. Indeed, Ronald Reagan's decisive victory over the incumbent Democrat, Jimmy Carter, in the 1980 presidential election demonstrated the conservative posture shared by most Americans, who were becoming increasingly annoyed by the Court's pronouncements. Even Americans who regarded themselves as liberals had become uneasy about Court decisions that freed criminals who were admittedly guilty and that supported institutionalized discrimination against nonentitled groups, particularly white males. These disenchanted middle-class voters became the "Reagan Democrats" and altered the balance of American political power.

Given this conclusive mandate by the voters in 1980 and again in 1984, it was inevitable that with the passage of time President Reagan would have the opportunity to reshape the Supreme Court. In the same year in which he was first inaugurated, 1981, Reagan's first Court opening appeared with the resignation of Associate Justice Potter Stewart. Reagan wanted a conservative, but he did not want his first Supreme Court appointment to become a prolonged, controversial, and divisive affair, as had happened to the last Republican president, Richard M. Nixon, with several of his nominations. So instead, Reagan located a relatively unknown but fairly conservative Arizona judge, Sandra Day O'Connor, and nominated her to become the first female Justice in the history of the Court. America's feminists finally got what they had been demanding, and Ronald Reagan had packed the Court with another conservative who, partly because she was a woman, faced little substantial opposition from Senate liberals. There were perhaps a half-dozen major philosophical battlegrounds that developed during the 1960's and 1970's, largely as a result of the Court's liberal decisions. One of the most important concerned sexuality generally, and procreative sexuality more specifically. Birth control, abortion, homosexuality, public and private nudity, and erotic literature and entertainment were all matters that came before the Court. A second battleground, often overlapping the first, revolved around the expanding definition of free speech. Incendiary statements, flag burning, the libel standards to be used against a supposedly free press, the rights of protesters to assemble and march, and the right to publish and read matter that some or most found offensive were issues that challenged the Court. A third battleground concerned affirmative action. Although a majority of Americans had supported the Civil Rights Act of 1964, a reactionary fervor had swept the nation as white males with superior test scores or more experience were denied jobs in favor of black or female applicants with lower test scores or less experience.

Another battleground concerned criminal procedure, the area of law that encompasses governmental law enforcement actions, including arrests, searches and seizures, questioning of suspects, jury selection, and presentation of evidence. Court decisions that had set guilty persons free due to technicalities (as the media often referred to Constitutional protections) infuriated the masses. A fifth battleground concerned the death penalty, which the Court had entirely struck down once, and which still seemed to be inoperable due both to Court-imposed restrictions and to the seemingly endless appeals that the law provided.

Unlike Chief Justice Burger, who had a reputation for aloofnesss among the other members of the Court and their clerks, Justice Rehnquist was generally thought of as modest, even self-effacing, gracious and friendly, albeit in a low-key manner. Rehnquist was never gregarious or demonstrative, but he could be charming and entertaining. His intelligence was undisputed even by his adversaries, and his cogent arguments and incisive analyses were legendary.

Rehnquist had followed the advice proffered to him years before by his friend and mentor Justice Douglas, and continued to cultivate his outside interests. In May, 1986, for example, the *New York Times* reported, "Associate Justice William H. Rehnquist of the Supreme Court accepted a bribe last week in the full view of several hundred witnesses, but no prosecution seems likely to result. Mr. Rehnquist was making a cameo appearance as the Solicitor in Gilbert and Sullivan's *Patience*. . . . Last Friday, resplendent in white wig and black robes, he was induced by the heroine to adjust a raffle over which he was presiding so that she won first prize." It was a perfect role for him, Chief Justice Rehnquist recently recalled, because he had no lines to memorize and because he had always loved the works of Gilbert and Sullivan.

Rehnquist also took up painting, primarily landscapes done in acrylics, in the mid-1980's. He studied in an evening class with other adult students, most of whom had no idea that the tranquil man painting meadows and streams amidst them was an Associate Justice of the Supreme Court. Rehnquist's modesty impressed another quiet, powerful man, President Ronald Reagan, who came to believe that a Court led by Rehnquist might accomplish that which the Burger Court had failed to do.

Clearly, the body politic was well prepared for the Court's conservative retrenchment. In May, 1986, Chief Justice Burger, during a private meeting with the president, dropped an entirely unexpected bombshell. He informed Reagan of his decision to resign from the Court. Reagan was stunned by Burger's announcement but did not try to dissuade him; the president had waited more than five years for such an opportunity.

After consulting Attorney General Edwin Meese and other close advisers, Reagan decided upon a difficult but virtually risk-free strategy. He would nominate Rehnquist for the office of Chief Justice, while at the same time nominating Antonin Scalia, a District of Columbia Court of Appeals judge, for Rehnquist's former position as Associate Justice, conditioned, of course, on the Senate's confirmation of Rehnquist for Chief Justice. Reagan knew that the opposition to Rehnquist would be both vociferous and organized; indeed, Rehnquist was no sure bet for confirmation, but even if rejected by the Senate, he would retain his seat on the Court as an Associate Justice.

Judge Scalia, on the other hand, was a very safe bet. Although he was a well-known conservative judge, Scalia carried none of the baggage that Rehnquist did and was much younger than Rehnquist. Scalia had not been intimately connected with the Nixon administration. The Senate would not have to vote on Scalia's confirmation unless Rehnquist was first confirmed as Chief Justice, and if Rehnquist, the far more problematic nominee, was confirmed, then Scalia would also be confirmed easily. If Rehnquist was not confirmed as Chief Justice, Scalia's nomination, conditioned entirely upon Rehnquist's confirmation, would become moot and Scalia, as a still-virginal Supreme Court nominee, could be resurrected and brought forth the next time there was an opening on the Court.

Thus, in the worst of all scenarios, the following would happen: (1) Rehnquist would be denied the post of Chief Justice and would remain on the Court as an Associate Justice; (2) Scalia's nomination would be mooted and he would emerge from the proceedings entirely unblemished and probably much enhanced by the national exposure; and (3) Reagan would look outside the Court for another suitable, and less controversial, nominee for the position of Chief Justice. The Court's makeup would eventually be the same whether Rehnquist was confirmed or not; of course, with Rehnquist as Chief Justice and Antonin Scalia as the new Associate Justice, Reagan's dreams of an effective, conservative Supreme Court might come to fruition. At any rate, it would be closer to such an actualization than it had ever been under the stewardship of Chief Justice Burger.

President Reagan announced his nominations, one conditioned upon the other, on June 18, 1986. The press conference was terse and awkward; Chief Justice Burger claimed to be leaving office so that he could devote his full energies to the bicentennial celebration of the Constitution, but no one really believed him. Burger denied that his health was failing and that he was tired of his position. The press conference had an eerie, unreal quality to it and was quickly adjourned.

It was not until more than a month later that the Senate Judiciary Committee began to consider the nominees in earnest. For Rehnquist it was virtually a repeat performance of his 1971 confrontation with that Senate body. In fact most of the same objections were raised, in addition to a few new ones discovered in the intervening decade and a half. The opposition to Rehnquist's nomination was perhaps the best-organized and best-funded opposition to a presidential judicial appointment in the history of United States politics. A coalition of feminists, civil rights activists, environmentalists, and others generally associated with the political left attacked the nominee on every front available.

Rehnquist was questioned about such matters as the minutiae of deed covenants that he had probably never read governing properties that he had long since ceased to own or control. The covenants, which purported to restrict resale to blacks, Jews, and other minority group members, were entirely unenforceable at law and had been so for many years. Senator Dennis DeConcini, a Democrat from Arizona, stated during the hearings, "I wonder how many of us on this committee could say that we have never owned a piece of property, either in trust or in escrow or in our names, that we haven't looked at every piece of the title."

In a revival of an old and entirely unproven allegation, persons from Arizona were brought to testify before the Committee that Rehnquist had harassed minority voters while working as an advisor to Republican poll-watchers in the 1950's and 1960's. But even taken at its face value, the testimony established nothing more than that Rehnquist was an aggressive challenger of potential voters. Although some may have found his actions offensive, there were no allegations of illegal acts. Meanwhile the Judiciary Committee had become embroiled in a debate with the White House, which was refusing to deliver memoranda written by Rehnquist when he served the Nixon administration from 1969 to 1971. President Reagan, claiming executive privilege, refused to supply the requested materials to the Committee. Reagan was not without allies in the Senate; Senator Strom Thurmond of South Carolina stated emphatically, "They have a right to exercise privilege. So far as I'm concerned that ends it."

Ironically, the most serious clash concerning executive privilege in recent history had come in 1974, when the Supreme Court, in *United States* v. *Nixon*,

418 U.S. 683 (1974), ruled against the president and ordered him to deliver audiotapes and other requested materials to the Congress. Associate Justice Rehnquist recused himself from the famous Nixon Tapes decision, and in fact was so eager to avoid the appearance of an impropriety that he declined even to observe the proceedings in the Court on that fateful day, although he longed to do so.

Eventually President Nixon relented and delivered the requested materials to the Senate Judiciary Committee. Among the memoranda were several that were highly offensive to certain groups. One in particular was a legal analysis of the proposed Equal Rights Amendment to the Constitution, in which Rehnquist opined that the Amendment might "hasten the dissolution of the family." Rehnquist's defense was that the memos were written pursuant to Rehnquist's role in the Justice Department as a "devil's advocate" and could not be construed to represent, necessarily, the private opinions of the nominee. This seemed a perfectly reasonable explanation to most members of the Senate Judiciary Committee, who voted, on August 15, 1986, to recommend that the full Senate confirm Rehnquist as Chief Justice. The vote was 13 to 5; all of the Senators who voted against the recommendation were Democrats, but three Democratic Senators voted in Rehnquist's favor. The Reagan administration's strategy had worked perfectly; the attention directed toward Antonin Scalia was minimal, and the Judiciary Committee voted unanimously to recommend his confirmation.

On September 18, 1986, the Senate met to decide whether William H. Rehnquist would become the sixteenth Chief Justice of the United States Supreme Court. His opponents had gathered steam in recent days, attacking him on every front, and had picked up substantial support in the Senate. Although victory appeared likely for Rehnquist, it was by no means certain. Two senators who would have supported Rehnquist, Republicans Jake Garn of Utah and Barry Goldwater of Arizona, were absent due to illness. Rehnquist's victory was decisive; sixty-five senators supported his nomination, while only thirty-three voted to deny him the position of Chief Justice. Almost as an afterthought, Antonin Scalia was confirmed unanimously to fill Rehnquist's seat as Associate Justice.

Although the battle had raged for three months, the Reagan administration's plan had worked perfectly, and now the Court appeared to be on the verge of being controlled by its conservative Justices. Although the numbers had not changed (retiring Chief Justice Burger had usually voted with Rehnquist in important cases), Rehnquist's persuasiveness coupled with Scalia's brash and perceptive conservatism were thought by Reagan's top aides to be sufficient to control and direct the Court. This theory would prove to be generally accurate, but not without some surprises along the way; although solidly conservative, Scalia was also entirely independent and often unpredictable. Some of Scalia's opinions reminded Court observers of Hugo Black, who had come to the Court as a conservative and become one of its most memorable defenders of civil liberties.

A case that illustrated both Rehnquist's nonpartisan approach to matters under consideration and his dedication to "judicial minimalism," as well as clearly showing the independent mind of Antonin Scalia, was *Federal Election Commission* v. *Massachusetts Citizens for Life Inc.*, 479 U.S. 238 (1986). The defendant corporation, a nonprofit antiabortion group in Massachusetts, had been penalized by the plaintiff federal agency for violating spending limitation laws that applied to corporations. The question before the Court was a narrow one: could Congress limit spending by small nonprofit corporations organized solely to promote an ideology, or did such limitations violate the First Amendment?

The opinion of the majority, written by liberal Associate Justice William Brennan and joined by fellow liberals Thurgood Marshall and Lewis F. Powell and conservatives Antonin Scalia and Sandra Day O'Connor, ruled in favor of the antiabortion group. The new Chief Justice dissented, along with the moderate Byron White and the usually liberal Harry Blackmun and John Paul Stevens. If Rehnquist had been a pure conservative ideologue rather than an objective jurist, he might have voted with the majority on a personal level. It is indisputable that Chief Justice Rehnquist was against abortion. But he dispassionately evaluated the facts and the law and came to the conclusion, as he stated in his dissent, that the law was permissible both to "rid the political process of corruption and appearance of corruption that accompany contributions to and expenditures for candidates from corporate funds."

Those who favored free access to abortions and other measures that safeguarded procreative privacy rights knew that Chief Justice Rehnquist was almost certain to vote to overturn the landmark decision of *Roe* v. *Wade* as soon as an appropriate vehicle presented itself to the Court. Indicative of Rehnquist's orientation in this regard was the case of *Thornburgh* v. *American College of Obstetrics*, 476 U.S. 747 (1986), whereby the defendants had challenged the constitutionality of Pennsylvania's Abortion Control Act. Justice Blackmun, writing for the majority, declared unconstitutional those portions of the Pennsylvania act that required that, prior to any abortion, medical authorities must inform the patient of: (1) the availability of medical assistance; (2) the financial responsibilities of the presumed father; and (3) all possible physical and psychological risks. Other portions of the act were also invalidated. Rehnquist joined in dissenting opinions that were filed by Justices White and O'Connor.

Justice Scalia was in complete disagreement with the Court's recognition of the right to privacy articulated in *Griswold* and expanded in *Roe* v. *Wade*, and it was clear that he would vote to overturn either of those opinions or any others based on the right to privacy. Thus, after the Senate confirmation of Rehnquist and Scalia prochoice abortion rights groups mounted a massive public relations effort in an attempt to bring public pressure upon the Court regarding any future challenges to *Roe* v. *Wade*. Because she was a woman, a mother, and someone who had faced enormous gender-based discrimination (her first job after law school was as a legal secretary because none of the major firms in California would hire her, Stanford degree or not), Sandra Day O'Connor was singled out as a lobbying target, and with some success. O'Connor, known as a states' rights conservative when she was confirmed, showed that she was more of a conciliator than an ideologue, much to the chagrin of the Reagan administration and her hard-core conservative brethren on the Court.

Rehnquist's first years as Chief Justice bore relatively few fruits for the conservatives in America. Instead of being the Court's lone dissenter, he instead was often joined by one or more of the Associate Justices. The sheer numbers of five-to-four and six-to-three decisions where Rehnquist was on the losing side were tantalizing to him and to the country's conservatives. An example of Rehnquist's inability to dictate the direction of the outcome of the Court's decisions was *Johnson* v. *Transportation Agency*, Santa Clara County, California, 480 U.S. 616 (1987). Johnson was a white man who was employed by Santa Clara County and who was denied a promotion, although his experience was far superior, in favor of a woman who was also employed by the county. Johnson challenged the county's affirmative action policy, and his appeal to the United States Supreme Court was supported by the Reagan administration. Their brief on his behalf lambasted the county's affirmative action program and criticized its results, i.e., the utterly blatant discrimination against white men employed by the county. Justice Brennan once again wrote the majority opinion, which not surprisingly supported the county's claim that statistics alone were sufficient to justify its affirmative action program. Joining Brennan were Justices Blackmun, Marshall, Powell, and Stevens and Justice O'Connor, who was becoming an increasing source of vexation for the administration. Justices White and Scalia wrote dissenting opinions, which were each joined in part by Chief Justice Rehnquist.

Rehnquist fared much better at controlling the direction of the Court when it came to criminal procedure cases. The Court's moderates, and even on occasion its liberal members, were more likely to join the Chief Justice when the rights of a criminal, as opposed to a common citizen, were in question. A case in point is *United States* v. *Salerno*, 481 U.S. 739 (1987). Anthony Salerno was one of New York City's best-known mobsters. He was, in fact, almost a caricature of a mobster of the 1940's or 1950's. Gravel-voiced, surly, and street-smart, with the disposition and physique of a bulldog, Salerno was seldom seen without his trademark, an unlit cigar butt as short and stubby as the man who clenched it in his teeth morning, noon, and night.

Salerno and another mobster, Vincent Cafaro, were arrested in March, 1986, by federal agents after a grand jury had charged the men with RICO (Racketeer Influenced and Corrupt Organizations Act) violations set forth in a twenty-nine-count indictment. Government attorneys moved at the arraignment proceedings to have the defendants detained without bail prior to trial, for which the law provided. The prosecution claimed that Salerno was the head, or "godfather," of New York City's Genovese crime family, one of five such families that made up New York City's Cosa Nostra, or Mafia. The prosecution also alleged that Cafaro was a captain, or "capo," in the Genovese family. Together, the five families of New York's Mafia were alleged to have more than 1,000 "made members" and perhaps three times as many "associates." The government claimed that the two mobsters had engaged in numerous criminal acts, including conspiracy to commit murder, and that no condition of release would assure the safety of the community.

The District Court granted the government's request for detention, but was overruled by the Court of Appeals. The Supreme Court granted certiorari to the government and heard the case argued in the autumn of 1986. Ironically, by the time the Court rendered its decision, in early 1987, Salerno's claim had been made moot because of the fact that he had already been brought to trial, convicted, and sentenced to 100 years in prison.

Chief Justice Rehnquist, writing for the majority, again demonstrated his nearly complete acquiescence to the legislature in areas of criminal law. In reversing the opinion of the Court of Appeals, which held that Salerno's pretrial detention was unconstitutional, Rehnquist stated in part:

> In our society liberty is the norm, and detention prior to trial or without trial is the carefully limited exception. We hold that the provisions for pretrial detention in the Bail Reform Act of 1984 fall within that carefully limited exception. The Act authorizes the detention prior to trial of arrestees charged with serious felonies who are found after an adversary hearing to pose a threat to the safety of individuals or to the community which no condition of release can dispel. The numerous procedural safeguards detailed above must attend this adversary hearing. We are unwilling to say that this congressional determination, based as it is upon that primary concern of every government, a concern for the safety and indeed the lives of its citizens, on its face violates either the Due Process Clause of the Fifth Amendment or the Excessive Bail Clause of the Eighth Amendment.

Thurgood Marshall's dissent was, as usual, a work of simplicity, clarity, and brutal frankness. Marshall began his dissent with this paragraph:

> This case brings before the Court for the first time a statute in which Congress declares that a person innocent of any crime may be jailed indefinitely, pending the trial of allegations which are legally presumed to be untrue, if the Government shows to the satisfaction of a judge that the accused is likely to commit crimes, unrelated to the pending charges, at any time in the future. Such statutes, consistent with the usages of tyranny and the excesses of what bitter experience teaches us to call the police state, have long been thought incompatible with the fundamental human rights protected by our Constitution. Today a majority of this Court holds otherwise. Its decision disregards basic principles of justice established centuries ago and enshrined beyond the reach of governmental interference in the Bill of Rights.

Throughout his judicial career, Rehnquist never displayed any qualms about shocking or disappointing anyone, including those who defined themselves as conservatives, especially those of the fundamentalist Christian persuasion. When the case of *Hustler Magazine* v. *Falwell*, 485 U.S. 46 (1988), came before the Court, it appeared to present a classic liberal versus conservative controversy. Larry Flynt was the publisher of *Hustler Magazine*, a periodical that displayed genitalia more graphically than a gynecology textbook. The magazine was vulgar and obscene by almost anyone's standards, but it most certainly conveyed important messages, many of them political and sociological, to its readers. There was no doubt, even in the minds of the most conservative jurists, that the magazine was entitled to all of the protections of the First Amendment.

The Reverend Jerry Falwell embodied all that Larry Flynt despised; Falwell was a nationally prominent fundamentalist preacher who railed against the likes of Flynt every time he was given the opportunity. Flynt responded by placing in his magazine an advertising parody that portrayed an intoxicated Falwell in a sexual tryst with his own mother, the incestual act being consummated in a rural southern outhouse. Falwell sued for libel and intentional infliction of emotional distress. The trial jury cleared *Hustler* of libel, but awarded damages to Falwell for the emotional distress claim. Flynt appealed to the Supreme Court, arguing that the judgment violated his First Amendment rights.

By an eight-to-zero decision, written by Chief Justice Rehnquist, the Court found in Larry Flynt's and *Hustler's* favor, shocking both liberal and conservative veteran court observers, and utterly enraging the religious right. The decision was perhaps Rehnquist's finest hour as a defender of the First Amendment, and these words from his decision show the true measure of both Rehnquist's intellect and his dedication to the provisions of the United States Constitution:

> This case presents us with a novel question involving First Amendment limitations upon a State's authority to protect its citizens from the intentional infliction of emotional distress. We must decide whether a public figure may recover damages for emotional harm caused by the publication of an ad parody offensive to him, and doubtless gross and repugnant in the eyes of most. Respondent would have us find that a State's interest in protecting public figures from emotional distress is sufficient to deny First Amendment protection to speech that is patently offensive and is intended to inflict emotional injury, even when that speech could not reasonably have been interpreted as stating actual facts about the public figure involved. This we decline to do. . . . At the heart of the First Amendment is the recognition of the fundamental importance of the free flow of ideas and opinions on matters of public interest and concern. "The freedom to speak one's mind is not only an aspect of individual liberty and thus a good unto itself but also is essential to the common quest for truth and the vitality of society as a whole."

Barnes v. *Glen Theatre, Inc.*, 501 U.S. 560 (1991), was another case that involved the First Amendment rights of a sexually oriented commercial enterprise. An Indiana theater that featured nude dancing challenged Indiana's public indecency law. The question presented to the Court was whether the state of Indiana had the right to require dancers to wear some semblance of clothing during their performances, or whether even this minimal requirement violated the dancers', and the theater's, First Amendment rights. Although Rehnquist's decision for the Court upheld Indiana's regulations, the Court specifically acknowledged that nude dancing was indeed a form of expression to which First Amendment rights attached. Stated Rehnquist, in a humorous opinion laced with double meanings, "[T]he governmental interest served by the text of the prohibition is societal disapproval of nudity in public places and among strangers. The statutory prohibition is not a means to some greater end, but an end in itself. It is without cavil that the public indecency statute is narrowly tailored; Indiana's requirement that the dancers wear at least pasties and a G-string is modest, and the bare minimum necessary to achieve the state's purpose."

It is interesting to note that in *Barnes* v. *Glen Theatre* Justice Scalia, while concurring in the majority opinion written by the Chief Justice, did not agree that the nude dancing in question deserved First Amendment protections at all. Scalia's opinion stated in part that "the challenged regulation must be upheld, not because it survives some lower level of First Amendment scrutiny, but because, as a general law regulating conduct and not specifically directed at expression, it is not subject to First Amendment scrutiny at all."

This was not to be the first or last instance in which Scalia played the role of conservative to Rehnquist's moderate; indeed, if in the Court of the early 1990's Chief Justice Rehnquist moved from being the Court's lone dissenter to being its intellectual center, then Justices Scalia and Thomas had taken his place at the Court's periphery.

It was not until 1989 that the Rehnquist Court finally began to take on a distinct identity of its own. Where his predecessor, Chief Justice Burger, had failed to stamp his own imprint on the Court, Chief Justice Rehnquist succeeded masterfully. Unlike Burger, Rehnquist understood the Court for what it was, an essentially undemocratic collection of nine highly individualistic jurists. Rehnquist suffered no illusions about judicial decision making; he stated repeatedly in his writings and speeches the need for common sense and for forging consensus opinions that would be suitable to at least five of the nine justices. In this sense, Rehnquist was an exceptionally practical Chief Justice, and although he was not willing to compromise on the meaning of the Constitution, or on the role of the Supreme Court in a tripartite government, Rehnquist was willing to define matters before the Court narrowly or broadly in such a way as to find common ground with the other Justices. Rehnquist's personable and gentle manner made this politicking easier, as did the appointments of individual Justices by conservative Republican presidents. But one additional factor that helps to explain the success of Chief Justice Rehnquist was his skill in assigning opinions to the individuals who served on his Court. More skillfully than most, Rehnquist matched opinions with jurists in such a way as to virtually assure that the opinions would be palatable to the majority.

In January of 1989, in the case of *Richmond v. J. A. Croson Co.*, 488 U.S. 469, the Court declared unconstitutional a provision of the city government of Richmond, Virginia, which mandated that general contractors who had been awarded city construction contracts subcontract thirty per cent or more of each contract to businesses owned by blacks, Hispanics, or other minority group members. Rehnquist had been largely unsuccessful in his efforts to overturn affirmative action plans, which he and other conservative Justices believed were unconstitutional under the Fourteenth Amendment because they affirmatively discriminated against whites in general and specifically against white males. *Richmond* offered Rehnquist's Court an excellent opportunity to strike a blow at affirmative action. The Richmond statute was exceptionally poorly written; no discrimination by general contractors had been proven, the thirty per cent minority subcontractor figure had apparently been drawn arbitrarily from thin air, no distinction was made whatever between those general contractors who allegedly had discriminated and those who had not, and the city had tried no less intrusive approaches to solving the perceived problem.

Rehnquist assigned the opinion to Sandra Day O'Connor. O'Connor had concurred with Justice Brennan's opinion in the case of *Johnson v. Transportation Agency of Santa Clara County*, 480 U.S. 614 (1987), which upheld the County's affirmative action employment schedule, but had voted against affirmative action in other cases. O'Connor would be sure to write an opinion that was moderate in tone and narrowly tailored to the specific facts of the case in question. By a five-to-three vote (O'Connor was joined in the decision, although not the full opinion, by Rehnquist, White, Scalia, and Kennedy) the Court greatly restricted governmental affirmative action plans. Again, Justice Scalia found himself on the Court's edge as he vigorously argued in his concurring opinion that racial preferences always violated the Fourteenth Amendment (O'Connor had opined that they were in some circumstances permissible).

Affirmative action, as incendiary a subject as it proved to be during the 1970's and 1980's, paled in comparison to the national debate over reproductive rights. Those in the prochoice movement strongly believed that at least five of the Court's Justices were of the opinion that *Roe v. Wade* had been wrongly decided and were simply waiting for a suitable case that presented issues sufficiently broad that *Roe v. Wade* could be overturned. *Webster v. Reproductive Health Services*, 492 U.S. 490 (1989), appeared to be that case. On July 3, 1989, the Court announced its decision in an opinion written by Chief Justice Rehnquist. Although the Court did not officially overturn *Roe v. Wade*, it narrowed the protections that that decision had previously been assumed to provide.

In *Webster* the state of Missouri's abortion regulations were challenged under the *Roe v. Wade* doctrine. Specifically, four sections of the Missouri legislation were at issue: (1) the Missouri act's preamble, which stated that unborn children had protectable interests; (2) the language that prohibited the use of public facilities or the services of public employees for the purposes of abortion; (3) the prohibited use of public funds for abortion counseling; and (4) the requirement that private physicians make a determination of fetal viability before performing an abortion.

Once again, Justice O'Connor demonstrated her independence and took a more moderate approach than did Rehnquist. Because of this, Rehnquist was able to forge only a plurality, rather than a majority, opinion. Rehnquist wanted to support the constitutionality of every part of the Missouri legislation, but at the end of the day the Court's decision would validate only Missouri's mandates concerning the use of public funds and services for abortions and abortion counseling, and for fetal viability testing.

Nevertheless, *Webster* was highly significant in that it clearly demonstrated that *Roe* v. *Wade* would likely be overturned if a suitable case found its way to the Chief Justice's conference table. The key to overturning *Roe* v. Wade appeared to be technological. The Missouri legislature, having determined that fetal viability could ensue at approximately twenty weeks, had mandated viability testing at that stage of development. This appeared to challenge the trimester standards of *Roe* v. *Wade*, although if one reads that decision closely, it is apparent that it does not do so. But by upholding the Missouri legislature's finding of potential viability, the Supreme Court had reconstructed the thinking behind *Roe* v. *Wade* in two ways, both of which could eventually destroy the viability of *Roe* v. *Wade* itself. First, the Court had acknowledged that changing technology could drastically alter fetal viability and, along with that, could change the date of fetal development at which point the State's interests in protecting the life of the fetus attached. Second, the Court acknowledged that determination of viability, in the light of new, post–*Roe* v. *Wade* scientific evidence, was a proper area for the state's legislature to regulate.

Although the difference seemed to concern only a few days or weeks of fetal development, the nature of the Court's *Webster* decision clearly illustrated the unworkability of the *Roe* v. *Wade* standards in light of changing technology and gave further impetus to the view that procreative rights could be far better secured through federal legislation than through repeated reconsiderations of *Roe* v. *Wade* and its nebulous right-to-privacy foundation.

It is highly unlikely that the Supreme Court would take seriously any challenge to federal legislation that guaranteed a woman's right to abortion as long as that legislation was grounded in a suitable constitutional clause or amendment. Those on the Court who most opposed the constitutional premises of *Roe* v. *Wade*, Chief Justice Rehnquist and Associate Justices Scalia, Kennedy, and O'Connor, were also the same Justices who were highly deferential to acts of the legislature. There was nothing in *Webster* or any other recent decision of the Court to indicate that these Justices had a particular personal interest in fighting abortion, per se, on ideological grounds.

One of Chief Justice Rehnquist's goals was to free the Supreme Court from the deluge of habeas corpus petitions that reached it each year, usually brought by death-row convicts in state prisons seeking to have their convictions, or their death sentences, overturned. It was clear from Rehnquist's public statements that he believed that there was an enormous abuse of the habeas corpus procedure, and that it was being used primarily as a delaying mechanism by lawyers who had run out of substantive grounds for objection.

On February 6, 1989, in a speech to the American Bar Association, Rehnquist referred to the death penalty appeals of the infamous serial murderer Ted Bundy as an example of how the Court could be manipulated and inconvenienced by the habeas corpus procedure. Noting that the Court considered, and ultimately rejected, three separate emergency appeals in the hours before Mr. Bundy's execution by the state of Florida, the Chief Justice said, "All three of these actions were being prosecuted simultaneously on the day before the execution of a prisoner who had been on death row for nine years. Surely it would be a bold person to say that this system could not be improved."

Noting that more than 11,000 federal appeals were filed annually in death penalty cases, Rehnquist made it clear that he was not against federal review but simply against what he perceived to be the abuse of the procedure. Rehnquist stated, "[T]o my mind, the flaw in the present system is not that capital sentences are set aside by Federal courts, but that litigation ultimately resolved in favor of the states takes literally years and years and years."

In March, 1990, the Court decided two cases that severely limited the rights of state prisoners to obtain federal review of their convictions or death sentences. *Butler* v. *McKellar*, 494 U.S. 407 (1990), and *Saffle* v. *Parks*, 494 U.S. 484 (1990), were both habeas corpus actions, and the question before the Court was similar in each of the cases: were the appeals based on a new rule of law, which was instituted subsequent to their convictions or sentencing, or were the appeals based on a rule of law that was in place at the time of their convictions or sentencing? In his opinion in *Butler* Chief Justice Rehnquist supported good-faith interpretations of existing precedents made by state courts even though they are shown to be contrary to later decisions.

In a fiery dissent to *Butler*, Justice Brennan stated that "a state prisoner can secure habeas relief only by showing that the state court's rejection of the constitutional challenge was so clearly invalid under then-prevailing legal standards that the decision could not be defended by any reasonable jurist." With this requirement, the Court has finally succeeded in its thinly veiled crusade to eviscerate Congress's habeas corpus regime.

Several months later the Court released its decision in the closely watched case of *Cruzan* v. *Director, Missouri Department of Health*, 497 U.S. 261 (1990). Nancy Beth Cruzan's parents and guardians were seeking judicial intervention that would allow them to terminate the means by which their daughter, who had been in a coma for some time and had no chance of recovery, was artificially fed and hydrated. The state of Missouri's laws demanded that clear and convincing evidence of such a person's pre-coma wishes to be withdrawn from such life-sustaining procedures be presented for such a request to be granted. Nancy Cruzan's parents were unable to meet Missouri's evidentiary requirement, but they were sure that they knew what Nancy would have desired.

In his opinion for the Court, Chief Justice Rehnquist rejected the Cruzans' claims and reinforced Missouri's asserted interest in protecting the lives of those unable to express their wishes in similar circumstances. "In this Court," Rehnquist stated in part, "the question is simply and starkly whether the United States Constitution prohibits Missouri from choosing the rule of decision which it did. This is the first case in which we have been squarely presented with the issue of whether the United States Constitution grants what is in common parlance referred to as a 'right to die.' . . . The principle that a competent person has a constitutionally protected liberty interest in refusing unwanted medical treatment may be inferred from our prior decisions."

But Rehnquist went on to say that the Court should not force the state of Missouri to substitute the wishes of Nancy Cruzan's parents for those of her own and that the state might have perfectly valid reasons for refusing to do so, that in fact the wishes of a patient's family members might be very much at odds with the purported wishes of a comatose or otherwise incompetent patient.

Arizona v. *Fulminante*, 499 U.S. 279 (1991), presented the Chief Justice with the best imaginable fact pattern for narrowing the *Miranda* doctrine, which defines and limits the rights of law enforcement personnel in regard to the questioning of criminal suspects. Coincidentally, the *Fulminante* case, like *Miranda*, pitted a criminal defendant against the state of Arizona. But Oreste Fulminante was not a man who could evoke much sympathy from any Justice of the Supreme Court, and although personal sympathy is not supposed to matter, it may have in Fulminante's case; he had been convicted of the murder of his eleven-year-old stepdaughter.

Fulminante was in prison on other charges when he met Anthony Savriola, a Mafia soldier turned snitch, who regularly passed information along to his FBI handlers. Savriola promised the physically diminutive Fulminante protection from other prisoners, but only if Fulminante would acknowledge his evil deeds to Savriola. Fulminante "confessed" to Savriola, unaware that Savriola would betray him. This confession was the first of a chain of events that led to a murder conviction and death sentence for Oreste Fulminante.

The Arizona Supreme Court overturned Fulminante's conviction, concluding that his purported confession had been coerced and violated the *Miranda* doctrine. But Rehnquist, who had little time for legal theories that overturned the convictions of patently guilty defendants, led the Court in a five-to-four decision that narrowed the application of *Miranda*. In his opinion, Rehnquist stated, "I am at a loss to see how the Supreme Court of Arizona reached the conclusion that it did. Fulminante offered no evidence that he believed that his life was in danger or that he in fact confessed to Savriola in order to obtain the proffered protection. . . . The facts of record in the present case are quite different from those present in cases where we have found confessions to be coerced and involuntary."

The Court was again faced with an important abortion case in the spring of 1991, and in another five-to-four decision written by Chief Justice Rehnquist, the Court once again demonstrated the predictability of its ever-solidifying moderate-conservative center. *Rust* v. *Sullivan*, 500 U.S. 173 (1991), challenged federal regulations implemented by the Reagan administration that prohibited all employees of medical or otherwise of federally funded family planning clinics from any discussion or dissemination of information regarding abortion.

The regulations were to have no small effect, as they would restrict the activities of more than 4,500 clinics nationwide, which offered services to millions of pregnant women. The case was argued on several grounds, foremost among them that the federal regulations violated the First Amendment rights of the clinics' employees. The plaintiffs also argued that the regulations violated the privacy rights of women, articulated under *Griswold and Roe* v. *Wade*, by denying them information that was necessary to make an informed decision regarding the termination of a pregnancy. Citing *Webster* v. *Reproductive Health Services*, Rehnquist stated,

> Here the Government is not denying a benefit to anyone, but is instead simply insisting that public funds be spent for the purpose for which they were authorized. The Secretary's regulations do not force the Title X grantee to give up abortion-related speech; they merely require that the grantee keep such activities separate and distinct from Title X activities. . . . We turn now to petitioners' argument that the regulations violate a woman's Fifth Amendment right to choose whether to terminate her pregnancy. . . . The Government has no constitutional duty to subsidize an activity merely because the activity is constitutionally protected and may validly choose to fund childbirth over abortion.

The judicial philosophy of William H. Rehnquist may be best summarized by this brief excerpt from one of his two books, *The Supreme Court: How It Was, How It Is*:

> The Supreme Court has on occasion been referred to as the conscience of the country, but I think this description has a considerable potential for mischief. . . . Many of us necessarily feel strongly and deeply about the judgements of our own consciences, but these remain only personal moral judgements until in some way they are given the sanction of supreme law.

SELECTED BIBLIOGRAPHY

A discussion of Justice Rehnquist's career up until his Supreme Court appointment can be found in Donald E. Boles, *Mr. Justice Rehnquist, Judicial Activist: The Early Years* (Ames: Iowa State University Press, 1987); his first four years as an Associate Justice are discussed in David L. Shapiro, "Mr. Justice Rehnquist: A Preliminary View" 90 *Harvard Law Review* 293 (1976). Sue Davis' *Justice Rehnquist and the Constitution* (Princeton, N.J.: Princeton University Press, 1989), and Jeff Powell's "The Compleat Jeffersonian: Justice Rehnquist and Federalism" 91 *Yale Law Journal* 1317 (1982), discuss Rehnquist's constitutional philosophy, while specific doctrines are examined in Derek Davis, *Original Intent: Chief Justice Rehnquist and the Course of American Church/ State Relations* (Buffalo: Prometheus Books, 1991), and Ursula Bentele, "Chief Justice Rehnquist, the Eighth Amendment, and the Role of Precedent," 28 *American Criminal Law Review* 267 (1991). Analyses of Rehnquist's leadership of the Court can be found in David G. Savage, *Turning Right: The Making of the Rehnquist Supreme Court* (New York: Wiley, 1992), and Sue Davis, "The Supreme Court: Rehnquist's or Reagan's?" 44 *The Western Political Quarterly* 87 (1991). The Rehnquist Court itself is examined in David M. O'Brien, "The Rehnquist Court and Federal Preemption: In Search of a Theory," 23 *Publius: The Journal of Federalism* 15 (1993). Justice Rehnquist is himself a prolific author; two of his many essays appear in Mark W. Cannon and David M. O'Brien, eds., *Views from the Bench: The Judiciary and Constitutional Politics* (Chatham, N.J.: Chatham House, 1985).

John Paul Stevens

☆ 1920–   ☆

APPOINTED BY GERALD R. FORD

YEARS ON COURT
1975–

by
LEONARD ORLAND

On August 9, 1974, as Gerald R. Ford became the thirty-eighth president of the United States, Richard Nixon's attorney general, John Mitchell, was attempting to extricate himself from charges of perjury and obstruction of justice. The subsequent felony convictions and imprisonment of Mitchell supported the judgment in Ford's acceptance speech that "Our Constitution works. Our great Republic is a government of laws and not of men." Ford's distinguished appointments of Edward Levi, president of the University of Chicago, as attorney general, and Federal Judge Harold R. Tyler, Jr., as deputy attorney general, underscored his inaugural theme of a government of laws and did much to reestablish the integrity of the United States Department of Justice.

Ford had been in office for almost a year when Justice William O. Douglas retired from the Court. This presented Ford with his only opportunity to make a Supreme Court appointment. On December 1, 1975, President Ford nominated John Paul Stevens, a fifty-five-year-old circuit judge for the Seventh Circuit, to succeed Douglas. Levi had known Stevens from the Illinois Bar and at the University of Chicago Law School, and Ford's heavy reliance on Levi's judgment was a critical factor in the nomination of Judge Stevens.

Born in Chicago on April 20, 1920, Stevens was elected to Phi Beta Kappa and graduated from the University of Chicago in 1941. He served as a naval officer from 1942 to 1945 and graduated, after two years, from Northwestern University Law School in 1947, magna cum laude, first in his class, with the highest record of academic achievement in the history of that law school. He served as a Supreme Court clerk to Justice Wiley B. Rutledge from 1947 to 1948.

Between 1948 and 1951 Stevens practiced law in Chicago. He returned to Washington in 1951 as associate counsel to the House Antitrust Subcommittee and worked on the subcommittee's Study of Monopoly Power. In 1952 Stevens returned to the private practice of law, specializing in antitrust counseling and litigation. He served on the attorney general's National Committee to Study the Antitrust Laws, authored several articles on antitrust issues, and taught antitrust law at both Northwestern Law School from 1952 to 1954 and the University of Chicago Law School from 1955 to 1956.

Stevens was sworn in as a judge of the United States Court of Appeals for the Seventh Circuit on November 2, 1970. His first judicial opinion, two months later, was a clearly written scholarly opinion in a case that questioned the authority of a legislature to use its contempt power to summarily imprison a political demonstrator. The claim arose after the Wisconsin legislature had, without trial or conviction, ordered the summary incarceration of the antiwar activist Reverend James E. Groppi for disrupting a legislative session. Groppi had been imprisoned for ten days when a United States District Court held that the action of the legislature had been unconstitutional. A three-judge panel of the Seventh Circuit reversed the District Court, and the reversal was upheld by the full Seventh Circuit en banc in *Groppi* v. *Leslie*, 436 F. 2d 331 (7th Circuit 1971).

Stevens' dissent from the en banc reversal foreshadowed his opinion writing in the Supreme Court in subsequent decades. The *Groppi* dissent, the first of many, not only demonstrated Stevens' view that constitutional restraints were needed to curb governmental repression of political protest, but also presaged Stevens' willingness to reach out in dissent to vindicate constitutional values. The "preservation of order in our communities," Stevens concluded, "will best be insured by adherence to established and respected procedures" rather than by "resort to procedural expediency [that] may facilitate an occasional conviction." Stevens dissenting view was ultimately vindicated by a unanimous Supreme Court the following year in *Groppi* v. *Leslie*, 404 U.S. 496 (1972).

At the Stevens confirmation hearings Attorney General Levi, a reflective and scholarly man with a tendency toward quiet understatement, described Stevens' Seventh Circuit opinions as "gems of perfection" and a "joy to read." The attorney general characterized Stevens as a man with a "built in direction system about how a judge should approach a problem, fairly, squarely, succinctly." Levi praised Stevens' "craftsmanship, his innate sense of what a judge is supposed to do," and concluded that Stevens had "the kind of judicial restraint and forthrightness which makes for a great judiciary."

Stevens' Seventh Circuit opinions were subject to meticulous analysis by the Standing Committee on the Federal Judiciary of the American Bar Association, which sought evaluations from six Harvard Law School professors. There is every reason to agree with the Bar Committee's conclusions:

> *Justice Stevens' opinions cover almost every field of federal law. . . . The opinions are of consistently high quality. . . . Several of the law professors who evaluated Judge Stevens' opinions noted the excellence of a particular opinion dealing with legal subjects in which they are expert. One professor characterized an opinion on federal jurisdiction as a "model of analysis;" one observed that Judge Stevens' opinions in complicated statutory interpretation cases are "excellent" and sometimes "brilliant"; an antitrust teacher pointed to "very thoughtful, sound and creative antitrust opinions."*

The Bar Association committee concluded that the "consistent excellence in opinion ranging over a broad spectrum of substantive areas" made Stevens highly qualified to sit on the Supreme Court. "Overall," the committee concluded, Stevens' opinions were "well written, highly analytical, closely researched and meticulously prepared. They reflect very high degrees of scholarship, discipline, open-mindedness, and a studied effort to do justice to all parties within the framework of the law." In retrospect, that committee's judgment is a fair characterization of Stevens' opinions in the United States Supreme Court.

Justice Stevens was sworn in as an Associate Justice of the Supreme Court on December 19, 1975. He wrote his first opinion, a routine denial of a stay, on February 17, 1976, in *Bradley* v. *Lunding*, 424 U.S. 1309 (1976).

At his confirmation hearings Stevens was quite explicit about what has become a central characteristic of his opinion writing and his entire Supreme Court tenure—an insistence on explaining, in brief opinions, reasons for joining the majority (or the dissenting minority) and exactly how his reasoning differs from that of his colleagues. "My own personal philosophy," Stevens noted at the hearings, "is that if I do not agree with the result of a majority, I dissent, even if it may be a very brief dissent, or if I find something in the reasoning that is unacceptable, I try to write a brief concurrence."

Stevens articulated several reasons for this approach: "I think the litigants are entitled to know how the judges appraised the arguments and to be sure that all of them understood the arguments that were presented." Equally important is the desirability of preserving "the fact that there was a diverse point of view of points expressed in the Court, making a record that will help at a future date when the same issue may be presented for reexamination."

Justice Stevens' opinions, over a fifteen-year period, are consistent with his articulated and quite unusual insistence on separate opinion writing. Traditionally a new Justice, in his first several terms on the Court, frequently joins with the opinions of other Justices rather than author separate concurrences or dissents. Justice William O. Douglas, for example, in his first full term of Court, never wrote an opinion that disagreed with Justice Hugo Black. In contrast Justice Stevens, with far greater frequency than any of his contemporaries or predecessors, has not hesitated to articulate his own reasoning in separate concurrences or dissents.

In the 1976–77 Supreme Court term, the first full term in which he participated, Justice Stevens wrote seventeen separate majority concurrences and twenty-seven separate dissents, far more than any other Justice. Stevens joined in dissents written by others without additional elaboration only twice. That pattern of independent voting has continued and has become the hallmark of Stevens' tenure on the Court. In the 1991–92 term Stevens wrote more dissenting opinions than any other Justice and was exceeded only by Justice Antonin Scalia in the number of concurring opinions. For the entire period from 1980 to 1990, Stevens wrote more opinions on average than any other

Justice; for nine of the ten years of that decade, Stevens wrote more opinions than any other Justice.

Another aspect of Stevens' independence is his apparent disinterest in consensus or bloc building within the Court. As one seasoned Court-watcher observed:

> [E]xceedingly bright and apolitical, Stevens liked to devise a unique position on every legal issue. He also steadfastly refused to adopt the thinking of his colleagues. He shunned chances to be a power broker. Even when he could sway the outcome of a case by joining either a liberal or a conservative coalition, Stevens often refused and wrote a separate opinion for himself.

Stevens, of course, is not unaware of this pattern; in a 1986 speech he wryly remarked that the "audience that I most frequently address does not always seem to be listening to what I have to say." One consequence of this approach is to reduce the impact Stevens has had on his colleagues and on the development of the law. Indeed, in the past fifteen years Stevens has not authored any of the major opinions of the Court in the great debates of the time. With the dramatic shift of the Rehnquist Court to the right, it appears unlikely that Stevens will author major opinions for the Court in the future.

Parallel to Stevens' proclivity for separate opinion writing is his remarkable record of nonalignment with any particular bloc or Justice. That pattern emerged in Stevens' first term on the court and has been maintained throughout his tenure, which, of course, has been marked by the Court's dramatic political shift to the right.

During the 1976–77 term Stevens voted with Chief Justice Warren E. Burger and Justice William Rehnquist only slightly less frequently than he voted with Justices William Brennan and Thurgood Marshall. The following table illustrates the frequency with which Stevens' vote was aligned with the other Justices during the 1976–77 term:

Justice	Per Cent That Stevens Voted with That Justice
Stewart	62.0
White	60.4
Powell	58.4
Marshall	56.9
Brennan	56.8
Blackmun	55.1
Rehnquist	52.4
Burger	51.5

The significance of this record of independence is underscored by the fact that during the same term Justice Rehnquist voted with Chief Justice Burger in 78.4 per cent of the cases while Justice Brennan cast his vote with Justice Marshall in 93.6 per cent of the cases. A similar pattern of Stevens' independence emerges in the voting patterns for the decade of the 1980's:

STEVENS IN THE 1980–90 DECADE

Justice	Per Cent That Stevens Voted with That Justice
Brennan	68.3
Blackmun	66.2
Marshall	65.9
White	60.1
O'Connor	58.2
Kennedy	57.3
Powell	56.6
Scalia	55.0
Rehnquist	54.3
Burger	53.5
Stewart	51.1

In the same decade Justice Brennan voted with Justice Marshall in 94.3 per cent of the cases; Justice Rehnquist voted with Justice Anthony Kennedy in 87.8 per cent of the cases and with Justice Burger in 85.1 per cent of the cases; and Justice Antonin Scalia voted with Justice Kennedy in 86.9 per cent of the cases. Stevens still demonstrated a somewhat muted but still discernable pattern of independence in the 1990–91 term.

STEVENS IN THE 1990–91 TERM

Justice	Per Cent That Stevens Voted with That Justice
Marshall	78.3
Blackmun	72.5
White	59.2
Souter	55.6
O'Connor	54.2
Kennedy	52.1
Rehnquist	49.2
Scalia	41.2

Although Stevens votes independently, a clear judicial philosophy has emerged. Foremost in Stevens' constitutional jurisprudence is a pervasive concern for the vulnerable—aliens, children, homosexuals, prisoners—and the belief that the Constitution should be utilized to protect the rights of those who traditionally have been powerless.

One of Stevens' first Supreme Court opinions dealt with the constitutional rights of aliens and reflected quite clearly this particular constitutional sensitivity. In *Hampton* v. *Mow Sun Wong*, 426 U.S. 88 (1976), Stevens, for a sharply divided Court, struck down as a violation of the Fifth Amendment Due Process Clause a civil service regulation barring resident aliens from competitive civil service employment. Steven's opinion suggested a new mode of analysis for examining claimed constitutional violations in cases where such violations would discriminate against those already suffering a handicap or disability:

> *The rule enforced by the Commission has its impact on an identifiable class of persons who entirely apart from the rule itself, are already subject to disadvantages not shared by the remainder of the community. Aliens are not entitled to vote and . . . are often handicapped by a lack of familiarity with our language and customs. The added disadvantage resulting from the enforcement of the rule—ineligibility for employment in a major sector of the economy—is of sufficient significance to be characterized as a deprivation of an interest in liberty. Indeed, we deal with a rule which deprives a discrete class of persons of an interest in liberty on a wholesale basis. By reason of the Fifth Amendment such a deprivation must be accompanied by due process.*

Five years later, in *Rosales-Lopez* v. *United States*, 451 U.S. 182 (1981), the Court found no reversible error in the trial court's refusal, at voir dire, to make specific inquiry as to jurors' racial prejudice against Mexican Americans. Stevens, joined by Brennan and Marshall, dissented:

> . . . *the voir dire was inadequate as a matter of law because it wholly ignored the risk that potential jurors . . . might be prejudiced against the defendant simply because he is a person of Mexican descent. Because the defendant's lawyer perceived a risk of such irrational prejudice . . . his request for a specific question concerning it should have been granted.*

Early in the 1976 term Justice Stevens (joined by Justices Brennan and Marshall) once again applied his concept of special concern for the vulnerable in his dissent from a ruling that upheld Social Security Act provisions that imposed greater burdens on illegitimate children seeking survivor benefits than legitimate children (*Mathews* v. *Lucas*, 427 U.S. 495 [1976]). To Stevens it was "radiantly clear" why the government "should not add to the burdens that illegitimate children inevitably acquire at birth." He wrote that the nation was "committed to the proposition that all persons are created equal. The Court's reason for approving discrimination against this class—'administrative convenience'—is opaque and insufficient." Justice Stevens' conclusion is an eloquent statement of his concern for the need to protect the rights of the underprivileged:

> *Illegitimates are . . . a traditionally disfavored class in our society. Because of that tradition of disfavor the Court should be especially vigilant in examining any classification which involves illegitimacy. For a traditional classification is more likely to be used without*

pausing to consider its justification than is a newly created classification. Habit, rather than analysis, makes it seem acceptable and natural to distinguish between male and female, alien and citizen, legitimate and illegitimate; for too much of our history there was the same inertia in distinguishing between black and white. But that sort of stereotyped reaction may have no rational relationship other than pure prejudicial discrimination to the stated purpose for which the classification is being made. . . .

I am persuaded that the classification which is sustained today in the name of "administrative convenience" is probably more the product of a tradition of thinking of illegitimates as less deserving persons than legitimates. The sovereign should firmly reject that tradition. The fact that illegitimacy is not as apparent to the observer as sex or race does not make this governmental classification any less odious.

A decade later Stevens was to return to the theme of "administrative convenience" as an insufficient basis for governmental restraints in his dissents in prisoner rights and criminal defense cases.

Stevens displayed a similar concern for poor school children in *Kadrmas* v. *Dickinson Public Schools,* 487 U.S. 450 (1988), where the Court upheld a North Dakota statute allowing certain school districts but not others to charge user fees for bus transportation. Stevens, in dissent, declared:

. . . there is no longer any justification at all for allowing the non-reorganized districts to place an obstacle in the paths of poor children seeking an education in some parts of the State that has been removed in other parts of the State. . . . [T]he Constitution requires a rational basis for the special burden imposed on the disfavored class as well as a reason for treating that class differently.

A similar Stevens sensitivity emerges in his dissent in *Bowers* v. *Hardwick,* 478 U.S. 186 (1986), where the majority held that the Georgia criminal sodomy statute did not violate the constitutional rights of homosexuals. Stevens joined in Harry Blackmun's anguished dissent, which condemned "the Court's almost obsessive focus on homosexual activity." However, Stevens also wrote a separate dissent, joined by Brennan and Marshall:

The essential "liberty" that animated the development of the law in cases like Griswold, Eisenstadt, *and* Carey *surely embraces the right to engage in nonreproductive sexual conduct that others may consider offensive or immoral. Although the meaning of the principle that "all men are created equal" is not always clear, it surely must mean that every free citizen has the same interest in "liberty" that the 12 members of the majority share. From the standpoint of the individual, the homosexual and the heterosexual have the same interest in deciding how he will live his own life, and more narrowly, how he will conduct himself in his personal and voluntary associations with his companions. State intrusion into the private conduct of either is equally burdensome.*

Stevens, beginning with his tenure on the Seventh Circuit, has been an eloquent spokesman for the constitutional rights of prisoners. In a 1974 case he declared,

[T]he view once held that an inmate is a mere slave is now totally rejected. The restraints and the punishments which a criminal conviction entails do not place the citizen beyond the ethical tradition that accords respect to the dignity and intrinsic worth of every individual.

"Liberty" and "custody" are not mutually exclusive concepts (United States ex re Miller *v.* Twomey, *479 F. 2d. 701, 712 [7th Cir., 1973], certiorari denied, sub nom.* Gutierrez *v.* Department of Public Safety of Illinois, *414 U.S. 1146 [1974]*).

In his initial years on the Supreme Court, Stevens expanded on the theme in a series of dissents in a sequence of prisoner rights cases; see *Meachum* v. *Fano*, 427 U.S. 215 (1976) due process in prisoner transfer; *Moody* v. *Daggett*, 429 U.S. 78 (1976), due process right of parolee to hearing on new charges; *Jones* v. *North Carolina Prisoners' Labor Union, Inc.*, 433 U.S. 119 (1977), no absolute prohibition on union organizing in prison; and *Estelle v. Gamble*, 429 U.S. 97 (1976), prisoner's right to medical treatment.

In ensuing years, as the Rehnquist Court handed down case after case denying the constitutional claims of prisoners, the pace and intensity of Stevens' quite eloquent prisoner rights dissents increased. In *Bell* v. *Wolfish*, 441 U.S. 520 (1979), the Court rejected a constitutional attack on double celling and related practices in a federal detention center on the ground the practice did not amount to punishment. Stevens, in dissent, declared that the majority had "confined the scope of punishment so narrowly that it effectively abdicates to correctional officials the judicial responsibility to enforce the guarantees of due process." "I think," Stevens concluded,

> *it is unquestionably a form of punishment to deny an innocent person the right to read a book loaned to him by a friend or relative while he is temporarily confined, to deny him the right to receive gifts or packages, to search his private possessions out of his presence, or to compel him to exhibit his private body cavities to the visual inspection of a guard.*

In *Penry* v. *Lynaugh*, 492 U.S. 302 (1989), the Court held that the Eighth Amendment does not flatly prohibit the execution of mentally retarded defendants because "there is insufficient evidence of a national consensus against executing mentally retarded people." Stevens' partial dissent concluded that the record "compels the conclusion that such executions are unconstitutional."

In *Connecticut Board of Pardons* v. *Dumschat*, 452 U.S. 458 (1981), the Court ruled that although the pardons board had granted seventy-five per cent of inmate requests to reduce life sentences, this rate of relief did not create a "liberty interest" protected by Due Process and hence did not require that the board give a statement of reasons to inmates who were denied clemency. Stevens dissented:

> *To some of us, it is "self-evident" that individual liberty has far deeper roots [than having been derived from state law]. . . . The question this case presents is not whether these respondents are mere slaves, wholly divested of any constitutionally protected interest in liberty; rather, the question is whether the Connecticut Board of Pardons refusing to commute their life sentences constitutes a deprivation of liberty entitling respondents to the protection of the Due Process Clause.*

In *Hudson* v. *Palmer*, 468 U.S. 517 (1984), the Court held that random searches of prisoners' cells do not invade a Fourth Amendment protected-privacy interest. Stevens eloquently dissented:

Measured by the conditions that prevail in a free society, neither the possessions nor the slight residuum of privacy that a prison inmate can retain in his cell, can have more than the most minimal value. From the standpoint of the prisoner, however, that trivial residuum may mark the difference between slavery and humanity. . . . To accord prisoners any less protection is to declare that the prisoners are entitled to no measure of human dignity or identity—not a photo, a letter, nor anything except standard-issue prison clothing would be free from arbitrary seizure and destruction. Yet this is the view the Court takes today. It declares prisoners to be little more than chattels, a view I thought society had outgrown long ago.

The premise of Stevens' dissent in *Hudson* is the special concern for the vulnerable that permeates his civil rights opinions:

The courts, of course, have a special obligation to protect the rights of prisoners. Prisoners are truly the outcasts of society. Disenfranchised, scorned and feared, often deservedly so, shut away from public view, prisoners are surely a "discrete and insular minority."

Perhaps the most clearly expressed part of Stevens' constitutional jurisprudence emerges in the plethora of Supreme Court cases addressing the constitutional rights of criminal defendants. The inherent tension between the protections of the Bill of Rights for criminal defendants and the desire to punish criminals in times of escalating criminal violence evokes strong political passions in the citizenry and sharp polarization in the Supreme Court.

Chief Justice Burger was particularly vigorous in his campaign against the exclusionary rule, while Chief Justice Rehnquist has moved to sharply limit the role of the Supreme Court in monitoring capital punishment. Both Burger and Rehnquist made it clear, in opinions and articles, that they consider the *Miranda* rule unworkable; that they favor eliminating the exclusionary rule; that the scope and frequency of federal collateral attack on state criminal convictions should be circumscribed; and that federal tort actions for claimed constitutional violations by the police should be limited. Justices Brennan and Marshall, with equal vehemence, have declared, in dozens of dissents and in unusually strong public statements, that the Burger/Rehnquist Court's holdings threaten to vitiate the fundamental protections of the Bill of Rights.

Stevens' position in the midst of this constitutional controversy not only gives insight into his own jurisprudence but also reveals the subtle as well as obvious movement in the Burger/Rehnquist Supreme Court. The decade from 1981 to 1991 marked the transformation of the Burger Court, and by 1992 Brennan and Marshall, the heart of the Burger Court, were gone. Only Justices Stevens, Blackmun, Byron White, and Rehnquist remained from the Burger Court. Sandra Day O'Connor replaced Potter Stewart in 1981; Antonin Scalia replaced Warren Burger in 1986 as William Rehnquist became Chief Justice; Anthony Kennedy replaced Lewis Powell in 1988; David Souter replaced William Brennan in 1991; and Clarence Thomas replaced Thurgood Marshall in 1992. By 1993 it had become clear that the Rehnquist Court saw its first duty as upholding the will of the majority and the rules of the government, not the constitutional rights of individuals.

This dramatic narrowing of the constitutional rights of criminal defendants has had an extraordinary impact on Stevens; he was forced from his traditional role as a centrist to become a consistent dissenter, frequently the sole dissenter. Stevens, along with Blackmun, according to Forward Sullivan in "The Justices of Rules and Standards," 106 *Harvard Law Review* 24 (1992), "took up posts as guardians of the Court's left flank."

In his first term on the Supreme Court, the 1976–77 term, Stevens found himself in the center of the Burger Court. His votes in twenty-four criminal rights cases during this term display Stevens' independence, his ability to move between results that favor the defendant and results that favor the government, and his reluctance to be associated with any particular group on the Court.

Stevens' position fifteen years later, however, in the 1990–91 term, stands in sharp contrast. In seventeen cases during this term when the Court denied the constitutional claim of a criminal defendant, Stevens dissented, often sharply and with increasing passion. These opinions display not a Justice who has become radicalized and moved to the left, but a consistent jurist in a Court that has made a dramatic shift to the right and in the process pushed a centrist Stevens into the honorable but lonely role of the great dissenter.

Stevens' criminal procedure opinions in the 1976 term are not amenable to a simplistic prodefendant or progovernment analysis. Stevens voted, without separate opinion, with a majority that included Chief Justice Burger and Justice Rehnquist and was opposed by Justices Brennan and Marshall in a number of cases circumscribing the constitutional rights of criminal defendants. These include *South Dakota* v. *Opperman*, 428 U.S. 364 (1976), which permitted a warrantless "inventory" search of an automobile impounded for multiple parking violations; and *Stone* v. *Powell*, 428 U.S. 465 (1976), which virtually eliminated federal habeas corpus relief in Fourth Amendment cases. Stevens also voted with the majority to hold that seizure of business records does not violate the Fourth and Fifth amendments (*Andresen* v. *Maryland*, 427 U.S. 463 [1976]); to deny Fourth Amendment protection to bank records (*United States* v. *Miller*, 425 U.S. 435 [1976]); to permit fixed checkpoint border searches (*United States* v. *Martinez-Fuerte*, 428 U.S. 543 [1976]); to sustain a conviction where an undercover agent had participated in a pretrial conference between the defendant and his attorney (*Weatherford* v. *Bursey*, 429 U.S. 545 [1977]); to validate the indictment of a witness for grand jury perjury although the witness was not told that he was a potential defendant (*United States* v. *Washington*, 431 U.S. 181 [1977]); and to reject the claim that New York's homicide statute, which placed the burden of proof of affirmative defenses on the defendant, was inconsistent with the presumption of innocence (*Patterson* v. *New York*, 432 U.S. 197 [1977]). Stevens wrote for the majority to limit the circumstances under which a prosecutor has a duty to disclose exculpatory evidence in *United* v. *Agurs*, 427 U.S. 97 (1976).

Stevens wrote narrow concurrences in *United States* v. *Santana*, 427 U.S.

38 (1976), which permitted the warrantless arrest of a defendant in the vestibule of her apartment building, and in *Wainwright* v. *Sykes*, 433 U.S. 72 (1977), which limited the availability of federal habeas corpus for state prisoners. In *Manson* v. *Brathwaite*, 432 U.S. 98 (1977), Stevens concurred in upholding a conviction in a case that involved suggestive eyewitness identification. And in *Doyle* v. *Ohio*, 426 U.S. 610 (1976), where the Court held it unconstitutional for a state prosecutor to cross-examine a defendant about his exculpatory statement by pointing to his silence after receiving *Miranda* warnings from the police, Stevens dissented, despite his conclusion that the prosecutor's conduct was improper.

Stevens also wrote a number of concurring or dissenting opinions that favored the constitutional rights of criminal defendants. These include *Jeffers* v. *United States*, 432 U.S. 137 (1977), where Stevens, joined by Brennan, Marshall, and Stewart, dissented from a holding that convictions for conspiracy and the substantive offense do not constitute double jeopardy. In *United States* v. *Ramsey*, 431 U.S. 606 (1977), Stevens, joined by Brennan and Marshall, dissented from a holding that the Fourth Amendment does not bar warrantless postal inspection, stating that "if the government is allowed to exercise the power it claims, the doors will be open to the wholesale secret examination of all incoming international mail." In *United States* v. *Martin Linen Supply Co.*, 430 U.S. 564 (1977), Stevens concurred in holding that the government may not appeal from a judgment of acquittal made on motion after a hung jury. In *Oregon* v. *Mathiason*, 429 U.S. 492 (1977), Stevens dissented from holding that a parolee's statement to the police was voluntary and did not violate *Miranda*. In *United States* v. *Donovan*, 429 U.S. 413 (1977), Stevens partially dissented from a ruling sustaining the legality of a wiretap. In *Ludwig* v. *Massachusetts*, 427 U.S. 618 (1977), Stevens, joined by Brennan, Stewart, and Marshall, dissented from the majority's upholding of the constitutionality of Massachusetts' two-tier criminal trial system.

Stevens also joined the majority in several important criminal justice rulings that upheld constitutional claims. In *Coker* v. *Georgia*, 433 U.S. 584 (1977), the Court held that capital punishment for rape violates the Eighth Amendment; in *United States* v. *Chadwick*, 433 U.S. 1 (1977), the Court held that a search of a footlocker taken from the trunk of a parked automobile without a warrant violated the Fourth Amendment; in *Hankerson* v. *North Carolina*, 432 U.S. 233 (1977), the Court held that the important presumption of innocence case of *Mullaney* v. *Wilber*, 421 U.S. 684 (1975), should be retroactively applied; in *Blackledge* v. *Allison*, 431 U.S. 63 (1977), the Court held that the opportunity for full evidentiary hearings on federal habeas corpus claims should not be unduly circumscribed; and in *Castaneda* v. *Partida*, 430 U.S. 482 (1977), the Court held that a Texas grand jury selection statute discriminated against Mexican Americans.

Stevens' vote in these twenty-four cases provides only a limited perspective on how Justice Stevens thinks or what his ultimate contribution to the jurisprudence of the Bill of Rights has been or will be. Those questions are better addressed by the opinions that reflect Stevens' pathfinding approach to constitutional questions and his dedication and ability to develop new and significant constitutional doctrine. Three difficult criminal procedure cases are illustrative.

Brewer v. *Williams*, 430 U.S. 387 (1977), involved a particularly brutal murder of a ten-year-old child. The defendant, an escapee from a mental hospital, surrendered to police on the advice of counsel. Counsel agreed with the police that no interrogation or mistreatment of the defendant would occur during the 160-mile drive that the defendant would have to make, unaccompanied by counsel, in a police car. The Supreme Court found that the police urging of the defendant, during this long drive, to help the police locate the victim's body to ensure a "Christian burial" for the victim was actually behavior designed to elicit a confession.

Justice Stewart, speaking for Justices Brennan, Marshall, Powell, and Stevens, held that the conviction was invalid because the defendant had been denied his constitutional right to counsel. Justices Blackmun, Rehnquist, and White and Chief Justice Burger bitterly dissented. "The result," the Chief Justice declared, which "ought to be intolerable in any society," continues the Court on the "much criticized course of punishing the public for the mistakes and misdeeds of law enforcement officers."

Justice Stevens' stated reason for concurring was "the strong language in the dissenting opinions." However, Justice Stevens' opinion did more than rationally respond to the dissenters' emotional attacks; instead the concurrence went on to make a compelling case for the demands of constitutional supremacy and the continuing viability of the exclusionary rule. At the same time Stevens enunciated a new perspective on the exclusion of statements of criminals taken by the police when the defendant is unprotected by his counsel which focused on the crucial role of counsel, in an ordered legal system.

"Nothing that we write," Stevens declared, "no matter how well reasoned or forcefully expressed, can bring back the victim of this tragedy." While the "emotional aspects of the case make it difficult to decide dispassionately," they "do not qualify our obligation to apply the law with an eye to the future as well as with concern for the result in the particular case before us." Stevens concluded,

> Underlying the surface issues in this case is the question whether a fugitive from justice can rely on his lawyer's advice given in connection with a decision to surrender voluntarily. The defendant placed his trust in an experienced Iowa trial lawyer who in turn trusted the Iowa law enforcement authorities to honor a commitment made during negotiations which led to the apprehension of a potentially dangerous person. Under any analysis, this was a critical stage of the proceeding in which the participation of an independent professional was of vital importance to the accused and to society. At this stage as in countless others in which the law profoundly affects the life of the individual, the lawyer is the essential

medium through which the demands and commitments of the sovereign are communicated to the citizen.

If, in the long run, we are seriously concerned about the individual's effective representation by counsel, the state cannot be permitted to dishonor its promise to this lawyer.

This brief opinion not only represents a vigorous reaffirmation of the values underlying the Sixth Amendment, but also presents a new theoretical basis for upholding the pivotal role of counsel in the criminal process—a theme that Stevens would return to in later years in such cases as *McNeil* v. *Wisconsin,* 111 S. Ct. 2204 (1991).

A second illustration of Stevens' ability to suggest new constitutional analysis is *Henderson* v. *Morgan,* 426 U.S. 637 (1976). The case raised the question of "whether a defendant may enter a voluntary plea of guilty to a charge of second degree murder without being informed that intent to cause the death of the victim was an element of the offense."

Stevens' legal resolution of this issue was imaginative and developed significant new constitutional doctrine: guilty pleas accepted without notice of all of the elements of the offense are unconstitutional because they are involuntary. Expanding on the waiver test of *Johnson* v. *Zerbst,* 304 U.S. 458, 464, 465 (1938), Stevens concluded that a guilty plea may be involuntary "either because the accused does not understand the nature of the constitutional protections that he is waiving" or because "he has such an incomplete understanding of the charge that his plea cannot stand as an intelligent admission of guilt." Accordingly, Stevens concluded that even though there was "overwhelming evidence of guilt available," and competent counsel advising the defendant, a guilty plea is invalid "unless it was voluntary in a constitutional sense"; a plea "could not be voluntary in the sense that it constituted an intelligent admission that he committed the offense unless the defendant received 'real notice of the true nature of the charge against him.' " This Stevens opinion, which made explicit a doctrine that had only been implicit in prior cases, represented the views of Justices Brennan, Stewart, White, Marshall, Blackmun, and Powell; Justice Rehnquist, joined by Chief Justice Burger, filed a sharp dissent.

A third effort at developing a new criminal constitutional perspective was *Gardner* v. *Florida,* 430 U.S. 349 (1977), a capital case in which the jury recommended life imprisonment, and the judge imposed the death sentence on the basis of confidential information in a presentence report—a result clearly permitted by Justice Black's opinion in *Williams* v. *New York,* 337 U.S. 241 (1949). Justice Stevens' plurality opinion sought to limit the *Williams* opinion in light of the Court's recognition that the death penalty differs from other forms of punishment.

Justice Stevens' opinion then imaginatively interpreted the Court's prior opinions to reach the conclusion that sentencing procedures demand Due Process. To Stevens, Due Process requires that "even though the defendant has no substantive right to a particular sentence within the range authorized by statute," sentencing "is a critical stage of the criminal proceeding." Accordingly, Stevens concluded that the defendant "was denied due process of law when the death sentence was imposed, at least in part, on the basis of information which he had no opportunity to deny or explain."

Stevens' opinions in *Brewer, Henderson,* and *Gardner* reflect sound analysis and realism, but they are genuinely imaginative; they display a Justice with a passionate commitment to the Bill of Rights and with the intellectual capacity and moral capability to develop sound new constitutional doctrine. These traits, quite evident in Stevens' first term on the Court, emerged more completely fourteen years later, when Stevens found himself confronting criminal constitutional issues in a quite different Court, the Rehnquist Court, with an apparent political mission to deny the constitutional claims of criminal defendants and to foreclose procedural opportunities for presenting those claims.

In the 1990–91 term Stevens dissented in seventeen cases in which the majority rejected constitutional claims of criminal defendants. The range of rejected claims is illustrated by eight cases in which Stevens joined the dissents of others (most frequently Marshall or Blackmun).

In *Arizona* v. *Fulminante,* 111 S. Ct. 1246 (1991), the Court, for the first time, held that the harmless error rule of *Chapman* v. *California,* 386 U.S. 18 (1967), was applicable to the admission of involuntary confessions. Justices Stevens, Marshall, and Blackmun joined Justice White in dissenting on this issue; quoting Justice Stevens' concurrence in *Rose* v. *Clark,* 478 U.S. 570, 577, 578, n.6 (1986), that use of a coerced confession "abort[s] the basic trial process" and "render[s] a trial fundamentally unfair." The dissenters "would adhere to the consistent line of authority that has recognized as a basic tenant of our criminal justice system . . . the prohibition against using a defendant's coerced confession against him at his criminal trial."

In *Florida* v. *Bostick,* 111 S. Ct. 2382 (1991), the Court held that random searches of passengers on intercity buses are not unconstitutional if the passenger does not object to the search. Justices Stevens and Blackmun joined Justice Marshall's passionate dissenting condemnation of "the suspicionless police sweep of buses in intrastate or interstate travel," which "bears all the indicia of coercion and unjustified intrusion associated with the general warrant."

In *County of Riverside* v. *McLaughlin,* 111 S. Ct. 1661 (1991), the Court sustained the constitutionality of a California county proceeding for arraignment and probable cause determination in light of *Gerstein* v. *Pugh,* 420 U.S. 103 (1975), which held that an individual detained following a warrantless arrest is entitled to a prompt judicial determination of probable cause as a prerequisite to a further restraint on liberty. Justices Stevens and Blackmun joined Justice Marshall's dissent stating that the Riverside, California, policy of combining probable cause determinations with arraignments was not sufficiently "prompt" under *Gerstein.*

In *Coleman* v. *Thompson,* 111 S. Ct. 2546 (1991), the Court concluded that it was constitutional for the federal court to not consider the defendant's habeas claims because of a variety of procedural defects. Justices Stevens and Marshall joined Justice Blackmun's dissent, which concluded that "the Court is creating a Byzantine morass of arbitrary, unnecessary, and unjustifiable impediments to the vindication of federal rights."

In *McCleskey* v. *Zant*, 111 S. Ct. 1454 (1991), the Supreme Court established new and quite rigorous standards for a criminal defendant to meet when his habeas corpus petition is challenged as "abusive." Justices Stevens and Blackmun joined Justice Marshall's acerbic dissent, which condemned the majority for departing "drastically from the norms that inform the proper judicial function" and for its "unjustifiable assault on the Great Writ." Marshall, with self-evident anger, concluded that "[w]hatever 'abuse of the writ' today's decision is designed to avert pales in comparison with the majority's own abuse of the norms that inform the proper judicial function."

In *Florida* v. *Jimeno*, 111 S. Ct. 1801 (1991), the Court held that a suspect's consent to search a car generally constituted consent to search closed containers within the car as well. Justice Stevens joined in Justice Marshall's dissent, which declared that

> when the Court speaks of practicality, what it really is talking about is the continued ability of the police to capitalize on the ignorance of citizens so as to accomplish by subterfuge what they could not achieve by relying on the knowing relinquishment of constitutional rights. (quoting Justice Marshall's dissent in Schneckloth v. Bustamante, 412 U.S. 218, 288 [1973]).

Finally, in *Mu'Min* v. *Virginia*, 111 S. Ct. 1899 (1991), the Supreme Court held that the defendant's Sixth Amendment right to an impartial jury was not violated when the trial judge, on voir dire, refused to question prospective jurors about the specific contents of news reports to which they had been exposed. Stevens and Blackmun joined in Marshall's dissenting condemnation of the majority for turning "a critical constitutional guarantee—the Sixth Amendment's right to an impartial jury—into a hollow formality."

The clearest expression of Stevens' views on the constitutional rights of criminal defendants emerges in seven cases in which Stevens wrote opinions dissenting from a Court rejection of a tendered constitutional claim. In *California* v. *Acevedo*, 111 S. Ct. 1982 (1991), the Court ruled that the police may search a closed container in the trunk of a car without a warrant; the holding eliminated the warrant requirement for closed containers that the Court had established in *Arkansas* v. *Sanders*, 442 U.S. 753 (1979). Justice Stevens, joined by Marshall and (in part) by White, dissented:

> No impartial observer could criticize this Court for hindering the progress of the war on drugs. On the contrary, decisions like the one the Court makes today will support the conclusion that this Court has become a loyal foot soldier in the Executive's fight against crime.
>
> Even if the warrant requirement does inconvenience the police to some extent, that fact does not distinguish the constitutional requirement from any other procedural protec-

tion secured by the Bill of Rights. It is merely part of the price that our society must pay in order to preserve its freedom. . . . [Thus] it is too early to know how much freedom America has lost today. The magnitude of the loss is, however, not nearly as significant as the Court's willingness to inflict it without even a colorable basis for its rejection of prior law.

In *California* v. *Hodari D.*, 111 S. Ct. 1547 (1991), the Court held that a police officer's pursuit of a fleeing juvenile is not a "seizure," and therefore the protections of the Fourth Amendment were not triggered until the officer physically tackled the offender. Stevens, joined by Marshall, authored one of his most important criminal procedure dissents:

The Court's narrow construction of the word "seizure" represents a significant, and in my view, unfortunate, departure from prior case law construing the Fourth Amendment. . . . [T]he Court now adopts a definition of "seizure" that is unfaithful to a long line of Fourth Amendment cases. Even if the Court were defining seizure for the first time, which it is not, the definition that it chooses today is profoundly unwise. In its decision, the Court assumes, without acknowledging, that a police officer may now fire his weapon at an innocent citizen and not implicate the Fourth Amendment as long as he misses his target.

The deterrent purposes of the exclusionary rule focus on the conduct of law enforcement officers, and on discouraging improper behavior on their part, and not on the reaction of the citizen to the show of force. . . . It is too early to know the consequences of today's holding. If carried to its logical conclusion, it will encourage unlawful displays of force that will frighten countless innocent citizens into surrendering whatever privacy rights they may still have. . . . Today's qualification of the Fourth Amendment means that innocent citizens may "remain secure in their persons . . . against unreasonable searches and seizures" only at the discretion of the police. . . . The Court's immediate concern with containing criminal activity poses a substantial, though unintended, threat to values that are fundamental and enduring.

In *Payne* v. *Tennessee*, 111 S. Ct. 2597 (1991), the Court held that the Eighth Amendment did not bar a capital sentencing jury from considering victim-impact evidence. Stevens, joined by Blackmun, dissented:

The notion that the inability to produce an ideal system of justice in which every punishment is precisely married to the defendant's blameworthiness somehow justifies a rule that completely divorces some capital sentencing determinations from moral culpability is incomprehensible to me. Also incomprehensible is the argument that such a rule is required for the jury to take into account that each murder victim is a "unique" human being. . . .

Given the current popularity of capital punishment in a crime-ridden society, the political appeal of arguments that assume that increasing the severity of sentences is the best cure for the cancer of crime, and the political strength of the "victims' rights" movement, I recognize that today's decision will be greeted with enthusiasm by a large number of concerned and thoughtful citizens. The great tragedy of the decision, however, is the danger that the "hydraulic pressure" of public opinion that Justice Holmes once described and that properly influences the deliberations of democratic legislatures has played a role . . . in the Court's decision. . . . This is a sad day for a great institution.

McNeil v. *Wisconsin*, 111 S. Ct. 2204 (1991), concerned a defendant's invocation of his right to counsel under the Fifth and Sixth amendments. The defendant had been arrested for a robbery and appeared at a preliminary hearing with counsel. Thereafter the defendant was interrogated again on a murder charge and made incriminating statements, which he sought to suppress. Justice Scalia, for the majority, held that the incriminating statements need not be suppressed. The majority, relying on a distinction between invocation of rights under the Fifth Amendment and the Sixth Amendment, concluded that "the accused's request for counsel at an initial appearance on a charged offense [does not] constitute an invocation of his Fifth Amendment right to counsel that precludes subsequent police interrogation on unrelated, uncharged offenses." Stevens, joined by Marshall and Blackmun, dissented:

> The Court's opinion demeans the importance of the right to counsel. . . . [T]oday's decision is ominous because it reflects a preference for an inquisitorial system that regards the defense lawyer as an impediment rather than servant to the cause of justice.
>
> The predicate for the Court's entire analysis is the failure of the defendant at the preliminary hearing to make a statement that can reasonably be construed to be an expression of a desire for the assistance of an attorney in dealing with custodial interrogation by the police. . . . If the petitioner . . . had made such a statement indicating that he was invoking his Fifth Amendment right to counsel as well as his Sixth Amendment right to counsel, the entire offense-specific house of cards that the Court has erected would collapse.

Stevens criticized the majority for departing from an entire line of cases that start with a critical view of police interrogation of suspects in the absence of counsel:

> Undergirding our entire line of cases requiring the police to follow fair procedures when they interrogate presumptively innocent citizens suspected of criminal wrongdoing is the long-standing recognition that an adversarial system of justice can function effectively only when the adversaries communicate with one another through counsel and when laypersons are protected from overreaching by more experienced and skilled professionals. Whenever the court ignores the importance of fair procedure in this context and describes the societal interest in obtaining "uncoerced confessions" from pretrial detainees as an "unmitigated good," the Court is revealing a preference for an inquisitorial system of justice. . . . The Court's refusal to acknowledge any danger of "subtle compulsion" in a case of this kind evidences an inability to recognize the difference between an inquisitorial and an adversarial system of justice.

In *Harmelin* v. *Michigan*, 111 S. Ct. 2680 (1991), the Court held that imposition of a mandatory sentence of life in prison without the possibility of parole did not violate the Eighth Amendment ban against cruel and unusual punishment. Stevens, joined by Blackmun, dissented:

> The death sentences that were at issue and invalidated in Furman were "cruel and unusual in the same way that being struck by lightning is cruel and unusual. . . ." In my opinion, the imposition of a life sentence without possibility of parole on this petitioner is

equally capricious . . . the notion that this sentence satisfies any meaningful requirement
of proportionality is itself both cruel and unusual.

In *Chapman* v. *United States*, 111 S. Ct. 1919 (1991), the Court held that a statute imposing a five-year mandatory minimum sentence for distributing more than one gram of a mixture of a substance containing LSD "required that the weight of the carrier medium must be included in determining sentence." Stevens, joined by Marshall, dissented:

The consequences of the majority's construction of [the relevant federal criminal statute]
are so bizarre that I cannot believe they were intended by Congress. . . . There is nothing
in our jurisprudence that compels us to interpret an ambiguous statute to reach such an
absurd result.

Finally, in *Hernandez* v. *New York*, 111 S. Ct. 1859 (1991), the Court found no violation of the bar to race-animated preemptory challenges developed by the Court in *Batson* v. *Kentucky*, 476 U.S. 79 (1986), when the prosecutor exercised peremptory challenges to two Hispanic-speaking Latino prospective jurors and justified the challenges by declaring that he doubted their ability to defer to the official translation of the anticipated Spanish-language testimony. The Court concluded that the "state courts came to the proper conclusion that the prosecutor offered a race-neutral basis for the exercise of his peremptory challenges." Justice Stevens dissented:

A violation of the Equal Protection Clause requires what our cases characterize as proof of
"discriminatory purpose." By definition, however, a prima facie case is one that is estab-
lished by the requisite proof of invidious intent. Unless the prosecutor comes forward with
an explanation for his peremptories that is sufficient to rebut the prima facie case, no
additional evidence of racial animus is required to establish an equal protection violation.
In my opinion, the Court therefore errs when it concludes that a defendant's Batson
challenge fails whenever the prosecutor advances a nonpretextual justification that is not
facially discriminatory. . . . The prosecutor's explanation . . . should have been rejected as
a matter of law.

Stevens has spoken forcefully in public of his concern that the Rehnquist Court is extinguishing the basic constitutional rights of criminal defendants. His message is both eloquent and blunt. Speaking of a century of progress of the Bill of Rights, Stevens offered this remarkably candid critique of the 1990–91 term of the Rehnquist Court:

In this country, while dozens of universities and communities throughout the land are
celebrating the bicentennial of the Bill of Rights, an extraordinarily aggressive Supreme
Court has reached out to announce a host of new rules narrowing the federal Constitution's
protection of individual liberties. The prosecutor's use of a coerced confession—no matter
how vicious the police conduct may have been—may now constitute harmless error. In a
totally unnecessary and unprecedented decision, the Court placed its stamp of approval on
the use of victim impact evidence to facilitate the imposition of the death penalty. The Court
condoned the use of mandatory sentences that are manifestly and grossly disproportionate
to the moral guilt of the offender. It broadened the power of the police to invade the privacy
of individual citizens, and even to detain them without any finding of probable cause or

reasonable suspicion. In perhaps its most blatant exercise of lawmaking power marching under the banner of federalism, the Court completely rewrote the procedural rules governing post-conviction proceedings to foreclose judicial review of even meritorious constitutional claims in capital cases. An attorney's untimely filing of a notice of appeal from a state court's refusal to grant post conviction relief—a negligent misstep that until this year merely would have foreclosed appellate review in the state's judicial system—now bars federal review of a claim that imposition of the death sentence on the attorney's client violated the Bill of Rights. (See "The Bill of Rights: A Century of Progress," 59 University of Chicago Law Review 13, 15 [1992].)

Perhaps as striking as Stevens' criticism of the harsh consequences of the Court's denial of constitutional claims of criminal defendants is his willingness to measure that denial in broader perspective:

Although the Court's extraordinarily disappointing performance in 1991 can only have a sobering influence on bicentennial celebrations [of the Bill of Rights] . . . the work product of a single term must be viewed from a broader perspective. Even while American judges are deprecating the value of liberty, there is a time when, thanks largely to the vision of Mikhail Gorbachev, and perhaps to the symbolic power of the Bill of Rights, the voices of freedom have produced the beautiful music of debate, controversy, and progress in most of Eastern Europe. Perhaps, in time, the free exchange of ideas in other parts of the world will give Americans the incentive and the courage to reexamine the reasons why our prison population and particularly the number of inmates on death row steadily expands at an alarming rate while armed conflict in the streets of our cities continues to flourish.

The Stevens that emerges from these decisions is a jurist with a meticulous yet compassionate devotion to the Fourth, Fifth, Sixth, Eighth, and Fourteenth amendments, a jurist skeptical of the value of wars on crime and drugs and deeply concerned about the impact of these wars on the constitutional rights of citizens, a jurist unwilling to sacrifice constitutional values in the name of administrative convenience, police burdens, or prosecutorial necessity, and a jurist who has become increasingly critical of a Court which in the area of criminal justice appears quite willing to advance political expediency over constitutional principles.

This recounting of Justice Stevens' votes in the criminal law field would indicate that he is the last of the Court's liberals. But as the earlier chart shows, he often voted with Justices Rehnquist (in fifty-four per cent of the cases) and Scalia (in fifty-five per cent of the cases), only somewhat less than the times he voted with Justices Brennan and Marshall (sixty-eight per cent and sixty-five per cent, respectively). Justice Stevens often struck out on his own and would present a different mode of analysis for many of the crucial issues coming before the Court, thus leading to what would appear to be an idiosyncratic voting pattern.

As an example of his approach, he voted in dissent (with only Chief Justice Rehnquist agreeing with him) in *United States* v. *Providence Journal Co.*, 485 U.S. 693 (1988), where the Court held that a special prosecutor appointed to litigate a contempt charge could not appear in the Supreme Court without the solicitor general's approval. Justice Stevens and Chief Justice Rehnquist alone believed that there was no separation of powers problem in letting the special prosecutor handle the case through the Supreme Court level.

Similarly, he voted with Justice Scalia (also in dissent) in *Tashjian v. Republican Party of Connecticut*, 479 U.S. 208 (1986), when the Court struck down a Connecticut law that restricted voters in a Republican primary to persons actually enrolled in the Republican Party. Justice Stevens believed that the restriction fit within the constitutional definition of eligible voters for both federal and state elections.

Justice Stevens often voted in favor of vigorous enforcement of the civil rights laws, but he approached the problems in a manner different from his brethren. He wrote the Court's opinion in *Cannon v. University of Chicago*, 441 U.S. 677 (1979), holding that Title IX of the Education Amendments of 1972 provided for a private cause of action in favor of women whom their school had discriminated against. He also wrote for the Court in *City of Los Angeles, Department of Water and Power v. Manhart*, 435 U.S. 702 (1978), where the Court held that a city pension plan that paid less to all women pensioners (on the ground that women generally live longer than their male counterparts) improperly discriminated on the basis of gender. He also wrote the majority decision in *Chisom v. Roemer*, 501 U.S. 380 (1991), holding that the Voting Rights Act applied to judicial elections.

Stevens often dissented in cases where the majority refused to recognize or uphold a litigant's constitutional or civil rights. Thus he dissented in *Bowers v. Hardwick*, 478 U.S. 1039 (1986), where the Court refused to strike down the Georgia sodomy statute on the grounds that it invaded the right of a plantiff, a homosexual, to engage in sexual acts in privacy with a consenting adult. He also dissented in a series of decisions where the Court did not enforce the civil rights laws as vigorously as he thought it should. Thus he did not believe that an aggrieved party should have to show intentional discrimination under Title VI of the 1964 Civil Rights Act, which prohibited discrimination by recipients of federal financial assistance.

In *Guardians Association v. Civil Service Commission*, 463 U.S. 582 (1983), Justice Stevens also thought that the Court had fashioned too stiff a test for granting immunity to governmental units when public officials violated a citizen's constitutional rights. He dissented in *Jett v. Dallas Independent School District*, 491 U.S. 701 (1989), when the Court held that a school board was not liable under 42 U.S.C. sec. 1981 for discrimination in employment but could only be sued under 42 U.S.C. sec. 1983, which required a showing that the discrimination was the result of a policy or custom of the employing school district. In *City of St. Louis v. Prapotnik*, 485 U.S. 112 (1988), he argued (again in dissent) that the Court's rules on governmental liability were unrealistically narrow and that the only test should be whether the official who performed the act in question had the potential of controlling governmental decision making. He dissented in another governmental case, *Oklahoma City v. Tuttle*,

471 U.S. 808 (1985), when the Court held that a city could not be liable under the civil rights laws for the single acts of low-level police officers.

He also dissented in *Will* v. *Michigan Department of State Police*, 491 U.S. 58 (1989), where the Court held that states were not suable under Section 1983. Among his other dissents were *City of Newport* v. *Fact Concerts*, 453 U.S. 247 (1981), where the Court held that cities could not be held for punitive damages under Section 1983, and *Town of Newton* v. *Rumery*, 480 U.S. 386 (1987), where the Court upheld an arrangement where the police were allowed to extract a release from liability from a person arrested for a criminal offense in exchange for dropping the charges.

Justice Stevens also wrote a series of decisions dealing with affirmative action. He explained in a dissent in *Wygant* v. *Jackson Board of Education*, 476 U.S. 267 (1986), that affirmative action programs cannot be squeezed into a narrow intellectual straitjacket. He agreed that government could not use race to decide who might serve on juries, use public facilities, or marry. But "race is not always irrelevant to sound governmental decisionmaking," and thus race might be taken into account by a school board in creating an integrated faculty. He concluded, contrary to the majority, that a school might retain later-hired minority teachers for purposes of utilizing the services of minority teachers for the mixed school population.

On the other hand, he voted against affirmative action programs in two of the most important cases decided by the Court, *Regents of University of California* v. *Bakke*, 438 U.S. 265 (1978), and *City of Richmond* v. *J. A. Croson Co.*, 488 U.S. 469 (1989). In *Bakke* he wrote that the affirmative action program adopted by the University of California medical school (under which a specific number of places in an entering class were set aside for minority students) was unconstitutional by reason of race.

In *Croson* (voting in opposition to his usual allies, Brennan, Marshall, and Blackmun, who dissented in that case), he rejected the strict scrutiny/rational relationship dichotomy that the Court had laid down in its Equal Protection analysis. Rather, he stated that a court must "identify the characteristics of the advantaged and disadvantaged classes that may justify their disparate treatment." Under that test, the set-aside program established by Richmond for minority contractors could not be upheld since it was based upon stereotypical analysis that violated the Equal Protection Clause.

The same pattern emerged in Justice Stevens' First Amendment cases. He was generally a vigorous supporter of First Amendment rights. Thus he dissented when the Court upheld a state law that placed restrictions on electioneering within 100 feet of a polling place (*Burson* v. *Freeman*, 112 S. Ct. 1846 (1992). He also dissented when the Court upheld a local law that prohibited any demonstrations of any kind, including carrying signs, in front of a residence. Justice Stevens began his dissent in the following way: " 'GET WELL CHARLIE—OUR TEAM NEEDS YOU.' In Brookfield, Wisconsin, it is unlawful for a fifth grader to carry such a sign in front of a residence" (*Frisby* v.

Schultz, 487 U.S. 474, 497 [1988]). He also dissented in *Fort Wayne Books* v. *Indiana*, 489 U.S. 46 (1989), where the Court upheld the use of the RICO statute against obscenity. Justice Stevens thought that the extraordinary reach of the law trod on First Amendment rights.

But he voted against the assertion of First Amendment rights in the two flag-burning cases that came before the Supreme Court in 1989 and 1990, *Texas* v. *Johnson*, 491 U.S. 397 (1989), and *United States* v. *Eichman*, 496 U.S. 310 (1990). In both cases, the majority held that the laws criminalizing flag burning were unconstitutional under the First Amendment as restricting the free speech rights of the demonstrators. Justice Stevens argued that "the Government may—indeed it should—protect the symbolic value of the flag without regard to the specific content of the flag burners' speech." He also wrote the Court's opinion in *Members of City Council* v. *Taxpayers for Vincent*, 466 U.S. 789 (1984), where the Court upheld an ordinance prohibiting the posting of signs on city property, despite strong dissents by Brennan, Marshall, and Blackmun. Justice Stevens found that a city's interest in protecting against visual clutter justified the law.

In the field of religious rights Justice Stevens appeared to be equally inconsistent. He wrote the Court's opinions in two leading establishment and free-exercise cases. In the first he held for the Court that an Alabama law providing for a moment of silence and meditation was unconstitutional, since it was a disguised sanction for school prayer. But he also wrote the Court's opinion in *Employment Division, Department of Human Resources* v. *Smith*, 485 U.S. 660 (1988), where the Court upheld the denial of unemployment benefits to two drug counselors who ingested peyote during a religious ceremony of the Native American Church.

John Paul Stevens has performed a unique role on the Supreme Court during his twenty-year tenure. He has steadfastly refused to accept casual resolution of the difficult issues facing the Court, and he has consistently eschewed pat verbal formulas as the solution to knotty constitutional problems. By offering new approaches to fundamental questions, he has challenged the conventional wisdom in key areas of criminal procedure, Equal Protection, establishment of religion, and free speech. Furthermore, he has displayed the highest acuity in analyzing the problems coming before the Court and an admirable craftsmanship in drafting his opinions. Consequently, the product and stature of the Supreme Court are enhanced by his analytic and verbal skills. He is, in the Holmesian tradition, a Great Dissenter.

SELECTED BIBLIOGRAPHY

The most comprehensive work on Stevens' judicial philosophy is Robert Judd Sickels, *John Paul Stevens and the Constitution: The Search for Balance* (University Park: Pennsylvania State University Press, 1988); another general work is William D. Popkin, "A Common Lawyer on the Supreme Court: The Opinions of Justice Stevens," 1989 *Duke Law Journal* 1087 (1989). Details of Justice Stevens' appointment to the Court are outlined in David M. O'Brien, "The Politics of Professionalism: President Gerald R. Ford's Appointment of Justice John Paul Stevens," 21 *Presidential Studies Quarterly* 103 (1991). Works by Justice Stevens include "The Life Span of a Judge-Made Rule," 58 *New York University Law Review* 1 (1983); "The Third Branch of Liberty," 41 *University of Miami Law Review* 277 (1986); and "Deciding What to Decide: The Docket and the Rule of Four" in Mark W. Cannon and David M. O'Brien, eds., *Views from the Bench: The Judiciary and Constitutional Politics* (Chatham, N.J.: Chatham House, 1985). Stevens' attitude towards capital punishment is examined in Scott Burris, "Death and a Rational Justice: A Conversation on the Capital Jusrisprudence of Justice John Paul Stevens," 96 *Yale Law Journal* 521 (1987) and his proposals to reduce the workload of the Supreme Court is replied to in Jeffrey J. Jones, "Justice Stevens' Proposal to Establish a Sub-Supreme Court," 20 *Harvard Journal on Legislation* 201 (1983).

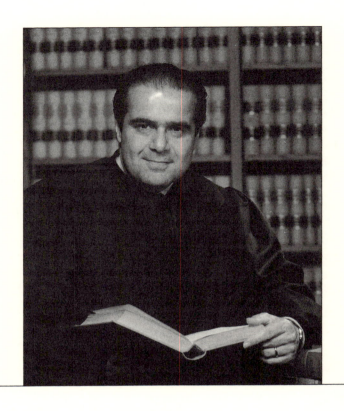

Antonin Scalia

☆ 1936–　　☆

APPOINTED BY RONALD REAGAN

YEARS ON COURT
1986–

by
JEFFREY ROSEN

Few Supreme Court Justices have claimed to be guided by a consistent judicial philosophy, but Antonin Scalia is a conspicuous exception. Since his appointment to the Court in 1986, he has distinguished himself by the confident sweep of his interpretive vision, and by the colloquial assertiveness of his opinions. Of the nine Justices on the Rehnquist Court, only Justice Scalia writes with flair: "It is instructive to compare this Nietzschean vision of us unelected, life-tenured judges, leading a Volk who will be tested by following, with the somewhat more modest role envisioned by the Founders," he wrote in *Planned Parenthood* v. *Casey*, 112 S. Ct. 2791 (1992).

Justice Scalia's speeches and opinions provide many details of the philosophy that he called, in his 1989 Holmes Lecture at Harvard, "The Rule of Law as a Law of Rules." In statutory interpretation, Justice Scalia claims to be a "textualist," refusing to look beyond the plain meaning of words for evidence of the original intentions of Congress. When interpreting the Constitution, however, Justice Scalia calls himself a "fainthearted originalist," insisting that each clause should be interpreted in light of the original understanding of its framers and ratifiers. Although he acknowledges the difficulties of reconstructing the intentions of long-dead legislators, Justice Scalia considers originalism, for all its practical defects, preferable to nonoriginalism as a methodological constraint. Finally, and most controversially, he says that judges should refuse to enforce rights that do not appear explicitly in the Constitution unless they are rooted in long-standing tradition or very specific historical practice.

Justice Scalia's interpretive principles—textualism, originalism, history, and tradition—are part of his broader claim that judges must find their answers in clear, generally applicable rules rather than in subjective standards. "[W]hen, in writing for the majority of the Court, I adopt a general rule, and say, 'This is the basis of our decision,' I not only constrain lower courts, I constrain myself as well. If the next case should have such different facts that my political or policy preferences regarding the outcome are quite the opposite, I will be unable to indulge these preferences; I have committed myself to the governing principle" ("The Rule of Law as a Law of Rules," 56 *University of Chicago Law Review* 1175, 1179 [1989]). Above all, Justice Scalia claims to be consistent. "The only checks on the arbitrariness of federal judges are the insistence upon consistency and the application of the teaching of the mother of consistency, logic." (Antonin Scalia, "Assorted Canards of Contemporary Legal Analysis," 40 *Case Western Reserve Law Review* 581, 588 [1990]).

Justice Scalia's intellectual energy and ambition have provoked lively interest among scholars; but scholarly evaluations of his jurisprudence have been mixed. Measuring him by his own exacting principles, many commentators have found Justice Scalia to be inconsistent. He sometimes seems to choose among competing interpretive principles in ways that appear scarcely more restrained than Justices who do not claim to be guided by systematic principles in the first place. Nevertheless, Justice Scalia deserves respect for articulating a coherent judicial philosophy, even if he does not always apply it coherently.

Antonin Scalia was born on March 11, 1936, in Trenton, New Jersey. His father, Eugene Scalia, emigrated to the United States from Sicily and became a professor of Romance languages at Brooklyn College. His mother, Catherine Scalia, taught elementary school. Antonin, their only child, was educated at a public school in Queens, and then at St. Francis Xavier, a Catholic military academy in Manhattan, where he graduated first in his class.

Scalia received his A.B. summa cum laude in history from Georgetown University in 1957, again graduating at the top of his class. At Harvard Law School, he was immersed in the Legal Process school in its heyday and served as note editor of the Law Review. He graduated magna cum laude in 1960, then spent a year traveling in Europe as a Sheldon Fellow. He joined the Cleveland law firm of Jones, Day, Cockley & Reavis in 1961 and practiced corporate financing, labor, antitrust, and real estate law. In 1967, he became a law professor at the University of Virginia, where he taught contracts, commercial, and comparative law, and in 1977 he moved to the University of Chicago, where he specialized in administrative law. As coeditor of *Regulation* and chair of the Administrative Conference of the United States, he became a prominent advocate of regulatory reform after the Chicago model. In the course of advocating broad presidential control over administrative agencies, he also distinguished himself as an academic opponent of the legislative veto.

In addition to his academic positions, Scalia served as general counsel in the White House Office of Telecommunications Policy under President Richard Nixon and as the assistant attorney general at the Office of Legal Counsel under President Gerald Ford. In August, 1982, President Ronald Reagan appointed him to the U.S. Court of Appeals for the D.C. Circuit, where he impressed observers with his devotion to law and order. In twenty-three decisions involving criminal defendants, media defendants, and civil plaintiffs, Judge Scalia ruled against them twenty times; and of his opinions concerning criminal procedure, four majority opinions and one dissent supported the prosecution. On June 17, 1986, President Reagan nominated Scalia to the Supreme Court. "I think it fair to say you would not regard me as someone who would be likely to use the phrase living constitution," Scalia confessed at his confirmation hearings. He was confirmed unanimously on September 17.

In criminal cases, Justice Scalia's interpretive methodology has sometimes pointed him toward positions that appear to be at odds with his political commitments. In an early review of Justice Scalia's criminal jurisprudence, George Kannar of the University of Buffalo concluded that "The Constitution becomes [for Scalia] a constricting and absolutely binding text that one is proud to follow closely because of, not in spite of, the fact that doing so sometimes frustrates one's desires" (George Kannar, "The Constitutional Catechism of Antonin Scalia," 99 *Yale Law Journal* 1297, 1320 [1990]).

Any suggestion that Justice Scalia's methodology usually leads him to favor defendants would be farfetched: a review of his votes in criminal cases shows that he supports the government about eighty per cent of the time. But in Fourth Amendment cases in particular, Justice Scalia's rigidly formalist analysis has sometimes led him to take the defendant's side. In *Arizona* v. *Hicks*, 480 U.S. 321 (1987), Justice Scalia held that the probable-cause requirement of the Fourth Amendment should not be relaxed, even for minimal intrusions. The police, after forcing their way into the apartment from which a shot was fired, searched it under the "exigent circumstances" doctrine. During the search, one officer noticed expensive stereo equipment and, suspecting that it might have been stolen, moved it slightly to examine its serial number. Justice Scalia held that the officer performed a search when he moved the stereo, triggering the full protection of the Fourth Amendment.

In the same spirit, Justice Scalia dissented from Justice O'Connor's holding that an arrested suspect may be held up to forty-eight hours without any judicial determination of probable cause (*Riverside County* v. *McLaughlin*, 112 S. Ct. 1661 [1991]). At common law, Justice Scalia noted, "a person arresting a suspect without a warrant [had to] deliver the arrestee to a magistrate 'as soon as he reasonably can.' " He then criticized the majority for holding that "a law abiding citizen wrongfully arrested may be compelled to await the grace of a Dickensian bureaucratic machine, as it churns its cycle for up to two days."

In a civil case concerning employee drug-testing programs, Justice Scalia tried to bring a measure of formalism to the Fourth Amendment's inherently subjective requirement that searches must be reasonable. In *National Treasury Employees Union* v. *Von Raab*, 489 U.S. 656 (1989), he dissented from the majority's immolation of privacy and human dignity in symbolic opposition to drug use. Focusing on what was "dispositively absent" from the government's case—"the recitation of *even a single instance* . . . in which any of the speculated horribles actually occurred . . ."—he concluded that the search was not reasonable.

In the service of Fourth Amendment formalism, Justice Scalia is hardly squeamish about unsettling settled doctrine. He has invoked the text and history of the Fourth Amendment, for example, to argue that a reasonableness requirement, rather than a warrant requirement, should govern all searches and seizures. In "The Rule of Law as a Law of Rules," he suggested that the Fourth Amendment requires a reasonableness inquiry not unlike the reasonable-care inquiry in tort cases: "Why should the question whether a person exercised reasonable care be a question of fact, but the question whether a search or seizure was reasonable be a question of law?" And in his concurring opinion in *California* v. *Acevedo*, 111 S. Ct. 1982 (1991), Justice Scalia emphasized that in the eighteenth and nineteenth centuries, juries, rather than judges, decided the legality of unwarranted searches: "An officer who searched or seized without a warrant did so at his own risk; he would be liable for trespass . . . unless the jury found that his action was reasonable." Justice Scalia's attempt to resurrect reasonableness as the touchstone of the Fourth Amendment would require dramatic changes in current doctrine. The exclusionary rule, as well as the warrant and probable-cause requirements, might have to be abandoned. Perhaps for this reason, his theory has not attracted wide support among other Justices.

In Fifth Amendment cases, Justice Scalia's textualism also leads occasionally to libertarian results. He has dissented from what he views as an insufficiently rigorous application of the Double Jeopardy clause in the context of multiple punishments. In *Jones* v. *Thomas*, 109 S. Ct. 2522 (1989), Justice Kennedy held that a defendant did not suffer from double jeopardy when he was sentenced to life after his fifteen year sentence was commuted. Ridiculing Kennedy's policy arguments, Justice Scalia took an impressively inflexible view of the Double Jeopardy clause: "A technical rule with equitable exceptions is no rule at all. Three strikes is out." On the other hand, Justice Scalia's narrow construction of the word "offense" in the Double Jeopardy clause has lead him to dissent from what he views as an overly expansive reading of the clause in the context of multiple prosecutions (*Grady* v. *Corbin*, 495 U.S. 508 [1990]). And in an acerbic dissent in *Minnick* v. *Mississippi*, 498 U.S. 146 (1990), Justice Scalia assailed his colleagues for prohibiting the resumption of an interrogation without counsel when the accused has already been refused counsel. The Court had produced, he said, a "veritable fairyland castle of imagined constitutional restrictions on law enforcement," and he added that "[w]hile every person is entitled to stand silent, it is more virtuous for the wrongdoer to admit his offense and accept the punishment he deserves."

In Sixth Amendment Confrontation clause cases similarly, textualism has sometimes led Justice Scalia to favor defendants. In *Coy* v. *Iowa*, 487 U.S. 1012 (1988), Justice Scalia held that an accused child abuser had a Sixth Amendment right to confront the child who had accused him. The trial judge had allowed a one-way screen to shield the accuser from the accused during testimony in court. Relying on etymology from ancient history to Hollywood

Westerns, Scalia held that the word "confrontation" had a settled and irreducible ordinary usage in American criminal cases. "Simply as a matter of English," said Justice Scalia, quoting Justice Holmes, "the confrontation clause confers at least 'a right to meet face to face all those who appear and give evidence at trial.' " And in *Maryland* v. *Craig*, 497 U.S. 836 (1990), Justice Scalia dissented from Justice O'Connor's opinion permitting child testimony to be received by closed-circuit television. Reaffirming the "unmistakable clarity" of the Sixth Amendment guarantee, he criticized the majority for "abstract[ing] from the right of confrontation to its purposes, and then eliminat[ing] the right."

In cases concerning affirmative action, Scalia appears to have been less successful in separating his personal views from his constitutional methodology. He has never disguised his scorn, as a second-generation immigrant from Sicily, at the idea that he should atone for the sins of earlier immigrants. In a vividly autobiographical essay written in 1979, he confessed his ethnic resentment of WASP judges like "the Wisdoms and the Powells and the Whites" whose ancestors oppressed blacks and who now try to rectify the error though affirmative action programs, at the expense of more recent immigrants. "My father came to this country as a teenager," Professor Scalia wrote. "Not only had he never profited from the sweat of any black man's brow, I don't think he had ever seen a black man" ("The Disease as Cure: In Order to Get Beyond Racism We Must First Take Account of Race," 1979 *Washington University Law Quarterly* 147). Scalia found it curious that recent white ethnic immigrants, like "Italians, Jews, Irish, Poles," who not only took no part in oppressing blacks but were themselves discriminated against by "the dominant Anglo-Saxon minority," are forced to a bear a disproportionate burden of affirmative action programs: "It is they who are the competitors with the urban blacks and Hispanics for jobs, housing, education—all those things that enable someone to scramble to the top of the social heap where one can speak eloquently (and quite safely) of restorative justice."

Given Justice Scalia's raw feelings on the subject, one would expect him to tread gingerly in considering the constitutionality of affirmative action programs. Instead, his opinions are notable for their failure to apply the originalist methodology and to examine the contemporary understanding of the Fourteenth Amendment. In *City of Richmond* v. *J. A. Croson Co.*, 488 U.S. 469 (1989), Justice O'Connor struck down a set-aside program for minority contractors, holding that states can discriminate on the basis of race only to "ameliorate the effects of past discrimination." In Justice Scalia's view, Justice O'Connor's position was too moderate: ". . . only a social emergency rising to the level of imminent danger to life and limb . . ." could justify an exception to "the principle embodied in the Fourteenth Amendment that '[o]ur Constitution is colorblind, and neither knows nor tolerates classes among citizens.' " Justice Scalia offered no historical support for this sweeping proposition, although he quoted James Madison on the dangers of faction and Alexander Bickel on the immorality of racism.

He ignored an amicus brief for the NAACP, written by Eric Schnapper of the Columbia Law School, arguing that the framers of the Fourteenth Amendment not only tolerated, but voted for, social welfare programs for the benefit of blacks. Administered by the Freedman's Bureau, some of the programs were open to all blacks, not only to recently freed slaves; and the assistance offered, which included land, education, job training, and employment set-asides, was not in any way tied to the amount of harm each individual had suffered. During the 1860s, Schnapper argued, only those members of Congress who opposed Reconstruction and the Fourteenth Amendment ever endorsed Justice Scalia's suggestion that the scope of race-conscious relief ought to match precisely the harm suffered by particular blacks. A Justice who claimed to be less bound by the specific understanding of the framers and ratifiers might be able to interpret the text of the Fourteenth Amendment, but Scalia offered no explanation for relaxing his originalist principles.

Justice Scalia's concurrence in *Croson* also seems to conflict, in important ways, with his dissent in *Rutan* v. *Republican Party of Illinois*, 497 U.S. 62 (1990). In *Rutan*, the Court held that the First Amendment forbids the government from engaging in patronage hiring. Justice Scalia objected that "the choice between patronage and the merit principle or, to be more realistic about it, the choice between the desirable mix of merit and patronage principles in widely varying federal, state, and local political contexts is not so clear that I would be prepared, as an original matter, to chisel a single, inflexible prescription into the Constitution." In *Croson*, he had excoriated "the enactment of a set-aside clearly and directly beneficial to the dominant political group, which happens also to be the dominant racial group." But in *Rutan*, he argued that patronage is desirable because it "enables racial and ethnic minorities to advance themselves by dominating a particular party machine . . . [and] acquir[ing] the patronage awards the machine had power to confer." Quoting a black newspaper, the *Amsterdam News*, Justice Scalia noted that "Every ethnic group that has achieved political power in American cities has used the bureaucracy to provide jobs in return for political support. It's only when Blacks begin to play the same game that the rules get changed."

In *Rutan*, Justice Scalia also seemed to shift from historical to textual interpretation of the Equal Protection clauses without providing a cogent explanation. In the course of arguing that political patronage was common at the time of the founding fathers, Justice Scalia found it necessary to confront *Brown* v. *Board of Education*, 347 U.S. 483 (1954). He argued that *Brown* was correctly decided because the text of the Thirteenth and Fourteenth Amendments clearly prohibited laws treating people differently on account of race:

> Moreover, even if one does not regard the Fourteenth Amendment as crystal clear on this
> point, a tradition of unchallenged validity did not exist with respect to the practice in

Brown. *To the contrary, in the 19th century the principle of "separate-but-equal" had been vigorously opposed on constitutional grounds, litigated up to this Court, and upheld only over the dissent of one of our historically most-respected Justices.*

As David Strauss of the University of Chicago has noted, the reference to the first Justice Harlan is entirely circular. The act that caused Harlan to be "one of our historically most respected Justices" was his dissent in *Plessy* v. *Ferguson*, 163 U.S. 537 (1896). And it is certainly odd that a constitutional challenge that garnered only a single dissent disestablished the segregation tradition, while the very strong movement against the spoils system that nearly succeeded in the Pendelton Act of 1883 did not disestablish the tradition of patronage (David A. Strauss, "Tradition, Precedent, and Justice Scalia," 12 *Cardozo Law Review* 1699, [1991]).

Drawing on his background as an administrative law scholar, Justice Scalia has made many of his most original contributions in the area of separation of powers. In a 1983 article, he discussed "The Doctrine of Standing as an Essential Element of the Separation of Powers" (17 *Suffolk University Law Review* 881 [1983]). The Court's distinction between constitutional and prudential standing was "unsatisfying," he said, "not least because it leaves unexplained the Court's source of authority for simply granting or denying standing as its prudence might dictate." Instead, Scalia proposed a clear alternative. If a person is the object of a legal regulation, he said, he should always have standing to challenge an agency's failure to enforce it; but sometimes even Congress cannot give an individual standing to regulate someone else. "There is a limit upon even the power of Congress to convert generalized benefits into legal rights—and that is the limitation imposed by the so-called core requirement of standing that individuals suffer concrete injury." In *Lujan* v. *Defenders of Wildlife*, 112 S. Ct. 2130 (1992), Justice Scalia won a majority for this proposition and wrote it into law.

For all of its analytical elegance, however, Justice Scalia's theory is arguably inconsistent with the original understanding and historical practice in England and America. Cass Sunstein has argued that the citizen suit was well established in the eighteenth and early nineteenth centuries; to establish standing throughout most of American history, parties merely had to show that Congress or the common law had given them a right to sue (see Cass R. Sunstein, "What's Standing After Lujan? Of Citizen Suits, Injuries, and Article III," 91 *Michigan Law Review* 163 [1992]). Justice Scalia's conclusion in *Lujan* that Congress can never grant standing to challenge the president's failure to enforce the law appears, in short, to be historically perverse. But instead of examining the historical evidence, Justice Scalia relied heavily on Justice William O. Douglas' much maligned opinion in *Association of Data Processing Service Org.* v. *Camp*, 397 U.S. 150 (1970), which has no pretense of historical support.

Other separation of powers opinions by Justice Scalia have been questioned on originalist grounds. In his solitary dissent in *Morrison* v. *Olson*, 487

U.S. 654 (1988), Justice Scalia argued that one branch of government cannot exercise any powers that have been granted, in the text of the Constitution, to another branch; and he criticized his colleagues for upholding the independent counsel provision of the Ethics in Government Act. As a textual and historical matter, Justice Scalia asserted, prosecution is a "purely executive power" because it "has always and everywhere—if conducted by Government at all—been conducted never by the legislature, never by the courts, and always by the executive." But Justice Scalia ignored briefs submitted by the Speaker and Leadership Group of the House of Representatives. Their extensive historical evidence suggested that, in the framers' world, prosecution had many nonexecutive qualities. Daniel N. Reisman has also argued that colonial prosecutions were largely private; and the shift to public prosecution during the eighteenth century did not invest prosecution with the qualities of a core executive function (Daniel N. Reisman, "Deconstructing Justice Scalia's Separation of Powers Jurisprudence: The Preeminent Executive," 53 *Albany Law Review* 49 [1988]).

Justice Scalia relied heavily on Chief Justice Taft's opinion in *Myers* v. *United States*, 272 U.S. 52 (1926), for the proposition that the president should have unlimited removal power over all principal executive officers. The *Myers* opinion, according to Justice Scalia, "exhaustively examin[ed] the historical records bearing upon the meaning of the applicable constitutional texts." Other commentators have been less kind in their assessment of *Meyers*. Reisman, for example, argues that Chief Justice Taft bypassed a rich history in which James Madison, among others, argued that the president's removal power varies according to the nature of the executive officer he seeks to remove.

Dissenting in *Mistretta* v. *United States*, 488 U.S. 361 (1989), Justice Scalia reiterated his view that any power exercised by officials in the executive branch is executive power and therefore should be subject to the complete control of the president. The Court upheld the Sentencing Reform Act of 1984, which authorized the U.S. Sentencing Commission to promulgate sentencing guidelines. Justice Scalia argued that the delegation of power was unconstitutional because the Sentencing Commission was independent of executive control. For Justice Scalia, "the power to make law cannot be exercised by anyone other than Congress, except in conjunction with the lawful exercise of executive or judicial power." He objected that the commission "neither exercises any executive power on its own, nor is subject to the control of the President who does."

Although Justice Scalia insists on consulting extrinsic evidence of the framers' intentions in constitutional interpretation, he refuses to do so in statutory interpretation. He explains the tensions between the two methodologies by insisting that nontextual sources such as legislative history—especially committee reports—are often unreliable evidence of the intentions of the average congressmen. Placing legislative intention before the text is a backward method of statutory interpretation, Justice Scalia argues, because legislative purpose can be gleaned only by "examining the language that Congress used" (*Moskal* v. *United States,* 498 U.S. 103 [1990]). Justice Scalia objects even more strenuously to the resort to legislative purpose in deciding whether old statutory language applies in a new setting: the " 'will of Congress' we look to is not a will evolving from Session to Session but a will expressed and fixed in a particular enactment" (*West Virginia University Hospital, Inc.,* v. *Casey,* 499 U.S. 83 [1991]).

On rare occasions, Justice Scalia appears willing to indulge in the benign fiction of guessing at legislative intent; but his concession is unrelated to legislative purpose. He assumes that the legislature intends to adopt clear background traditions to avoid absurd results (see *K Mart Corp.* v. *Cartier, Inc.,* 486 U.S. 281, 324, note 2 [1988]). He is also willing to favor a permissible reading over the ordinary meaning of a statutory text, but only when established canons of construction support the choice (*Chisom* v. *Roemer,* 111 S. Ct. 2354, 2373 [1991]). He is willing to consult the text of related statutes to illuminate the text of the disputed provision (*Pennsylvania* v. *Union Gas Co.,* 109 S. Ct. 2237, 2295 [1989]). But Justice Scalia will consider the purpose of a law only to determine how the legislature used language at the time of the statute's adoption (*Crandon* v. *United States,* 494 U.S. 152 [1990]).

In statutory as in constitutional interpretation, Justice Scalia has been criticized for inconsistency. In *Boyle* v. *United Technologies Corp.,* 487 U.S. 500 (1988), Justice Scalia held for the Court that a serviceman could not sue a military contractor for tort damages. State law, he concluded, was preempted, not by a federal statute, but by a rule of federal common law. The opinion is difficult to reconcile with an earlier opinion, in which Justice Scalia had condemned the Court's efforts to derive immunity rules for the military that have no basis in statutory law (*United States* v. *Johnson,* 481 U.S. 681, 692 [1987]).

Dissenting in *Johnson* v. *Transportation Agency, Santa Clara County,* 480 U.S. 616, 670 (1987), Justice Scalia urged the Court to overrule *United Steelworkers* v. *Weber,* which held that Title VII does not prohibit voluntary affirmative action by private employers. Justice Scalia claimed that the text of Title VII clearly prohibits all discrimination on the basis of race and sex. But although Title VII says explicitly that employers are not required to hire on the basis of race, it says nothing about voluntary racial preferences. The principle of *expresio unius,* which Justice Scalia has invoked in other cases, suggests that by failing to prohibit voluntary preferences, Congress may not have meant to prohibit them in all circumstances.

In other cases, Justice Scalia's methodology appears to have thwarted Congress' intentions even when they are clearly expressed. In 1982, for example, Congress amended the Voting Rights Act to prohibit unintentional as well as intentional discrimination. Congress clearly intended the amendment to extend the scope of the Act, which had always been understood to cover the election of state judges as well as state legislators. Dissenting in *Chisom* v.

Roemer, 111 S. Ct. 2354 (1991), however, Scalia pounced on language in the amendment about giving voters the chance "to elect representatives of their choice." He argued that " here is little doubt that the ordinary meaning of 'representatives' does not includes judges," and that judicial elections should not be covered by the extended Voting Rights Act. Justice Stevens, by contrast, emphasized the "broad remedial purpose of rid[ding] the country of racial discrimination in voting." He also noted that the Louisiana Bar Association had characterized state Supreme Court members as "representatives."

Justice Scalia is a fervent defender of judicial deference to agency interpretations of ambiguous statutes. He has acknowledged however, that the deference required by *Chevron* v. *Natural Resources Defense Council,* 467 U.S. 837 (1984), does not rest on an explicit congressional directive:

> [T]o tell the truth, the question for the "genuine" legislative intent is probably a wild-goose chase anyway. In the vast majority of cases I expect that Congress neither (1) intended a single result, nor (2) meant to confer discretion upon the agency, but rather (3) didn't think about the matter at all. If I am correct in that, then any rule adopted in this field represents merely a fictional, presumed intent, and operates principally as a background rule of law against which Congress can legislate (Antonin Scalia, "Judicial Deference to Administrative Interpretations of Law," 1989 Duke Law Journal 511, 516–517).

Scalia's candor about indeterminacy might be expected to make him skeptical about *Chevron,* because he claims that textualism is the proper form of statutory interpretation. Instead, Scalia assuages his doubts by focusing on the meaning of "ambiguous" in the *Chevron* analysis. The test for ambiguity does not require, he has taken pains to point out, that the arguments for conflicting interpretations are equally plausible. Rather a provision may be ambiguous even though one reading is preferable. "One who finds *more* often (as I do) that the meaning of a statute is apparent from its text and from its relationship with other laws, thereby finds *less* often that the triggering requirement for *Chevron* deference exists. It is thus relatively rare that *Chevron* will require me to accept an interpretation which, though reasonable, I would not personally adopt."

In *I.N.S.* v. *Cardoza-Fonseca,* 480 U.S. 421 (1987), Justice Scalia clashed with Justice Stevens, the author of *Chevron,* about how congressional intent should be determined. In his concurring opinion, Justice Scalia rejected Justice Stevens' reliance on "traditional tools of statutory construction"—including legislative purpose and legislative history—which he called an "evisceration of *Chevron.*" Legislative intention, expressed in legislative history, should never trump a clear statutory text, he argued. Justices Stevens and Scalia have continued their debate in subsequent opinions. In *Sullivan* v. *Everhart,* 494 U.S. 83 (1990), Justice Scalia, writing for the Court, found ambiguity in the provision of the Social Security Act concerning recovery of overpayments; accordingly, he insisted on *Chevron* deference. The statute stated that "[w]henever the Secretary finds that more or less than the correct amount of payment has been made to any person . . . proper adjustment or recovery shall be made." The Secretary determined that an overpayment was the netted difference between past over and underpayment. In Justice Scalia's view, if Congress had meant to specify that monthly overpayments and underpayments should not be netted, the statute would refer to "any payment," rather than "payment." Justice Stevens dissented, asserting "clear congressional" intent as the primary interpretive criterion. "Our duty is to ask what Congress intended, and not to assay whether Congress might have stated that intent more naturally, more artfully, or more pithily."

Justice Scalia has articulated a tradition-bound approach to the Due Process clauses of the Fifth and Fourteenth Amendments. He relies on history to determine how much process is due, and on tradition to determine which unenumerated rights and liberties are to be considered fundamental.

Concurring in *Pacific Mutual Life Insurance Co.* v. *Haslip*, 499 U.S. 1 (1991), Justice Scalia suggested that procedures consistent with the traditional practice of American courts necessarily constitute due process as long as they do not violate the Bill of Rights. The Court upheld a punitive damage award four times larger than the compensatory damage award; but Justice Scalia would have resolved the constitutional question without asking whether Alabama's procedural safeguards were reasonable. Traditionally, Justice Scalia argued, quoting Coke, Blackstone, and Cardozo, juries have had broad discretion to set punitive damage awards; and "no procedure firmly rooted in the practices of our people can be so 'fundamentally unfair' as to deny due process of law." At the same time, Justice Scalia noted that state legislatures and courts have the power to abolish the common law practice of punitive damages; and perhaps, when the legislative process has purged a historically approved practice, the Due Process clause would permit the Supreme Court to announce that it is no longer in accord with the law of the land. This observation is consistent with Justice Scalia's broader search for objective, textual evidence of current social practice, such as his interesting suggestion that courts should consult past and present state constitutions in deciding whether most people today consider capital punishment cruel and unusual (see, e.g., *Stanford* v. *Kentucky*, 492 U.S. 361 [1989]).

In *Michael H.* v. *Gerald D.*, 492 U.S. 110 (1989), Justice Scalia made it clear that he accepts the doctrine of substantive due process: "It is an established part of our constitutional jurisprudence that the term 'liberty' in the Due Process Clause extends beyond freedom from physical restraint." He then described, and radically narrowed, the circumstances in which he would consider enforcing an unenumerated right. Michael H. was the natural father of a child whose natural mother had been married to another man. A state statute conclusively presumed that a child born to a woman living with her husband was a child of the husband. The effect of the statute was to deny visitation rights to Michael H., and he challenged it as a violation of the Due Process clause. Justice Scalia, writing for a plurality of the Court, declared that in construing the substantive component of the Due Process clause, the Court had "insisted not merely that the interest denominated as a 'liberty' be fundamental (a concept that, in isolation, is hard to objectify), but also that it be an interest traditionally protected by our society." Under this standard, Michael H.'s claim was easy to reject, since he could not prove that society had traditionally accorded fathers in his situation parental rights.

Justice Brennan, in dissent, objected that Justice Scalia was construing the disputed tradition too narrowly. The relevant question was that American tradition protected parenthood in general, not the rights of natural fathers of children conceived in adultery. In the celebrated footnote #6, from which Justices O'Connor and Kennedy dissociated themselves, Justice Scalia replied: "Though the dissent has no basis for the level of generality it would select, we do: We refer to the most specific level at which a relevant tradition protecting, or denying protection to, the asserted right can be identified."

Despite the intense scholarly criticism that footnote 6 has provoked, Justice Scalia has not gone out of his way to apply it in subsequent cases. In *Burnham* v. *Superior Court*, 110 S. Ct. 7229 (1990), for example, Justice Scalia, writing for a plurality, held that California could assert personal jurisdiction over a New Jersey resident during his brief trip to the state. Without lingering over the question of how abstractly the relevant tradition should be identified, Justice Scalia surveyed English and American common law to support his conclusion. He argued convincingly that most states shared the same conception of personal jurisdiction over transient cases when the Supreme Court decided *Pennoyer* v. *Neff*, 95 U.S. 714 (1878). But Justice Scalia failed to note that *Pennoyer* explicitly exempted divorce actions from its holding. By failing to examine the most specific tradition of the constitutionally required process for divorce proceedings, Justice Scalia arguably failed to follow his own methodology.

In other cases, Justice Scalia has rejected substantive due process claims without engaging in extended historical analysis. His most passionate and at times vituperative opinions have been in abortion cases, in which he argues that *Roe* v. *Wade* should be openly overruled. He has ridiculed the "illusion" that the Court has the authority to devise "an Abortion Code" (*Hodgson* v. *Minnesota*, 497 U.S. 417 [1990]); and he has lamented that the political issue of abortion, "to the great damage of the Court, makes it the object of the sort of organized public pressure that political institutions in a democracy ought to receive," (*Webster* v. *Reproductive Health Services*, 492 U.S. 490 [1989]). In *Casey* v. *Planned Parenthood*, 112 S. Ct. 2791 (1992), he criticized the circularity of the majority's claim that overturning Roe "under fire" would make the Court look political and illegitimate: "We have no Cossacks, but at least we can stubbornly refuse to abandon an erroneous opinion that we might otherwise change to show how little [the pro-life] protesters intimidate us."

Nevertheless, Justice Scalia joined Chief Justice Rehnquist's dissenting opinion arguing that "the historical traditions of the American people [do not] support the view that the right to terminate one's pregnancy is 'fundamental.' " The single paragraph that Rehnquist devotes to this claim is too vague to be adequate. Rehnquist maintains that in 1868, when the Fourteenth Amendment was adopted, twenty-eight out of thirty-seven states had laws banning or limiting abortion. He emphasizes that the common law made abortion after fetal "quickening" an offense. He fails to emphasize, however, that from the time of the founding until well into the nineteenth century, few states banned abortion before fetal quickening. Based on the common law understanding, it is at least arguable that the traditions of the American people do support a right to terminate pregnancy before quickening. But Justice Scalia and Chief Justice Rehnquist's position is also plausible. In light of the nineteenth-century movement toward more restrictive abortion laws, perhaps the tradition supporting a right to abort before quickening is not deeply rooted enough to be considered fundamental. This much, at least, seems clear: having decided to acknowledge "tradition" as an independent source of constitutional rights, Justice Scalia has an obligation to explain, more carefully than he did in *Casey*, exactly how and when traditions get measured; and how long they must endure before judges can enforce them.

During Justice Scalia's first term on the Court, he questioned the Court's test for policing the Establishment clause in *Lemon* v. *Kurtzman*, 403 U.S. 602 (1971). In *Edwards* v. *Aguillard*, 482 U.S. 578 (1987), a seven-member majority struck down a Louisiana law requiring all public schools to teach creation science whenever they taught evolution. In a scathing dissent based on his (unexpected) scrutiny of legislative history, Justice Scalia concluded that the law had been enacted with a secular purpose. He also advocated abolishing the secular-purpose requirement of the *Lemon* test, contending that the "cases interpreting and applying [it] have made . . . a maze of the Establishment clause."

Justice Scalia launched a more sustained attack on *Lemon* in *Lee* v. *Weisman*, 112 S. Ct. 2649 (1992). A five-to-four majority held that it is unconstitutional to recite a nondenominational prayer (actually a paraphrase of Micah 6:8) at a public high school graduation. At the beginning of his dissent, Justice Scalia confessed his personal views: "To deprive our society of [this] important unifying mechanism, in order to spare the nonbeliever what seems to me the minimal inconvenience of standing or even sitting in respectful nonparticipation, is as senseless in policy as it is unsupported in law." In attacking the majority, Justice Scalia did not bother to conceal his anger. The Court's "psychojourney" is "nothing short of ludicrous." Although Justice Scalia dismissed the majority opinions as "conspicuously bereft of any reference to history," Justice Souter's concurrence, in fact, reviewed the evidence of the framers' intentions in meticulous detail, concluding that "history neither contradicts nor warrants reconsideration of the settled principle that the Establishment clause forbid" nonpreferential as well as preferential support for religion. Justice Scalia, however, ignored Justice Souter's arguments about the intent of the framers. Instead, he shifted his focus from original intention to subsequent practice or tradition, noting that presidents have traditionally issued thanksgiving proclamations. The move was methodologically surprising. In a footnote in his abortion dissent, Justice Scalia had argued that tradition can never trump a right explicitly enumerated in the Constitution.

Justice Souter again criticized Justice Scalia for methodological inconsistency in decisions construing the Free Exercise clause of the First Amendment. In *Employment Division, Department of Human Resources v. Smith*, 494 U.S. 872 (1990), Justice Scalia, writing for the majority, upheld Oregon's decision to include "religiously inspired peyote use" within the reach of its general criminal statutes. In the course of upholding the Oregon statute, Justice Scalia rejected the long-established principle of *Sherbert v. Verner*, 374 U.S. 398 (1963), that the proper standard for determining violations of the Free Exercise clause was whether the state could show a compelling governmental interest to justify the substantial burden it was placing on religious practice. Instead, Justice Scalia announced a new rule: there was no need to prove a compelling state interest "if prohibiting the exercise of religion . . . is not the object of [a law] but merely its incidental effect." In his concurring opinion in *Church of the Lukumi Bablu Aye, Inc. v. Hialeah*, 113 S. Ct. 2217 (1992), Justice Souter, drawing on widespread scholarly criticism, meticulously attacked Justice Scalia's opinion on two levels. He demonstrated that Justice Scalia's opinion had mischaracterized the precedents on which it claimed to rely; and he argued that Justice Scalia's theory was also inconsistent with the intentions of the framers of the Free Exercise clause. Justice Scalia has not yet responded to the widespread criticisms of the *Smith* opinion; and Congress has considered several bills to repudiate it.

Although Justice Scalia can hardly be called a traditional First Amendment libertarian, his analytical formalism has led him, in some opinions, to protect speech in unconventional ways. In *R.A.V. v. St. Paul*, 112 S. Ct. 2538 (1992), Justice Scalia ingeniously extended the First Amendment, holding that even the traditional exceptions to the First Amendment, such as obscenity, defamation, and fighting words, are "not entirely invisible to the Constitution," and government may not regulate them selectively to "handicap the expression of particular ideas." Accordingly, Justice Scalia struck down a St. Paul ordinance prohibiting the display of symbols "including, but not limited to, a burning cross or Nazi swastika, which one knows or has reasonable grounds to know arouses anger, alarm or resentment in others on the basis of race, color, creed, religion or gender." In his ambitious opinion for the Court, Justice Scalia noted that "[s]pecial hostility toward the particular biases thus singled out . . . is precisely what the First Amendment forbids." Minnesota could pass a general statute banning fighting words, but it could not single out only those fighting words that provoke violence on the basis of race or sex.

Justice Scalia has invoked similar logic, however, to justify broad regulation of obscene speech. In *FW/PBS, Inc.* v. *Dallas*, 493 U.S. 215 (1990), he developed a novel theory for regulating the sale of sexually explicit material. A Dallas zoning ordinance had been enforced against the owners of adult bookstores; and the Court concluded that the ordinance was not on its face unconstitutional. Justice Scalia suggested that although he would prohibit communities from suppressing particular books or films, he would allow blanket bans on adult bookstores and theaters on the grounds that pandering sex for profit is illegal: "The Constitution does not require a State or municipality to permit a business that intentionally specializes in, and holds itself forth to the public as specializing in, performance or portrayal of sex acts, sexual organs in a state of arousal, or live human nudity." Similarly, in *Pope* v. *Illinois*, 481 U.S. 497 (1987), the Court ruled that the third prong of the *Miller* obscenity test should be governed by whether the ordinary member of any community would find serious value in the allegedly obscene material. Justice Scalia concurred with the holding because he felt the "objective" test was most faithful to the true intentions of *Miller* v. *California*, 413 U.S. 15 (1973). But he added that, in his view, "[i]t is quite impossible to come to an objective assessment of (at least) literary or artistic value, there being many accomplished people who have found literature in Dada, and art in the re-publication of a soup can." The legal fiction of the reasonable man, he noted, cast little light on this esoteric inquiry.

Finally, in *Austin* v. *Michigan State Chamber of Commerce*, 494 U.S. 652 (1990), the Court upheld a Michigan statute restricting corporate spending in connection with state elections. The statute prohibited corporations from supporting or opposing candidates for state offices, but allowed them to make contributions from segregated funds used only for political purposes. "Attention all citizens," Justice Scalia wrote in dissent. "To assure the fairness of elections by preventing disproportionate expression of the view of any single powerful group, your Government has decided that the following associations of persons shall be prohibited from speaking or writing in support of any candidate." Unsatisfied by the Court's argument that corporate speech may be regulated because corporations often "amass vast wealth" because of their protections under state law, Justice Scalia felt the Court was conflating two bad arguments. The state was not entitled to extract First Amendment forfeitures in exchange for corporate benefits; and it could not suppress political speech based on aggregations of wealth without embracing prohibitions against individuals whose "net worth is above a certain figure."

Radical self restraint, scrupulous attention to text and history, methodological consistency—these are exacting principles, but Justice Scalia properly demands to be judged by them, and he deserves to be taken seriously. In many cases, Justice Scalia's principles do restrain his passions, but in some of the cases he feels most deeply about, his passions have led him to betray his principles. Even as a flawed formalist, however, Justice Scalia deserves respect as one of the few Justices on the Rehnquist Court who has tried to articulate an objective jurisprudence against which his decisions can be measured.

SELECTED BIBLIOGRAPHY

The best introduction to Justice Scalia's jurisprudence are his own speeches and scholarly articles. See, e.g., Antonin Scalia, "Assorted Canards of Contemporary Legal Analysis," 40 *Case Western Reserve Law Review* 581, 588 (1990); "The Rule of Law as a Law of Rules," 56 *University of Chicago Law Review* 1175 (1989); "Originalism: The Lesser Evil," 57 *University of Cincinnati Law Review* 849 (1989); "Judicial Deference to Administrative Interpretations of Law," 1989 *Duke Law Journal* 511; "The Doctrine of Standing as an Essential Element of the Separation of Powers," 17 *Suffolk University Law Review* 881 (1983).

Justice Scalia's jurisprudence has provoked more academic commentary than that of any other sitting Justice. The most wide-ranging discussion is found in a symposium on "The Jurisprudence of Antonin Scalia," 12 *Cardozo Law Review* 1593, 1867 (1991). For an earlier assessment, see George Kannar, "The Constitutional Catechism of Antonin Scalia," 99 *Yale Law Journal* 1297, 1320 (1990). Other selections from the extensive secondary literature include David B. Anders, "Justices Harlan and Black Revisited: The Emerging Dispute Between Justice O'Connor and Justice Scalia over Unenumerated Fundamental Rights," 61 *Fordham Law Review* 895 (1993); William D. Popkin, "An 'Internal' Critique of Justice Scalia's Theory of Statutory Interpretation," 76 *Minnesota Law Review* 1133 (1992); Steven G. Gey, "Justice Scalia's Death Penalty," 20 *Florida State University Law Review* 67 (1992); David Boling, "The Jurisprudential Approach of Justice Antonin Scalia: Methodology over Result?" 44 *Arkansas Law Review* 1137 (1991); Beau James Brock, "Mr. Justice Antonin Scalia: A Renaissance of Positivism and Predictability in Constitutional Adjudication," 51 *Louisiana Law Review* 623 (1991); Arthur Stock, "Justice Scalia's Use of Sources in Statutory and Constitutional Interpretation: How Congress Always Loses," 1990 *Duke Law Journal* 160; James Edward Wyszynski, Jr., "In Praise of Judicial Restraint: The Jurisprudence of Justice Antonin Scalia," 1 *Detroit College of Law Review* 117 (1989); Daniel N. Reisman, "Deconstructing Justice Scalia's Separation of Powers Jurisprudence: The Preeminent Executive," 53 *Albany Law Review* 49 (1988).

Anthony M. Kennedy

☆ 1936–   ☆

APPOINTED BY RONALD REAGAN

YEARS ON COURT
1987–

by
THEODORE EISENBERG

Anthony M. Kennedy was nominated to the Supreme Court on November 11, 1987, by President Ronald Reagan. He was born on July 23, 1936, the son of a Roman Catholic California lawyer and lobbyist, and a mother well known for her work with volunteer organizations. Justice Kennedy grew up in Sacramento, California, received his undergraduate degree from Stanford University in 1958, his law degree cum laude from Harvard Law School in 1961, and he spent a year studying at the London School of Economics. He began his legal career at a San Francisco law firm, but within the year his father died and Kennedy returned to Sacramento to take over his father's law and lobbying practice.

While a Stanford undergraduate, throughout law school, and as a practicing lawyer, he showed a strong interest in constitutional law. He taught constitutional law at the McGeorge School of Law from 1965 until his Supreme Court appointment. He also developed expertise in tax law and gained prominence through a measure that combined his interests in constitutional law and tax law. He helped California governor Ronald Reagan's administration draft a state ballot proposition to limit state spending. Although that proposition was rejected by the voters, Kennedy had caught the attention of the state administration. In 1975, at the young age of thirty-eight, he was appointed to the United States Court of Appeals for the Ninth Circuit. He served on the Ninth Circuit for twelve years.

Justice Kennedy's appointment to the Supreme Court arose under an unusual set of circumstances. He was President Reagan's third choice to fill the seat left vacant by Justice Powell's resignation. His nomination followed the failed nominations of Robert Bork and Douglas Ginsburg. As an academic and judge, Bork had left a lengthy paper trail that provided specific targets for his opponents. He was receptive to and underwent one of the most intensive public interrogations of any Supreme Court nominee. His nomination failed in the Senate (42 for confirmation, 48 against) for a combination of reasons. One of the most important was his restrictive view of constitutional interpretation. Judge Ginsburg's nomination was withdrawn after it was revealed that he had smoked marijuana. By the time Kennedy was nominated, the Senate and potential opponents had expended much energy contesting the president's nominees. And Justice Kennedy's paper record was not cluttered with controversial views on major issues.

Kennedy even received some support from traditionally liberal groups and individuals. He had taught for many years at McGeorge Law School. The La Raza Law Students Association of McGeorge Law School, a liberal organization dedicated to Hispanic and related social issues, unanimously endorsed his nomination to the Supreme Court. The Hispanic National Bar Association and the AFL-CIO did not oppose him. Harvard Law School professor Laurence Tribe, a leading opponent of Judge Bork and a critic of conservative jurisprudence, testified in support of Kennedy's appointment, as did Susan Westerberg Prager, dean of the UCLA Law School.

Several civil rights groups did express concern. He was opposed by the National Organization for Women, the Americans for Democratic Action, the National Gay & Lesbian Task Force, the National Lawyers Guild, and other groups. The Mexican-American Legal Defense Fund expressed serious reservations about him. He was strongly endorsed by police and law enforcement organizations. But the depth of feeling marshaled against Judge Bork never materialized and, on February 3, 1988, the Senate confirmed his nomination by a vote of ninety-seven to zero. Justice Kennedy joined the Court on February 18, 1988.

As might be expected, no single unifying theme explains Justice Kennedy's views during his first five years on the Court. For most Justices, five years is too brief a period for a unified judicial philosophy to emerge. Some Justices, such as Justice Scalia, seem to arrive on the Court with a fixed philosophy. Most others are more willing to allow their views to evolve on a case-by-case basis, and Justice Kennedy appears to be in this group. Even without the benefit of a unifying philosophy, however, some useful statements summarizing Justice Kennedy's performance can be made.

First, those liberal supporters who testified on behalf of Kennedy are almost certainly disappointed with his performance to date. On balance, he has been a consistent member of the Court's conservative majority on practically every issue. His cautious approach applies both to judicial technique and to substantive results. The most obvious feature of his judicial technique is a strong respect for precedent. On occasion, however, Justice Kennedy is not a technical conservative. At times, his analytical path to a restrictive result tramples precedent and operates on the basis of questionable empirical assumptions.

Aside from technique, the range of views one usually associates with conservative jurisprudence does apply to Justice Kennedy. He usually sides with the government against the individual, strongly believes in state powers, and views unfavorably an expansive approach to access to federal courts. Justice Kennedy's work also reflects a genuine streak of independence. He is not an idealogue on most issues. When he believes precedent dictates a result he disfavors, he usually will side with precedent. On occasion, he will depart from the conservative majority and stake out a position on his own, sometimes even more restrictive than that of other conservatives. Furthermore, the 1991 term seemed to reflect both a change and a growing independence in Justice Kennedy's views. He proved more willing to modify his own prior views and less willing to join an increasingly strident Justice Scalia. Whether this proves to be a one-term phenomenon or a long-term development cannot yet be determined.

Justice Kennedy quickly joined Chief Justice Rehnquist and Justices White, O'Connor, and Scalia to form a conservative majority. In his first term, a partial term, he agreed with each member of the new conservative majority in at least eighty-two per cent of the cases. According to the *Harvard Law Review*, his highest rate of agreement with one of the other four Justices was sixty-eight per cent (with Justice Stevens). This early pattern grew in intensity in the 1988 term. His lowest rate of agreement with any member of the conservative majority was eighty-five per cent (with Justice Scalia); his highest rate of agreement with any other Justice was sixty-three per cent (with Justice Stevens). This pattern continued in Kennedy's third term, the 1989 term, with a slight decrease in the solidity of the conservative majority but a growing gap between the two wings of the Court. Outside of the conservative bloc, Justice Kennedy's highest rate of agreement fell to fifty-six per cent (with Justice Blackmun).

For his first few terms, the statistics are a reasonable proxy of Justice Kennedy's views. But raw numbers are not a fully satisfactory measure of a Justice's work. Although early and properly viewed as a conservative Justice, Kennedy also quickly showed a willingness to subordinate personal views to what he believed the Constitution mandates. The flag-burning case, *Texas* v. *Johnson*, 491 U.S. 397 (1989), was one of the most publicized issues of Justice Kennedy's early years. After burning an American flag as a form of political protest, Johnson was convicted of violating Texas' flag desecration law. The state conceded that Johnson's conduct was expressive conduct and thereby implicated the First Amendment. The case was, in the opinion of many, a litmus test of one's belief in freedom of expression.

One of the core principles of the First Amendment is that expressions of unpopular views, even if abhorrent to the majority, are protected. To many, there is no more abhorrent symbolic act of protest than desecrating the flag. It is the national symbol. Johnson could have burned copies of the Declaration of Independence or the Constitution without the emotional effect triggered by flag burning. The question in *Johnson* was whether an act so knowingly and deeply offensive to so many could find protection in the First Amendment. Yet as a matter of First Amendment principle the case seemed easy. The depth of feeling against Johnson's conduct could not supercede his First Amendment rights.

The strong emotional feelings about the issue produced an unusual five-to-four alignment within the Court. Two members of the usual conservative majority, Justices Scalia and Kennedy, joined Justices Brennan, Marshall, and Blackmun to strike down Johnson's conviction. Although he joined Brennan's majority opinion, Justice Kennedy was obviously disturbed by the case. In a brief concurring opinion, Kennedy wrote about the personal toll that cases exact. Clearly, Kennedy abhorred Johnson's conduct. He stated how this was a rare instance in which a Justice pauses to express distaste for a result compelled by the Constitution. But he ultimately sided with free expression and invoked the flag's image as transcending and encompassing the Johnsons of the world:

> The flag is constant in expressing beliefs Americans share, beliefs in law and peace and that freedom which sustains the human spirit. The case here today forces recognition of the costs to which those beliefs commit us. It is poignant but fundamental that the flag protects those who hold it in contempt.

This was judging at its finest: strongly held personal beliefs cast aside to yield a result that is believed to be commanded by the Constitution.

In most other areas, Justice Kennedy's detailed views, reviewed below, fit the more conservative mold. In his first few terms, Kennedy joined in opinions that represented noticeable shifts to, or furthered the development of, conservative trends in the Court's approach to several important issues. He was a reliable vote in support of Chief Justice Rehnquist's continuing effort to restrict the scope of federal habeas corpus. He authored or joined in a series of restrictive interpretations of federal civil rights statutes that were eventually overruled by Congress in the Civil Rights Act of 1991. He was a vigorous critic of affirmative action. And he seemed on the verge of joining in the view that *Roe* v. *Wade*, 410 U.S. 113 (1973), should be overruled.

With few exceptions, Justice Kennedy joined in a major retrenchment of the scope of federal habeas corpus. The retrenchment occurred primarily along two fronts. First, by limiting federal habeas review of state convictions to cases in which no new legal rule is sought to be created, the Court erected a new procedural barrier to federal habeas corpus claims. Second, the Court and Justice Kennedy substantially expanded the circumstances under which procedural defaults would preclude the availability of federal habeas relief. In implementing these changes, Justice Kennedy was the author of important opinions for the Court in *Saffle* v. *Parks*, 494 U.S. 484 (1990) and *McCleskey* v. *Zant*, 111 B.Ct. 1454 (1991), and he joined in several other opinions.

The new procedural barrier, the no-new-rule standard, was constructed in perhaps the most important habeas corpus decision of Justice Kennedy's early years, *Teague* v. *Lane*, 489 U.S. 288 (1989). In *Teague*, Kennedy joined an opinion that erected a substantial new barrier to the ability of state prisoners to obtain federal habeas corpus relief for constitutional violations. Until *Teague*, the Court had been willing to adjudicate habeas corpus claims asserting constitutional violations in much the same fashion it adjudicated direct appeals from state courts. If the Court determined that a constitutional violation had occurred, it gave the petitioning prisoner the benefit of the rule proscribing the government's behavior. The Court left to subsequent cases the question of whether the rule should be applied to other prisoners whose claims predated that of the petitioning prisoner. New constitutional limits on state behavior, announced in the petitioning prisoner's case, were not always applied to all other prisoners.

In part to avoid this seeming inequality, the Court announced in *Teague* that federal habeas-corpus cases would no longer be a vehicle in which the Court could announce new behavioral standards. If the federal habeas petitioner sought to benefit from a new rule, one to be announced in the petitioner's case, the federal district court would have to dismiss his or her petition.

Teague was a major shift in federal habeas corpus doctrine. It cut off one important avenue for the development of constitutional criminal procedure rules. Some of the Court's most important pronouncements in the area of criminal procedure had been announced in habeas corpus cases. Under *Teague*, a prisoner's chance of benefiting from a new rule of constitutional criminal procedure depends on the slim possibility that the Supreme Court will agree to hear his or her case on direct review of his or her state court conviction, in contrast to a postappeal collateral attack on that conviction through a federal habeas corpus action. Since the Court agrees to hear a tiny fraction of all cases in which review is sought, only freakish good luck could lead to the development of a new rule for a specific prisoner.

The Court, with Justice Kennedy joining, made it clear that the *Teague* approach to habeas corpus would not be narrowly confined. In *Penry* v. *Lynaugh*, 492 U.S. 302 (1989), the Court stated that *Teague*'s no-new-rule requirement would be applied even to the sentencing phase of capital cases. Penry claimed that the trial court unconstitutionally failed to instruct the jury on how to weigh mitigating factors in answering a set of special inquiries about the defendant's acts. The instructions given to the jury seemed to require a death sentence even if the jury found substantial mitigating factors to be present, because the instructions did not specify how the jury should balance mitigating circumstances against factors in the case that would support a death sentence.

The Court found in the *Penry* case that the habeas corpus petitioner was not seeking application of a new rule and allowed the case to go forward. The Court relied on two precedents. In *Lockett* v. *Ohio*, 438 U.S. 586 (1978), a plurality of the Supreme Court had decided that an Ohio death penalty statute that limited the jury's consideration to specified mitigating circumstances violated the constitutional requirement of individualized sentencing in capital cases. In *Eddings* v. *Oklahoma*, 455 U.S. 104 (1982), the *Lockett* view commanded a majority. The Court held that a sentencing judge's refusal to consider mitigating evidence concerning a defendant's family history and upbringing was constitutional error. *Lockett* and *Eddings*, the Court concluded, clearly governed the *Penry* claim. The Court stated that, at the time of Penry's conviction, it was clear that a state could not prevent the jury from considering and giving effect to evidence relevant to the defendant's background or character or to mitigating evidence. Justice Kennedy and two other Justices joined Justice Scalia's dissent from the majority's conclusion that *Penry* did not involve a new rule.

The question of whether a habeas petitioner's claim involved assertion of a new rule became a fertile, hypertechnical branch of federal habeas doctrine. The no-new-rule requirement asks not what the law is or what the law should be but whether the legal standard sought by the petitioner "was susceptible to debate among reasonable minds" at the time the habeas petitioner's conviction became final (*Butler* v. *McKellar*, 494 U.S. 407 [1990]).

The reasoning in *Penry* is central to understanding Justice Kennedy's subsequent opinion for the Court in *Saffle* v. *Parks*, 494 U.S. 484 (1990). There, on facts not altogether different from *Penry*, Kennedy was able to command a majority against allowing the habeas claim to go forward. Parks had been convicted of capital murder. During the sentencing phase of the trial, Parks offered testimony by his father, who described Parks' background and character. Parks' counsel relied on this mitigating testimony, arguing to the jury that Parks' youth, race, school experience, and broken home were mitigating factors that the jury should consider in deciding whether to sentence Parks to death. By instructing the jury, the trial judge told the jury to avoid any influence of sympathy, sentiment, passion, prejudice, or other arbitrary factor when imposing sentence. Eventually, Parks filed a petition for a writ of habeas corpus in federal district court, arguing that the antisympathy component of the jury instruction violated the Eighth Amendment because it, in effect, told the jury to disregard the mitigating evidence that Parks had presented.

Under *Teague* v. *Lane*, Parks faced the preliminary hurdle of convincing the Court that he was not seeking the application of a new rule. The antisympathy instruction was not a new rule, he asserted, because it was implicit in *Lockett*, in *Eddings*, and in *Penry*. Justice Kennedy's opinion for a five-to-four majority rejected the claim. Kennedy stated that *Lockett* and *Eddings* did not address the same issue as *Saffle*. He described the issue in *Saffle* as being "whether the State may instruct the sentencer to render its decision on the evidence without sympathy." This he viewed as being a question of *how* a jury must consider mitigating evidence. *Lockett* and *Eddings*, in contrast, concerned a question of what mitigating evidence a jury must be allowed to consider. Justice Kennedy also rejected the view that *Penry* foreshadowed the relief sought in *Saffle*. Again, his opinion emphasized that *Penry* addressed what evidence death sentence juries must be allowed to hear, not how they must hear it.

These differences between *Saffle* and earlier cases, perhaps obvious only to a legal analyst, were enough to prevent federal review of Parks' death sentence. Yet it would have been easy to state the holdings of *Lockett*, *Eddings*, and *Penry* at a level of generality that supported Parks' claim that he was not requesting a new rule. Those earlier cases could have been viewed as instances where juries were allowed to fully consider mitigating evidence bearing on death sentences. This statement is broad enough to encompass both the kinds of mitigating evidence juries must have access to as well as how the mitigating evidence should be weighed against the circumstances pointing toward a death sentence.

Thus, in dissent in *Penry* and writing for the majority in *Saffle*, Justice Kennedy used a highly technical approach—constructing subtle distinctions among cases—to a highly technical standard that he had helped create—the no-new-rule standard. The combined result is a hypertechnical interpretation that severely limits the power of federal courts to review death sentences. This hardly seems like an area in which technicality should be piled on technicality to yield a result.

In *Stringer* v. *Black*, 112 S. Ct. 1130 (1992), Justice Kennedy, again writing for the Court, delivered a less restrictive interpretation of the no-new-rule standard. *Stringer*, which involved a Mississippi death sentence, required the Court to determine whether a state statute involving aggravating circumstances that could justify a death sentence was unduly vague. In *Godfrey* v. *Georgia*, 446 U.S. 420 (1980), the Court had invalidated a death sentence imposed under a state law that deemed an aggravating circumstance a killing that was "outrageously or wantonly vile, horrible and inhuman." The Court held this standard to be too vague, thereby inviting arbitrary and capricious application of the death penalty. In *Maynard* v. *Cartwright*, 486 U.S. 356 (1988), the Court applied *Godfrey* to invalidate a state statute that deemed an aggravating circumstance a killing that was "especially heinous, atrocious, or cruel." By the time of *Clemons* v. *Mississippi*, 494 U.S. 738 (1990), the *Godfrey* principle had been applied to Mississippi's aggravating circumstance statute, which contained aggravating circumstance language identical to that in *Maynard*.

In *Stringer*, the state argued that, at the time Stringer's conviction became final, applying *Godfrey* and *Maynard* to Mississippi's aggravating circumstance statute would constitute application of a new rule. The Court rejected the claim. It noted that in *Clemons* itself the state had failed to argue that there was no constitutional requirement to define, with precision, aggravating factors under Mississippi's sentencing scheme. Justice Kennedy wrote that differences between Mississippi's sentencing scheme and that invalidated in *Godfrey* pointed toward more definite application of the *Godfrey* standard.

Prior to *Teague*, and well before Justice Kennedy's appointment to the Court, the most significant modern restriction on federal habeas corpus was announced in *Wainwright* v. *Sykes*, 433 U.S. 72 (1977). There, the Court held that procedural defaults in state criminal proceedings bar subsequent federal habeas corpus review unless the state prisoner shows cause for the failure to comply with state procedures and prejudice to his case from the state's refusal to hear his claim. The cause and prejudice standard, as developed in subsequent cases, effectively precluded most state prisoners from raising an issue for the first time in a federal habeas corpus petition. The cause and prejudice standard undermined the "deliberate bypass" standard announced in *Fay* v. *Noia*, 372 U.S. 391 (1963). Under *Fay*, a prisoner would not be deemed to have waived an issue unless the prisoner deliberately bypassed state proceedings.

In *Coleman* v. *Thompson*, 111 B. Ct. 2546 (1991), Justice Kennedy joined Justice O'Connor's opinion for a six-Justice majority that extended the cause and prejudice standard. Coleman, who had been sentenced to death, had defaulted his entire state collateral appeal by filing late. This was an inadvertent error, as the state conceded. Nevertheless, the Supreme Court concluded that *Wainwright*'s cause and prejudice standard had to be satisfied. Justice Blackmun, joined by Justices Marshall and Stevens in dissent, accused the majority of erecting "petty procedural barriers to block federal court consideration of constitutional claims.

In *McCleskey* v. *Zant*, 111 B. Ct. 1454 (1991), Justice Kennedy's opinion for the Court further extended the cause and prejudice standard. McCleskey had been convicted of murder and sentenced to death. At trial, he renounced a prior confession. To rebut McCleskey's testimony, the prosecution called Evans, who had occupied a jail cell next to McCleskey's. Evans testified that McCleskey admitted to having committed the crime. McCleskey appealed the conviction to the Supreme Court of Georgia on several grounds, one of which was that the trial court erred in allowing evidence of McCleskey's statement to Evans because the prosecutor had deliberately withheld the statement in violation of *Brady* v. *Maryland*, 373 U.S. 83 (1963). The Georgia court rejected this claim because disclosing the evidence would not have helped McCleskey. The Supreme Court denied review of the case and McCleskey brought a postconviction proceeding in state court. In that proceeding, McCleskey alleged that the prosecution should have disclosed an agreement to drop pending escape charges against Evans in return for his cooperation and testimony. He also alleged that admission of Evans' testimony violated his right to counsel because the situation had been designed to elicit incriminating statements from McCleskey without the assistance of counsel. The court denied relief and both the Supreme Court of Georgia and the U.S. Supreme Court denied review.

McCleskey next brought a federal habeas corpus petition where he renewed the claims based on nondisclosure of Evans' testimony and nondisclosure of the prosecution's agreement with Evans. This proceeding succeeded in the district court, but the court of appeals reversed and the Supreme Court, after reviewing the question whether Georgia's capital sentencing procedures were unconstitutional, denied relief. A second state postconviction proceeding was unsuccessful and McCleskey filed a second federal habeas corpus petition.

In the second federal habeas petition, McCleskey renewed the claim, made in his first state postconviction proceeding, that the prosecution had denied him the assistance of counsel in eliciting statements from him through Evans. This claim, which was not made a basis for McCleskey's first federal habeas petition, was the central issue before Justice Kennedy in *McCleskey*. In support of the denial-of-counsel claim in the second federal petition, McCleskey relied on a twenty-one-page signed statement that Evans had made to the police two weeks before McCleskey's trial began. The police had furnished the statement to McCleskey one month before he filed his second federal petition.

The statement prompted the federal district court to conduct hearings. After extensive testimony, the court concluded that Evans had been used by the police to obtain incriminating evidence from McCleskey in violation of McCleskey's right to counsel. The state opposed the petition in part on the grounds that raising this claim in the second habeas petition (and not in the first) constituted an abuse of the writ of habeas corpus. The federal district court ruled that McCleskey did not deliberately abandon the claim after raising it in his first state postconviction proceeding. The district court excused the earlier failure to renew the claim because, at the time of the first federal petition, McCleskey did not know about the key twenty-one-page document or about a key witness that the document led to. After the court of appeals reversed the district court on the abuse of the writ claim, Justice Kennedy wrote for the Supreme Court.

He might have taken the view that, even considering the new testimony, there remained no substantial doubt about McCleskey's guilt. Relief could have been denied on that score with little doctrinal innovation. But, as in *Teague*, Justice Kennedy and the Court's majority seemed eager to reshape federal habeas corpus doctrine. Kennedy's opinion for the Court made a major new pronouncement about the scope of the writ. He wrote that abuse of the writ of habeas corpus is not confined to instances of deliberate abandonment. A petitioner may abuse the writ by failing to raise a claim through inexcusable neglect as well as deliberate decision. By combining unintentional failures with intentional failures, Justice Kennedy was able to ease the analysis toward the state procedural default line of cases, discussed above, where many failures to raise claims stem from simple neglect.

His opinion links the standards governing abuse of the writ to the standards governing procedural default. He concluded that the same standard used to determine whether to excuse state procedural default should govern the determination of inexcusable neglect in abuse of the writ cases. Although much of the rhetoric of procedural default cases had been based on the need for federal courts to respect the procedures and sovereignty of states and their courts, this possibly limiting principle was quickly cast aside. The doctrines of procedural default and abuse of the writ are both designed "to lessen the injury to a state that results through reexamination of a state conviction on a ground that the state did not have the opportunity to address at a prior, appropriate time."

The linking of abuse-of-the-writ doctrine to state procedural defaults meant that abuse cases would be governed by the cause and prejudice standard. Justice Kennedy's embrace of the standard was based on an extreme, but empirically unsupported, view of recent habeas corpus experience. In a revealing passage, he wrote, "The cause and prejudice standard should curtail the abusive petitions that in recent years have threatened to undermine the integrity of the habeas corpus process."

Habeas corpus was out of control, and he would help curtail it. The passage explains the Court's efforts to reach out and decide issues that a truly conservative approach to jurisprudence would not countenance. It also helps explain the specific result in the case.

The practical impact of Justice Kennedy's new abuse standard could only be assessed by how it would be applied to specific facts. And his application of it to the facts in *McCleskey* suggests that he was eager to curtail habeas corpus. For even under the cause and prejudice standard, McCleskey had a plausible claim. The ineffective assistance of counsel claim had not been pursued in the first federal habeas proceeding because the twenty-one-page document that prompted McCleskey to renew the claim was not available at the earlier time. In the second federal proceeding, the district court found that neither the document nor the key witness it led to were known or discoverable before filing the first federal petition.

To avoid the logical implications of this finding, Justice Kennedy distinguished between two issues: whether McCleskey could have discovered the twenty-one-page document and whether he knew about or could have discovered the evidence that the document contained, namely, Evans' jail-cell conversations. Based on a review of the record that, in most cases, would have been left in the first instance to a lower court, Kennedy concluded that McCleskey could have discovered the evidence the statement contained at an earlier time. After all, McCleskey had participated in the conversations reported in the document.

This reasoning seems to ignore a fundamental reality of criminal law practice. Without the twenty-one-page statement, McCleskey's counsel had only the uncorroborated testimony of his client to support the denial of counsel claim. Since the state denied any arrangement with Evans and since the first state postconviction proceeding had rejected the denial of counsel claim, McCleskey's counsel might reasonably have concluded that it was pointless to repeat the claim in the first federal habeas proceeding. The twenty-one-page document gave credibility to the suspicion that the state had used Evans as an agent and failed to reveal that fact at trial. It may be that counsel could have discovered the contents of the document at an earlier time. But Justice Kennedy's opinion places no weight on the state's seemingly deliberate efforts to hide its arrangement and to delay releasing the key document until after a sentence of death had been imposed. Surely the state's effort made counsel's task more difficult. Why the burden of that increased difficulty should be borne by the defendant and not the state is far from clear.

On balance, Justice Kennedy's and the Court's performance on the abuse standard has not been a model of reasoning. Few would equate negligently failing to raise an issue with an abuse of a legal process. The Court seemed moved more by its perceptions of the federal docket than any reasoned legal analysis.

Yet Kennedy was not prepared to go quite as far as most of the Court's other conservative members in applying the cause and prejudice standard to curtail federal habeas corpus relief. In *Keeney* v. *Tamayo-Reyes*, 112 B. Ct. 1715 (1992), he dissented from a denial of access to federal court in an opinion that, like his statement in *McCleskey*, revealed much of the basis for his willingness to restrict access in so many other cases. In *Keeney*, a Cuban immigrant with almost no knowledge of English had been charged with murder. Tamayo-Reyes was provided with a defense attorney and an interpreter. After a hearing where he signed a form in English, which the interpreter translated, explaining the rights he was waiving by entering the plea, he pled nolo contendere to manslaughter. Tamayo-Reyes later brought a collateral attack on his plea in state court. He alleged that he did not understand the elements of the crime of manslaughter and that he thought he was agreeing to be tried for manslaughter.

After a hearing, the state court denied relief and Tamayo-Reyes brought a federal habeas corpus action. He alleged that the facts concerning the translation were not adequately developed at the state-court hearing. Under *Townsend* v. *Sain*, 372 U.S. 293 (1963), he alleged that this required a federal evidentiary hearing on whether his plea was unconstitutional. The court of appeals determined that material facts had not been developed due to the negligence of postconviction counsel. Because counsel's negligent failure to develop the facts did not amount to a deliberate bypass under *Fay* v. *Noia*, the court of appeals ruled that Tamayo-Reyes was entitled to a federal hearing. The question before the Supreme Court was whether the "deliberate bypass" standard of *Fay* v. *Noia* continued to be the standard for excusing a habeas petitioner's failure to develop a material fact in state-court proceedings or whether the "cause and prejudice" standard would apply.

A five-to-four majority held that the cause and prejudice standard applied. Justice Kennedy joined Justice O'Connor's dissenting opinion and filed a dissent of his own. In his dissenting opinion, he made clear the premises underlying his usual willingness to curtail federal habeas corpus doctrine. He stated that the number of cases in which the factual record in state court proceedings is inadequate "will be few in number" and that "there is no clear evidence that this particular classification of habeas proceedings has burdened the dockets of the federal courts" (112 S. Ct. at 1727).

Justice Kennedy's restrictive view of prisoner's rights also emerged in a non–habeas corpus case addressing prison conditions. *Wilson* v. *Seiter*, 111 S. Ct. 2321 (1991), questioned whether a prisoner claiming that conditions of confinement constitute cruel and unusual punishment under the Eighth Amendment must show a culpable state of mind on the part of prison officials. In a five-to-four decision, Kennedy joined Justice Scalia's opinion for the Court holding that a culpable state of mind is necessary. The Court refused to draw a distinction between isolated instances—onetime conditions—and systemic prison conditions. In cases of alleged systemic violations, *Wilson* seems to give prison officials a surprising defense. Even if heating, food, and living conditions are objectively inadequate, the Eighth Amendment is not implicated unless the prison authorities subjectively intend that the conditions be punishment. This was a less than generous interpretation of the Eighth Amendment's scope.

Justice Kennedy's enthusiastic support of limited interpretations of federal habeas corpus doctrine and prisoners' rights suggests that he has adopted several Justices' somewhat hysterical views of federal prisoner litigation. In *McCleskey* v. *Zant* and *Keeney* v. *Tamayo-Reyes*, he all but expressed the view that growing prisoner caseloads required restrictive doctrinal interpretation. Under this view, as articulated in Supreme Court opinions and elsewhere, the Court has intentionally curtailed habeas corpus and other prisoner cases with an eye on the docket. Prisoners, the reasoning goes, have become too litigious and occupy a disproportionate part of federal judicial time and energy.

Justice Kennedy's and other Justices' frustration with prisoner claims is especially visible in death penalty cases. In *Delo* v. *Stokes*, 495 U.S. 320 (1990), Justice Kennedy, writing for himself, Chief Justice Rehnquist, and Justice Scalia took the unusual step of, in effect, lecturing the court of appeals about its procedures. He criticized the lower court for not having a set of rules that would reduce the need for delaying executions when prisoners brought late challenges to their death sentences.

Curtailing doctrine based on the premise of overly litigious prisoners is problematic. Courts should not be able to eliminate or pare down classes of cases simply because they find them numerically troublesome. Congress confers jurisdiction on the federal courts and, however legitimate it may be to refuse to adjudicate in individual cases, it cannot be for the courts to decide when there are too many cases of a given kind.

Even more disturbing is that Justices who curtail doctrine based on perceived overloads do so on the basis of possibly inaccurate observations. They routinely fail to note that the number of prisoners has increased at least as dramatically as the number of prisoner filings. The U.S. prison population increased from about 240,000 inmates in 1975 to over 700,000 by 1989. When one adjusts the number of prisoner federal court filings to take account of the number of prisoners, there has been no real growth in prisoner filings. In fact, the number of federal court filings per prisoner decreased during the 1980s and, by this measure, habeas corpus filings decreased quite dramatically.

In Justice Kennedy's brief tenure on the Court, federal habeas doctrine has been changed more radically than in any other period of comparable length. He has been a central part of that movement. By unreflectively accepting stereotypical views of prisoner litigation, Kennedy has helped constrict doctrine based on what is at least in part a faulty premise—the increasing litigiousness of prisoners.

Outside the area of federal habeas corpus, the most important criminal procedure development during Justice Kennedy's early years on the Court was the development of rules limiting the use of peremptory challenges to jurors. Such rules have the potential to affect juror selection in every civil and criminal case.

Justice Kennedy joined in expanding prohibitions on race-based exclusions from juries. In *Batson* v. *Kentucky*, 476 U.S. 79 (1986), which occurred before he joined the Court, the Court had held that a defendant may challenge a prosecutor's use of peremptory challenges to exclude members of the defendant's race from the jury panel. In *Powers* v. *Ohio*, 111 B. Ct. 1364 (1991), the Court held that a criminal defendant may object to the use of peremptory challenges to exclude jurors on the basis of race, whether or not the defendant and the excluded juror are of the same race. Thus, a white defendant could protest the race-based exclusion of black jurors. Justice Kennedy's opinion for the Court emphasized service on juries as an aspect of citizenship and viewed race-based exclusion as "a practice that forecloses a significant opportunity to participate in civic life."

In *Edmonson* v. *Leesville Concrete Company, Inc.*, 111 S. Ct. 2077 (1991), again writing for the Court, Justice Kennedy pushed the *Batson* principle to one of its outer limits. *Edmonson* holds that a private litigant in a civil case may not use peremptory challenges to exclude jurors on account of race. This necessitated the expansion of *Batson* and *Powers* to the civil context, a process that required emphasizing service on juries as an attribute of citizenship rather than focusing on the rights of criminal defendants. And since the Fourteenth Amendment only limits government action, extending *Batson* to civil cases also requires holding that the acts of private litigants in using their peremptory challenges could be attributed to the state for purposes of the Fourteenth Amendment. In expanding the exclusion to the civil context, Justice Kennedy relied on the harm to the excluded juror and the deprivation of that juror's right to participate in the system of justice. In holding that acts by private litigants constitute state action, Kennedy expanded the concept of state action. In *Georgia* v. *McCollum*, 112 S. Ct. 2348 (1992), Justice Kennedy joined Justice Blackmun's opinion for the Court, extending the *Batson* rule to bar criminal defendants from exercising peremptory challenges on racial grounds.

To hold that race-based exclusions are forbidden is one thing. To find that such exclusions have in fact occurred is another. An early chance to apply the

Batson standard came in *Hernandez* v. *New York,* 111 S. Ct. 1859 (1991). Kennedy, writing the plurality opinion for four members of the court, rejected a challenge to a prosecutor's exclusion of two Spanish-speaking Latino prospective jurors. *Hernandez* involved Hispanic victims, Hispanic defendants, and Hispanic witnesses. The Spanish-language testimony would be interpreted by a court interpreter, whose translation would be official. The prosecutor defended the exclusion of Spanish-speaking prospective jurors on the grounds that they might not accept the official translation of testimony and might have an undue impact upon the jury. The prosecutor argued that the Hispanic status of the victims in the case gave him no reason to wish to systematically exclude Hispanics from the jury.

Hernandez argued that Spanish-language ability bears a close relation to ethnicity and that it therefore violates the Equal Protection Clause to use peremptory challenges on the grounds of language ability. Justice Kennedy acknowledged that the prosecutor's exclusion criterion might result in the disproportionate exclusion of Latino jurors. But he emphasized the deference due the trial judge on questions of fact and declined the defendant's request to adopt a more aggressive standard of review.

Nevertheless, sustaining the prosecutor's reasoning was difficult. The prosecutor's argument could easily be generalized to exclude all Spanish-speaking prospective jurors from juries in cases involving Spanish testimony. Such a rule would not be quite the same as an express rule implementing an ethnicity-based exclusion—some non-Hispanics speak Spanish—but it is uncomfortably close to such a standard. Where a rule has such a massively disproportionate impact, it is tempting to equate the impact, exclusion of Latinos, with an intent to exclude that group. Justice Kennedy's deferential approach to review would lead to few successful challenges on *Batson* grounds.

Justices Blackmun, Stevens, and Marshall dissented. They relied on the severe disparate impact and the availability of alternatives. Justice Stevens' dissenting opinion noted that bilingual jurors could have been instructed to bring to the judge's attention any disagreement they may have had with the official translation. Alternatively, the translator could be the only person to hear the witness' words, thereby limiting the jury to the official translation.

Outside the area of jury selection, Justice Kennedy regularly voted to limit or curtail criminal defendants' procedural rights. In *Nedina* v. *California,* 112 S. Ct. 2572 (1992), Kennedy, writing for the Court, held that a defendant who alleges incompetence to stand trial may be made to bear the burden of proving incompetence by a preponderance of the evidence. Justice Kennedy has advocated a narrow view of the Fourth Amendment. Indeed, some of his pre–Supreme Court notoriety came from his dissent at the court of appeals level from a holding to craft good faith exception to the Fourth Amendment's exclusionary rule. In *United States* v. *Leon,* 468 U.S. 817 (1984), his dissenting view prevailed in the Supreme Court on review of his court of appeals decision. This narrow view of the Fourth Amendment continued after he joined the Supreme Court. In *Skinner* v. *Railway Labor Executives Association,* 489 U.S. 602 (1989), Justice Kennedy's opinion for the Court sustained federal railroad regulations authorizing drug and alcohol testing of railroad employees. The regulations, he wrote, were reasonable under the Fourth Amendment even though no warrant was required and testing could be done without suspicion that any particular employee might be impaired. In *James* v. *Illinois,* 493 U.S. 307 (1990), Justice Kennedy, in a dissent joined by three other Justices, believed that the exception to the exclusionary rule, which allows illegally seized evidence to be used to impeach a defendant, should be extended to permit the prosecution to impeach the testimony of all defense witnesses.

Even though he is quite restrictive of criminal procedure rights, Justice Kennedy is not the most restrictive Justice. For example, in *Doggett* v. *United States,* 112 B. Ct. 2686 (1992), he joined Justice Souter's opinion for the Court in holding that an eight-and-a-half-year delay between indictment and trial violated the Sixth Amendment's speedy trial requirement. Justices O'Connor, Thomas, and Scalia, and Chief Justice Rehnquist would have held that it did not.

In a dissenting opinion early in his Supreme Court career, Kennedy demonstrated a reluctance to protect a suspect's right to counsel. In *Edwards* v. *Arizona,* 451 U.S. 477 (1981), the Court had held that a suspect who has said that he wishes to deal with the police only through counsel is not subject to further interrogation until counsel has been made available or the suspect initiates further communications with the police. *Arizona* v. *Roberson,* 486 U.S. 675 (1988), raised the question of whether there was an exception to *Edwards* for cases in which the police wish to interrogate a suspect about an offense that is unrelated to the subject of their initial investigation. A six-Justice majority declined to endorse an exception.

Justice Kennedy, in an opinion joined only by Chief Justice Rehnquist, dissented. He argued that the majority's rule was not necessary to protect suspects' rights and that it deprived the police of a legitimate investigative tool. Police, he argued, should be able to give *Miranda* warnings with respect to a separate investigation and, if the suspect agrees, to interrogate the suspect with respect to a crime unrelated to that for which he had insisted on speaking only through counsel. This second warning reduces the opportunity for police coercion in the second investigation.

Based on *Roberson,* in which not even Justice Scalia would join Justice Kennedy's dissent, Kennedy might have been thought to be extremely reluctant to restrict police interrogations. Yet, in *Minnick* v. *Mississippi,* 111 S. Ct. 486 (1990), Kennedy refused to curtail the *Edwards* rule. The Mississippi Supreme Court interpreted *Edwards* to mean that the police may ask about a different crime once the suspect has consulted with counsel. This cramped interpretation of *Edwards* might have rendered its holding meaningless. Justice Kennedy, writing for the Court, stated that a "single consultation with an attorney does not remove the suspect from persistent attempts by officials to persuade him to waive his rights, or from the coercive pressures that accompany custody and that may increase as custody is prolonged."

Had Justice Kennedy been unremittingly hostile to the *Edwards* rule, *Minnick* presented him with an opportunity to express his dissatisfaction. Instead, his majority opinion reaffirmed *Edwards* and triggered a dissent from Justice Scalia, joined by Chief Justice Rehnquist. Justice Scalia threw back at Justice Kennedy language from Kennedy's dissent in *Roberson*, suggesting that *Edwards* should be strictly limited.

Justice Kennedy has been restrictive in his interpretation of civil rights statutes and remedies. From employment-discrimination claims to procedural issues to voting rights, he regularly votes against civil rights plaintiffs unless the legal issue is almost completely clear in their favor. His reluctance to recognize civil rights interests combines with a strongly felt opposition to the use of affirmative action unless it is limited to remedying identifiable past discrimination.

Patterson v. *McLean Credit Union*, 491 U.S. 164 (1989), questioned whether a claim of racial harassment in employment could be brought under 42 U.S.C. SS 1981, a surviving portion of the Civil Rights Act of 1866. In *Runyon* v. *McCrary*, 427 U.S. 160 (1976) and *Jones* v. *Alfred H. Mayer Co.*, 392 U.S. 409 (1968), the Court had interpreted section 1981 and a companion provision, 42 U.S.C. SS 1982, to reach private racial discrimination in contractual and property relations. After the initial oral argument in *Patterson*, the Court, on its own motion, ordered the case reargued. It asked the parties to address the question whether *Runyon's* interpretation of section 1981 should be overruled.

Few procedural orders in the Court's history have generated such a substantial reaction. Many observers interpreted the *Patterson* reargument order as foreshadowing the reversal of the prior twenty years' practice of applying sections 1981 and 1982 to private discrimination. The reargument order prompted sharp dissents from Justices Blackmun and Stevens, each joined by Justices Brennan and Marshall. The majority responded by taking the unusual step of defending a reargument order in writing. The reargument order generated intense attention on the pending case. Following the second oral argument, Justice Kennedy wrote the Court's opinion. As he would later in the *Planned Parenthood* plurality opinion, Justice Kennedy relied on the doctrine of stare decisis and the Court unanimously declined to overrule *Runyon*.

But the rest of Kennedy's treatment of *Patterson*, which prompted four dissents, was a flawed technical performance that provided a nearly irrational interpretation of section 1981. Section 1981 provides that all persons shall have the same right to make and enforce contracts as white citizens. Justice Kennedy stated that the right to make and enforce contracts does not extend to conduct by an employer after establishment of the contractual relation, including Patterson's claim of posthiring racial harassment. Under this view, employers could not discriminate on the basis of race in hiring workers, but section 1981 would not prevent them from discriminating on the basis of race after the initial hiring. Analogously, private schools, whose behavior is also covered by section 1981, could not discriminate on the basis of race in admitting students but could keep them in segregated classrooms. It is difficult to imagine a rational legislator voting for such a bizarre set of results.

Part of the problem Justice Kennedy faced was not of his creation. There was a respectable argument that neither section 1981 nor section 1982 reaches private discriminatory behavior. But the Court had held otherwise in *Jones* v. *Mayer* and *Runyon* v. *McCrary* and Justice Kennedy was not ready to overrule those cases. Once one accepts that section 1981 applies to private behavior, it should be applied in a logical manner. Justice Kennedy's hypertechnical and implausible reading of section 1981 seems to be the result of a combination of frustration with the institutional constraints on overruling prior cases, together with a sense that section 1981 should be limited to the point where the prior cases were in effect largely overruled anyway.

Congress reacted to *Patterson* and other decisions by passing the Civil Rights Act of 1991, which overruled *Patterson*'s narrow reading of section 1981. President Bush's veto of the Civil Rights Act of 1990 was not based on a defense of the result in *Patterson*. In the lengthy and vigorous debates over the Civil Rights Acts of 1990 and 1991, few would defend either the *Patterson* result or the reasoning in Justice Kennedy's opinion.

Justice Kennedy's restrictive approach to civil rights issues emerged in several other cases overruled or modified by the Civil Rights Act of 1991. In *Wards Cove Packing Co.* v. *Atonio*, 490 U.S. 642 (1989), a five-to-four decision, Justice Kennedy joined a majority that issued several controversial interpretations of Title VII of the Civil Rights Act of 1964. In *Martin* v. *Wilks*, 490 U.S. 755 (1989), Justice Kennedy was part of a five-to-four majority that restrictively interpreted the scope of a consent decree designed to promote the hiring of black firefighters in Birmingham, Alabama. In *Lorance* v. *A T & T Technologies, Inc.*, 490 U.S. 500 (1989), Kennedy joined a six-Justice majority in narrowly interpreting the timely filing requirements of Title VII. In *EEOC* v. *Arabian American Oil Company*, 111 S. Ct. 1227 (1991), Kennedy was part of a six-Justice majority holding that Title VII does not apply to the employment practices of United States employers who employ United States citizens abroad.

Price Waterhouse v. *Hopkins*, 490 U.S. 228 (1989), raised the question of Title VII's application to cases in which an employment decision resulted from a mixture of legitimate and illegitimate motives. A majority of the Court rejected the argument that plaintiffs must establish tainted motives as the "but-for" cause of the discrimination. Tainted motives need only be a substantial factor contributing to the employment decision and evidence of a tainted motive requires that the employer show that the challenged action would have been taken anyway. Justice Kennedy, in an opinion joined by Chief Justice Rehnquist and Justice Scalia, dissented. He argued that unless tainted motives are found to be *the* cause of a discriminatory decision, the defendant who relied on other factors should not be viewed as having discriminated. In the Civil Rights Act of 1991, Congress expanded on the majority's view in *Price Waterhouse*. It declared that mixed-motive cases do constitute unlawful discrimination. Defendants who can prove they would have fired a worker for valid reasons as well as invalid reasons could have that factor taken into account in assessing the remedy.

Justice Kennedy's restrictive views of civil rights statutes and individual liberties were not limited to cases overruled by the Civil Rights Act of 1991. In *Chisom* v. *Roemer*, 111 S. Ct. 2354 (1991), a six-Justice majority held that state judicial elections are covered by the Voting Rights Act of 1965. Justice Kennedy joined Justice Scalia's dissenting opinion, which was also joined by Chief Justice Rehnquist. In *Presley* v. *Etowah County Commission*, 112 S. Ct. 820 (1992), Justice Kennedy wrote for a six-Justice majority in finding that the Voting Rights Act did not effect a change in the decision-making authority of elected members of county commissions when it appeared that the changes were precipitated by black officials occupying those county offices for the first time in recent history. In *Will* v. *Michigan Department of State Police*, 491 U.S. 58 (1989), Kennedy joined a five-to-four majority opinion limiting civil rights litigants' power to sue states in state courts. In *DeShaney* v. *Winnebago County Department of Social Services*, 489 U.S. 189 (1989), Justice Kennedy joined an opinion holding that the state has no constitutional duty to protect a child not in its custody.

He also took a restrictive view of the kinds of civil rights actions that ought to give rise to a cause of action under 42 U.S.C. SS 1983. In *Golden State Transit Corp.* v. *City of Los Angeles*, 493 U.S. 103 (1989), Kennedy, in a dissent joined by Chief Justice Rehnquist and Justice O'Connor, acknowledged that, under the National Labor Relations Act, a city lacked power to condition renewal of a taxicab franchise upon the settlement of the taxicab company's labor dispute. He argued, however, that a cause of action for damages to enforce this right under section 1983 was not available. Nevertheless, he believed that injunctive relief was available under other federal statutes. In *Dennis* v. *Higgins*, 111 S. Ct. 865 (1991), Kennedy, in an opinion joined by Chief Justice Rehnquist, dissented from a holding that Commerce Clause claims may be brought under section 1983. In *Dellmuth* v. *Muth*, 491 U.S. 223 (1989), a five-to-four decision, Justice Kennedy's opinion for the Court held that the Education of the Handicapped Act, which seeks to assure that handicapped children receive an appropriate free public education, did not abrogate a state's Eleventh Amendment immunity.

Although a minority opinion, Justice Kennedy's views of section 1983 in *Golden State Transit* and *Dennis* could draw support from the historical context in which section 1983 was enacted. As part of the post–Civil War era civil rights legislation, section 1983 was originally enacted out of concern for the rights of newly freed slaves in the South. Its original focus was not on broad structural rights such as those implicated by the Commerce Clause. Modern era cases such as *Maine* v. *Thiboutot*, 448 U.S. 1 (1980), had extended section 1983 to nontraditional areas, including statutory claims. And the statute's language is not limited to particular kinds of constitutional claims. The challenge for Justice Kennedy was to reconcile his narrow view of section 1983 with the prior expansive interpretations and statutory text. Rather than confront precedent and text directly, he relied on an argument, linguistically strained, that Commerce Clause rights are not rights "secured" under section 1983.

The underlying motivation for Justice Kennedy's restrictive views of section 1983 in *Golden State Transit* and *Dennis* was not hostility to the rights being asserted. He acknowledged the availability of injunctive relief. The real stakes, as articulated in his *Dennis* dissent, were whether attorneys' fees could be recovered by a prevailing plaintiff. Fees would be available for a cause of action brought under section 1983 but not available for an injunctive action brought under other federal statutes.

Justice Kennedy also took a narrow view of federal court's remedial powers in cases in which there plainly was a cause of action. In *Missouri* v. *Jenkins*, 495 U.S. 33 (1990), a five-to-four decision in a school desegregation case that spanned more than a decade, the question arose as to how to fund an expensive remedial decree. The majority held that to fund a desegregated school system after years of resistance to desegregation, a local government with taxing authority may be ordered to levy taxes in excess of the limits set by state statutes. Kennedy, writing for the four dissenters, all but ridiculed the breadth of the district court's order. He pointed out that the plan to upgrade the schools included a performing arts middle school, a twenty-five-acre farm, a twenty-five-acre wildlife area, and a high school that would offer programs ranging from heating and air conditioning to cosmetology and robotics. Ultimately, however, he did not rely on the breadth of the remedial program. Kennedy's was a more structural argument. He argued that the power to tax rests in the legislature, not the judiciary, and that the remedial order transcended the federal judiciary's power.

In *Freeman* v. *Pitts*, 112 S. Ct. 1430 (1992), Justice Kennedy's opinion for the Court showed great deference to a district court's judgment that some aspects of a school desegregation decree could be terminated. The school district's expert testified that continued racial imbalance in the school system resulted from massive demographic shifts that had left the county residentially segregated. The district court credited this testimony and held that the school district had achieved the "maximum practical desegregation" in light of the changed residential pattern. Justice Kennedy held that the district court had discretion "to order an incremental or partial withdrawal of its supervision and control" even though some vestiges of segregation remained in areas that continued to be supervised by the court. The Court remanded the case for more specific findings about whether continued supervision over pupil assignments would help eliminate vestiges of segregation in other areas.

Despite his substantive and remedial reluctance in civil rights matters, Justice Kennedy has not been the most restrictive interpreter of civil rights. In *Hudson* v. *McMillan*, 112 S. Ct. 995 (1992), he joined a seven-Justice majority that refused to make serious injury a prerequisite to a prisoner's claim of cruel and unusual punishment under the Eighth Amendment. Justices Thomas and Scalia would have done so.

In affirmative action cases, Justice Kennedy has been unsupportive of benign governmentally backed race-based distinctions. In *City of Richmond* v. *J. A. Croson Company*, 488 U.S. 469 (1989), Richmond required prime contractors to whom the city awarded construction contracts to subcontract at least thirty per cent of the dollar amount of the contract to minority business enterprises. For purposes of *City of Richmond*, Justice Kennedy applied a standard that subjected racial preferences to rigorous scrutiny by the courts. Applying this standard, and joining with five other Justices to make a majority, he found that Richmond's minority business enterprise requirements for the construction industry were invalid under the Fourteenth Amendment. The city council did not explore the nature and the scope of the discrimination that it sought to remedy, the extent of the city's involvement in prior discriminatory acts, and the precision with which the set-aside requirement related to the injury it was designed to address.

One key distinction between *City of Richmond* and *Fullilove* v. *Klutznick*, 448 U.S. 448 (1980), an earlier case allowing an affirmative action program, was the entity adopting the program. *Fullilove* involved a minority set-aside program not unlike that in *City of Richmond*, but the program in *Fullilove* had been adopted by Congress. Some Justices in *City of Richmond* placed great emphasis on the differences between congressional and state and local legislation and were willing to show greater deference to Congress.

Justice Kennedy's concurrence in *City of Richmond* intimated that he was prepared to reject any distinction based on differences between Congress and other legislative bodies and to strike down almost all racial preferences not tied to remedying unlawful discrimination. It was not necessary to adopt such a drastic rule for purposes of *City of Richmond* because the remedial program was not one of Congress' making. And he acknowledged that such a holding would be a significant departure from past affirmative action cases.

In *Metro Broadcasting, Inc.* v. *F.C.C.*, 110 S. Ct. 2997 (1990), a different majority emerged to sustain an affirmative action program. Justice Kennedy, in dissent, expressly adopted the view he had intimated in *City of Richmond* v. *Metro Broadcasting* that questioned the constitutionality of two FCC minority preference policies. First, the FCC awarded an enhancement for minority ownership and participation in management when comparing competing applications for new radio or television broadcast licenses. Second, the FCC had a "distress sale" policy that allowed a radio or television broadcaster whose qualification to hold a license had come into question to transfer that license without the normally required comparative hearing. But it could do so only if the transferee were a minority enterprise meeting certain requirements.

A majority of the Court, in an opinion by Justice Brennan, viewed the FCC preference policies as attributable to Congress. As such, the FCC's policies enjoyed the protection of *Fullilove*'s deference to Congress rather than the more active level of judicial review relied on to strike down the minority set-aside program in *City of Richmond*. Since the congressional policies served an important government objective—promotion of broadcast diversity—they were constitutional. The Court did not require that the preferential treatment for minorities be tied to a remedy for past discrimination, as it had insisted on in *City of Richmond* for a noncongressional remedial program.

In addition to joining Justice O'Connor's dissenting opinion, Justice Kennedy wrote a dissent joined by Justice Scalia. He pointed out some of the difficulties with a government policy designed to assist only those minority groups favored by minorities on an official list. The policies upheld, he claimed, served to exclude the many racial and ethnic minorities not on the FCC's list of favored minorities. The policies approved also required identifying racial groups. He noted that the FCC found it necessary to trace an applicant's history to 1492 to conclude that the applicant was Hispanic for the purpose of a minority tax certificate policy.

In joining Justice O'Connor's opinion, he distinguished *Metro Broadcasting* from *Fullilove*. First, *Fullilove* had relied on Congress' powers to enforce the Fourteenth Amendment to apply a less stringent standard of review to a racial classification. Second, *Fullilove* involved a congressional measure that sought to remedy identified past discrimination. In *Metro Broadcasting*, Justice Kennedy's separate opinion characterized the government interest—broadcast diversity—as trivial.

His separate opinion, joined only by Justice Scalia, rejected the argument that the race-based classification in *Metro Broadcasting* could be characterized as benign. Justice Kennedy equated this reasoning with that of the Court in *Plessy* v. *Ferguson*, 163 U.S. 537 (1896), which viewed the stamp of inferiority of segregation as arising "solely because the colored race chooses to put that construction on it."

Justice Kennedy's opinions in *City of Richmond* and *Metro Broadcasting* are among his most sharply worded opinions. He plainly has deeply held feelings about the lawfulness and wisdom of affirmative action programs not tied to specific remedies for identifiable past acts of discrimination.

In his first few years on the Court, Justice Kennedy often provided a crucial fifth vote to establish a conservative majority. By the 1990 term, Justice Souter had replaced Justice Brennan. Justice Souter's high rate of agreement with the conservative majority reduced the influence of Justice Kennedy's vote. His formerly key fifth vote was now one of six votes. The dominant conservative majority could afford a defection. And, with the addition of

Justice Souter, the number of five-to-four decisions, in which one Justice's vote could play a critical role, diminished from the prior two terms. The 1988 and 1989 terms had yielded thirty-three and thirty-nine five-to-four decisions, respectively. Justice Kennedy voted with the majority in seventy-five per cent of these seventy-two cases. The 1990 term yielded only twenty-one five-to-four decisions and Justice Kennedy was in the majority in sixty-two per cent of them. With the addition of Justice Thomas, the 1991 term continued the trend. The 1991 term yielded only fourteen five-to-four decisions, with Justice Kennedy in the majority in sixty-four per cent of them.

With the 1991 term, many observers expected the growing conservative majority to generate a new burst of conservative decision making. Justice Thomas, replacing Justice Marshall, was expected to provide an additional reliable conservative vote. The conservative momentum gathering since Justice Souter had replaced Justice Brennan seemed on the verge of becoming overwhelming. Yet the 1991 term proved to be one of the most surprising in recent Supreme Court history. For rather than take a sharper-than-ever conservative turn, the Court seemed to stabilize and clearly failed to fulfill the hopes of its most conservative members.

Justice Kennedy's votes during the 1991 term were a central part of its surprising status. He showed a greater willingness to depart from some conservative Justices than he had in any previous term. Whereas in his first two terms his lowest rate of agreement with the decisions of Rehnquist, Scalia, O'Connor, or White had been over eighty per cent, in the 1991 term his highest rate of agreement with any of them was sixty-eight per cent (with Justice White). The addition of Justice Thomas had measurably pulled the Court to the right (Justices Thomas and Scalia agreed in eighty-six per cent of the cases), but Kennedy refused to be fully pulled along.

At the specific case level, no vote was more central or more surprising than his vote in the 1991 term's leading abortion case. Justice Kennedy's position on abortion rights initially coincided with, but later parted from, that of the Court's most vehement critics of *Roe* v. *Wade,* 410 U.S. 113 (1973). In a 1989 ruling, *Webster* v. *Reproductive Health Services,* 492 U.S. 490 (1989), Justice Kennedy seemed on the verge of willingness to overrule *Roe* v. *Wade. Webster* involved a constitutional challenge to a Missouri statute regulating the performance of abortions. The statute: (1) required a physician, prior to performing an abortion on a woman whom he has reason to believe is twenty or more weeks pregnant, to ascertain whether the fetus is viable by performing medical tests; (2) prohibited the use of public employees and facilities to perform or assist abortions not necessary to save the mother's life; and (3) made it unlawful to use public funds, employees, or facilities for the purpose of encouraging or counseling a woman to have an abortion not necessary to save her life.

Justice Kennedy did not write a separate opinion in *Webster.* He did join a majority opinion by upholding the Missouri law's restrictions on the use of public employees and facilities for the performance or assistance of nontherapeutic abortions and by dismissing as moot the challenge to the provisions relating to encouraging or counseling a woman to have an abortion. He, along with Justice White, also joined a plurality opinion by Chief Justice Rehnquist construing the twenty-week testing requirement to require only those tests that are useful to ascertain the fetus' viability. The Chief Justice's opinion would have rejected *Roe* v. *Wade*'s trimester framework and sustained the testing requirement because it is reasonably designed to ensure that abortions are not performed where the fetus is viable—an end that all concede is legitimate. That is sufficient to sustain its constitutionality. Although it would have rejected the trimester framework of *Roe*, the plurality opinion viewed the case as sufficiently different from *Roe* v. *Wade* to consider overruling *Roe* inadvisable. The plurality Justices therefore refused to join Justice Scalia's call to overrule *Roe*.

After *Webster*, many believed that Justice Kennedy would provide a crucial vote in the outright overruling of *Roe* v. *Wade*. In *Webster*, he had cast his lot with Chief Justice Rehnquist and Justice White, whose reluctance to overrule *Roe* in *Webster* stemmed from crucial differences between the cases and not from a belief in the correctness of *Roe*. When Justices Souter and Thomas replaced Justices Brennan and Marshall, *Roe*'s days seemed numbered.

In *Planned Parenthood of Southeastern Pennsylvania* v. *Casey*, 112 S. Ct. 2791 (1992), Chief Justice Rehnquist and Justice White, as expected based on their plurality opinion in *Webster*, did join Justice Scalia and the newly appointed Justice Thomas in an opinion that would have overruled *Roe*. But neither the third member of the *Webster* plurality, Justice Kennedy, nor Justice Souter, the most likely sources of the crucial fifth vote, joined that opinion. Instead, they and Justice O'Connor followed the extraordinary procedure of jointly announcing and delivering a plurality opinion. The opinion cannot be attributed to an individual Justice.

The *Planned Parenthood* plurality opinion expressly considered but declined to overrule all of *Roe*. It replaced *Roe*'s trimester analysis with a line drawn at viability. Before viability, a woman has the right to choose to terminate her pregnancy. But the plurality stated that before viability the state is not prohibited from taking steps "to ensure that this choice is thoughtful and informed." States are free to enact laws "to provide a reasonable framework for a woman to make a decision that has such profound and lasting meaning" so long as the state regulation does not impose an undue burden on a woman's ability to decide. After viability, the state may, as in the third trimester in *Roe*'s framework, regulate and even proscribe abortion except where it is medically necessary for the preservation of the life or health of the mother.

The plurality opinion triggered an unusual and powerful statement from Justice Blackmun, the then eighty-three-year-old author of *Roe*. In the face of what must have been adamant efforts to persuade at least one plurality member to join in gutting *Roe,* they had stood fast. "Make no mistake," Justice Blackmun wrote, "the joint opinion of Justices O'Connor, Kennedy, and Souter is an act of personal courage and constitutional principle."

Justice Kennedy's performance in *Planned Parenthood* and other 1991 term cases led some to argue that he had been "Blackmunized." The term refers to Justice Blackmun's early conservative stance and his later move toward more liberal views about individual rights and criminal procedure. Upon learning of the phrase being applied to Justice Kennedy after the 1991 term, Justice Blackmun is said to have penned a note to Kennedy reading, "Don't worry. It's not fatal."

Viewed in retrospect, the 1991 term may prove to be considered a watershed in Justice Kennedy's career. His position in *Planned Parenthood* was the most surprising of any of the Justices. *Tamayo-Reyes,* also decided during the 1991 term, is one of his rare refusals to contract habeas corpus doctrine. And in *Wright* v. *West,* 112 S. Ct. 2482 (1992), Justice Kennedy, writing only for himself, indicated that he was not prepared to restrict the traditional power of federal district judges to engage in de novo review of constitutional issues that involve mixed questions of law and fact.

Justice Kennedy's approach to First Amendment issues reveals a less conservative bent than his approach to most other issues. As discussed above, he cast aside personal views to support First Amendment freedoms in the flag-burning case. In *Lee* v. *Weisman,* 112 S. Ct. 2649 (1992), writing for a five-to-four majority, he rejected an appeal to loosen constitutional controls on behavior that might run afoul of the First Amendment's establishment of religion clause. Providence, Rhode Island, had allowed public school principals to invite clergy members to offer prayers as part of the graduation ceremonies for middle and high schools. Attendance at graduation was not compelled. One middle school principal invited a rabbi to provide nonsectarian prayers at graduation.

Under *Lemon* v. *Kurtzman,* 403 U.S. 602 (1971), the government violates the Establishment Clause when it acts (1) with a nonsecular purpose, (2) with the purpose or primary effect of endorsing religion, or (3) in a manner that fosters excessive government entanglement with religion. In *Weisman,* the United States argued that the Court should discard the *Lemon* framework in favor of an approach that focused on the coercive nature of government-sponsored religious activity. Justice Kennedy wrote that the case did not require revisiting the *Lemon* framework:

> *The government involvement with religious activity in this case is pervasive, to the point of creating a state-sponsored and state-directed religious exercise in a public school.*

In responding to the argument that attendance was voluntary, and therefore the government did not mandate religious activity, Justice Kennedy emphasized the importance of graduation ceremonies:

To say a teenage student has a real choice not to attend her high school graduation is formalistic in the extreme. . . . Everyone knows that in our society and in our culture high school graduation is one of life's most significant occasions.

In *International Society for Krishna Consciousness, Inc.* v. *Lee,* 112 S. Ct. 2711 (1992), Justice Kennedy cast a crucial vote in cases involving bans on solicitation and distribution in airports. In his concurring opinion, Kennedy rejected Chief Justice Rehnquist's analysis, which held that solicitation can be banned in airport terminals because they are not public facilities. The test of a public forum, according to the majority, is whether a public property's "principle purpose" is for "the free exchange of ideas." Since airports were meant to supply transportation, not conversation, they could not be public forums under this test. Justice Kennedy's analysis emphasized whether expressive activity would significantly interfere with the property's uses, whether the property shares physical similarities with more traditional public forums, and whether the government has permitted or acquiesced in broad public access to the property. He believed in a more evolving concept of a public forum. Kennedy concluded that the government cannot prohibit distribution of literature in airports because such a prohibition is too broad and does not leave sufficient room for alternative channels of communication. He viewed the ban on solicitation of funds, however, as a reasonable regulation of speech because it did not ban requests for funds, only "solicitation and receipt of funds." He felt the restriction on transfer of funds protected travelers from fraud and was not aimed at the content of any ideas.

If any characteristic dominates Justice Kennedy's method, it is his reluctance to overrule precedent, even that with which he disagrees. In *Patterson* v. *McLean Credit Union* and *Planned Parenthood,* he sustained prior interpretations that, in the first instance, he might not have adopted. When he has sustained prior habeas corpus doctrine, as in *Keeney,* it is in the name of preserving precedent. But Justice Kennedy's willingness to join majorities that run roughshod over prior habeas corpus doctrine suggests that his commitment to curing what he perceives to be the ailments of a flawed habeas system outweighs his respect for precedent. Thus, in *McCleskey* v. *Zant,* troublesome precedents were cast aside in the name of reforming habeas corpus.

Kennedy parses matters very finely and is quite adept at distinguishing prior cases. Yet his legal analysis sometimes seems to cut too finely. Thus, the distinction in *Patterson* v. *McLean Credit Union* between making contracts and postformation contract matters, the distinction between the habeas corpus cases of *Saffle* v. *Parks* and *Penry,* the logic-chopping reasoning used to deny McCleskey a hearing in *McCleskey* v. *Zant,* and the finely tuned position distinguishing among constitutional rights in *Golden State Transit Corp.,* all have a detached scholastic quality, perhaps reflecting his years as a constitutional law instructor. Yet these refinements ultimately seem rather thin bases for distinguishing cases in the context of constitutional decision making or interpreting important federal civil rights statutes.

Justice Kennedy has absorbed at least one of the less pleasing tricks of a Supreme Court Justice's trade. It is common for a dissenter to chastise the majority when the majority decides an issue not strictly necessary for resolution of a case before the Court. But this righteous indignation is usually reserved for cases in which the Justice disagrees with the majority's resolution of the merits of the case. When the Justice is in the majority, such prudential considerations are given less weight.

In *Missouri* v. *Jenkins*, Justice Kennedy relied on this criticism. When the Court held that federal judges could order taxing authorities to exercise their powers, he strenuously objected that the Court's statements were not necessary for its judgment and should not be viewed as precedent for the future. Yet in the employment discrimination case of *Wards Cove Packing*, the Court could have effectively disposed of the case on the narrow grounds that the plaintiff had failed to make an adequate statistical showing. Nevertheless, the majority, joined by Justice Kennedy, went out of its way to resolve issues governing the burden of proof and the requisites for a Title VII plaintiff's evidence. The majority did so in the name of providing guidance for the lower courts yet triggered the debate that led to the Civil Rights Act of 1991. The same justification could have supported the pronouncements that Justice Kennedy was so critical of in *Missouri* v. *Jenkins*.

SELECTED BIBLIOGRAPHY

Materials on Justice Kennedy may be found in *Nomination of Anthony M. Kennedy to be Associate Justice of the Supreme Court of the United States: Hearings Before the Senate Judiciary Committee*, 100th Cong., 1st Sess. (1987); Terry Carter, "Crossing the Rubicon," *California Lawyer* (Oct. 1992), p. 39; Cynthia Gorney, "A Cautious Conservatism; Judge Kennedy Lives by the Rules," *Washington Post*, Dec. 14, 1987, p. Al; Robert Reinhold, "Man in the News; Restrained Pragmatist Anthony M. Kennedy," *New York Times*, Nov. 12, 1987, p. 1; Richard C. Reuben, "Man in the Middle," *California Lawyer* (Oct. 1992), p. 34; Reynolds Holding, "Kennedy's High Court Decisions Stem from Belief in Precedent," *San Francisco Chronicle*, July 1, 1992, p. A4.

Sandra Day O'Connor

☆ 1930–   ☆

APPOINTED BY RONALD REAGAN

YEARS ON COURT
1981–

by
ALAN FREEMAN AND ELIZABETH MENSCH

The United States Supreme Court decided in 1873, in *Bradwell* v. *Illinois*, 83 U.S. (16 Wall.) 130, that the state of Illinois had not violated the U.S. Constitution when it denied Myra Bradwell a license to practice law solely on the basis of her gender. In his concurring opinion Justice Joseph P. Bradley gratuitously pointed out that women's "natural and proper timidity and delicacy . . . unfits [them] for many of the occupations of civil life."

Exactly 120 years later a woman was named by the *National Law Journal* as "lawyer of the year" and the occupant of the "lawyer's seat" on the United States Supreme Court because she was "moved by the facts of the case and existing law" rather than by ideological agendas. The same woman was also described in a 1993 issue of the *ABA Journal* as "arguably the most influential woman official in the United States." She was Sandra Day O'Connor, who has served on the high court since 1981. The first and until recently the only woman on the Court, she represents a dramatic refutation of Justice Bradley's assumptions.

The groundwork for O'Connor's ascent to the Supreme Court was laid in the same decade that Bradley rendered his decision; the 1870's was when her paternal grandfather, Henry Clay Day, left his native Vermont and moved to the Arizona Territory. There he acquired a 300-square-mile tract of desert land and turned it into a cattle ranch, the Lazy B, whose main dwelling was a four-room adobe house without running water or electricity. The Lazy B was where the future Justice would spend much of her childhood learning to mend fences, shoot rifles, ride horses, and (by the age of ten) drive a truck.

The first child of Ada Mae and Harry Day, Sandra Day O'Connor was born in El Paso, Texas, on March 26, 1930. At that time, the Lazy B still did not have running water or electricity. O'Connor would not know such luxuries until age six, when she was sent to El Paso to live with her maternal grandmother for the school year.

An extraordinarily hard worker, O'Connor believes that her determination and persistence "came out of my background, growing up as I did on a cattle ranch, where one learns to work and do things for oneself.'' That same ranch experience also instilled in her a commitment to local community cooperation as a way of life. "Certainly that was very strongly true in the western tradition in which I grew up," she remembered. "For many years ranches would have their annual round-ups, for example. In the early days each rancher would send his crew to help the other. This was just the way people lived and did things. We always tried to help other people." In a commencement address at Stanford University in 1982, she would urge cooperative negotiation rather than litigation as a way to resolve disputes, suggesting that "you remember the golden rule: Do unto others as you would have them do unto you. That might make you a little more generous, save you a lot of time and money and make my job a lot easier."

O'Connor regards her maternal grandmother, Mamie Scott Wilkey, as the woman who most influenced her life. Wilkey was strong willed as well as devoted to her obviously intelligent granddaughter; she expected O'Connor to live up to her potential and was always "supportive of all the things I tried to do." While staying with her grandmother in El Paso, O'Connor attended first the exclusive Radford School for Girls and then Austin High School, from which she graduated at age sixteen.

O'Connor's father had always wanted to attend Stanford University, but he had given up his college plans to run the family ranch after his father died. Sandra applied solely to Stanford and was accepted. She wound up completing both her undergraduate and law studies there, and in only five years. She has attributed her desire to study law to one of the school's professors, Harry J. Rathbun, who taught undergraduate as well as graduate courses in business law. Rathbun was known campuswide for his end-of-the-semester lectures, in which he would discuss the meaning of life and the role individuals could play as citizens of the world and in the evolution of the human spirit.

O'Connor proved to be a top-notch student at Stanford. She was named an editor of the *Stanford Law Review* (where she met her future husband, John O'Connor, who was a class behind her) and graduated from law school with a ranking of third in her class, just behind William H. Rehnquist, the future Chief Justice of the Supreme Court. She was only twenty-two years old at the time.

Despite her extraordinary academic achievement, O'Connor quickly encountered the legal profession's deeply entrenched assumption that women were unfit to practice law. She applied to major law firms; none had ever hired a woman, and none were about to do so. Her only job offer was to be a legal secretary in the prestigious Los Angeles firm of Gibson, Dunn and Crutcher. (At the time William French Smith was a partner in the firm. Years later, as United States Attorney General, he would be instrumental in securing O'Connor's nomination to the Supreme Court.)

Rebuffed by the major private firms, O'Connor fared better in the public sector. She worked for two years as a deputy county attorney in San Mateo

County, California, then moved to Germany and worked as a civilian lawyer for the Quartermaster's Corps when her husband, who had joined the Judge Advocate General's Corps, was stationed there. In 1957, the same year that she gave birth to the first of her three sons (Scott, Brian, and Jay), the couple moved to Phoenix. There Sandra, along with another lawyer, opened a neighborhood law office that handled "every kind of problem that would come in the door."

In 1960, after the birth of her second son, O'Connor left her practice and spent the next five years raising her children. In her spare time she volunteered for so many civic and law-related activities that, she recalls, "I decided I needed a paid job so that my life would be more orderly."

In 1965 O'Connor returned to full-time employment in the public sector as an assistant attorney general in Arizona. At first she specialized in mental health regulations, but she quickly became generally indispensable. In 1969 she was appointed to fill a vacant state Senate seat. Subsequently elected to a full term, she was chosen by her Republican colleagues (all but two of whom were men) as majority leader—the first woman in the United States to hold such a position. Her hard work, toughness, and intelligence became known and respected. According to state senator Alfredo Gutierrez, "It was impossible to win a debate with her. We'd go on the floor with a few facts and let rhetoric do the rest. Not Sandy, she would overwhelm you with her knowledge." Her close attention to statutory detail (she once offered an amendment to a bill in order to insert an important missing comma) and complete mastery of facts is especially notable in light of her future judicial methodology.

Anxious to return to law in 1974, O'Connor won a seat as a trial judge on the Maricopa Superior Court. Four years later, U.S. senator Barry Goldwater and the Arizona Republican party encouraged her to run for governor against Democrat Bruce Babbitt. After seriously considering their suggestion, she decided to remain on the superior court bench.

In 1980 Babbit, who had been elected governor, appointed O'Connor to the Arizona Court of Appeals (an intermediate appellate court). Babbitt was accused of using the appointment to remove a potentially powerful political rival; he responded to the charge by saying that O'Connor fulfilled his commitment to place the finest legal talent available on the state bench. "Her intellectual ability and her judgment are astonishing," Babbitt said.

Commentators at the time of O'Connor's Supreme Court nomination hastily concluded that because her appeals court opinions were not about broad constitutional questions, they served little predictive value for her likely Supreme Court performance. The cases she decided raised the usual run of state-court appellate issues: workers' compensation cases; a sprinkling of tort, property, and contract cases; a few routine criminal appeals; two equal protection cases; and a miscellany of state statutory cases.

A careful reading of her state court opinions, however, reveals the basic methodological blueprint that O'Connor would take with her to the Supreme

Court, especially her characteristic approach to what might be termed hard cases. She always sought to identify the extreme positions on each side and then sought to find the precise fault line between them. Facts were carefully described and compared to those of other decided cases.

O'Connor was not a mechanical formalist. She paid a legal realist's attention to underlying purposes of both statutes and common law doctrines. Nor did she like to take big steps with her decisions; in fact, she tended to find the closest analogic move that would decide the outcome without extending the doctrine any more than necessary. She paid scrupulous attention to detail, searching out whatever was required to decide the case, including legislative history, English legal history, out-of-state cases if Arizona law was unsettled, economic realities, overall statutory schemes, and business contexts. While not a formalist, she did have a refined sense of precise legal doctrine, which she took seriously while valuing the underlying goals of such doctrines over any formalist categories.

In short, O'Connor's judging represented exactly what Karl Llewellyn described as the "common-law tradition," which can best be demonstrated by examining in detail one of her stated opinions. The case, *Food Products Corp.* v. *Industrial Commission of Arizona*, 129 Ariz. 208 (App.) (1981), is representative both because of its utterly ordinary subject matter—workers' compensation—and because O'Connor's characteristic methodology was evident in even so brief (three and a half pages) an opinion.

The issue before her was whether a particular injury "arose out of and in the course of" employment. O'Connor started by carefully and precisely stating the facts. The case involved a deliveryman who, in the course of his work during the morning rush hour, had encountered a stranded car; he stopped to help the driver push the car to the curb and was hit from behind. Some of the facts were sympathetically told: "The stalled car was in the fast lane of a six-lane thoroughfare. A young child was visible in the car, and a woman was unsuccessfully struggling to push the car to the curb." O'Connor was careful to state, however, the precise contours of employer permission: the deliveryman was forbidden to conduct personal business, but there had been no discussion of assistance to stranded motorists.

The hard question in the case was the causal one, whether the deliveryman's humanitarian response to an emergency situation could be said to arise "out of" his employment. On that question, O'Connor found an Arizona case that laid out the dilemma precisely as she conceived it: some injuries arise from a risk distinctly work-related and others from risks that are personal and in no way work-related. Those are the "easy cases." In between are the middle category of cases, the hard cases, and they must be determined "on a case-by-case basis, keeping in mind the purposes and intent of the Workmen's Compensation Act in the particular jurisdiction."

O'Connor then examined two Arizona cases in which compensation had been allowed. In the first the employer had given an ambulance driver implied permission to help a patient during a plane flight; that implied permission was apparently determinative. In the other a bank security guard had left the employer's bank to help investigate an accident on an adjacent highway; there the court had focused upon the "reasonableness" of the worker's action, which would bring it within the scope of risk incident to employment. In a third Arizona case, however, the court had denied compensation when a worker was test-flying an airplane (which crashed) during work time for a friend, even though permission had been granted by the employer. In that case the court had applied a benefit test, pointing out that the worker's action benefited his friend, not his employer.

O'Connor rejected a mechanical application of a benefit test, which would have denied compensation to the deliveryman as well; she also rejected, citing an Oklahoma case, a meaningless expansion of benefit that would presume employer benefit from any employee display of humanitarianism. O'Connor saw that interpretation as stretching the doctrine "so thin as to become fiction." Similarly, the search for a fictional "implied permission" or its absence would have been misleading. Instead, she distinguished the deliveryman from the test pilot on the basis of the former's *reasonable* response to an emergency situation, as in the case of the bank security guard; she also described a Massachusetts case in which a worker who often had to travel was injured while removing a hazardous obstruction from the road because it posed a danger to other drivers. The court had stated that an attempt to remove danger, like a reasonable rescue effort, is "one of the risks of the employment, an incident of the service, foreseeable, if not foreseen, and so covered by the statute." Also citing a law review comment on workers' compensation and the Good Samaritan, she concluded that the deliveryman's action was reasonable under the circumstances and thus, despite the lack of express or implied permission, an act "in the course of and arising out of" his employment.

Notably, O'Connor in this opinion rejected the two mechanical tests that could have been invoked to decide the case—consent and benefit. Nor did she see cause as an objective thing—either there or not there. Instead, in utterly Cardozian fashion, she described cause in relational terms as the connection between risks undertaken and injury sustained, a connection drawn by reasonableness of action—terms incapable of mechanical definition.

Although O'Connor rejected mechanical rules that could themselves be manipulatively turned into mere fictions, she did not see judging as utterly open-ended or as appropriately responsive to sentiment alone. However sympathetic his case, the deliveryman would not have been compensated if he had been on a family excursion. Close factual analysis was required because this was a hard case; otherwise, the results would be easily predetermined. Within the hard case category, there was clearly room for judicial creativity, yet such creativity was also constrained—not by doctrinal tests as such, but by the facts of other cases, which she described in detail. Hence her carefully researched description of facts from both Arizona cases and cases from other jurisdictions. In what kinds of situations had a causal relationship been found or not found? Her conclusion was not deduced from a rule but induced from a reading of situations that had raised the same doctrinal issue—a classic instance of, in Llewellyn's phrase, "situation-sense."

As might have been predicted at the time, O'Connor would later employ the same methodology on the Supreme Court. This point necessarily highlights a complex pair of questions: first, whether a Llewellynesque common law approach is coherent in its own terms (recall the manipulative genius of the great realist common law judge, Benjamin Cardozo, both in refashioning the doctrine to which he deferred and in selectively choosing relevant contextual facts), and second, whether that approach can provide coherence to a constitutional tradition, whose very framework and presuppositions may be in question.

On July 7, 1981, President Ronald Reagan nominated Sandra Day O'Connor to become the first woman Justice on the Supreme Court, adroitly announcing her as a "person for all seasons." O'Connor herself viewed the nomination as "a classic example of being the right person in the right spot at the right time. Stated simply, you must be lucky."

The nomination, while politically brilliant, was not without controversy. As a presidential candidate Reagan, facing a serious gender gap, had answered criticism on questions of women's rights by promising to appoint a woman to the Supreme Court. In choosing O'Connor he fulfilled that pledge. There is little doubt that gender was her determinative qualification. The American Bar Association gave O'Connor a mere "qualified" (as opposed to "highly qualified") rating on experience, because she had never served at the federal level. Law professor and Supreme Court historian G. Edward White stated frankly that "a man with O'Connor's background would probably not be nominated to the Supreme Court."

On the other hand, one might speculate that, had O'Connor's career opportunities at the outset not been foreclosed by gender alone, she might well have achieved a record of accomplishment by 1980 akin to that of her classmate William H. Rehnquist. As suggested, her state court opinions (like those of her more recently appointed colleague, David Souter) reveal a high level of judicial skill.

O'Connor's nomination quickly won approval from liberal Democrats and most conservative Republicans. Women's groups were enthusiastic; for example, Eleanor Smeal of the National Organization for Women called the nomination a "major victory for women's rights." Representative Morris Udall of Arizona reassured fellow Democrats that "if we're going to have a Reagan appointee to the Court, you couldn't do much better," because O'Connor "is about as moderate a Republican as you'll ever find being appointed by Reagan."

As a moderate, O'Connor was nevertheless philosophically compatible with the Reagan administration, even if not as ideological as many partisan Reaganites. The administration's painstaking background research had showed a political record of "mainstream pragmatic Republicanism." While her judicial experience had offered little opportunity for constitutional decision making, she had revealed some key predispositions in a lecture given as part of a symposium at William and Mary Law School in January, 1981, and later published as "Trends in the Relationship Between the Federal and State Courts from the Perspective of a State Court Judge," 22 *William and Mary Law Review* 801–15 (1981). After reviewing with customary care cases and apparent trends in federal court review of state criminal cases as well as federal civil cases reviewing the actions of state officials, she questioned the core assumption of liberal activists of the 1960's and 1970's—that federal courts were better than state courts for litigation in pursuit of justice and should therefore be open and available to every federal claim as early as possible during litigation. O'Connor challenged the premise central to that assumption: that state judges were inherently less competent, less independent, and less hospitable to constitutional claims. Her overall theme pointed toward increased respect for the integrity of state judicial process and a diminished role for federal courts in reviewing state matters generally. Chief Justice Warren Burger, a participant in the William and Mary symposium, was impressed by O'Connor (not surprisingly, given his advocacy for the reduction of federal court caseloads), as were Reagan administration officials, who generally supported states' rights.

O'Connor was not only philosophically congenial but also personally and politically well connected. In Phoenix the O'Connors had resumed their Stanford friendship with the Rehnquists; when asked, Rehnquist endorsed O'Connor, as did Chief Justice Burger. Barry Goldwater, by then a longtime friend and neighbor, recommended *only* O'Connor to the White House. Dean Myers of Stanford Law School and former Stanford professor William Baxter (then in the Reagan Justice Department) provided further endorsement. And an utterly pleasant interview with the president apparently sealed the choice.

The only serious political objection to O'Connor came from extreme social conservatives, who objected to her support as a state senator for the Equal Rights Amendment (ERA) and her votes against a number of antiabortion measures. The exact meaning of those votes was ambiguous (she had opposed attaching a completely nongermane antiabortion amendment to other legislation, for example, and had opposed the state's proposing a constitutional amendment to overrule Roe), but they were enough to lead the evangelist Jerry Falwell to urge every good Christian to oppose O'Connor. Goldwater retorted, "I think every good Christian ought to kick Falwell right in the ass." Intense media focus on the ERA and abortion issues distorted coverage of her legislative record otherwise, which included careful mental health review reform, probate code reform, flood control funding, and the restoration of the death penalty.

At her confirmation hearings, O'Connor dealt with the abortion issue by expressing her personal opposition to abortion (as she apparently did in the interview with Reagan, who did not demand a litmus test statement on *Roe*), by explaining her votes as state senator, and then by refusing to take any explicit stand on how as Justice she would vote on *any* case that came before her, insisting that "personal views" on a subject should be set aside in resolving matters before the Court. Her refusal thus to commit herself on abortion led one conservative senator on the Judiciary Committee to abstain—but on the floor even he voted to confirm.

At the hearings and in her opening statement, O'Connor made a point of emphasizing the importance of the states' role in the federal system. Deftly avoiding commitment on specific substantive issues, O'Connor generally welcomed the growing number of women in the legal profession, voiced her personal support for the death penalty, indicated serious reservations about forced school busing, and expressed reservations about overly rigid application of the exclusionary rule. In general she said she opposed a judicial activism that would *change* the law on account of changing social mores but carefully stated her views so as not to preclude judicial *reinterpretation* of constitutional provisions. O'Connor's performance was by all accounts an adroit one, and one for which she had, typically, meticulously prepared herself; despite a lack of federal experience, O'Connor knew her cases. The full Senate voted ninety-nine to zero to confirm her, and she took the oath of office to become Associate Justice on September 25, 1981.

Those eager to predict O'Connor's future on the Court could with some confidence foresee considerable concern with federalism and separation of powers questions, given her role in all three branches of state government, her William and Mary lecture, her opening statement to the Judiciary Committee, and her perceived (although not uniform) pattern of deference to lower courts and legislators during her brief tenure as state appellate judge. In light of her past record and her disavowal of policy-oriented or ideological judicial activism, many predicted a reluctance to overrule statutes on constitutional grounds and in general expected her opinions to demonstrate a closely crafted attention to facts, statutory language, and precedent. She was generally thought likely to favor limits on defendants' rights in criminal cases. For feminists, of course, a key question was whether she would construe her opposition to gender discrimination so far as to regularly support affirmative action, abortion rights, or equality rights. Some who were skeptical of her ability and distrustful of her conservatism thought she would be little more than an overshadowed clone of her friend Rehnquist (the "Arizona twins"), while others more favorably predicted that her consensus-building skills and acknowledged tact would usher in a new rosy era of happy unity on the Court.

By the end of Justice O'Connor's first term, the Court clearly remained far from unified; some observers, in fact, noted "increased bitterness" as the

Court's conservative trend gained strength. On the other hand, O'Connor was not just an "Arizona twin" of Rehnquist. Whereas many new Justices suffer from the "freshman effect" as a result of being inexperienced newcomers to the uniquely demanding work of the Court, O'Connor immediately staked out independent ground. In the 1981 term she did vote with the "conservative bloc" (then Lewis Powell, Burger, and Rehnquist) 77 per cent of the time and with Rehnquist specifically 81.6 per cent of the time. (For statistics on O'Connor's first term, see "The Supreme Court, 1981 Term," 96 *Harvard Law Review* 304–11 [1982].) Nevertheless, although she was assigned fewer opinions than any other Justice during the 1981 term (a typical courtesy to a new Justice), she asserted herself vigorously through separate concurring opinions, for which she ranked fourth. (In about twenty per cent of the cases in which she agreed with Rehnquist as to result, for example, she did so on grounds different from his.) By her second term she ranked fifth overall in writing opinions for the Court. (John Scheb II and Lee Ailshie, "Justice Sandra Day O'Connor and the 'Freshman Effect,' " 69 *Judicature* 9–12 [June-July, 1985].) These were telling early patterns: by the end of the 1991 term, her agreement rate with Rehnquist had fallen to sixty-three per cent, and for that term she was third in number of opinions written and second in opinions for the Court. (For the statistics see "The Supreme Court, 1991 Term," 106 *Harvard Law Review* 378–85 [1992].) She had clearly seized control of the independent ground that she had shrewdly started to stake out for herself during the first term and had turned it into a position of leadership.

Predictably, O'Connor's earliest opinions showed meticulous attention to fact, precedent, and statutory language. Substantively, her commitment to judicial restraint was evident in her deference to state and federal legislation and especially in her respect for state sovereignty. In criminal cases she did tend to favor "law and order" results; for example, in the twelve cases involving federal habeas corpus petitions from state prisoners challenging their convictions, she voted to deny all twelve.

In one of those, *Engle* v. *Isaac*, 456 U.S. 107 (1982), she wrote the opinion for the majority in a five-to-four decision. Echoing the spirit of her William and Mary lecture, O'Connor emphasized the importance of finality in criminal cases and the attendant respect for federalism entailed by deference to finality. She quoted Justice John Harlan (the grandson) at some length on the finality point, noting that the "writ [habeas] undermines the usual principles of finality" and its liberal allowance "degrades the prominence of the trial itself." Her special concern with the significance of federalism was explicit:

> [T]he Great Writ imposes special costs on our federal system. The States possess primary authority for defining and enforcing the criminal law. In criminal trials they also hold the initial responsibility for vindicating constitutional rights. Federal intrusions into state criminal trials frustrate both the States' sovereign power to punish offenders and their good-faith attempts to honor constitutional rights.

Nevertheless, in the same opinion she made clear by reference to its history and common law roots that the writ of habeas corpus was "today, as in prior centuries . . . a bulwark against convictions that violate 'fundamental fairness.' "

One might dismiss such language as empty rhetoric, yet even in O'Connor's first term, despite her agreement with the conservatives in the criminal cases, she showed in her concurring opinions that she was more concerned with factual context than ideology and was given to careful statutory analysis. A good example is *Smith* v. *Phillips*, 455 U.S. 209 (1982), a six-to-three habeas denial in which (despite her agreement with the majority opinion written by Rehnquist, which found insufficient evidence of juror bias in the factual record) she wrote separately to insist that the Court's opinion should not be read to "foreclose the use of 'implied bias' in appropriate circumstances."

Even her dissent in *Enmund* v. *Florida*, 458 U.S. 782 (1982), in which the majority (by a five-to-four vote) applied the Eighth Amendment to bar the execution of a mere accomplice in a felony-murder case, was more contextual than doctrinaire. Despite her strong objection to the flat ban announced by the majority, she would have remanded the case for resentencing because the record suggested failure to consider all mitigating factors. Moreover, in *Eddings* v. *Oklahoma*, 455 U.S. 104 (1982), another death penalty case, O'Connor's vote was determinative in obtaining a remand for a defendant in which, as with her reading of *Enmund*, the record suggested that the trial judge might have felt unduly precluded from considering relevant mitigating circumstances.

In *Eddings* the defendant was only sixteen at the time of the murder; of the three (of thirty-two) criminal cases in which O'Connor voted for the defendant, two involved youthful offenders—a fact taken by some as evincing a special concern for young people. That impression found support in *Mills* v. *Habluetzel*, 456 U.S. 91 (1982), in which the Court found a denial of equal protection for illegitimate children and accordingly struck down a one-year statute of limitations for paternity suits. O'Connor concurred to emphasize that a subsequently enacted four-year statute might also be invalid, as might even longer periods of limitation. She took care, in fact, to describe the social and financial obstacles faced by mothers of illegitimate children in filing suits.

A concern for children also characterized O'Connor's concurrence in *New York* v. *Ferber*, 458 U.S. 747 (1982), in which the Court denied First Amendment protection to child pornography. She insisted that "works depicting minors engaged in explicit sexual conduct" could not be saved by claims of even "serious social value":

> [A] 12-year old child photographed while masturbating surely suffers the same psychological harm whether the community labels the photograph "edifying" or "tasteless."

O'Connor's concern with child welfare, however, did not translate into a "children's rights" agenda as such. In *Board of Education* v. *Pico*, 457 U.S. 853

(1982), O'Connor dissented from the Court's conclusion that the First Amendment limited a local school board's discretion in removing books from secondary school libraries. While she did not personally agree with some of the actions taken by the board, she explained that "it is not the function of the courts to make the decisions that have been properly relegated to the elected members of school boards. It is the school board that must determine educational suitability."

Superficially, *Mills* and *Pico* seem inconsistent—O'Connor was for children in one, but against children in the other. But her views are inconsistent only if one conceives of the cases solely in rights terms. O'Connor's concern with the proper functioning of groups within the polity charged with particular social responsibilities emerged even in her first term. In the *Mills* and *Pico* pairing one finds two entities—parents and local school board—charged with caring for the welfare of children. In the first case, the mother's parental task should not arbitrarily be made more onerous nor should the father be relieved of responsibility by operation of legal technicality. On the other hand, a local school board charged with responsibility for the moral and intellectual training of the young needs to be afforded considerable discretion and not have its work unduly impeded by federal courts in the name of rights. O'Connor's concern, in other words, is with the integrity of those "mediating structures" that fall between nation-state and individual rights-holder; she resists reducing every question to a state/individual model.

Where explicit federal rights are at stake, however, O'Connor has not been hesitant to demand their enforcement. *FBI* v. *Abrahamson*, 456 U.S. 615 (1982), involved the scope of the exemption for "records compiled for law enforcement" under the Freedom of Information Act. Such records need not be disclosed when requested. The majority, in a five-to-four decision, found the particular records within the exemption; O'Connor dissented, accusing the majority of usurping its authority by rewriting the statute. A long quotation from a Felix Frankfurter essay on the reading of statutes that appears in her opinion is telling with respect to her approach toward statutes in particular and judging in general. The quotation reads in part:

> [T]he only sure safeguard against crossing the line between adjudication and legislation is an alert recognition of the necessity not to cross it and instinctive, as well as trained, reluctance to do so. (456 U.S. at 633, quoting Frankfurter, "Some Reflections on the Reading of Statutes," 47 Columbia Law Review 527, 533, 535 [1947].)

Like Frankfurter's, one of O'Connor's principal concerns is with federalism. Traditionally, states were the most important politically constituted mediating structure within the federal system. O'Connor stated her theoretical commitment to protecting state autonomy with uncharacteristically florid prose in her first-term dissent in *Federal Energy Regulatory Commission [FERC]* v. *Mississippi*, 456 U.S. 742 (1982). There the Court upheld a public utilities regulatory act against facial challenge by Mississippi. The act required state regulatory commissions to implement certain FERC regulations and "consider" adoption of other specific standards and procedures. The Court held that the Constitution was not violated because Congress had the power under the Commerce Clause to preempt the entire field of utility regulation. O'Connor dissented on broad federalist principle:

> The Court's conclusion . . . rests upon a fundamental misunderstanding of the role that state governments play in our federalist system.
>
> State legislative and administrative bodies are not field offices of the national bureaucracy. Nor are they think tanks to which Congress may assign problems for extended study. Instead, each State is sovereign within its own domain, governing its citizens and providing for their general welfare. While the Constitution and federal statutes define the boundaries of that domain, they do not harness state power for national purposes. The Constitution contemplates "an indestructible Union, composed of indestructible States," a system in which both the state and national governments retain a "separate and independent existence."

As wryly noted by Justice Harry Blackmun in his majority opinion, O'Connor's rhetoric was colorful: she accused the majority of "conscript[ing] state utility commissions into the national bureaucratic army," of approving the "dismemberment of state government," of making state agencies "bureaucratic puppets of the Federal Government," and of permitting Congress "to kidnap state utility commissions." Blackmun chided O'Connor for her rhetoric, yet her persistent concern for federalism would later gain considerable acceptance on the Court.

O'Connor also expressed her concern for federalism in another first-term case, *Zobel* v. *Williams*, 457 U.S. 55 (1982), in which she concurred with the Court's judgment to strike down an Alaska plan to distribute income from its oil wealth to its citizens based on length of residence. In concurring, O'Connor rejected the commonplace of constitutional law teachers: that the Equal Protection Clause has basically swallowed up the Interstate Privileges and Immunities Clause of Article IV, Section 2. She argued for a distinctive jurisprudence of that provision, which would offer a nuanced approach to difficult issues of federalism like that in *Zobel*. In her view, "a generalized desire to reward citizens for past endurance, particularly in a State where years of hardship only recently have produced prosperity, is not innately improper." Yet under a federalist structure the unequal treatment of new residents by a state "conflicts with the constitutional purpose of maintaining Union rather than a mere 'league of States.' " Showing particular attention to the proper source of applicable doctrine, she argued that the Interstate Privileges and Immunities Clause would offer a sound and appropriate basis for analyzing these delicate questions of federalism and the right of interstate travel, a position she would develop in the future.

Apart from federalism, and unlike Justice Frankfurter (who wrote the notorious opinion in *Goesaert* v. *Cleary*, 335 U.S. 464 [1948]), O'Connor's second area of outspoken concern was sex discrimination. Her first term gave her the opportunity to write, for a five-to-four majority, what has remained a major opinion in this area, one that arguably supersedes the Court's 1976 opinion in *Craig* v. *Boren*. In *Mississippi University for Women* v. *Hogan*, 458 U.S. 718 (1982), the Court, speaking through O'Connor, held (over the dissent of Justices Burger, Blackmun, Powell, and Rehnquist) that a state-supported nursing school violated the Equal Protection Clause in refusing to admit a male student. O'Connor seemed to augment the showing required by intermediate scrutiny in her insistence that the state show "an exceedingly persuasive justification for the [gender] classification." More significantly, O'Connor countered the state's claim that it was compensating for past harms done to women, seeing the policy as serving only to "perpetuate the stereotyped view of nursing as an exclusively woman's job," thereby reinforcing traditional, often inaccurate, assumptions about the proper roles of men and women. Her opinion was applauded by feminists.

After *Hogan*, commentators inevitably speculated as to whether O'Connor would bring to the Supreme Court a woman's perspective—and, more subtly, exactly what a woman's perspective might mean. By the mid-1980's, O'Connor had made evident her own awareness of the importance of her role as the first woman on the Supreme Court. In talks (often given to women's professional groups) and in writings she has reflected on the role of women in law. Typical examples are the introduction she wrote for the October, 1985, *New York Bar Journal* issue devoted to achievements of women in the legal profession and her speeches during bicentennial events on women and the Constitution (such as the one given at the Carter Center of Emory University on February 11, 1988).

She has also good-humoredly but pointedly tweaked sexist assumptions. When in September, 1983, the *New York Times*, in a cutesy "Topics" column on Washington, D.C., "shorthand," reported that the "nine men who interpret [the laws] are often the SCOTUS [Supreme Court of the United States]," O'Connor responded with a letter to the editor:

> *According to the information available to me, and which I had assumed was generally available, for over two years now SCOTUS has not consisted of nine men. If you have any contradictory information, I would be grateful if you would forward it as I am sure the POTUS [President of the United States], the SCOTUS and the undersigned (the FWOTSC [first woman on the Supreme Court]) would be most interested in seeing it.*

In 1990, at a centennial celebration of Gibson, Dunn and Crutcher, the law firm that had offered her a job as legal secretary, O'Connor noted:

> *I have calculated from looking at Martindale-Hubbell that had this firm offered me a job in 1952 as a lawyer, and had I accepted it, remained in the firm and progressed at the usual rate, I would now be at least the tenth ranking lawyer in the firm, which today numbers 709 attorneys. . . . I want to thank Bill Smith. I can remember as if it were yesterday when he telephoned me on June 26, 1981, to ask if I could go to Washington, D.C. to talk about a position there. Knowing his former association with your firm, I immediately guessed he was planning to offer me a secretarial position—but would it be as Secretary of Labor or Secretary of Commerce? Of course, it was not. He had something else in mind.*

That O'Connor is well aware of her historic role seems clear. What is less clear is whether one can speak meaningfully of a feminist jurisprudence, and whether O'Connor exemplifies such a thing if it does exist. In gender discrimination cases O'Connor has been willing to break with the conservatives. In *North Haven Board of Education* v. *Bell*, 456 U.S. 512 (1982), she voted with the liberals to apply Title IX sex discrimination prohibitions to employees as well as students of educational institutions—over the dissent of Powell, Burger, and Rehnquist, who charged that such an interpretation "tortures the language" of the statute. In *Grove City College* v. *Bell*, 465 U.S. 555 (1984), however, she was somewhat more restrictive, joining the majority in holding Title IX to be limited to programs actually receiving direct or indirect aid. And in *Arizona Governing Committee* v. *Norris*, 463 U.S. 1073 (1983), she joined Justice Thurgood Marshall's majority opinion holding that retirement plans paying lower benefits to women violated Title VII but by her swing vote made liability prospective only and in concurrence emphasized that the Court had not decided the broader issue—whether *any* sex-based payment plan is discriminatory, even if freely chosen. Her concurring opinion, typically, was narrowly crafted to the facts of the case.

Nothing so disappointed some feminists as O'Connor's second-term offering on the abortion issue—a strenuous dissent in *City of Akron* v. *Akron Center for Reproductive Health*, 462 U.S. 416 (1983). There O'Connor laid out an analysis of the abortion question that departed from the stark privacy right rationale of *Roe*. O'Connor argued instead that the state's interest in potential life exists throughout pregnancy. In some memorable phrases, she described the *Roe* framework as "on a collision course with itself" and made clear her view that "there is no justification in law or logic for the trimester framework adopted in Roe." Thus for O'Connor regulations are constitutionally acceptable so long as they do not "unduly burden" women seeking abortions, a standard that requires a contextual, fact-oriented judgment. Such a nuanced approach to the abortion issue outraged those who had hoped for an unequivocal endorsement of a woman's reproductive rights.

O'Connor accordingly became characterized by some as a mere token advance for women: "Feminists are left with a symbolic achievement for women but no positive, concrete gains in women's rights." When the New York Women's Bar Association announced plans to give its award for outstanding prominence in law or public service to O'Connor at its fiftieth annual dinner, sixty-six female lawyers protested, calling the award an "affront" to those seeking gender and racial equality.

Paradoxically, other feminists, drawing on the work of Carol Gilligan, had been criticizing the abstract rights approach to legal decision making as overbearingly male in contrast to the more contextual, relational approach said to be more typical of women. In that sense, while O'Connor did not advance a thoroughgoing "feminist" agenda, she did seem, some said, to speak in a "feminine" voice. Suzanna Sherry, in an influential article, "Civic

Virtue and the Feminine Voice in Constitutional Adjudication," 72 *Virginia Law Review* 543 (1986), made that argument in its most comprehensive form.

Sherry described two important strands in O'Connor's decision making. First was O'Connor's (by then frequently noted) preference for close, fact-based contextual judgment, which Sherry identified as consistent with female, rather than male, moral development. In *Wilson v. Garcia*, 105 S. Ct. 1938 (1985), for example, O'Connor was the sole dissenter from the Court's decision to apply a uniform statute of limitations to all Section 1983 claims. In *Charles D. Bonanno Linen Service* v. *NLRB*, 454 U.S. 404 (1982), the majority adopted a uniform rule prohibiting employer withdrawal from multiemployer bargaining units when negotiations had reached impasse, while Burger and Rehnquist argued in dissent for an equally uniform rule permitting such withdrawal. O'Connor wrote separately to argue that the answer should depend on the "circumstances surrounding and following that impasse."

The same insistence on contextual judgment had continued to run through her criminal cases; even the choice of applicable legal test, O'Connor had argued, should be contextual. In a case involving revocation of probation for an indigent, she argued that the Court should not simply focus mechanically on whether the correct test should be strict scrutiny (equal protection) or minimal rationality (due process). This approach, said O'Connor, was too formulaic. Quoting Harlan, she stated:

> Whether analyzed in terms of equal protection or due process, the issue cannot be resolved by resort to easy slogans or pigeonhole analysis, but rather requires a careful inquiry into such factors as "the nature of the individual interest affected, the extent to which it is affected, the rationality of the connection between legislative means and purpose, [and] the existence of alternative means for effectuating the purpose." (Bearden v. Georgia, 461 U.S. 660, 666–67 [1983], quoting Williams v. Illinois, 399 U.S. 235, 260 [1970] [Harlan, J., concurring].)

As Sherry also pointed out, O'Connor had been concerned in the criminal context with protecting the *process* of individualized decision making, to the point of disagreeing with the conservatives and joining prodefendant liberal opinions when she thought that process had been impeded; on the other hand, she had little patience for technical criminal "rights" that seemed peripheral to the real truth-finding function of the criminal justice system.

This emphasis on contextual rather than formulaic analysis is related to a second, somewhat more elusive dimension of O'Connor's opinions: her concern for discrete, responsible, participatory decision-making bodies within the polity. As was already evident in her first term (e.g., the *Pico* dissent), the relevant model for O'Connor was not necessarily one of individual rights–holders confronting the state but rather one of discrete community and political entities and office-holders, each charged with doing responsible "good government" decision making. O'Connor emphasized in an interview with Bill Moyers her commitment to "workable government." For O'Connor, as

Sherry pointed out, the integrity of decision-making processes may be a more compelling concern than the question of individual rights as such.

In *Caldwell* v. *Mississippi*, 105 S. Ct. 2633 (1985), for example, in which a jury had arguably been misled, Marshall's opinion rested on the resulting violation of the defendant's rights, whereas O'Connor, agreeing with Marshall as to result, emphasized in her concurring opinion that "the prosecutor's remarks were impermissible because they were inaccurate and misleading in a manner that diminished the jury's sense of responsibility. . . . [Those remarks, about subsequent review, inappropriately] sought to minimize the sentencing jury's role."

According to Sherry, this emphasis on protecting the integrity of the decision-making process of various groups within the polity has its historical roots in Jeffersonian republicanism as small-group, participatory democracy— the yeoman farmer model that was at least partially displaced by the Madisonian and Hamiltonian emphasis on a national state and a national economy. (One might add Alexis de Tocqueville's observation that the strength of American democracy would last only so long as various voluntary, *apolitical* mediating structures, such as churches, also retained their vigor.) Any small, participatory community, however, carries the potential for exclusivity. On this issue, Sherry offers some interesting observations, for she finds in O'Connor a special concern for the destructive potential of that exclusivity.

One of O'Connor's most important early contributions was in the area of church/state relations. Much analysis of that troubling area had reached a self-contradictory impasse, seemingly incapable of resolving the tension between the Establishment Clause and the Free Exercise Clause. O'Connor's reformulation of the standard *Lemon* test for Establishment Clause cases gave new emphasis to establishment as a question of community. Rejecting both the purity of the strict separationists and the seemingly indifferent clarity of those conservatives who advocated invalidating only official establishment or coerced compliance, O'Connor focused on whether or not government sends an exclusionary message of endorsement or disapproval in a particular case:

> Endorsement sends a message to nonadherents that they are outsiders, not full members of the political community, and an accompanying message to adherents that they are insiders, favored members of the political community. Disapproval sends the opposite message.
> (Lynch v. Donnelly, 465 U.S. 668, 687–88 [1985].)

Thus her focus went more to the question of the proper constitution of communities than to the question of individual rights in relation to state power.

O'Connor's concern for community integrity was also evident, Sherry suggested, in her willingness to sanction the use of federal power to put a stop to the intimidating and threatening danger of mob rule despite the arguable violation of federalism constraints such deployment of power entails. In 1983, in *United Brotherhood of Carpenters* v. *Scott*, 463 U.S. 824, O'Connor broke with the conservatives to join Justices Blackmun, Brennan, and

Marshall in dissenting from the majority's refusal to extend the Reconstruction-era civil rights conspiracy statute, Section 1985(3), to a case in which union members assaulted and severely injured nonunion employees. Sherry suggested that for O'Connor, with her concern for community, mob violence may be seen as the "time-tested method of keeping outsiders on the outside."

Ten years later, in 1993, O'Connor joined Justices Blackmun and John Paul Stevens to dissent from the Court's refusal to extend the same statute to protesters blocking access to abortion clinics. In *Bray* v. *Alexandria Women's Health Clinic*, 113 S. Ct. 753 (1993), O'Connor in her separately written dissent characterized the problem as those who "act in organized groups to overwhelm local police forces and physically blockade the entrances to respondents' clinics." Later in her opinion she observed, "The controversy associated with the exercise of those [abortion] rights, although legitimate, makes the clinics and the women they serve especially vulnerable to the threat of mob violence." The *Bray* dissent seems consistent with Sherry's observation about the earlier vote in *Carpenters*. So, too, does O'Connor's opinion for a six-to-three Court in *Frisby* v. *Schultz*, 487 U.S. 474 (1988), also involving abortion protest, which discounts the First Amendment claim of the protesters and upholds a ban on targeted residential picketing as protective of the residential privacy of one's home.

However insightful Sherry's readings of O'Connor's opinions, her analysis does not necessarily support her main point that O'Connor is the Court's feminine voice. For one thing, the "contextual" analysis accurately identified as such by Sherry is contextual in the sense that the common law tradition, at its best, has always been contextual—requiring a close reading of facts *in relation to* and *constrained by* precedent, and where applicable, by statutory language. There is nothing particularly feminine about that approach to judging. While some are less inclined than O'Connor to follow an essentially common law methodology in constitutional decision making (and while many judges are less skilled than she in using it), that is hardly a difference that seems to follow gender lines—as O'Connor's frequent reliance on John Harlan, the legacy of Lewis Powell, and Souter's similar methodology makes clear. O'Connor herself, citing Sherry, rejected any "New Feminism" that would perpetuate "old myths we have struggled to put behind us." In fact, she finds the gender differences cited approvingly by Sherry and others "surprisingly similar to stereotypes from years past."

So too with O'Connor's emphasis in her opinions on the role of various responsible mediating structures within a national polity. Such an emphasis may evoke the historical tradition of Jeffersonian republicanism, which Sherry herself describes at length, or a vision of American life captured by de Tocqueville. It might also draw on the cooperative spirit of the Western roundup, which O'Connor has cited as formative in her experience, or the experience of trying to do "good government" at the state level rather than drawing on any distinctively feminine outlook. It may also, of course, derive chiefly from her theoretical interpretation of Madisonian federalism.

If one sets aside the gender issue in regard to O'Connor's decision making, questions of considerable significance remain. First, can the supposed constraints of the common law tradition of decision making, which O'Connor seems to exemplify, serve to resolve the theoretical dilemmas and the political polarization that have beset the Court in recent years? Can one, in other words, convincingly contain theoretical contradiction simply by doing "good judging" in the common law sense? Second, can the O'Connor focus on the proper role of mediating structures (e.g., her emphasis on federalism) be taken as a serious constitutional resolution of the state/individual problem, or is it just a nostalgic invocation of a bygone era, irrelevant to a modern nation-state with a massive federal bureaucracy and national economy and fundamentally alien to a constitutional structure that was in large measure designed by its founders (as O'Connor recognizes) to *limit* the role of participatory localism?

Madisonian constitutionalism is at least in part a product of Enlightenment political theory, reflecting, for example, the rationalism of David Hume (and, some would say, the skepticism of Thomas Hobbes) along with Hume's distrust of unmediated democracy. The resultant American version of popular sovereignty is securely located in a constitutional form and a national federalist structure, not in the direct voice of people—hence the perennial, intractable problem of explaining the legitimacy of constitutional law decision making (especially judicial review) in a democracy.

As early American legal theorists such as Alexander Hamilton and John Marshall understood (along, perhaps, with James Madison himself) the constitutional structure, however much a product of Enlightenment rationalism, depends for its legitimacy on a decidedly pre-Enlightenment tradition of reasoning—the common law tradition. As a *legal* text the Constitution was not to be interpreted according to an Enlightenment version of natural law but rather through the "reason" of customary common law traditionalism—Lord Coke's "artificial reason" (77 *Eng. Rep.* 1342, 1343 [K.B. 1608]). As Hamilton emphatically stated in the *Federalist*:

> The interpretation of the laws is the proper and peculiar province of the courts. A constitution is, in fact, and must be regarded by the judges, as a fundamental law. It therefore belongs to them to ascertain its meaning.

John Marshall made exactly the same claim in *Marbury* v. *Madison*: "It is emphatically the province and duty of the Judicial department to say what the law is" (5 U.S. [1 Cranch] 137, 177 [1803]).

Notably, this tradition had been discredited by Enlightenment natural rights theorists like John Locke and Tom Paine and had been challenged as well by the epistemological skeptic Hobbes. Nor was it wholly compatible even with pre-Enlightenment versions of natural law, since its claim was not one that could be defended by rational principle but rather depended on a "thick description" of *craft*—hence the great common law theorist Matthew Hale could answer Hobbes' theoretical assault only through evocative description of the changing changelessness of tradition, not by logical argument.

H. Jefferson Powell has thus described, in *The Moral Tradition of American Constitutionalism: A Theological Interpretation*, the common law background to American constitutionalism as rooted in a nonphilosophic conception of reason. A rule's validity and its appropriate application to particular cases is governed by "resoun"—a word more complex and bound to traditional craft than our modern conception of reason:

> For classical common lawyers, rules were discovered in, debated in terms of, and decided with reference to stories of past situations and decisions. A rule of broad generality might emerge from such stories, but its application in future circumstances was always open to further narrative argument. It was not possible, even in theory, to establish in advance a metarule that would determine the proper application of a rule to all the varied circumstances of human life. Even a putatively general rule was limited to cases that a lawyer well schooled in the profession's traditions of argument would agree fell within the resoun of the rule. One learned how to be a good legal reasoner by reading and hearing good arguments by lawyers and judges with the virtues of insight, discrimination, judgment, integrity, and so on.

Thus the common law tradition represents not just analogy and precedent but the use of that methodology in the service of the larger goal "of discerning and applying substantive standards of justice and reasonability through the forms of law."

Some critics from within the American legal realist tradition have attacked the neutrality and hence the legitimacy of judicial decision making with Hobbesian skepticism. Toward the end of his career, the great legal realist Karl Llewellyn defended (echoing Matthew Hale in the seventeenth century) the "reckonability" of appellate-court decision making by invoking craft and tradition. Llewellyn's defense was not a logical, structured argument but a rich, evocative narrative of courts and judges and case-by-case doctrinal development combined with an often elusive (and hyphenated) description of method—situation-sense (the most important), craft-controlled, law-conditioned, rule-type, authority-leeways, craft-practice, etc. (For a good summary, see Charles Clark and David Trubek, "The Creative Role of the Judge: Restraint and Freedom in the Common Law Tradition," 71 *Yale Law Journal* 255 [1961].) Situation-sense was most important, being for Llewellyn "not a creature of mere reason" but rather "what reason can recognize in the nature of man and of the life conditions of the time and place." A reason capable of that recognition is a reason schooled by craft, very much the pre-Enlightenment "resoun" described by Powell.

Agreeing with critics of the Supreme Court, Llewellyn feared that the Court had lost its common law moorings and had turned to broad theory or

simple result orientation rather than employing the Grand Tradition of common law doctrinal development:

> *I find in my own reading . . . signs and patterns . . . that have troubled me far more than*
> *could any particular decisions. Frankfurter can want his own doctrine until it is to hell*
> *with the Court and with his duty as a teamplayer. Douglas can twist a case beyond all legal*
> *decency or honesty, and use it, straightfaced, as if it supported his conclusion. Black can*
> *whittle authorities into shavings, and who knows, from this, where he is at? Warren can*
> *put out a principle as broad as all outdoors, and then disregard it in the next case, as soon*
> *as one touch of the phrasing becomes uncomfortable. . . . What our study shows . . . is (1)*
> *that a court ought always to be slow in uncharted territory, and, in such territory, ought*
> *to be narrow, again and again, in any ground for decision. Until the territory has been*
> *reasonably explored. But what our study shows is (2) that once there is clearish light, a*
> *court should make effort to state an ever broader line for guidance. And (3) so long as each*
> *such line is promptly and overtly checked up and checked on and at need rephrased on each*
> *subsequent occasion of new illumination. Such informed questing after broader lines is of*
> *the essence of good appellate judging.*
>
> *What the [critics of the Court] are really complaining of, in this connection, is a*
> *Warrenish type of broad generalization not built in care on and out of eight or eighteen*
> *prior cases but framed ad hoc to support the conclusion for the case in hand. That is of*
> *course out of line. Anybody can see that, who gets far enough away to use two eyes.*

Sandra Day O'Connor can best be understood as operating within the
craft tradition described by Llewellyn. The question is whether that (pre-
Enlightenment) tradition can salvage constitutionalism by successfully mediating (post-Enlightenment) philosophical tensions built into it. More
specifically, the question is whether O'Connor's common law methodology
can serve as an effective antidote to the jurisprudence of ideology that has
become so characteristic of the Supreme Court or whether ideological clashes
are inevitable, given that the Constitution is an expression of political theory
as much as it is a legal document.

Over the past two decades (at least), both ideological conservatives and
ideological liberals on the Supreme Court have implicitly adopted the state/
individual model of the modern political and constitutional dilemma—with
the liberals tending to side with the individual in areas of personal liberty
and criminal rights but with the state in areas of economic rights, while the
reverse is usually true of the conservatives. So too, the liberals will side
with equality rights while conservatives will tend to protect those liberty
interests that necessarily entail inequality (e.g., property). At the level of
pure logic, neither side is clearly right—which makes the choices seem logically uncompelled and hence political. Not just the outcome of individual
cases but the whole general framework of analysis is in dispute. That logical
dilemma may not be *solved* by an almost prelogical exercise of craft, but it
is contained or mediated (or perhaps just obfuscated) through an arguably
apolitical methodology. Can the "resoun" of O'Connor adequately replace
a "reason" that is no longer considered valid? If not, the ever-recurring

sense of constitutional crisis may eventually lead to complete, corrosive politicization.

While there is no necessary logical connection between a commitment to common law craft and a concern with protection of independent sources of authority—mediating structures—within the polity, both may show a similar resistance to adopting a single, sweeping ideology. Both also represent a rejection of the stark state-versus-individual formulation of constitutional issues. O'Connor's focus has consistently been on the proper constitution of community *within* the polity rather than on the definition of individual rights as against state authority. A law clerk has said that O'Connor is "one of those people who believes that a lot of problems governments have to face have good-government solutions, which people of good will can agree on without having to adopt one broad ideological solution." If there are good, nonideological law solutions to concrete cases, then presumably there are "good-government solutions" to particular problems that can be achieved by a variety of distinct authoritative bodies within the polity—each doing its distinct job—ranging from the local school board to the U.S. Congress.

Again, however, this is not necessarily to answer the theoretical dilemma set in motion by Madisonian constitutionalism—here the conflict is between government by the local participatory community and government by a nationalized structure. The great rallying cry of the English civil war, "the voice of the People is the voice of God," led all too easily to anarchy and chaos, as Hobbes understood and feared. And it was that tendency of the local "people out of doors" toward unruly irrationalism—mob rule (a problem O'Connor has recognized), *not* good government—that led Madison to favor an expanded national territory and a federal institutional structure that stifled faction and filtered democratic passion out of public life. Hume's oft-quoted statement is usually taken to be Madison's inspiration:

> In a large government, which is modelled with masterly skill, there is compass and room enough to refine the democracy from the lower people, . . . to the higher magistrates, who direct all the movements.

Given the rejection of the tradition of pure participatory republicanism at the outset—including, one might add, the rejection of the republican repudiation of the common law (as in James Harrington and Tom Paine)—the role of more localized sources of authority is at least problematic. As noted, moreover, O'Connor herself finds federal power legitimately exercised as against what she sees as illegitimate (unruly, or unduly exclusionary) localized community authority despite what might otherwise be taken as compelling federalism constraints (*Bray*). One then has to ask exactly how one can, in a principled way, decide when states or localities can legitimately claim autonomy. The courts of an earlier era believed some matters were "by their very nature" local, an essentialist conviction that is now not commonly held. Where, then, does one find the boundaries that mark spheres of autonomy? In effect that problem is also epistemological, and the question is whether the common law methodology O'Connor employs can successfully resolve it.

O'Connor's independent voice on the Court has become both more significant and more frequently determinative in the years since the beginning of the 1986 term, when Antonin Scalia joined the Court. O'Connor has often found herself trying to establish a position simultaneously distant from the heavy-handed result orientation of either Rehnquist or Brennan (until he retired in 1990) on the one hand and from the rigid formalism of Scalia, which has sought to dominate the conservative majority, on the other. In doing so, she has demonstrated a methodology that retains the character of her Arizona opinions.

An early illustrative case is *O'Connor* v. *Ortega*, 480 U.S. 709 (1987), a Section 1983 civil action brought by a former public employee claiming that his employer violated the Fourth Amendment in searching his office, desk, and files. O'Connor, writing for a plurality of four, focused on the operational realities of the government workplace. Thus, while she conceded there might be a reasonable expectation of privacy (unlike the Solicitor General, who had argued for none) for public employees, it was one that might be reduced by actual office practices and must be assessed in light of the employment relation. O'Connor, typically, opted for a reasonableness standard to be applied on a case-by-case basis, rejecting a Fourth Amendment formalism that would have insisted on a warrant and probable cause as in a criminal context. O'Connor placed great emphasis on the real problem faced by public employers dealing with the "inefficiency, incompetence, mismanagement, or other work-related misfeasance of its employees."

Scalia, concurring only in the result, jumped on O'Connor's call for a case-by-case approach, dismissing it as "a standard so devoid of content that it produces rather than eliminates uncertainty in this field." Scalia's own approach would reduce the issue to one of neat binary categories—if one's office is private, the Fourth Amendment automatically applies, regardless of whether the employer is public or private; because the place is protected, the identity of the searcher (police or supervisor) is irrelevant. Yet as one begins to think Scalia's formalism will offer more protection to employees than O'Connor's approach does, Scalia points out that only unreasonable searches are outlawed by the Fourth Amendment and maintains that because private employers routinely search employee offices, desks, and files to retrieve work-related materials or investigate misconduct, it is *per se* reasonable for public employers to do the same.

The dissenting liberals, on the other hand, also denied context, insisting in effect that a search is a search is a search. Thus Blackmun argued that the only expectation of privacy is that offered by the Fourth Amendment in its purity—requiring probable cause and a warrant prior to search (unless there is special need, not involved in this case). However uncertain O'Connor's approach will be in the long run, it does seem more sensibly responsive to the government workplace setting than either the full-fledged rigidity of criminal due process in the workplace (the dissent) or Scalia's lip service to a protection that is none at all.

O'Connor's unwillingness to be cabined by doctrinal rigidity is nowhere more evident than in *Michael H. v. Gerald D.*, 109 S. Ct. 2333 (1989), in which Scalia's plurality included only himself and Rehnquist, with O'Connor concurring with the opinion except to one footnote and Justice Anthony Kennedy taking that position with her. (Stevens concurred in the result, to make a majority.) The case, brought by a natural father who had fathered a child as a consequence of an adulterous relationship with the married mother, involved his challenge to the 100-year-old California conclusive statutory presumption that the husband was the father of the child. Scalia, while conceding that the issue was the meaning of liberty in the Fourteenth Amendment and that the word might mean more than freedom from physical restraint (thus giving some license to substantive due process), confined its meaning by a very specific notion of tradition. For Scalia, the clear tradition was that of protecting the marital father. Brennan, in dissent, invoked traditions of parenthood and the right "not to conform." O'Connor, while agreeing with Scalia as to result, made clear that she did not wish to "foreclose the unanticipated by the prior imposition of a single mode of historical analysis."

At times O'Connor's disagreement with Scalia has led him to join with the liberals in dissent. In *Maryland v. Craig*, 497 U.S. 836 (1990), O'Connor, writing for the majority in a five-to-four decision, upheld a state procedure that allowed a six-year-old victim of sexual abuse to testify against the perpetrator by one-way closed-circuit television, thereby denying the defendant the opportunity for face-to-face confrontation required by the Confrontation Clause of the Sixth Amendment. O'Connor concluded that while the clause expressed a "preference" for face-to-face confrontation, the requirement was not "absolute" if other protections were available. Her solicitude for the child victims in such cases was evident in her recognition of the "trauma of testifying against the alleged perpetrator."

Scalia in dissent (along with Brennan, Marshall, and Stevens) accused O'Connor and the majority of conspicuously failing "to sustain a categorical guarantee of the Constitution against the tide of prevailing current opinion." His basic accusation: "subordination of explicit constitutional text to currently favored public policy."

By way of testament to O'Connor's tendency to draw close factual distinctions, the Court on the same day as *Craig* decided *Idaho v. Wright*, 497 U.S. 805 (1990), in which O'Connor, speaking for a majority of five (herself, Brennan, Marshall, Stevens, and Scalia), held that the admission of hearsay statements by a child victim of sexual abuse to a pediatrician violated the defendant's Confrontation Clause rights, requiring reversal of the conviction. Here too she focused on the particular facts of the case, earning a dissent from Kennedy, Rehnquist, White, and Blackmun.

A year later, in another instance of insistence on formalist absolutism, Scalia in dissent (again with the liberals) invoked O'Connor's *Craig* opinion against her sarcastically. In *County of Riverside* v. *McLaughlin*, 500 U.S. 44 (1991), O'Connor—speaking for herself, Rehnquist, White, Kennedy, and Souter—held that the Fourth Amendment's requirement of a "prompt" judicial determination of probable cause following a warrantless arrest and pre-trial detention would be presumptively satisfied by a forty-eight-hour rule, which would protect individual rights while allowing local government some room for flexibility and experimentation as well as financial savings. Scalia joined Marshall, Blackmun, and Stevens in dissent but wrote separately, insisting on an absolute twenty-four-hour rule. In so doing, he observed (perhaps with O'Connor especially in mind, because *Webster* [discussed below] had been decided two years earlier) that "this Court's constitutional jurisprudence . . . alternately creates rights that the Constitution does not contain and denies rights that it does. Compare *Roe* v. *Wade* [citation omitted] (right to abortion does exist) with *Maryland* v. *Craig* [citation omitted] (right to be confronted with witnesses, Amdt. 6, does not)."

One of the most striking illustrations of O'Connor's success in distancing herself from the formalism of Scalia on the one hand and from the formulaic liberalism of Blackmun, Brennan, and Marshall on the other is her opinion for the Court in *City of Richmond* v. *J. A. Croson Co.*, 488 U.S. 469 (1989), which has become the definitive decision on the constitutionality of affirmative action. Richmond, Virginia, whose city council had a black majority (five to four), had enacted a set-aside plan mandating that thirty per cent of construction subcontracts be awarded to minority business enterprises. The plan was based on generalized findings of past discrimination, especially the statistic that whereas blacks comprised fifty per cent of Richmond's population, minority businesses had received only .67 per cent of construction contracts from the city.

Scalia, who concurred in the judgment, maintained that the constitution is color-blind and therefore any race-based affirmative action is per se illegal except in a case in which an identifiable victim is being compensated (which is not affirmative action at all). The dissenting liberals, on the other hand, would have deemed the racial classification merely benign or remedial and therefore not subject to more than medium constitutional scrutiny, a standard they thought the plan satisfied. Given the two positions at the extreme, the question posed by the case was whether in the area of affirmative action there exists any principled middle position.

O'Connor, in an opinion that was generally denounced by liberals at the time, insisted on strict scrutiny where race was at issue and found that the specific plan was not narrowly tailored enough to remedy particularized local instances of past discrimination and was therefore invalid. She did not, however, rule out more carefully structured plans that would satisfy the constitutional standard in future cases. With some distance and a better sense of

O'Connor's overall constitutional outlook, *Richmond* gains stature. For one thing, it is clearer today than it once was that heavy-handed affirmative action has its destructive downside, especially for its supposed beneficiaries. A growing critical literature recognizes this reality. (E.g., Shelby Steele, *The Content of Our Character*, 1990; Stephen Carter, *Reflections of an Affirmative Action Baby*, 1991.) Thus O'Connor may have been more insightful than many supposed when she observed in *Richmond* that

> *Classifications based on race carry a danger of stigmatic harm. Unless they are strictly reserved for remedial settings, they may in fact promote notions of racial inferiority and lead to a politics of racial hostility.*

Moreover, O'Connor's focus on the particular politics of Richmond that produced the plan in question is consistent with her continuing concern with the integrity of local political process despite her federalism concerns. The seemingly inclusionary move (the set-aside) can become a tool of exclusion (in the hands of a political majority who can promulgate such a plan based on generalities alone); it can also be a source of corruption. Nevertheless, O'Connor does recognize that the historical and continuing reality of racial discrimination is such that there must be some in-between space, however ill-defined, that allows for remedial efforts that go beyond mere formal equality of opportunity but stop short of categorical demands for equality of results. While such a middle category gives scant logical comfort to anyone, it may nevertheless be the one that is most simultaneously sensitive to historical, political, and experiential reality.

Shaw v. *Reno*, 113 S. Ct. 2816 (1993), posed a similar problem with respect to voting districts. The North Carolina General Assembly had passed a reapportionment plan that contained a majority-black voting district of a bizarre snakelike shape obviously designed for purposes of including African Americans. (A state legislator commented that "if you drove down the interstate with both car doors open, you'd kill most of the people in the district.") Under the plan whites still remained a voting majority in a disproportionate number of districts, and the state had sent its first black representative since Reconstruction to the U.S. Congress.

As with *Richmond*, the two possible extreme positions were easily identified: all race-conscious districting could be prohibited, or any race-conscious districting could be allowed so long as it served the benign purpose of increasing minority representation. Typically, O'Connor, writing for the majority in subjecting the plan to strict scrutiny and remanding for further review, rejected either extreme. She conceded that in its redistricting plans the legislature, inevitably "always is *aware* of race when it draws district lines, just as it is aware of age, economic status, religious and political persuasion, and a variety of other demographic factors." There are, after all, no natural district lines—they are always contrived to accommodate a variety of political and social constituencies. Nevertheless, she argued, in this case the lines were *so* peculiarly drawn according to race alone as to bear "an uncomfortable resemblance to political apartheid" and to reinforce the stereotypical assumptions of racial bloc voting.

Justice Souter, who often shares O'Connor's methodological approach, dissented in *Shaw*, objecting that the test O'Connor had stated was unclear as to both derivation and content—in effect, a new "configuration 'so bizarre' " category for redistricting plan cases based, as O'Connor conceded, on appearance alone ("appearances do matter"). Recall, in the classic racial gerrymandering case of *Gromillion* v. *Lightfoot*, 364 U.S. 339 (1960), Justice Frankfurter's virtually determinative characterization of the territorial rearrangement in question as "from a square to an uncouth twenty-eight-sided figure," a description quoted twice by O'Connor in her *Shaw* opinion.

Any appearance standard is bound to be less than fully satisfying. Perhaps her opinion omitted other arguably relevant factors, such as numbers and history, yet any effort to impose limits on race consciousness short of complete prohibition will inevitably lack clarity.

During her career on the Court, O'Connor has had a great impact on a wide range of legal areas. Perhaps her least-publicized contributions are her notable opinions in several areas of federal statutory law. For example, in her second term she applied her common law methodology to write what became the first opinion successfully explaining the "tax benefit" rule, a judge-made rule of tax law. Her opinion in *Hillsboro National Bank* v. *Commissioner of Internal Revenue*, 460 U.S. 370 (1983), became an instant classic and has proved to be an excellent teaching tool.

A year later she entered a real thicket, "tying arrangements" under federal antitrust law. In *Jefferson Parish Hospital* v. *Hyde*, 466 U.S. 2 (1984), she wrote a characteristic O'Connor concurring opinion, trying to distance herself from the liberal formalism that dominated antitrust law in the late 1960's and early 1970's without yielding to an equally wooden conservative formalism (which in its extreme form would argue that all business practices are legal except hard-core price-fixing). Her carefully researched and thoughtful opinion makes a real effort to clarify the issues in terms of business context and economic realities.

Another area of significant impact has been intellectual property, especially copyright law. (For a review of her work in this area, see Marci Hamilton, "Justice O'Connor's Intellectual Property Opinions: Currents and Crosscurrents," 13 *Women's Rights Law Reporter* 71 [1991].) Particularly notable were her opinions in *Harper & Row Publishers, Inc.* v. *Nation Enterprises*, 471 U.S. 539 (1985), which extended copyright protection to the unauthorized publication of excerpts from Gerald Ford's then-unpublished memoirs, and *Feist Publications Inc.* v. *Rural Telephone Co.*, 499 U.S. 340 (1991), in which she refused on constitutional grounds to extend copyright protection to the white pages of a telephone directory, pointing out that "originality is a constitutionally mandated prerequisite for copyright protection" and mere "industry" is not enough.

In addition to her impact on federal statutory law, O'Connor has shown special concern for and been immensely influential on a number of more substantive and more controversial areas, namely federalism, religion, gender, and children. O'Connor has penned well-thought and significant opinions in each of these fields and has in many cases profoundly shaped Supreme Court policy.

Justice O'Connor has emphasized from the outset of her Supreme Court career that her concern for federalism and the autonomy of states within the national federal structure is paramount. In her opening testimony at her confirmation hearings, her first two substantive points were (1) that she was "honored" to be "the first woman to be nominated as a Supreme Court justice" and (2) that "my experience as a State court judge and as a State legislator has given me a greater appreciation of the important role the States play in our federal system." And as noted above, her most stinging first-term dissent was in a federalism case, *FERC* v. *Mississippi*.

She offered another forceful dissent in 1985, in *Garcia* v. *San Antonio Metropolitan Transit Authority*, 469 U.S. #528. The Court, by a five-to-four vote in *Garcia*, overruled its 1975 decision in *National League of Cities* v. *Usery*, 426 U.S. 833. *National League of Cities* had sought to resurrect the Tenth Amendment as a constitutional check on the power of Congress to interfere with state autonomy, in particular with the imposition of federal minimum wage laws on state and local governments as employers. That decision represented the first such use of the Tenth Amendment since it had been deemed a mere "truism" by the New Deal Court in 1941 in *United States* v. *Darby*, 312 U.S. 100.

National League of Cities, which was followed by a bewildering series of seemingly incoherent decisions, barely lasted a decade. Justice Blackmun, whose concurring vote had clinched the original decision, switched to join the five-to-four majority in *Garcia*. O'Connor began her *Garcia* dissent with the observation that the "Court today surveys the battle scene of federalism and sounds a retreat." Her position was nothing less than "fundamental disagreement with the majority's views of federalism and the duty of this Court." Given that the Court was itself overruling a precedent, it seemed clear that O'Connor would seek in time to restore that precedent, whose overruling she deemed illegitimate (both O'Connor and Rehnquist as much as said so in their *Garcia* dissents). Because her position would come to prevail by 1992, her *Garcia* dissent bears a careful reading.

For O'Connor, the "central issue of federalism is, of course, whether any realm is left open to the States by the Constitution—whether any area remains in which a State may act free of federal interference." She firmly believes that the essence of federalism is that "the States as States have legitimate interests which the National Government is bound to respect even though its laws are supreme." Taking on the challenge of Madisonian constitutionalism, O'Connor concedes that the framers "envisioned a National Government capable of solving national problems" yet believes they just as surely "envisioned a republic whose vitality was assured by the diffusion of power not only among the branches of the Federal Government, but also between the Federal Government and the States."

Quoting Madison, O'Connor offers his account of a "compound republic," where power is divided between two distinct governments and then further subdivided within each into "distinct and separate departments." The upshot is that a "double security arises to the rights of the people. The different governments will control each other; at the same time that each will be controlled by itself."

O'Connor understands that national government must deal with national economic problems, and that the Court has generously interpreted the Commerce Clause to that end. Yet she insists that the Court must also enforce affirmative limits on federal regulation of the states as well. She is unwilling to trust what she terms Congress's "underdeveloped capacity for self-restraint."

While recognizing the failure of *National League of Cities* to produce "bright lines defining the scope of the state autonomy protected," she is content, as usual, to take a case-by-case approach that at least weighs "state autonomy as a factor in the balance." She simply insists that the state as subject of regulation should not be treated as if it were just a private litigant.

As if to leave no uncertainty as to her seriousness in this area, O'Connor, joined only by Brennan, dissented from the Court's seven-to-two decision in *South Dakota* v. *Dole*, 483 U.S. 203 (1987), upholding congressional insistence on a twenty-one-year-old drinking age as a precondition to receipt of federal highway funds. Similarly, she wrote the opinion for a five-to-four majority in 1989 refusing to extend respondent superior liability to local governments sued for damages in civil rights actions under Section 1981. (*Jett* v. *Dallas Independent School District*, 491 U.S. 701).

An important sign that O'Connor was gradually prevailing on the federalism concern was the Court's 1991 decision in *Gregory* v. *Ashcroft*, 501 U.S. 452, a statutory construction case with a heavy constitutional edge. The precise issue was whether the federal Age Discrimination in Employment Act prevented Missouri from enforcing a state constitutional provision requiring mandatory retirement of state judges at age seventy. The narrow but sufficient answer of the Court was that because the judges in question were policymaking officials within the meaning of the federal law, they were exempt from its coverage and could be retired involuntarily. O'Connor's opinion for the Court is not so narrowly tailored, however; it contains a lengthy celebration of the virtues of a federal system (similar to her *Garcia* dissent) and makes clear that in interpreting the federal law the state position would prevail unless one could be "absolutely certain" that Congress intended the opposite.

The transitional character of the *Gregory* decision, along with its constitutional significance, became clear with the Court's 1992 decision in *New York* v. *United States*, 112 S. Ct. 2408, in which O'Connor, writing for a six-to-three majority, invoked the Tenth Amendment (for the first time since 1975) to strike down a federal law—one that O'Connor characterized as a congressional attempt to "use the States as implements of regulation." The case involved a complex scheme for regulating the disposal of low-level radioactive waste, but the gist of O'Connor's opinion is that while Congress may regulate directly in appropriate areas and may even encourage state regulation, it may not go so far as to compel states to regulate, thereby bypassing state legislative process.

The case may be of minimal impact, restricted to its peculiar facts. The decision turns specifically on the fact that Congress offered the states two choices: regulate, or take title—neither of which, in O'Connor's view, could have been legislated in a singular command. Thus she found the offer of choice to be equally invalid. She insisted at the outset of her opinion (perhaps unconvincingly) that the decision in *New York* v. *U.S.* leaves otherwise intact the entire line of cases from *National League of Cities* (1975) to *Gregory* v. *Ashcroft* (1991). Thus *National League of Cities* remains overruled, *Garcia* is still good law, etc.

Given its explicit invocation of the Tenth Amendment, however, along with O'Connor's long-standing views in this area, the case may well signal a new era of Supreme Court activism (albeit a selective and contextual one) in promoting the state side of the federal/state balance. The last part of O'Connor's opinion suggests at least that the case is other than *sui generis*. Beginning with the observation that "Some truths are so basic that, like the air around us, they are easily overlooked," O'Connor points out that the Constitution "divides power among sovereigns and among branches of government precisely so that we may resist the temptation to concentrate power in one location as an expedient solution to the crisis of the day." The Constitution, she maintains, " 'leaves to the several States a residuary and inviolable sovereignty' . . . reserved explicitly to the States by the Tenth Amendment." Such language is likely to find itself cited and urged upon the Court in future litigation.

Given O'Connor's commitment to federalism, with its concomitant deference to state and local authorities acting within their spheres of authority, and her belief in the firm enforcement of criminal law, it is hardly surprising that she has been reluctant to extend federal rights to state prisoners claiming abuse by correctional officials. Yet even in this area, where predispositions were predictable, she has sought to offer an independent voice at times. In *Hudson* v. *Palmer*, 468 U.S. 517 (1984), she agreed with the majority that a prisoner claiming that his cell was searched and his property seized maliciously and as harassment by prison officials could not invoke a Fourth Amendment claim, because the privacy guaranteed by that amendment does not extend to prison cells. Nevertheless, rather than join the majority opinion, O'Connor concurred in order to emphasize that seizure or destruction of property, even that of a prisoner, might be actionable under the Due Process and Takings Clauses of the Constitution in an appropriate case, although the particular one was not ripe on that issue as yet.

She took a position of extreme deference in her opinion for a five-to-four Court in *Whitley* v. *Albers*, 475 U.S. 310 (1986), in which she wrote that the infliction of pain in the course of enforcing prison security was actionable under the Eighth Amendment's proscription of cruelty only if inflicted "unnecessarily and wantonly," a standard not met by the shooting of a prisoner without prior verbal warning during the quelling of a riot. Nevertheless, in 1992 she wrote for a seven-to-two majority, over the dissent of Scalia and Thomas, that a prisoner who satisfies the *Whitley* standard of "wanton and unnecessary" need not also establish that serious injuries were suffered in order to have a federal claim. O'Connor, reflecting her unwillingness to extend the individual rights/state model to every institutional setting, leaves prison officials with wide discretion yet makes clear that at some point their exercise of authority may become illegitimate.

One unusual area where O'Connor is willing to overturn state court judgments is that of punitive damage awards. In *Browning-Ferris Industries* v. *Kelco Disposal, Inc.*, 492 U.S. 257 (1989), the Court refused to apply Eighth Amendment limitations to punitive damages awarded in civil actions by a state court. O'Connor in dissent argued on the basis of extensive reference to English legal history that punitive damages fall within the excessive fines language of the Eighth Amendment because they are a modern version of thirteenth-century amercements, payments due to the Crown because of a variety of offenses that at the time were not categorized as either criminal (against the state) or civil (against another private individual). Blackmun, writing for the majority, found O'Connor's historical argument "somewhat intriguing" but did not adopt it because later history seemed to him to suggest that the Excessive Fines Clause derived specifically from historically rooted fear of *government* abuse.

Kelco left open the question of due process limitations on punitive damages, which had not been properly raised in the case. In *Pacific Mutual Life Insurance Co.* v. *Haslip*, 499 U.S. 1 (1991), an insurance fraud case, the Court did hold that due process standards could be applied to state procedures for awarding punitive damages. Justice Blackmun, however, writing for the Court, refused to find the particular guidance offered to juries in Alabama sufficiently open-ended to violate due process standards; Scalia, concurring in the result, insisted that the Court had no authority to impose due process standards at all because punitive damages have been a traditional part of state common law decision making.

O'Connor, dissenting, argued that serious due process scrutiny should require something more than unfettered jury discretion both as to whether punitive damages are awarded (here the jury was told, in effect, to do whatever it felt like) and as to amount. While this scrutiny requires some Court interference with the local, traditional institutions to which O'Connor usually defers, she appears to be calling for dialogue between the Court and the states. O'Connor suggests that had the states on their own adopted some reasonable check on absolute discretion, the Court would not have had to intervene, and that once the Court announces some guidelines, it should leave the states considerable leeway in fashioning more rational procedures. Echoing her concern over the dangers of mob rule, O'Connor charges the Alabama punitive damages procedure with giving "free reign to the biases and prejudices of individual jurors, allowing them to target unpopular defendants and punish selectively. In short, it is the antithesis of due process."

The issue was revisited in *TXO* v. *Alliance Resources*, 113 S. Ct. 2711 (1993), in which the Court recognized an implicit due process limitation to punitive damage awards. A plurality defined this limitation as more essentially procedural than substantive and found insufficient reason to overturn $10 million in punitive damages over and above only $19,000 in actual damages. O'Connor, writing in dissent, charged the majority with abandoning *Haslip*'s promise of sufficient constitutional scrutiny to "restore fairness to what is rapidly becoming an arbitrary and oppressive system" and to check the "caprice, passion, bias, and prejudice" that are "antithetical to the rule of law." Here O'Connor read the record as suggesting the likelihood that the jury was influenced by the fact that TXO was a large, wealthy out-of-state corporation.

In *Honda* v. *Oberg*, 114 S. Ct. 2331 (1994), however, the Court, with only two dissenters, did strike down a punitive damages award in a products liability suit against Honda. Stevens, writing for the majority, read both *Haslip* and *TXO* as imposing a substantive limit (despite the absence of bright-line guidelines) to punitive damages, but in *Oberg* the Court could focus on the defectiveness of Oregon's procedure: an amendment to the Oregon Constitution prohibited judicial review of the amount of punitive damages awarded by a jury unless the Court could affirmatively say there was no evidence to support the verdict. This absence of review the Court found out of line with both traditional common law safeguards and constitutional constraints as stated in *Haslip*.

In 1989, in *County of Allegheny* v. *ACLU*, 492 U.S. 573, Justice Blackmun, in an opinion announcing the judgment of the Court, proclaimed that the best available approach for deciding establishment clause cases was one that had been introduced by O'Connor in a determinative concurring opinion five years earlier in *Lynch* v. *Donnelly*, 465 U.S. 668 (1984). In *Lynch*, the Court upheld the inclusion of a creche in the annual Christmas holiday display funded by the city of Pawtucket, Rhode Island. Chief Justice Burger, in *Lynch*, had rejected any *per se* Establishment Clause test—including the three-prong *Lemon* test that had often been invoked by liberals to maintain a strict separation of church and state for the sake of insuring a supposed state neutrality toward religion. While Burger did not explicitly overrule the *Lemon* test, he did insist that the "line between permissible relationships and those barred by the Clause can no more be straight and unwavering than due process can be defined in a single stroke or phrase or test." Burger's own opinion, upholding the municipal display in light of its overall secular character, proposed that the Court reject its prior categorical insistence on strict separation and adopt instead a more contextual approach to Establishment Clause cases. He offered, however, little doctrinal clarification.

O'Connor, concurring, sought to clarify the meaning of *Lemon* so as to retain traditional Establishment Clause doctrine while at the same time allowing, like Burger, for a more contextualized and accommodationist approach. She stressed what she took to be the central purpose of the Establishment Clause—to prohibit government from "making adherence to a religion relevant in any way to a person's standing in the political community," which could be done either through "excessive entanglement" or "endorsement or disapproval." The latter, in turn, could occur when there was either a "purpose" to endorse or disapprove or when a government act had the "effect" (from the vantage point of an objective observer) of endorsement or disapproval. True to Llewellynesque legal realism, she urged that the traditional three prongs of the *Lemon* test (purpose, effect, and entanglement) be understood in light of the underlying purpose of the Clause and applied according to a more contextualized standard (often shortened to endorsement) that did not insist upon *strict* separation but did stay true to what she considered the real meaning of Supreme Court doctrine in the area.

In 1985, the Court revisited Establishment Clause doctrine in *Wallace* v. *Jaffree*, 472 U.S. 38. The state of Alabama had enacted three statutes relating to public school prayer: one calling for a period of silence "for meditation," another (three years later) calling for a period of silence "for meditation or voluntary prayer," and a third (a year after that) explicitly authorizing teachers to lead willing students in school prayer. The third had already been found unconstitutional, and the validity of the first was not in issue. Thus the only question before the Court was the validity of the second statute.

Justice Stevens, for the majority, applied the *Lemon* test to find the second moment-of-silence statute unconstitutional, especially focusing on the purpose prong of the test. In doing so, Stevens emphasized the individual rights dimension of the Establishment Clause—"the individual's freedom to choose his own creed is the counterpart of his right to refrain from accepting the creed established by the majority." Justice Powell wrote a concurring opinion expressly to affirm the strict *Lemon* test against O'Connor's position that the test should be "reexamined and refined" as in Lynch but not overruled and against a mounting conservative assault that would discard the test altogether.

O'Connor found herself alone in the center. The liberals were insisting on an unmodified test, but the conservatives were now challenging the whole formulation of *Lemon* as, in Rehnquist's view resting upon a premise about a supposed "wall of separation" that was supposedly ungrounded in the history of the First Amendment and had led to incoherently disparate results. In Rehnquist's view, the Establishment Clause prohibits only the literal establishment of a state church or preferential discrimination among denominations. Burger, also dissenting, reiterated his impatience with *Lemon*, especially criticizing the "naive preoccupation with an easy, bright-line approach for addressing constitutional issues." For Burger the Court's "responsibility is not to apply tidy formulas by rote" but "to determine whether the statute or practice at issue is a step toward establishing a state religion." Thus Burger, while not adopting Rehnquist's formalist non-preferentialism, did seem close to Rehnquist in proposing a drastic overhaul of Establishment Clause doctrine.

O'Connor, as in *Lynch*, refused to abandon *Lemon* altogether but stressed the need for its clarification with the goal of articulating doctrine that could be applied with some consistency. Returning precisely to her formulation in *Lynch*, she stated that her "endorsement" test did not "preclude government from acknowledging religion or taking religion into account in making law and policy. It does preclude government from conveying or attempting to convey a message that a particular religious belief is favored or preferred." Proving that the focus on endorsement, while accommodationist, nevertheless constituted a serious limitation, O'Connor agreed with the majority that Alabama had violated the Establishment Clause by clearly indicating a "purpose" to endorse religion. She explained that "moment of silence laws are not *per se* unconstitutional" and examined the "peculiar features" of the Alabama law that rendered it unconstitutional: the question in any moment of silence case is "whether the State has conveyed or attempted to convey the message that children should use the moment of silence for prayer," a question that can only be answered contextually, by examining "the history, language and administration of a particular statute to determine whether it operates as an endorsement of religion." Here the statute in question was added to a pre-existing moment of silence statute for the sake specifically of adding prayer as an activity, a purpose stated in the particular legislative history.

Here O'Connor again represented a middle ground between two extremes, a middle ground based on careful interpretation of doctrine, neither mechanical on the one hand nor wholly open-ended on the other but rooted in an effort to understand core doctrinal meaning and combined with careful contextual consideration of each individual case in light of that meaning. The precise relation between the purpose prong of the *Lemon* test and O'Connor's primary concern with community (where presumably the relevant focus should be on how children actually experience the practice as administered, not on the arguably irrelevant comments of a state legislator) remains somewhat unclear. Yet to ignore purpose would be to abandon the traditional test, a step O'Connor was unwilling to take.

Dramatically, less than one month after *Jaffree*, O'Connor's doctrinal approach had gained acceptance as the Court's Establishment Clause doctrine. In *School District of Grand Rapids* v. *Ball*, 473 U.S. 373 (1985), Justice Brennan, writing for the majority, stated that the core question under the Establishment Clause is the endorsement or disapproval one. He then employed O'Connor's version of the *Lemon* effects test—whether government action is likely to be perceived as endorsement—to strike down some cooperative public school/parochial school programs. O'Connor and Burger filed opinions concurring in part but indicating disagreement as to the particular factual nature of the cooperative programs in question (e.g., exactly how many public school teachers involved in one program were once teachers in the parochial schools to which they were assigned). Thus while *Grand Rapids* indicated a growing consensus that endorsement was the appropriate test, it also showed the extent to which endorsement does depend upon the eye of the beholder as well as upon the inherently manipulable description of factual context. While her approach had helped to clarify the core doctrinal concern in public symbolic display/religious speech cases, the ironic fact of O'Connor's dissent in *Grand Rapids*, a case in which the majority explicitly adopted her test, signaled that her approach was less useful in resolving public-funding cases.

In 1989 the Court had to pass judgment on two more holiday displays. In *County of Allegheny* v. *ACLU*, 492 U.S. 573, Justice Blackmun, announcing the judgment of the Court, simply stated that O'Connor's concurring opinion in *Lynch* "provides a sound analytic framework for evaluating governmental use of religious symbols" and claimed that the dissenters in *Lynch* differed only as to its application, not formulation; he also took *Grand Rapids* to stand for the Court's adoption of O'Connor's endorsement test.

Blackmun then distinguished the *Lynch* display, which had been full of gaudy nonreligious items, from one of the displays before the Court, a single isolated creche with an angel declaring "Glory to God in the Highest," whose more straightforward (and more tasteful) design constituted endorsement. The second display in question was more difficult, consisting as it did of a menorah next to a Christmas tree under a sign saluting liberty. Blackmun focused on the fact that the menorah was the only available symbol for Chanukah and that both the (secularized) Christmas tree and the menorah taken together could be interpreted as standing for the fact that both "Christmas and Chanukah are part of the same winter-holiday season, which has attained a secular status in our society." Thus the display did not communicate endorsement. O'Connor, writing in concurrence, agreed with the result as to each display but characterized the second one somewhat differently—she thought that the menorah retained its distinct religious character but that the display as a whole conveyed a permissible message of pluralism.

Justices Kennedy, White, and Scalia dissented, objecting to the endorsement test as requiring an inherently unpredictable "jurisprudence of minutiae." Nevertheless, O'Connor's approach seems to have been adopted in symbolic display and religious speech cases—although the most recent case, *Lee* v. *Weisman*, 112 S. Ct. 2649 (1992), rested on the per se invalidity of school prayer and did not need to explore the endorsement issue. In the 1994 *Kiryas Joel* case, 114 S. Ct. 2481, however, O'Connor herself conceded that "endorsement" as such provided little useful guidance in school funding cases, as *Grand Rapids* had effectively demonstrated. In *Kiryas Joel*, the Satmar Hasidian village of Kiryas Joel had been allowed by special state legislation to form a separate school district. The purpose was to provide a government-supported, secular program of special education for handicapped students within the community. (Other Kiryas Joel students were sent to private schools for religiously based instruction.) Originally, special-education classes had been provided in an annex to one of the private religious schools, but in response to *Grand Rapids* and a similar holding in *Aquilar* v. *Felton*, that arrangement had been discontinued; the children were then sent to a district school outside the community, where they suffered "panic, fear and trauma" and were, except in one case, withdrawn. In some cases they had received no subsequent special education services until the new district was formed.

The Court, with Justice Souter writing for the majority, struck down the special Kiryas Joel district, but not on *Lemon* or endorsement grounds. Souter's emphasis was on the state's delegation of government authority to a group defined solely by its religious identity. (Justice Kennedy, in a concurring opinion, made explicit the implicit comparison to *Shaw*.) In addition, given the singularity of the legislation (which related only to Kiryas Joel) the state could offer no assurance that other similarly situated groups would be similarly accommodated.

O'Connor, concurring in part and in the judgment, agreed that the school district constituted an improper "legislatively drawn religious classification" designed specifically to benefit one particular religious group. She added, however, that the Court had erred in the past in disallowing remedial services to parochial schools (*Aquilar*) and had created the Kiryas Joel problem in the first place. Moreover, acknowledging that the Court's "slide away from Lemon's unitary approach" was well underway, O'Connor conceded that Establishment Clause jurisprudence could not be reduced to any single test. While she suggested endorsement was still the appropriate test for cases about government speech on religious topics and urged retaining "some of the insights" *Lemon* had provided, she clearly signaled its abandonment in school funding and special benefit cases (like *Kiryas Joel*) as well as in cases involving government decisions pertaining to religious doctrine.

While the endorsement approach has proved workable for some Establishment Clause cases, O'Connor's initial suggestions that the same test might resolve free exercise cases by identifying limits to the government's license to promote the free exercise of religion (*Wallace*, 472 U.S. at 82–83 [O'Connor, J., concurring]) has not taken hold. Thus a basic theoretical dilemma remains:

either of the two religion clauses, if expanded to logical extreme, would threaten to devour the other, a problem that had been exacerbated by earlier Establishment Clause doctrine mandating a supposed stance of state neutrality.

In 1986 the Court decided a pair of cases in which O'Connor dissents seemed to suggest a particularly strong concern with free exercise rights. In the first, *Goldman* v. *Weinberger*, 475 U.S. 503, the Court upheld the air force in prohibiting an Orthodox rabbi from wearing his yarmulke on base. In dissent O'Connor sought, typically, to identify those consistent themes that seemed to run through the Court's precedent—first, whether the interest asserted by the government as against the free exercise claim was unusually important (compelling, overriding, etc.), and second, whether granting the requested exemption would do substantial harm to that interest (as in a "least restrictive means" test or "not otherwise served" test). That high standard she found clearly was not met by the facts of the case.

Similarly, in *Bowen* v. *Roy*, 476 U.S. 693 (1986), the Court upheld the requirement that Native American parents can be forced to provide a child's social security number as a precondition to receiving government benefits. Chief Justice Burger stated the position that under the Free Exercise Clause any facially neutral and uniformly applicable government requirement relating to the administration of government benefits is valid so long as it is a "reasonable means of promoting a legitimate public interest." Again, O'Connor, dissenting in part, insisted that only an "especially important" government interest pursued by "narrowly tailored means" could justify withholding benefits. On the facts, she found the government's interest in preventing welfare fraud to be easily accomplished without requiring social security numbers from the few who might have religious objections.

Given her record of insisting on strict standards in free exercise cases, O'Connor's later majority opinion in *Lyng* v. *Northwest Indian Cemetery Protective Association*, 485 U.S. 439 (1988), was puzzling and disturbing to many. The Court upheld, five to four, a Forest Service decision to allow timber harvesting and road construction in an area of national forest traditionally used for religious purposes. O'Connor conceded the religious significance of the land but found the Indians' claims not distinguishable from *Roy* (in which she had *dissented*), emphasizing that in neither case was the government prohibiting religious exercise or coercing action inconsistent with religious belief. Without applying the strict test she suggested in *Roy*, she seemed to take *Lyng* almost as a question about the government's property rights. She said Indians' claims cannot "divest the Government of its right to use what is, after all, *its* land" (emphasis in original), and she worried that Indian beliefs could "easily require *de facto* beneficial ownership of some rather spacious tracts of public property." In dissent, Brennan criticized what seemed to be an overly formalist distinction between prohibiting or compelling on the one hand and preventing on the other.

In *Employment Division* v. *Smith*, 494 U.S. 872 (1990), which upheld a drug prohibition as applied to Native Americans who used peyote in traditional ceremonies, O'Connor returned to her insistence that free exercise claims be evaluated according to a strict standard. Concurring, she argued that Justice Scalia in writing for the majority had distorted precedent in asserting that neutral laws of general applicability were, in effect, per se valid, regardless of effect on religion, unless other constitutional rights were impaired. She insisted that a compelling state interest and narrowly tailored means test was appropriate and stated that established doctrine clearly required a careful weighing of competing interests, not Scalia's categorical rule. Nevertheless, she was unwilling to overrule Oregon's judgment that the "possession and use of controlled substances, even by only one person, is inherently harmful and dangerous." Even one person's use of a harmful substance, she said, was contrary to the "purpose of the laws that prohibit them" (citing prohibition of handling poisonous snakes, also upheld by the Court).

With respect to the law of gender discrimination, O'Connor made her mark early, fashioning the applicable doctrine for future constitutional sex discrimination cases in her first-term opinion in *Mississippi University for Women* v. *Hogan*. With respect to her subsequent performance on the Court, however, her own gender has been far from determinative. Despite Suzanna Sherry's best efforts to the contrary, O'Connor cannot be reduced to a feminine voice on the Court; her faithfulness to common law tradition seems a more convincing characterization. She also has been criticized by some feminists for failing to promote a particularized feminist agenda, especially in the controversial area of abortion. This criticism becomes muted if one concedes that feminists, more generally understood as people concerned about the lives and welfare of women, may well reach different conclusions on controversial political or moral issues, including abortion.

Nevertheless, there is a sense in which O'Connor's historic role as first woman on the Court seems to influence her opinions insofar as they display a sensitivity to the actuality of women's lives. In this sense, there may be a slight gender tilt in her judicial role. In *Wimberly* v. *Labor and Industrial Commission*, 479 U.S. 511 (1987), O'Connor, for a unanimous Court, made her view clear (as in *Hogan*) that equality for women did not mean preferential treatment for women and therefore the prohibition against singling out pregnancy for unfavorable treatment cannot be transformed into a mandate for preferential treatment of women who leave work because of pregnancy. Yet in *Johnson* v. *Transportation Agency, Santa Clara County*, 480 U.S. 616 (1987), O'Connor, over the dissents of Byron White, Scalia, and Rehnquist, concurred in approving an affirmative action hiring plan for women in the county transportation agency. While her rhetoric is formally consistent with that eventually employed in *Richmond*, there does seem an extra stretch to uphold the gender-based plan. She notes, for example, that at "the time the plan was adopted, not one woman was employed in respondents' 238 skilled craft positions, and the plan recognized that women are not strongly motivated to seek employment in job classifications where they have not been traditionally employed because of the limited opportunities that have existed in the past for them to work in such classifications."

In 1989 O'Connor contributed significantly to Title VII sex discrimination law with her concurring opinion in *Price Waterhouse* v. *Hopkins*, 490 U.S. 228. Ann Hopkins had been denied promotion to partnership in the prestigious Price Waterhouse accounting firm despite a record of business success. The record did show that she was "overly aggressive, unduly harsh, difficult to work with and impatient with staff." Yet the same record showed also that she was perceived by partners as behaving inappropriately given her gender: one partner advised her to "walk more femininely, dress more femininely, wear make-up, have her hair styled, and wear jewelry."

In view of such evidence that sex stereotyping played a role in the partnership decision, the Court held that Price Waterhouse had the burden of proving that it would have reached the same decision regardless of gender. O'Connor joined the six-to-three majority reaching that conclusion on the facts of the case over the dissent of Kennedy, Rehnquist, and Scalia, who would not have shifted the burden of proof to the employer. Yet O'Connor, in a characteristic concurrence, tried to be fair to the employer while emphasizing in no uncertain terms the need to shift the burden of proof in appropriate cases.

With careful analogy to both tort law (recall her state court opinions) and equal protection law, O'Connor concluded that once the plaintiff shows, as Hopkins did in this case, that an illegitimate criterion was a *substantial* factor in the adverse employment decision, "the employer may be required to convince the factfinder that, despite the smoke, there is no fire." Most interesting is O'Connor's own retelling of the record:

> It is as if Ann Hopkins were sitting in the hall outside the room where partnership decisions were being made. As the partners filed in to consider her candidacy, she heard several of them make sexist remarks in discussing her suitability for partnership. As the decision-makers exited the room, she was told by one of those privy to the decisionmaking process that her gender was a major reason for the rejection of her partnership bid. (490 U.S. at 272–273.)

She concludes that "one would be hard pressed to think of a situation where it would be more appropriate to require the defendant to show that its decision would have been justified by wholly legitimate concerns."

O'Connor, moreover, generalizes from the facts of *Price Waterhouse* to reflect on problems of women in the professional world, noting "mounting evidence that [Hopkins] is not alone in her inability to pinpoint discrimination as the precise cause of her injury."

> Particularly in the context of the professional world, where decisions are often made by collegial bodies on the basis of subjective criteria, requiring the plaintiff to prove that one

factor was the definitive cause of the decisionmakers' action may be tantamount to declaring Title VII inapplicable to such decisions.

While her opinion is not as liberal as Brennan's for the plurality and may have disappointed some feminists, it seems realistic and hardly insensitive to the plight of women in the workplace.

Two other O'Connor opinions, both dissents in seven-to-two decisions, illustrate her concern for the contextual reality of women's lives. In *Mansell* v. *Mansell*, 490 U.S. 581 (1989), the Court held that military retirement pay that had been waived by a former husband in order to receive veterans' disability benefits was not community property divisible upon divorce. O'Connor, along with Blackmun, dissented from Marshall's opinion for the majority. While basically disagreeing with the majority's interpretation of the federal Uniformed Services Former Spouses Protection Act, O'Connor in so doing goes out of her way to detail the plight of military wives and especially ex-wives: "Military wives face special difficulties because frequent change-of-station moves and the special pressures placed on the military spouse as a homemaker make it extremely difficult to pursue a career affording economic security, job skills and pension protection," leading to the "dire plight of many military wives after divorce." One cannot help but recall that O'Connor accompanied her husband when he was stationed in Germany as a JAG officer in the 1950's.

The other striking dissent is in the recent case of *United States* v. *Burke*, 112 S. Ct. 1867 (1992), which concerned the tax treatment of a back pay award in a Title VII sex discrimination case. The majority of seven, speaking through Blackmun, held such awards to be taxable income not included in the statutory exemption for "damages received . . . on account of personal injuries." O'Connor, dissenting along with Thomas, reemphasized her position in *Price Waterhouse* that Title VII is most analogous to tort law and that discrimination in the workplace is a serious form of personal injury. In so doing, she worked to clarify the classic common law distinction between contract (the majority) and tort in a case where, arguably, that line makes all the difference.

In *J.E.B.* v. *Alabama*, 114 S. Ct. 1419 (1994), the Court struck down gender-based peremptory challenges used by the state in a paternity and child support case that resulted in an all-female jury. The state argued that an all-female jury would be more sympathetic to its suit against the father, but the majority of the Court found that striking potential jurors solely on the basis of their gender served only to perpetuate the sort of stereotypes that historically had led to barring women from jury service. O'Connor concurred but wrote a separate opinion to voice some reservations. She hesitated to subject the jury selection process to yet further constitutional oversight, noting that the peremptory challenge was of ancient origin and deeply rooted in the "common law heritage." In particular, scrutiny would force lawyers to articulate and defend reasons that were often quite properly based on good lawyer's intuition. Moreover (and notable in light of her attitude toward stereotypes), O'Connor stated that in response to some cases (such as rape), gender differences may be a fact of life even if not constitutionally allowed to be legally relevant. Since the *J.E.B.* holding would almost surely be extended to criminal defendants as well as private litigants, its somewhat disturbing effect was to exalt the right to sit on juries over the right even of criminal defendants.

Given that O'Connor is, among other things, the first mother to sit on the Supreme Court, it is perhaps unsurprising that what could be called a maternal perspective, namely a special solicitude for the welfare of children and their families (when otherwise consistent with her judicial methodology and outlook), should occasionally inform her decision making, at least at the margin.

Thus in *Hicks* v. *Feiock*, 485 U.S. 624 (1988), O'Connor joined conservatives in dissent to object to excessive due process restrictions on enforcement of child support payments. Dissenting for herself, Rehnquist, and Scalia, O'Connor, in a five-to-three decision, characterized the case as one illustrating "how difficult it can be to obtain even modest amounts of child support from a noncustodial parent." She characterized the judgment as below as incorrect as a matter of federal law in its insistence on criminal procedure due process standards and regarded the judgment as one that turns the child support order into "a worthless piece of scrap" and "hampers the enforcement of support orders at a time when strengthened enforcement is needed."

On the other hand, O'Connor joined liberals Brennan and Marshall in dissenting from the denial of a writ of certiorari in *Gregory* v. *Town of Pittsfield*, 470 U.S. 1018 (1985), in which a town in Maine had denied general assistance to Cindy Gregory and her husband because she had quit her job and used her AFDC check to obtain her husband's release from jail. O'Connor, writing for the dissenting trio, found the state court's conclusion "that an applicant for general assistance does not have an interest protected by the Due Process Clause . . . unsettling in its implication that less fortunate persons in our society may arbitrarily be denied benefits that a State has granted as a matter of right," since there was "no dispute that Mrs. Gregory was entitled under Maine law to the general assistance benefits denied to her."

Even though O'Connor has been consistently favorably disposed toward the death penalty, she balked at the execution of a fifteen-year-old murderer, providing the deciding vote against execution in *Thompson* v. *Oklahoma*, 487 U.S. 815 (1988). While refusing to adopt the majority's categorical objection to such executions, she found the particular Oklahoma procedural scheme sufficiently defective to vacate the death sentence in question. Scalia, writing for the dissenters, attacked O'Connor's determinative opinion:

> The concurrence's approach is a Solomonic solution to the problem of how to prevent execution in the present case while at the same time not holding that the execution of those under 16 when they commit murder is categorically unconstitutional. Solomon, however,

was not subject to the constitutional constraints of the judicial department of a national government in a federal, democratic system.

Even a year later, when O'Connor went along with death sentences imposed, respectively, on seventeen- and sixteen-year-old murderers, she wrote separately, refusing to join Scalia's plurality opinion and leaving room for her own proportionality approach in a future case (*Stanford* v. *Kentucky*, 492 U.S. 361, 380–382 [1989]).

Child welfare concerns seemed paramount in *Clark* v. *Jeter*, 486 U.S. 456 (1988), in which O'Connor's concurring opinion in *Mills* v. *Habluetzel* was vindicated. In *Mills*, when the Court struck down a one-year statute of limitations for paternity suits, O'Connor emphasized the plight of mothers of illegitimate children and suggested that even a four-year statute might be invalid. In *Clark*, O'Connor, for a unanimous Court, struck down even a six-year statute as violative of the Equal Protection Clause, despite her usual deference to state procedural rules.

Displaying similar concern, O'Connor wrote for a seven-to-two majority in *Baltimore City Department of Social Services* v. *Bouknight*, 493 U.S. 549 (1990), denying a mother's right to invoke her Fifth Amendment privilege against self-incrimination by resisting a court order to produce her child where there was a history of serious physical abuse and the child had been judicially declared a "child in need of assistance." "Once Maurice [the child] was adjudicated a child in need of assistance, his care and safety became the particular object of the State's regulatory interests."

And in a 1991 case in which a father had been convicted of murdering his infant daughter, O'Connor agreed as to admissibility of evidence that the child had a history of serious abuse but emphasized the need for special instructions as to such evidence: "The fact that a 6-month-old child was repeatedly beaten in the course of her short life is so horrifying that a trial court should take special care to inform the jury as to the significance of that evidence" (*Estelle* v. *McGuire*, 112 S. Ct. 475).

Just recently, in *Reno* v. *Flores*, 113 S. Ct. 1439 (1993), while agreeing with the majority in rejecting a facial attack on Immigration and Naturalization Services regulations involving alien juveniles in deportation proceedings, O'Connor, joined by Souter (with whom she shares a traditional common law judicial sensibility), wrote separately to emphasize that "these children have a constitutionally protected interest in freedom from institutional confinement." In so doing she observed that "in our society, children normally grow up in families, not in governmental institutions" and that " 'the consequences of an erroneous commitment decision are more tragic where children are involved. [C]hildhood is a particularly vulnerable time of life and children erroneously institutionalized during their formative years may bear the scars for the rest of their lives.' "

The most awesome responsibility borne by judges is that of deciding cases that literally involve life or death choices, all the more awesome when, as on the Supreme Court, one knows that one has the last word on the issue. That responsibility is eased somewhat if one can comfortably and regularly take the side of life as against death or can evade responsibility by treating the option for death as someone else's decision. In modern society, or perhaps in any world of fallible humans, the inescapable reality is that death is regularly chosen for some and life for others. Consequently, Sandra Day O'Connor's judicial record in cases concerning the death penalty, abortion, and the "right to die" are of special interest to contemporary observers.

O'Connor's views on the death penalty were clear from the outset. At her confirmation hearings, she reported that as a legislator she had participated rather extensively in the subcommittee effort that led to Arizona's reenactment of the death penalty following the Supreme Court's decision in *Furman v. Georgia;* she had "voted for that measure after it was drafted and brought to the floor" and "had occasion to, in effect, apply it as a judge in the trial court in Arizona in some criminal cases." Following those remarks came the following colloquy with Senator Arlen Specter:

> *SENATOR SPECTER. Have you changed your views since you voted in favor of the death penalty?*
>
> *JUDGE O'CONNOR. Mr. Chairman, Senator Specter, I felt it was an appropriate vote then and I have not changed my view.*

Nevertheless, O'Connor has not joined those who would routinely uphold death sentences out of deference to state process. Beginning in her first term, she stated her view that the prisoner sentenced to be executed must be "afforded a process that will guarantee, as much as is humanly possible, that the sentence was not imposed out of whim, passion, prejudice or mistake" (*Eddings* v. *Oklahoma*, 455 U.S. 104, 117–19 [(1982]). In that case—which incidentally involved a sixteen-year-old defendant—O'Connor's concurrence led to a remand requiring full consideration of mitigating evidence including the defendant's family background and personal history over the dissent of Burger, White, Blackmun, and Rehnquist, who would have affirmed the judgment.

And in *Ford* v. *Wainwright*, 477 U.S. 399 (1986), while disagreeing with the majority that the Eighth Amendment forbids the execution of an insane prisoner, she concurred in the result on the ground that Florida law prohibits such executions and that Florida had failed to provide even minimal due process to make the determination required by its own law.

Writing for the Court in *Penry* v. *Lynaugh*, 492 U.S. 302 (1989), O'Connor, over the dissent of Scalia, Rehnquist, White, and Kennedy, rejected a categorical Eighth Amendment exemption from execution for the mentally retarded but remanded nevertheless. O'Connor again stressed mitigating evidence, offering her sense of appropriateness with respect to death sentences:

> [P]unishment should be directly related to the personal culpability of the criminal defendant. If the sentencer is to make an individualized assessment of the appropriateness of the

death penalty, "evidence about the defendant's background and character is relevant be-
cause of the belief, long held by this society, that defendants who commit criminal acts that
are attributable to a disadvantaged background, or to emotional and mental problems, may
be less culpable than defendants who have no such excuse."

The defendant in question had offered mitigating evidence of his mental retardation and abused childhood as the basis for life imprisonment instead of execution, but "the jury was never instructed that it could consider the evidence offered by Penry as mitigating evidence and that it could give mitigating effect to that evidence in imposing sentence." Thus, remand was required.

On the other hand, where she found that "a rational factfinder could have found that respondent both relished the crime and inflicted gratuitous violence on the victim," O'Connor, writing for a five-to-four majority over the dissent of Blackmun, Brennan, Marshall, and Stevens, upheld a death sentence based on "aggravating circumstances" under state law that treated as such the commission of murder "in an especially heinous, cruel, and depraved manner" (*Lewis* v. *Jeffers*, 497 U.S. 764 [1990]). Yet a year later she was on the other side of a five-to-four decision, in which the state supreme court had failed to give adequate consideration to mitigating circumstances (*Parker* v. *Dugger*, 498 U.S. 308 [1991]).

The pattern has continued with three additional cases. In *Herrera* v. *Collins*, 113 S. Ct. 853 (1993), O'Connor joined a six-to-three majority upholding the death sentence but did so in a close concurrence limited to the record in the particular case; however, in *Graham* v. *Collins*, 113 S. Ct. 892 (1993), she dissented along with Stevens, Souter, and Blackmun from the majority's denial of federal relief to the condemned prisoner; and in *Arave* v. *Creech*, 113 S. Ct. 1534 (1993), she wrote for a seven-to-two majority upholding the death sentence in question.

With respect to abortion, O'Connor's singular contribution has been her insistence that abortion, no less than capital punishment, is a life or death issue. Yet that insistence neither mandates *Roe* v. *Wade* in its pure form nor requires that it be overruled so as to return plenary authority over abortion to the states.

As with her endorsement approach to the Establishment Clause, O'Connor's undue burden approach to abortion cases has finally won a majority of the Court. Beginning with her 1983 *Akron* dissent, O'Connor registered her dissatisfaction with *Roe*'s trimester approach and her willingness to permit state regulation throughout pregnancy unless it "unduly burdens" the right to seek an abortion.

Her approach became the effective majority when in *Webster* v. *Reproductive Health Services*, 492 U.S. 490 (1989), the Court upheld restrictions on access to abortion but did not overrule *Roe* v. *Wade*. O'Connor supplied the crucial fifth vote but did so in a concurring opinion employing her undue burden approach. She also made clear that the state can "directly promote its interest in potential life when viability is possible." O'Connor was scathingly denounced by Scalia in his *Webster* dissent, especially for her reliance on "judicial restraint" to avoid a formal reconsideration of *Roe* itself. Then in 1991 O'Connor dissented along with Blackmun, Marshall, and Stevens in *Rust* v. *Sullivan*, 500 U.S. 173, the gag rule case. O'Connor would have construed the relevant statute in light of the First Amendment and held that the regulations in question exceeded statutory authority.

Then came *Casey*, with O'Connor—joined by Souter (predictably) and Kennedy (more enigmatically)—occupying the literal center of the Court to make a majority of five for the survival, albeit in altered form, of *Roe* v. *Wade* (*Casey* v. *Planned Parenthood of Eastern Pennsylvania*, 112 S. Ct. 2791 [1992]). Four justices would have overruled *Roe* altogether (Rehnquist, White, Scalia, and Thomas); two would have reaffirmed it entirely (Blackmun and Stevens). Neither extreme would prevail, for the determinative opinion was a joint one written by three justices, all of whom had been appointed by Republican presidents elected on the plank of an absolutist opposition to abortion. That joint opinion may in fact mark the beginning of a process that will lead to workable compromise on this most controversial of issues.

The joint opinion in *Casey* bears O'Connor's characteristic mark in its methodology, in its protection of precedent, and in its substance, which represents the formal adoption of O'Connor's *Akron* dissent and *Webster* concurrence as the law in this area. The joint opinion affirms that the state has "a legitimate interest in promoting the life or potential life of the unborn" from the outset of pregnancy yet also affirms a woman's right to choose abortion prior to fetal viability. Thus the states may regulate abortions, even where such regulations have the "incidental effect of making it more difficult or more expensive to procure an abortion": "Only where state regulation imposes an undue burden on a woman's ability to make this decision does the power of the State reach into the heart of the liberty protected by the Due Process Clause." The Court in *Casey* considered five provisions of Pennsylvania law that regulated abortions: informed consent, a twenty-four-hour wait with mandatory counseling, parental consent for minors, spousal notification, and mandatory record keeping and reporting. All but the spousal notification provision were upheld.

Thus while *Roe* was reaffirmed, its trimester framework was not, nor was its absolutist conception of a right to privacy. After *Casey*, it seems clear that *Roe* was essentially a substantive due process case after all, one about the meaning of liberty under the Fourteenth Amendment as understood in light of history, tradition, and convention. In this respect O'Connor is once again following Justice Harlan, who took the same approach in his concurring opinion in the famous Connecticut birth control case, *Griswold* v. *Connecticut*, 381 U.S. 479 (1965).

Nowhere in the joint opinion is *Roe* reaffirmed on its merits; the threesome stops short of saying it was correctly decided. The margin that keeps the core holding of *Roe* at least partially intact is precedent; a long Part III of the opinion deals with this issue, opening with the enigmatic observation that "the obligation to follow precedent begins with necessity, and a contrary necessity marks its outer limit," and declining to place *Roe* in the same category as either *Lochner* v. *New York*, 198 U.S. 45 (1905), or *Plessy* v. *Ferguson*, 163 U.S. 537 (1896), both of which are seen as cases properly overruled by the Court.

Scalia, in dissent, enjoys a sarcastic romp, deriding the opinion's supposed lack of logic. The authors characterized *Roe*, when decided, as a "mistake"—"legally problematic at best, sociologically inaccurate, and politically disastrous." Nevertheless, *Casey* may represent a first step toward achieving a workable compromise. The premise of *Roe* itself was a backward one: that the Court could freeze reality and make the abortion issue disappear. Forgotten was the inevitable dynamic of law, that judicial decisions contain a historical agency of their own. Thus, Scalia notwithstanding, the precipitous overruling of *Roe*, which would immediately have sent the issue back to state legislatures with no constitutional guidelines, might similarly have loosed a dynamic that would have been worse than accepting with patience a gradual realignment on this painful question. There was simply no way to recapture January, 1973, as if *Roe* had never happened. That is perhaps why the joint opinion's reliance on precedent ultimately makes practical sense (in the best common law tradition). The Court as an institution, after all, had triggered the political battles over abortion; as an institution the Court bears continuing responsibility for the consequences it has produced. Thus *Casey* seems consistent with O'Connor's usual impulse to make only gradual readjustments, invite dialogue, and leave room for further development.

As medical technology advances, the very meaning of death becomes problematic, an issue the Court faced in the 1990 "right to die" case, *Cruzan* v. *Director, Missouri Department of Health*, 497 U.S. 261. Nancy Cruzan was an auto accident victim relegated to a "persistent vegetative state" and kept alive by artificial life support. Her parents wanted to terminate the life support, but Missouri refused in the absence of "clear and convincing evidence" that Nancy herself would so choose. The Court took the case to decide whether Nancy had a constitutional right to require the hospital to withdraw the life-sustaining treatment.

By a five-to-four decision, the Court upheld Missouri's decision. O'Connor, concurring, found herself not atypically situated between extremes, although in this case even the extremes were muted in tone and restrained in scope. Rehnquist, writing for the majority, emphasized the state's interest "in the protection and preservation of human life," analogized to laws prohibiting suicide, and held that since the "choice between life and death is a deeply personal decision of obvious and overwhelming finality," Missouri "may legitimately seek to safeguard the personal element of this choice through the imposition of heightened evidentiary requirements." Rehnquist recognized that there might be at stake a relevant personal liberty interest in the individual (presumably sufficient to protect enforcement of a living will), but that interest must be balanced against an "unqualified interest in the preservation of human life" on the part of the state. Scalia, concurring, would have gone further, simply announcing "clearly and promptly, that the federal courts have no business in this field: that American law has always accorded the State the power to prevent, by force if necessary, suicide—including suicide by refusing to take measures necessary to preserve one's life."

The dissenters (Brennan, Marshall, Blackmun, and Stevens) moved toward the opposite extreme, ready to embrace a more libertarian constitutional "right to die," although stopping short of locating such a right in the absoluteness of "privacy right" doctrine. For Brennan this was Nancy Cruzan's "fundamental right to be free of unwanted artificial nutrition and hydration," because she is "entitled to choose to die with dignity." Stevens asserted his belief that "the Constitution requires that the individual's vital interest in liberty should prevail over the general policy."

O'Connor, concurring, agreed with the dissenters that the "liberty guaranteed by the Due Process Clause must protect, if it protects anything, an individual's deeply personal decision to reject medical treatment, including the artificial delivery of food and water." Her concurrence is limited to the lack, in this particular case, of "clear and convincing evidence" of Nancy Cruzan's choice. She acknowledged that this is a "difficult and sensitive problem" as to which "no national consensus has yet emerged." O'Connor implied strongly that the solution will lie in state procedures giving effect to the decisions of surrogate decision makers (as with a "living will") and suggested that there may be a constitutional duty to give effect to such decisions in order to "protect the patient's liberty interest in refusing medical treatment."

In characteristic O'Connor fashion, she limits *Cruzan* to its facts:

> Today we decide only that one State's practice does not violate the Constitution; the more challenging task of crafting appropriate procedures for safeguarding incompetents' liberty interests is entrusted to the "laboratory" of the States.

Looking at O'Connor's approach in *Cruzan*, one cannot help but think that the same methodology, applied to *Roe* v. *Wade* in the first instance (e.g., recognizing a liberty interest, striking down the Texas criminal law, and otherwise leaving the issue to the states), might have avoided many years of public strife.

SELECTED BIBLIOGRAPHY

A brief overview of Justice O'Connor's background, appointment, and career in relation to women's rights can be found in Orma Linford, "Sandra Day O'Connor: Myra Bradwell's Revenge" in Frank P. LeVeness and Jane P. Sweeney, eds., *Women Leaders in Contemporary U.S. Politics* (Boulder, Colo.: Lynne Rienner, 1987). Analyses of O'Connor's judicial decisions can be found in Donald L. Beschle, "The Conservative as Liberal: The Religion Clauses, Liberal Neutrality, and the Approach of Justice O'Connor," 62 *Notre Dame Law Review* 151 (1987); Richard A. Cordray and James T. Vradelis, "The Emerging Jurisprudence of Justice O'Connor," 52 *University of Chicago Law Review* 389 (1985); and Arnold H. Loewy, "Rethinking Government Neutrality Towards Religion Under the Establishment Clause: The Untapped Potential of Justice O'Connor's Insight," 64 *North Carolina Law Review* 1049 (1986). More hostile critiques of O'Connor include Richter H. Moore, Jr., "Justice Sandra Day O'Connor: Law and Order Justice?" 63 *International Social Science Review* 147 (1988), and Jeffrey Rosen, "Gerrymandered," 209 *New Republic* 12 (25 October 1993). Susan Behuniak-Long attempts to analyze the impact of O'Connor's gender on her judicial philosophy in "Justice Sandra Day O'Connor and the Power of Maternal Legal Thinking," 54 *Review of Politics* 417 (1992).

David Hackett Souter

☆ 1939– ☆

APPOINTED BY GEORGE BUSH

YEARS ON COURT
1990–

by
EDWARD DE GRAZIA

When David Hackett Souter was sworn in on October 9, 1990, as the Supreme Court's 105th Justice, he promised to exercise his judicial authority "according to the light that God gives me"; and said that he would try to pass it on "in as vigorous condition as I have received it this afternoon from Justice Brennan." At the age of eighty-four, it was a frail Justice William J. Brennan, Jr., who sat among the audience on that day. Ten weeks earlier, the great jurist had unexpectedly stepped down, following thirty-six years of service and a mild stroke. David Souter undoubtedly disappointed some conservatives in the audience at his swearing-in when he assured them that Brennan would go down in history as "one of the most fearlessly principled guardians of the American Constitution that it has ever had, and ever will have."

Many conservatives hoped that the little-known judge from New Hampshire would distinguish himself from Brennan by lending his weight to the conservative majority dominating the Court's work. This majority now included the Court's Chief Justice, William Rehnquist, Jr., and Justices Antonin Scalia, Anthony Kennedy, Sandra Day O'Connor, and the Kennedy appointee Byron White. For liberals the situation pre-Souter was bad enough, for the ascendancy of a militant conservative bloc had placed in jeopardy three decades of humanistic accomplishments of the Warren Court, including that Court's egalitarian extension of individual rights and civil liberties; its heightening of constitutional protections for criminal defendants; the ban it placed on sanctioned prayer in public schools; its freeing from censorship sexual expression in books, movies, magazines, and other media of communication; and its respecting of the privacy of a woman's decision whether to bear a child or prevent its creation. Now if Souter were to align himself with the conservatives' voting pattern, the antiliberal tilt would go to six to three. Moreover, although no one yet knew this, by the end of the new term the liberal presence on the Court would be further depleted with the resignation of Justice Thurgood Marshall and his prompt replacement by Clarence Thomas, a certified conservative jurist then sitting on the United States Court of Appeals for the District of Columbia Circuit.

Only three days after Justice Brennan informed George Bush that he was retiring, the president announced he had found the man to replace him. Emphasizing Souter's considerable experience as New Hampshire attorney general and a judge of the New Hampshire Supreme Court, Bush said Souter was like Brennan for being "largely a product of the State court system" and possessing "the same dedication to public service and strength of intellect exemplified by Justice Brennan." The president went on, however, to allude to a possible difference between his appointee and Brennan: David Souter, he said, was "committed to interpreting not making the law." When a reporter asked the president how he expected Souter to vote "if *Roe* v. *Wade* came before the Court during the new term," Bush responded that Souter "will interpret the Constitution, not legislate from the Federal bench." In fact, during Souter's second term on the Court, when *Roe* v. *Wade* did more or less return, the president's wish was fulfilled, although not perhaps in ways entirely to his liking: Justice Souter showed he understood what every intelligent and conscientious judge knows—that there is no way to interpret the Constitution without creating law, and that to overrule a constitutional precedent for political reasons—for example, because the president and his constituents would like you to—is no doubt the most irresponsible sort of judicial legislation.

David Hackett Souter was born in Melrose, Massachusetts, on September 17, 1939, the only child of Joseph Alexander and Helen Adams Hackett Souter. When Souter was eleven, his family moved to a town near Concord, New Hampshire, called Weare, which he still calls his hometown. At Concord High School young Souter was voted "most literary," "most sophisticated," and "most likely to succeed." In Harvard College, his senior honors thesis dealt with judicial positivism as adumbrated by Justice Oliver Wendell Holmes. According to Souter, Holmes' philosophy signified that good judges should never act on the basis of political predilections or ideology. He graduated from Harvard magna cum laude and a member of Phi Beta Kappa and spent the next two years at Oxford studying law and philosophy on a Rhodes scholarship. Deeply religious, Souter is said to have been one of the few young men at Oxford who regularly went to chapel and took communion. When, during recess, the others abandoned Oxford for Paris, Rome, or the Swiss Alps, Souter stayed behind to catch up on his reading. After that he entered Harvard Law School, where if he did not make *Law Review* neither did he flunk out. A friend at Harvard who became an Episcopal minister said that all young Souter really wanted out of life was to be a judge; some friends addressed him as "Mr. Justice Souter." While he was "great fun to have dinner with," he was also "formal, reserved, and intensely private." Some people said he was "in the 18th-century mold" and "very patriotic," and thought the reason he went into law was to defend American values.

After graduation from Harvard Law School David Souter joined a local firm in Concord known as Orr and Reno where he "spent two unhappy years." Public interest law was more rewarding. Once he joined the office of attorney general of New Hampshire he worked closely for the next twelve years with the man who would serve as his mentor and, eventually, as his official U.S. Senate sponsor to the Supreme Court—then attorney general Warren B. Rudman. In 1976 David Souter himself became attorney general of New Hampshire, placed in the post by Governor Thomson. Two years later Thomson started Souter up the judicial ladder by appointing him to superior court and, five years after that, the next governor of the state, John H. Sununu, elevated Souter to the state's highest judicial bench, a five-member court, on which Souter served for seven years—writing more than 200 opinions. Sununu was the man who later, as President George Bush's chief of staff, energetically advised the president to replace Brennan with this judge from the backwoods of New Hampshire, this bachelor with the tumbledown house and the unmowed lawn, who was thought of by everyone who knew him as a conservative even if no one could be sure what kind of conservative he was, or might turn out to be, once he reached the Supreme Court.

David Souter led a quiet, unassuming life in New Hampshire, which did not change much even when he moved to Washington. He likes to drive subcompact cars; his current one is a 1987 Volkswagen Golf. He likes to lunch every day on the same thing—cottage cheese and an apple. And he likes to wear clothes so drab that donning his black judicial robe is said to add color to his attire. From Weare, neighbors reported that Souter was a vestryman at St. Andrew's Episcopal Church (in nearby Hikinton) and could be found regularly on Sundays walking the same old lady home from church. On Sundays, just as regularly, Souter drove to Concord to see his aged mother at the nursing home there. Everyone says he is courteous, loyal, unaffected, and upright. A man who lived a mile from him for forty years said that he does not put on airs and is very down to earth. The financial statement that Souter was required to file when he joined the Supreme Court shows his net assets at between $65,000 and $150,000; by contrast, Justices Sandra Day O'Connor and John Paul Stevens are millionaires.

The American Bar Association assigned to David Souter its highest judicial rating, which is to say it reported him "well qualified" to sit on the nation's highest bench. At the time of the appointment the uppermost question in many Court observers' minds was whether Souter would rest content to become one more conservative Justice or instead try to take his brothers and sisters up more highly principled constitutional paths. At the time of Souter's nomination the hottest, most sensitive issue facing the nation, the nominee, and the Senate Judiciary Committee was abortion, and the new term was expected to bring abortion-related cases before the Court, including *Rust* v. *Sullivan*. Conservatives and liberals alike wondered how Souter would stand on that, for as the next Justice he could provide the vote that would overturn *Roe* v. *Wade*. And so, by the end of Souter's confirmation hearings, abortion proved to be the issue—felt by some to be the most divisive to face the country since slavery—about which everyone learned the least about Souter's thinking.

The Senate Judiciary Committee hearings on the nomination of Judge Souter endured for twenty hours; they were at the time the second longest in history held to consider the fitness of a Supreme Court candidate, trailing only President Reagan's failed nomination three years earlier of Judge Robert H. Bork. Indeed, the ghost of Bork appeared sometimes to fill the Senate committee room, shaping the questions Souter was asked, the answers or nonanswers given by him, and the overriding desire of almost everyone to avoid another bloody, Bork-like battle and give the recently appointed federal First Circuit judge the benefit of the doubt. In the end the only member of the committee who voted against Judge Souter was Senator Edward Kennedy. In due course the nominee was confirmed as Justice Souter by a ninety-to-nine vote of the Senate.

President Bush's selection of the quiet, solitary judge from New Hampshire marked a deliberate departure from the considerations that had entered into the ill-fated nomination of Judge Bork by President Reagan. Whereas the American Bar Association committee that evaluates judicial nominees gave Bork a damaging ambivalent rating, it unanimously gave Judge Souter its highest rating. Where Bork appeared to be pugnacious or even belligerent, Souter had an emollient, low-key personality which he displayed throughout the hearings. Judge Bork, a prolific and controversial writer while teaching at the Yale Law School, was widely known as a constitutional scholar at the outer edges of conservatism. Moreover, it was remembered that as President Nixon's solicitor general, Bork played a key role in the Saturday Night Massacre, seeking to save Nixon from being impeached.

Judge David Souter, on the other hand, had never published a book, an article, or even a speech. Where Bork's paper trail enabled his opponents to gather ample ammunition for the heated battle to kill his confirmation, Souter's "blank slate" gave the Senate committee little ground to anticipate the character of Souter's future moorings on the Court. There were, of course, the 200 legal opinions he had written while on the New Hampshire Supreme Court, but only a few of these involved constitutional issues. There was also his undergraduate senior thesis on the jurisprudence of Justice Oliver Wendell Holmes, but that had been written twenty-nine years earlier. And whereas Bork refused to be prepped by the administration for his Senate confirmation hearings, Souter not only agreed to the procedure but spent a good deal of time carefully studying what had gone on during Bork's interrogation.

Mixing forthrightness with strategies of avoidance, Souter readily obtained the Senate's blessing. Somewhat unexpectedly, he did come forward with positions on several controversial issues—expressing opposition to any flat ban on the death penalty; exposing his belief that the Supreme Court had a constitutional obligation to enforce fundamental rights; and depicting the *Miranda* ruling as pragmatic and so, presumably, not lightly to be cast aside. Souter even said he was opposed to using original intent as a method of constitutional jurisprudence and sidestepped the loaded question of how he would vote on abortion. Echoing President Bush—who stated publicly that he did not know and had not asked Souter his personal views on abortion— Souter avoided or declined all direct and most indirect questions regarding abortion and the stability of *Roe* v. *Wade*. He noted that the Code of Judicial Ethics states that "a judge should abstain from public comment about a pending or impending proceeding in any court."

Souter's studied comments during the confirmation hearings complemented a lean legal and judicial record. Very few of the 200 opinions delivered by him during his tenure on the New Hampshire Supreme Court gave his opponents grounds even to attempt a Bork-like attack. His brief two months of service on the federal First Circuit had yielded no written opinions at all. On the other hand, the few state cases that offered any insights into Souter's constitutional jurisprudence were examined by the committee and by commentators in the press. In 1986, he had dissented in a state case, *In re Estate of Dionne*, which concerned the validity under the New Hampshire Constitution of a law requiring people to pay special fees to probate judges. Souter argued that the majority had failed in its interpretive task of determining the meaning of the state constitutional language "as it was understood when the framers proposed it and the people ratified it as part of the original constitutional text that took effect in June, 1784." Although the language in this opinion pointed toward an "original understanding" approach to constitutional interpretation—a view that helped bring about Judge Bork's defeat—Judge Souter was quick to assure the Senate Judiciary Committee that this was not his prevailing view on interpreting the Constitution. "My approach to interpretation is not a specific intent approach." Additionally, Souter said he thought that the Ninth Amendment, which provides that the people retain rights against the government that the Constitution does not make explicit, suggested that the rights enumerated in the Constitution were not necessarily meant to be exhaustive. This contrasted sharply with Judge Bork's comment that the Ninth Amendment was meaningless, "a water blot on the Constitution." Souter added that he would seek to define "unenumerated rights" as did Justice Harlan, another avowed hero of his. Harlan spoke of looking to American tradition and history in order to understand "what might be called the bedrock concept of liberty."

Several opinions written by State Justice Souter showed respect for individual liberties. A 1988 opinion of his in *Richardson* v. *Chevrefils* held that state welfare officials violated a man's constitutional right to due process of law by placing his name on a list of child abusers without notice or a chance to object. In another 1988 opinion, Judge Souter ruled in favor of a nonprofit organization set up under state law to provide legal services to indigent disabled people. He held that the state law that barred the center from serving people who were not poor violated the First Amendment's guarantee of freedom of association, because that prohibited any state interference with an organization's right to speak on public issues. On the other hand, in 1987, Souter had signed an advisory opinion stating that New Hampshire might constitutionally prevent homosexuals from serving as adoptive or foster parents, because the prohibition was rationally related to the proposed bill's purpose of providing appropriate role models for children. In a rape prosecution, Judge Souter overturned a man's conviction because the trial judge erroneously excluded evidence about the alleged victim's own behavior prior to the incident, and stated that the state's rape shield law could not bar directly relevant evidence about the circumstances of the crime. "[S]uch a statute's reach has to be limited by a defendant's state and national constitutional rights to confront the witnesses against him and to present his own exculpatory evidence."

The only case that Souter ever considered touching on the issue of abortion was handed down in 1986; there he joined a unanimous bench's conclusion that a woman might sue her obstetrician for failing to warn her that a case of measles during her pregnancy put her at serious risk of bearing a child with severe birth defects. The woman, whose baby was born with serious defects, alleged in her suit that had she been properly informed she would have had prenatal testing and considered having an abortion. In a separate concurrence Souter pointed out that "a physician with conscientious scruples against abortion" might discharge his professional obligation to the patient by making a timely referral to other physicians who were not similarly constrained, an issue not presented to the court. In another abortion matter, in 1981, when Souter was sitting on superior court, he authored a letter to a state legislative committee officially expressing the opposition of superior court judges to a provision in a proposed bill that would have given teenagers the option of seeking a judge's consent, rather than a parent's, before having an abortion. Judge Souter said the wording of the provision would force the judges to engage in "acts of unfettered personal choice," impinging upon the principle of legality.

Souter's previous tenure as New Hampshire's attorney general likewise raised a number of short-lived concerns. He had filed a brief opposing the classification of state employees by race, prosecuted and sought bail denials for protesters at the Seabrook Nuclear Power Plant, and defended the state's efforts to fly the American flag at half-staff on Good Friday by contending that this would be a historical rather than religious tribute. While opponents of Souter tried to highlight such actions as indicative of his likely performance as an Associate Justice, the Senate committee gave them only a passing nod, noting correctly that, unlike a judge, the New Hampshire attorney general was the sort of appointed official who was expected to defer to state policies.

Although Souter's "rather Spartan existence" in a small New Hampshire town raised some senatorial doubts—several senators wondered "whether he [had] the background to really understand the problems of those who are less fortunate in our society"—these swiftly faded as Souter demonstrated his "first-rate legal mind." Overall, Souter's performance befit the nickname he received in the press—the "Stealth nominee." Describing himself as undogmatic and middle-of-the-road in judicial temperament, Judge Souter frustrated conservatives and liberals alike by refusing to endorse a traditional conservative philosophy. Conservatives felt frustrated because President Bush may have failed to pick someone conservative enough. Liberals felt frustrated because they could not believe that Souter, nominated by Bush and endorsed by Sununu, would really be open-minded in his jurisprudence. Souter refused to be baited in supplying instances where the Supreme Court had gone too far in recognizing constitutional rights, responding instead with a long, low-key defense of Warren Court rulings, particularly the controversial landmark *Miranda* decision requiring the police to inform criminal suspects of their rights. He alarmed some conservative senators by a declaration that in his judgment if Congress failed to carry out its obligations under the Fourteenth Amendment, the Court had a responsibility to act to fill the vacuum, citing as his example the Warren Court's historic decision in *Brown* v. *Board of Education.*

Of additional concern to liberals and conservatives were Souter's views regarding precedent. Souter stated that one factor a judge should consider when deciding to adhere to precedent is "whether private citizens in their lives have relied upon it in their own planning to such a degree that, in fact, there would be a great hardship in overruling it now." Such a statement especially bothered conservatives because a similar argument had been made by supporters of the result in *Roe* v. *Wade,* in the context of the many hardships that would occur if that decision were overturned. While Souter's testimony pleasantly surprised some liberal senators and interest groups, others remained wary, even hostile, because to them so much of Souter's testimony seemed evasive and vague. For example, while Souter did state that he supported *Griswold* v. *Connecticut*—the 1965 birth-control information case that recognized the existence of a constitutional right to marital privacy that safeguarded from government interference the dissemination of information regarding the use of contraceptives—he declined to state whether he thought it correct to extend that right to unmarried couples (which was done a few years later), or whether the Court had properly expanded the right of privacy to include abortion. Judge Souter stated that in his mind it was "an open question" whether unmarried persons had a fundamental right to privacy.

Souter's disinclination to directly affirm liberal doctrine led to attacks upon his candidacy by some women's organizations, including the National Abortion Rights Action League and the Planned Parenthood Action Fund, as well as by a few other organizations, including the NAACP—organizations that had spearheaded the successful campaign to defeat the Bork nomination. Their leaders claimed that in their questioning of Judge Souter's jurisprudence, Senate Judiciary Committee members were discriminating against constitutional issues concerning women. They contended further that while the judge was forthcoming about the legal principles he would use to test violations of the First or the Eighth Amendment, the committee had acquiesced in Souter's reticence when it came to discussing the legal principles he would use to test violations of women's rights. However, this confrontation proved short-lived. Many of the liberal organizations that had opposed Robert Bork three years earlier stood by silently now, hesitating to attack the quiet judge from New Hampshire because they were sure they could not get a less conservative nominee from President Bush. In the end, their silence encouraged the Judiciary Committee to give Souter the go-ahead. Congratulating itself on having conducted some of "the best hearings . . . pertaining to a judicial nominee" in history, the Senate Judiciary Committee decided to leave such burning questions as whether David Souter believed that unmarried persons had a constitutional right to privacy or that women had the constitutional right to choose abortion to be answered by *Justice* David H. Souter.

The first few days of argument during the 1990–91 term took place without David Souter. Although the term opened as usual in October, 1990, the first important cases did not come down until January. On January 22, the Court decided a drug-related, first-degree murder death sentence case, *Parker* v. *Dugger*, 111 S. Ct. 731 (1991), in which Souter's vote proved crucial and swung the decision five to four in the defendant's favor, reversing the sentence of death that had been imposed upon him by a Florida trial judge in the teeth of a sentencing jury's recommendation that the sentence be life imprisonment, not death. The majority opinion, which Souter joined, was written by Justice Sandra Day O'Connor; also joining her were Justices Thurgood Marshall, John Paul Stevens, and Harry A. Blackmun. Although few Court observers perceived this at the time, what happened in *Dugger* carried tidings of things to come in a number of contentious areas where the minority configurations of liberal and conservative Justices on the Court were sharply divided, and a somewhat enlarged shifting nucleus of centrists—Souter, O'Connor, Kennedy, and White—became empowered to decide the open questions. In *Dugger*, according to dissenters Rehnquist, White, Scalia, and Kennedy, the Court had resumed the practice it "long ago gave up" of "second-guessing State supreme courts" in death penalty cases.

In two important cases decided relatively early in Souter's first term, the freshman Justice declined to follow the conservative Chief Justice into dissent, linking himself instead to liberal-centrist majorities. In neither of these cases was Souter's vote pivotal; the results would have been the same had he voted with the Chief Justice. In the first of these, *McNary* v. *Haitian Refugee Center*, 111 S. Ct. 888 (1991), the Court decided seven to two to give aliens standing to challenge the government's administration of the refugee amnesty program. Dissenters Rehnquist and Scalia complained that the Stevens-led majority had rewritten the federal law involved to favor persons who were illegally present in the United States. In the second, *Dennis* v. *Higgins*, 111 S. Ct. 865 (1991), over the heated dissents of Kennedy and Rehnquist, the Court ruled seven to two that state officials could be sued for violating the federal civil rights of persons to engage in interstate commerce.

Justice David Hackett Souter wrote his first opinion for the Court on February 19, 1991, in *Ford* v. *Georgia*, 111 S. Ct. 850 (1991). Here the Court unanimously invalidated a Georgia Supreme Court rule that prevented a black defendant, facing trial in a death penalty case, from asserting an equal protection claim that the state had applied the impermissible criterion of race to exclude venire members from the jury that convicted him. One month later, in the politically sensitive area regarding judicial admission of coerced confessions in criminal trials, Souter provided the pivotal fifth vote needed by Chief Justice Rehnquist to undercut a Warren Court doctrine that had worked for over twenty years to automatically invalidate criminal convictions involving the use of involuntary or coerced confessions, even in cases where the use could be considered "harmless error" because of the adequacy of other evidence to support the conviction obtained independently of the confession. The case, *Arizona* v. *Fulminante*, 111 S. Ct. 1246 (1991), was almost certainly one in which the Court would on this issue have reached the opposite conclusion had Justice William J. Brennan, Jr., not retired. However, in ruling on the case's second issue the Court's new coerced confession doctrine was itself undercut by a different majority division of the bench; this ruled that the admission of Fulminante's confession could not be deemed harmless error; a retrial of Fulminante was ordered to proceed without benefit of his confession. In a strong dissent issued against the first part of the Court's action, Justice Byron White charged the majority with overturning a "vast body of precedent" and truncating "one of the fundamental tenets of our criminal justice system." White pointed out that "permitting a coerced confession to be part of the evidence on which a jury is free to base its verdict of guilty is inconsistent with the thesis that ours is not an inquisitional system of justice." It was White also who led the different division of the Court holding that the erroneous admission in evidence of the confession made by the defendant was in this case not "harmless beyond a reasonable doubt." Joining him were Justices Marshall, Blackmun, Stevens, and Scalia. Inexplicably, Justice Souter did not vote (for either side) in this part of the case. The coerced confession in the *Fulminante* case had been obtained by a prison inmate acting as an informer for the Federal Bureau of Investigation who offered to protect Fulminante from violence in prison if Fulminante gave him a complete account of the murder of his eleven-year-old stepdaughter. Commenting on the doctrinal revision effected by the Rehnquist Court (by way of what, however, was essentially obiter dictum), the president of the National Association of Criminal Defense Lawyers called the decision a "troublesome one" giving "subtle encouragement to law enforcement officials to break the rules." Henceforth, a police-coerced confession admitted at trial would no longer automatically effect a reversal of conviction. According to Justice White, the change in the applicability of harmless error doctrine to coerced confessions abandoned what until now the Court has treated as "axiomatic"—namely, that a defendant in a criminal case is deprived of due process of law "if his conviction is founded, in whole or in part, upon an involuntary confession, without regard for the truth or falsity of the confession."

Two months later, Souter was voting with Chief Justice Rehnquist and Justices Scalia and White, dissenting, in a five-to-four decision in which a Stevens-orchestrated majority overturned an Idaho death sentence (*Lankford v. Idaho*, 111 S. Ct. 1723 [1991]). This was the first nonunanimous decision of the term in which Justice Souter found himself on the side opposed to that of Justice O'Connor. Until then, Souter had voted the same way O'Connor did in some twenty-five split-decision cases; no other pair of Justices had so constantly agreed. In *Lankford*, Justices O'Connor, Marshall, Blackmun, and Kennedy joined the majority opinion of Justice John Paul Stevens in holding that the failure of a state judge to notify a defendant at his sentencing hearing that he would consider imposing the death penalty violated the Due Process Clause of the Fourteenth Amendment. Souter joined the dissenting opinion written by Justice Scalia which complained that the majority had created a new defense to the imposition of the death penalty based on the defendant's "unreasonable expectations" or "ignorance of the law."

Probably the most controversial decision of Justice Souter's first term was the Court's five-to-four ruling in *Rust* v. *Sullivan*, 111 S. Ct. 1759 (1991), handed down on May 23, 1991, in which Souter once more aligned himself with a conservative Rehnquist-led majority and once again voted in opposition to Justice O'Connor. The case was a double blow to liberals because it upheld a federal regulation promulgated by the Department of Health and Human Services (HHS) that impinged both upon First Amendment freedom and the constitutional right to privacy supporting a woman's right to have an abortion. Under the HHS regulation—which had been suspended pending the outcome of this case during three years of litigation—doctors and other persons employed in some 4,500 federally financed family planning clinics were prohibited from discussing abortion with, or providing medical information about abortion to, pregnant patients. Under the controversial rule, which involved an administrative reinterpretation of a seventeen-year-old federal law, the clinics were forbidden to help women locate doctors willing to perform abortions; if a woman inquired about ending an unwanted or unhealthy pregnancy, she was required to be told only that "the project does not consider abortion an appropriate method of family planning." A pro-life spokeswoman for Americans United for Life made the following comment on the decision: "It's encouraging to have Justice Souter on the record even in this tangential case." Said the pro-choice director of the Women's Legal Defense Fund: "When David Souter showed his true colors today . . . the Supreme Court put *Roe* v. *Wade* in immediate peril." In *Rust*, Chief Justice Rehnquist justified the effect of the Court's decision to allow the government to deny poor women access to abortion on the ground that such women would be "in no worse position than if Congress had never enacted Title X"—the provision of the federal family planning statute under which the clinics affected were funded and regulated.

In dissent, Justice O'Connor accused the Rehnquist-led majority of overreaching, arguing that they should not have taken up the constitutional issues in the case; they should instead have ruled that the challenged regulation was an improper application or interpretation of Title X, which, as the majority itself conceded, was "ambiguous and unenlightening" in its purport. In fact, throughout the first seventeen years of the law's administration—until the final year of the Reagan administration—the questioned regulation had construed the federal law, Title X, in an obverse way. During that period clinic employees were *required* to provide patients with information about abortion as well as about childbirth. It was Rehnquist's view, which Souter joined, that the law's ambiguity made it incumbent upon the Court to give "substantial deference" to the correctness of its present interpretation by the agency that administered it. And, in such a situation, it was only if an administrative construction of statutory language was not plausible that the courts should find it impermissible.

Justice Souter's performance in this case disappointed some Court observers who had hoped the freshman Justice would adhere to a position like that put forward by Justice O'Connor in dissent. In part this was because during the oral argument of *Rust* Souter had directed several questions at Solicitor General Kenneth W. Starr that suggested he viewed as questionable the statutory authority for and validity of the Title X regulation. At argument, Justice Souter seemed to think scarcely credible the administration's position that a valid regulation could keep a physician from performing "his usual professional responsibility" and "preclude professional speech." In the opinion Souter joined, the Chief Justice explained why the regulation did not involve an abridgment of "the free speech rights of private health care organizations that receive Title X funds, of their staff, and of their patients, and why it did not discriminate invidiously in its subsidies in such a way as to aim at the suppression of dangerous ideas." Although the regulation plainly did prohibit "counseling, referral, and the provision of information," this was because the regulation was "designed to ensure that the limits of the federal program are observed." And "a doctor who wished to offer prenatal care to a project patient who became pregnant could properly be prohibited from doing so because such service is outside the scope of the federally funded program" and the bans on "abortion, counseling, and referral are of the same ilk. This is not a case of the Government 'suppressing a dangerous idea,' but of a prohibition on a project grantee or its employees from engaging in activities outside its scope."

David Souter's first written dissenting opinion grew out of an important five-to-four decision involving the federal sentencing guidelines in *Burns* v. *United States*, 111 S. Ct. 2182 (1991), in which Justice Thurgood Marshall delivered the Court's opinion. Although the guidelines did not expressly require that advance notice be given a defendant of the fact that a judge preparing to sentence him intended to "depart upwards" from the prescribed guidelines, the Marshall-led majority ruled that a provision of adequate notice specifying the ground upon which the court contemplated an upwards departure had to be read into the sentencing procedure, not only to satisfy the guidelines' opportunity-for-comment provisions, but to prevent a serious question from being raised as to whether the guidelines did not violate the Due Process Clause. According to Marshall, in analogous situations where the legislature had been silent regarding a need to give individuals both notice and a meaningful opportunity to be heard prior to a deprivation of liberty interests, the Court had not hesitated to impose such requirements upon the procedure contemplated by statute. Chief Justice Rehnquist and Justices White and O'Connor joined Justice Souter's dissenting opinion, which maintained that Congress did not intend that notice and an opportunity to be heard were required to be given to a defendant in any case of judicially contemplated "upward departure." And, while it was the opinion of Souter, joined by White and O'Connor, that the sentencing part of a criminal proceeding, like the trial process itself, "must satisfy the requirements of the Due Process Clause, the Chief Justice showed that he thought otherwise by not joining this part of Souter's opinion. The conclusion reached by all four dissenters, however, was the same—namely, that there was no requirement established by the guidelines and none required by the Fifth Amendment's due process provisions for notice to be given of a judicially contemplated upwards departure in sentencing. The Court's decision was one of its most important interpretations of the new sentencing guidelines under which federal judges apply relatively precise formulas to their sentencing process designed to prevent the exercise of excessive judicial discretion.

A week later, in *Barnes* v. *Glen Theatre*, 111 S. Ct. 2456 (1991), the Chief Justice put together a five-to-four majority that upheld an Indiana statute banning nude dancing of the barroom type. Rehnquist's plurality opinion was not joined by Souter, who nevertheless voted to uphold the law. According to Rehnquist, although such dancing might be said to imply "communication" adequate "to bring into play the First Amendment," a sufficiently important governmental interest "in protecting order and morality" justified the Indiana ban. In his separate concurrence Souter indicated that the "moral views" of society cited by the Chief Justice were not sufficient grounds, in his opinion, upon which to rest an abridgment of the expressive element in nude dancing. Instead Souter defended his vote to uphold the ban "on the basis of the State's substantial interest in combatting the secondary effects of adult entertainment establishments," namely, "the interest asserted by [Indiana] in preventing prostitution, sexual assault, and other criminal activity" of the type allegedly associated with nude-dancing establishments. The dissenters in *Glen Theatre*, led by Justice Byron White, rejected the dubious reasoning of the Chief Justice that in proscribing nude dancing Indiana was not seeking to prohibit the erotic communicative message in the dancing but the noncommunicative and morally offensive nudity in the dancing. In White's words, "The Indiana law, as applied to nude dancing, targets the expressive activity itself; in Indiana nudity in a dancing performance is a crime because of the message such dancing communicates." Under settled First Amendment doctrine such content or message suppression is plainly unconstitutional.

In another five-to-four First Amendment case decided during Souter's first term, *Cohen* v. *Cowles Media*, 111 S. Ct. 2513 (1991), handed down four days after *Glen Theatre*, Justice Souter and Justice White switched roles. It was now White who wrote an opinion for the Court holding that the free press guarantee was not violated by upholding a damage action brought against newspapers which had violated promises made to a news source (the plaintiff) to keep his identity confidential. It was Souter who, dissenting, wrote that the Court was taking too narrow a view of the First Amendment protection that was meant to be accorded both to the press and to the public receiving information from the press. Applying a balancing test of the sort often resorted to by the Court in resolving First Amendment issues, Souter found that "the State's interest in enforcing a newspaper's promise of confidentiality [is] insufficient to outweigh the interest in the unfettered publication of the information revealed in this case." In saying this he was joined by Justices Marshall, Blackmun, and O'Connor.

The final six weeks of the October, 1990, term saw a large number of decisions handed down by a divided court that affected the rights of criminal suspects, criminal defendants, imprisoned persons, and persons convicted of crimes punishable by death. Mostly the decisions were close ones that went against these persons, and usually Souter was to be found siding with the conservative-centrist majorities that controlled the outcomes. In *County of Riverside* v. *McLaughlin*, 111 S. Ct. 1661 (1991), the Court interpreted the Fourth Amendment's ban on unreasonable searches and seizures—as applied to police arrests without warrant—to require that a judicial determination of probable cause take place within forty-eight hours after the arrest. Here the arrestee argued, as the Ninth Circuit court of appeals ruled, that except in exigent circumstances thirty-six hours should be the maximum period of detention allowed pending a judicial determination of probable cause; and that it was unreasonable and unconstitutional to fail to provide a probable cause hearing prior to the time within which an arraignment must take place. Under the rules of the county where the arrest occurred, it was possible for an individual arrested without a warrant late in the week to be held for as long as five days before receiving a judicial probable cause determination; over the Thanksgiving holiday, a seven-day delay might take place. With Justices Scalia, Marshall, Blackmun, and Stevens dissenting, Justice Souter voted with the Chief Justice and Justices O'Connor, White, and Kennedy to give local law enforcement authorities the power to detain a person arrested without a judicial warrant on a misdemeanor or felony charge only up to forty-eight hours without bringing the person before a judicial officer for a probable-cause determination. The theory of the majority, as articulated in the opinion delivered by Justice O'Connor, was that the clear and definite forty-eight-hour rule not only struck a proper balance between the state's "strong interest in protecting public safety" and the individual's competing concern with avoiding "prolonged detention based on incorrect or unfounded suspicion," but also eliminated the otherwise irreducible vagueness and uncertainty inherent in applications of a rule tied to standards like "reasonable," as derived from the text of the Fourth Amendment, and "prompt," as used in the leading precedent on the issue, *Gertein* v. *Pugh*, 420 U.S. 103 (1975). Dissenting separately, Justice Scalia came up with a twenty-four-hour limit that was rooted in an eloquently stated plea made by him for a return to common-law principles for the protection of persons against unlawful arrest; these excluded from the equation considerations of administrative convenience. In joining Justice O'Connor's majority opinion in *McLaughlin*, Justice Souter probably was responding positively to the propositions contained in it that the forty-eight-hour rule showed "proper deference to the demands of federalism" (recognizing that "state systems of criminal procedure vary widely") and that the Fourth Amendment did "not impose on the states a rigid procedural framework." In *Gerstein*, the rules that the Supreme Court outlawed had permitted persons arrested without warrants in Florida to be detained for as long as thirty days without any judicial determination of probable cause.

In two cases involving the use of peremptory challenges to remove persons from prospective juries because of their race, *Powers* v. *Ohio*, 111 S. Ct. 1364 (1991), and *Edmonson* v. *Leesville Concrete Co.*, 111 S. Ct. 2077 (1991), Justice Souter voted with seven-to-two and six-to-three majorities respectively to hold that the race-based exclusion of white jurors in a criminal case involving a black defendant violated the Equal Protection Clause, and that the race-based exclusion of black jurors in a civil case in which the plaintiff was black also did that. In both cases, Chief Justice Rehnquist and Justice Scalia dissented, decrying the Court's penchant for overturning state court criminal trial verdicts and civil trial judgments because of alleged misuses of peremptory challenges that probably in no way affected the merits of the trials' results. In *Powers*, Scalia took the opportunity to attack a bête noire of conservatives, charging that the majority's reasoning was "a reprise, so to speak," of *Miranda* v. *Arizona*, 284 U.S. 436 (1966), inasmuch as "the Court uses its key to the jailhouse door not to free the arguably innocent, but to threaten release upon society of the unquestionably guilty." Joined by the Chief Justice, he went on to predict that "if for any reason the State is unable to reconvict Powers for the double murder at issue here, later victims may pay the price for our extravagance." Dissenting in *Edmonson*, Scalia complained that by the Court's action "yet another complexity is added to an increasingly Byzantine system of justice that devotes more and more of its energy to sideshows and less and less to the merits of the case." Justice O'Connor also dissented in *Edmonson*, in an opinion which the Chief Justice joined.

Justice Souter's second term on the Court opened with 108 cases calendared for decision, including an antiabortion law case, and with a new conservative Justice, Clarence Thomas, on the bench. During his confirmation hearings Thomas had seemed to be evasive in responding to the *Roe* v. *Wade* questions put to him by Judiciary Committee members and—since Justice Souter had voted with the Court's conservative bloc in the only case decided during the previous term bearing at all on abortion, *Rust* v. *Sullivan*—there was even greater anxiety among Court watchers during this term than during the last about this explosive issue.

In the first well-publicized decision of his second term on the bench, Justice Souter joined a unanimous Court, led by Justice Sandra Day O'Connor, in holding unconstitutional New York's "Son of Sam" law (*Simon & Schuster* v. *New York Crime Victims Board*, 112 S. Ct. 501 [1992]). Enacted in 1977, New York's law was designed to redistribute to the victims of crimes, and to creditors, any moneys that convicted criminals might receive from selling the stories of their crimes to book publishers or other producers of works describing or depicting the crime. Statutes having similar objectives subsequently were enacted by the federal government and most of the states. Citing the well-settled First Amendment principle that "regulations which permit the government to discriminate on the basis of the content of the message cannot be tolerated," the Court struck down the New York law and, inferentially, all extant similar laws as well. The challenge to the law's constitutionality had been brought by Simon & Schuster, to escape liability to the New York Crime Victims Board for moneys paid by it to a career criminal named Henry Hill who had helped author Nicholas Pileggi to write a book the plaintiff published as *Wiseguy: Life in a Mafia Family*.

In four other major free speech cases decided during the October, 1991, term, Justice Souter voted for expansive readings of the First Amendment's protection. In *International Society for Krishna Consciousness* v. *Lee*, 112 S. Ct. 2701 (1992), Souter dissented from a Rehnquist-led six-to-three majority ruling that the First Amendment's free speech guarantee was not violated by a public airport terminal's total ("viewpoint-neutral") ban on the expressive activity involved in the solicitation of funds by persons and groups inside the terminal. Writing for Justices Blackmun and Stevens as well, Justice Souter disagreed sharply with the majority's holding that the public areas of the New York City–area air terminals involved were not "public forums" from which the government was prevented by the First Amendment from excluding speech, including solicitations. The majority held that such terminals were, instead, nonpublic forums with regard to which government could, consistently with the First Amendment, "reasonably limit solicitations by restricting them to the public sidewalks outside the terminals." Said Souter, "The practical reality of the regulations, which this Court can never ignore, is that it shuts off a uniquely powerful avenue of communication for organizations like the International Society for Krishna Consciousness, and may, in effect, completely prohibit unpopular and poorly funded groups from receiving funds in response to [constitutionally] protected solicitation."

However, in a companion case involving the same parties decided the same day, *Lee v. International Society for Krishna Consciousness*, 112 S. Ct. 2709 (1992), the Court held invalid under the First Amendment bans that were established by the same airport terminals on the distribution of literature—even in the absence of solicitation activity—inside the terminals. The opinion for the Court here was per curiam, "for the reasons expressed" in the separate opinions (concurring and dissenting) of Justices Souter, Kennedy, and O'Connor in the solicitation ban case. Dissenting from this decision awarding First Amendment protection to leafleting inside public airport terminals were the Chief Justice and Justices White, Scalia, and Thomas. Justice Souter was especially critical of Chief Justice Rehnquist's conclusions in both cases that because airport terminals were not traditional public forums, they were disqualified from treatment as such. This reasoning, he said, "has no warrant in a Constitution whose values are not to be left behind in the city streets that are no longer the only focus of our community life." And, "if that were the level of our [jurisprudential] direction, we might as well abandon the public forum doctrine altogether." In this pair of decisions Justices O'Connor and Kennedy cast the pivotal votes that allowed the Court to uphold (six to three) per Rehnquist the ban on solicitation, and to strike down (five to four) per curiam, the ban on leafleting. In both cases, Justice Souter was aligned with the Court's liberal Justices Stevens and Blackmun.

In another major free speech case of the term, the Court struck down as unconstitutional on its face a St. Paul, Minnesota, hate-speech ordinance that criminalized the use on public or private property of symbols such as "a burning cross or Nazi swastika" that knowingly "arouse anger, alarm, or resentment in others on the basis of race, color, creed, religion, or gender"— because the law sought to "handicap the expression of particular ideas." Said Justice Scalia, in an opinion that Justice Souter as well as Justices Kennedy and Thomas and the Chief Justice joined: "The First Amendment does not permit St. Paul to impose special prohibitions on those speakers who express views on disfavored subjects," citing the "Son of Sam" law decision handed down earlier in the term. "The point of the First Amendment," according to Scalia, "is that majority preferences must be expressed in some fashion other than silencing speech on the basis of its content" (*R. A. V.* v. *City of St. Paul,* 112 Sup. Ct. 2538 [1992]).

In two other cases, Souter voted on free speech grounds to strike down a Tennessee statute prohibiting the solicitation of votes, displays, and the distribution of campaign materials within 100 feet of the entrance to a polling place; and a Georgia ordinance that permitted a government official to set fees for assembling or parading in accordance with his estimates of the costs of maintaining public order. In the first case, *Burson* v. *Freeman*, 112 S. Ct. 1846 (1992), Justices Souter and O'Connor joined Justice Stevens' dissenting opinion. In the second one, *Forsyth County* v. *Nationalist Movement*, 112 S. Ct. 2395 (1992), Souter was part of the five-to-four majority that struck down the statute. In both cases, Justice Blackmun wrote the Court's opinions; in both cases, Souter was on the side opposed to that of Chief Justice Rehnquist and Justice Scalia.

In one of the most politically charged and significant decisions of the term, *Lee* v. *Weisman*, 112 S. Ct. 2649 (1992), Justice Souter cast a pivotal vote enabling the Court to rule (five to four) that the inclusion in a public high school graduation ceremony of a religious exercise consisting of short prayers violated the religion clauses of the First Amendment that were made applicable by the Fourteenth Amendment with "full force to the States and their school districts." This put Chief Justice Rehnquist and Justices White, Scalia, and Thomas into dissent. The decision marked a further extension of Establishment Clause doctrines that were a hallmark of Warren Court jurisprudence; they have been used to nullify any "entanglement of Government, negatively or positively, with the religious beliefs and practices of the people." The decision was brought about when Justices Kennedy, O'Connor, Blackmun, Stevens, and Souter agreed to reject the argument presented by the Justice Department, appearing for the United States as amicus curiae, urging the Court to reinterpret the Establishment Clause to permit an expanded role for the expression of religious ceremonies and beliefs in public life and institutions—by holding that government constitutionally might *endorse* religion so long as it did not *coerce* religious conformity. The result of the case—which arose out of an attempt by a graduating senior and her father to enjoin school officials from permitting nonsectarian religious prayers to be offered at graduation exercises by a rabbi—disappointed those who expected the enlarged conservative bloc on the Court to revamp the Court's Establishment Clause doctrine. Justice Kennedy's majority opinion held that "the government involvement with religious activity in this case is pervasive, to the point of creating a state-sponsored and state-directed religious exercise in a public school," and that such "formal religious observance" was in conflict with the Court's "settled rules pertaining to prayer exercise for students." Quoting from the leading Warren Court case on Establishment Clause questions, *Engel* v. *Vitale*, 370 U.S. 421, 425 (1962), the opinion reiterated the "conservative principle" that "it is no part of the business of government to compose official prayers for any group of American people to recite as a part of a religious program carried on by government," and that "the central meaning of the Religion Clauses is that all creeds must be tolerated and none favored," including even a so-called civil religious creed—i.e., a nonsectarian one which "permits once conflicting faiths to express the shared conviction that there is an ethic and a morality which transcend human invention." Justice Souter's separate twenty-three-page concurrence in *Weisman*, joined by Justices Stevens and O'Connor, was perhaps his most significant opinion to date, one in which he took a stand on constitutional interpretation that was not only strongly principled but expressly opposed to the stand taken by the Court's staunchest conservatives—Chief Justice Rehnquist and Justice Scalia. In doing this, he also repaired a weakness in the fabric of the Court majority's opinion, which dissenting Justice Scalia described as being "conspicuously bereft of any reference to history" and characterized as laying "waste [to] a tradition that is as old as public school graduation ceremonies themselves, and that is a component of an even more long-standing American tradition of nonsectarian prayer to God at public celebrations generally." Souter effectively refuted Scalia's insistence that history ran against the Court's jurisprudence on freedom of religion by pointing to numerous instances in the historical setting of the Religion Clauses where several of the framers themselves departed from the tradition painted by Scalia. "President Jefferson, for example, steadfastly refused to issue Thanksgiving proclamations of any kind, in part because he thought they violated the Religion Clauses." And, "during his first three years in office, James Madison refused to call for days of thanksgiving and prayer," though later, "amid the political turmoil of the War of 1812, he did so on four separate occasions." Souter went on to show that although the leaders of the young Republic "engaged in some of the practices that State-Church separationists like Jefferson and Madison criticized . . . those practices prove, at best, that the Framers simply did not share a common understanding of the Establishment Clause, and, at worst, that they, like other politicians, could raise constitutional ideals one day and turn their backs on them the next." Justice Souter in this case also exposed as fitful or manipulative the use to which history has sometimes been put by Court conservatives like Scalia and Rehnquist in the interpretation of constitutional text. In reviewing the history of the First Amendment, Souter used the historical evidence to rebut the Chief Justice's view that the Constitution forbids government only from preferring one particular religion over another, showing instead that it requires the government to adhere to a position of neutrality not only between different sects, but as between believers and nonbelievers.

Justice Souter's emerging independent views regarding constitutional interpretation took even firmer hold in the most controversial case decided during the October, 1991, term, *Planned Parenthood of Southeastern Pennsylvania v. Casey*, 112 S. Ct. 2791 (1992), in which Souter's liberal views on interpreting the Due Process Clause trumped the cramped reading of that clause favored by Chief Justice Rehnquist and Justices White, Scalia, and Thomas. Given the extraordinary political contexts of *Casey*, both on the Court and in the nation at large, the unusual sixty-page-long majority opinion—jointly authored by Justices Souter, O'Connor, and Kennedy and joined by Justices Blackmun and Stevens—suggests that in Souter the Court may have found a Justice sufficiently dedicated to the Constitution's basic values and the over-arching rule of law. He appeared sufficiently adept at the arts of mobilizing judicial consensus and crafting principled opinions, to blunt the apparent agenda of the Court's conservative present Chief Justice, which is to bring the Court's constitutional jurisprudence into closer parity with the executive branch policies of the Republican administrations of the past dozen years.

The decision in *Casey* upheld several sections of Pennsylvania's abortion law for the reason that they did not impose on the right to abortion "an undue burden," meaning a "substantial obstacle in the path of a woman seeking an abortion before the fetus attains viability." The provisions passing constitu-tional muster required a pregnant teenager wanting an abortion to obtain the consent of a parent or a judge, and a pregnant adult woman to listen to a medical presentation that is designed to discourage her from having an abor-tion and then to wait twenty-four hours before going ahead. The validated laws also stipulate what medical emergency conditions will warrant a waiver of these requirements for abortion and require that all doctors and clinics involved with abortion decisions make statistical reports to the state govern-ment. On the other hand, and more significantly, the Court invalidated a provision of the Pennsylvania law requiring a married woman to notify her husband of her intent to have an abortion, saying: "A State may not give to a man the kind of dominion over his wife that parents exercise over their children." This ruling had the abiding side effect of confirming the vitality of the ideological principles and societal implications of *Roe* v. *Wade*, which effectively guarantees to mature women constitutional immunity from state laws that would criminalize abortion procedures undertaken prior to fetus viability. According to the joint Souter-Kennedy-O'Connor opinion, the Court's 1973 decision in *Roe* v. *Wade* established a "rule of law and a compo-nent of liberty we cannot renounce"; its "rare precedental force" might be overturned "under political fire" only "at the cost of both profound and unnecessary damage to the Court's legitimacy, and to the nation's commit-ment to the rule of law." As bluntly noted in the joint opinion's first para-graph, the White House had, through the Justice Department, pressured the Court to overrule *Roe* on six separate occasions over the previous decade. This the Court declined to do.

It was a critical and surprising aspect of the decision in *Casey* that Justices Kennedy and O'Connor moved away from the conservative right wing of the Court onto a common doctrinal ground with Justice Souter and the same decisional ground as Souter and the Court's liberals; and that Justice Souter may indeed even have brokered the consensus to reaffirm, not overrule, the basic holding of *Roe* v. *Wade*.

By the end of his second term on the High Bench, Justice Souter had placed his weight behind liberal-centrist Court majorities that upheld the constitutional contentions of criminal defendants in a number of important criminal cases. In *Morgan* v. *Illinois*, 112 S. Ct. 2222 (1992), he joined Justice Byron White's majority ruling that Fourteenth Amendment due process required that a capital defendant in a state case be permitted to challenge for cause any prospective juror who would automatically vote to impose death if the defendant was convicted of a capital offense. In *Dawson* v. *Delaware*, 112 S. Ct. 1093 (1992), Souter joined an eight-to-one majority (only Justice Thomas dissented) holding that the First Amendment precludes irrelevant evidence of a capital prisoner's beliefs and associations being admitted at his sentencing hearing. In *Hudson* v. *McMillian*, 112 S. Ct. 995 (1992), Souter joined another eight-to-one majority (Thomas again dissenting) to hold that the use of excessive force against a state penitentiary prisoner may violate the Eighth Amendment's prohibition against cruel and unusual punishment even if the prisoner does not suffer serious injury as a result. In *Jacobson* v. *United States*, 112 S. Ct. 1535 (1992), Souter and Thomas helped make up a five-to-four majority led by Justice White that overturned a federal child pornography conviction (having free speech implications) on the ground of entrapment, when a fifty-six-year-old veteran-turned-farmer without any criminal record was enticed by post office police to order a magazine containing child pornography from a fictitious trading company and federal agents arrested him upon delivery of the magazine. According to Justice White, "In their zeal to enforce the law, Government agents may not originate a criminal design, implant in an innocent person's mind the disposition to commit a criminal act, and then induce commission of the crime so that the Government may prosecute."

Near the close of the October, 1991, term, Justices Souter, O'Connor, and Kennedy banded together in *Wright* v. *West*, 112 S. Ct. 2482 (1992), to reject a Bush Justice Department argument that would have required federal judges in habeas corpus proceedings to defer without independent evaluation to the conclusions reached by state court judges. As Justice O'Connor pointed out, since Congress had "refused on 13 occasions to amend the habeas corpus law as requested by the White House to require deference from federal judges, the Court should not itself take such a step." In reaching this decision, the Court redressed some of the damage done to the long-established federal habeas law the previous term in *Keeney* v. *Tamayo-Reyes*, 112 S. Ct. 1715 (1992). There Justice Souter and Thomas had joined a five-to-four majority opinion written by Justice Byron White that overruled a 1963 Warren Court precedent. There were notably strong dissents from Justices O'Connor and Kennedy in *Keeney* because of the extent to which the majority already had gone in undercutting the ability of state prisoners to bring into federal court constitutional challenges to state convictions and sentences. In *Keeney*, the petitioner's lawyer negligently failed to present essential facts about an inadequate Spanish translation of the terms of a negotiated guilty-plea agreement and about the circumstances of the agreement; but the White-led majority ruled that the federal writ should not be issued unless a newly announced standard of cause were met, and that attorney error did not qualify as cause.

Souter also joined Court majorities in two cases where the liberties of mentally ill criminal defendants were at stake. In *Riggins* v. *Nevada*, 112 S. Ct. 1810 (1992), the Court held that a pretrial criminal defendant has a Fourteenth Amendment due process interest in avoiding the involuntary administration of an antipsychotic drug during the course of his murder and robbery trial. And, in *Foucha* v. *Louisiana*, 112 S. Ct. 1780 (1992), the Court held that a criminal defendant found not guilty by reason of insanity and thereafter committed to a psychiatric hospital could not be kept confined until such time as he might be able to demonstrate that he was no longer dangerous. According to the Court, if an inmate is found by a court at any time to still be dangerous but no longer mentally ill, he has a due-process right to release from confinement.

Justice David Souter's judicial behavior during his second term on the bench worked to stabilize the Court's political balance and restore some of its faded ideological integrity. By combining advantageously with the Court's liberal and centrist blocs in cases where the bench was deeply divided, Souter helped produce decisions and opinions that showed a decent respect for the Court's own precedents, a healthy mistrust of executive branch advocacy, and a sensitivity to principled modes of constitutional interpretation. Justice Souter was in the majority in thirteen of the fourteen cases that were decided by five-to-four votes during his second term—including the Pennsylvania abortion case, the high school graduation prayer case, and the Georgia demonstration-permit free speech case. One result of Souter's positioning during the term was to put the Court's three most conservative members—Clarence Thomas, Antonin Scalia, and William H. Rehnquist—into dissent in eleven nonunanimous cases. Rehnquist himself dissented in a total of nineteen such cases during the term.

SELECTED BIBLIOGRAPHY

Justice Souter's appointment to the bench was widely covered in the media; for example, the August 6, 1990, issue of the *National Law Journal* contains a number of articles on the issues surrounding Souter's appointment and his personal background (see pp. 1, 45). Justice Souter's New Hampshire decisions concerning Fourth, Fifth, and Sixth Amendment rights are analyzed in John. F. Brigden, "Justice Souter's Impact on the Supreme Court's Criminal Procedure Jurisprudence," 29 *American Criminal Law Review* 133, and a number of his opinions before his appointment to the Supreme Court have been compiled by University of Southern California law professor Judith Resnik and the USC Law Library reference staff as *Souter on Issues of Freedom* (Los Angeles: University of Southern California Law Library, 1990). Justice Souter's first term as a Supreme Court Justice is discussed in Scott P. Johnson, "David Souter's First Term on the Supreme Court: The Impact of a New Justice," 75 *Judicature* 238. An overview of Souter's life and judicial career with a special emphasis on his role in crafting the *Casey* decision can be found in David J. Garrow, "Justice Souter Emerges" *New York Times Magazine*, September 25, 1994, p. 36.

Clarence Thomas

☆ 1948–   ☆

APPOINTED BY GEORGE BUSH

YEARS ON COURT
1991–

by
SUSAN THOMAS

Clarence Thomas, the 106th Justice of the United States Supreme Court, was the second African American to be appointed to the Court. The seat Thomas filled had been vacated by Thurgood Marshall, the first African-American Justice and a hero of the civil rights movement whose liberal views had been marginalized by an increasingly conservative Court. Ideologically, Thomas more closely resembled Robert Bork, the conservative judge he had replaced on the District of Columbia court of appeals one year earlier.

At his Senate confirmation hearings, Thomas professed that he would approach the bench "stripped down like a runner," without preconceptions either about issues on which he had previously expressed views, such as affirmative action, or about issues on which his views were not known, such as abortion. During his first term on the Supreme Court, Thomas' judicial philosophy did not diverge significantly from the conservative views he had espoused during his political career with the Reagan and Bush administrations. Thomas promptly allied himself with the Court's most conservative Justice, Antonin Scalia, adopting Scalia's history-based approach to constitutional interpretation, his modest view of the role of the federal courts, and much of his disdain for stare decisis. Voting with Scalia and frequently with Chief Justice Rehnquist, Thomas signaled his willingness to overrule uncongenial precedents on subjects ranging from criminal procedure to abortion to the Establishment Clause and to rechart the Court's direction.

In a significant number of cases, however, Thomas revealed a distinct voice. Although Thomas borrowed Scalia's confident rhetoric, his own version of originalism struggled to mediate between history and precedent in a more complex manner than Scalia's purer views would allow, and his version of an appropriately modest judicial role sometimes allowed for judicial intervention in the service of goals Thomas had not yet clearly defined. Thomas also brought a unique and complex perspective to issues involving race, a subject of critical importance in his life and previous work.

During his confirmation hearings and throughout his earlier career,

Thomas presented his own success story as a vindication of his view that equality must be achieved by individuals and not by group-based solutions such as affirmative action. Born in 1948 to a poor mother in the evocatively named Pin Point, Georgia, Thomas spent much of his early life in a largely segregated society. At the age of six, he moved to Savannah, where he was raised by his grandparents. At about the same time as the Supreme Court decision in *Brown* v. *Board of Education,* Thomas' grandfather, a self-employed tradesman, enrolled Thomas and his brother in private Catholic schools. As one of the few black students at local schools and later at the Immaculate Conception Seminary in rural Missouri, Thomas suffered the barbs of racism. Thomas left the South for Holy Cross College in Massachusetts and then Yale Law School. Both institutions had affirmative action programs; later critics were to chide Thomas for disfavoring affirmative action when he himself appeared to have been its beneficiary. This early history was only one of the ways in which Thomas' identity as a racial minority and the views he adopted about race were to become a dominant theme of his life and career, even after he had moved from Pin Point to New England and ultimately to the affluent suburbs of Washington, D.C.

After graduating from Yale Law School, Thomas considered returning to Georgia to practice law, but found that the law firms of Atlanta still treated blacks differently. Instead, he took a job with Republican John Danforth, then attorney general of Missouri, from 1974 to 1977. During this time, Thomas registered as a Republican, changing his party affiliation. In 1977, Thomas took a job as in-house counsel to the Monsanto Chemical Corporation working on environmental issues. Two years later, Danforth, having been elected senator from Missouri, brought Thomas to Washington as his legislative assistant. From there, Thomas' position as a conservative black Republican sponsored by an influential senator led to his meteoric rise in the Reagan administration. In 1981, Thomas was named assistant secretary for civil rights at the Department of Education, where he was responsible for enforcing civil rights laws as they applied to schools and universities. This was the first job in which Thomas' views on race became relevant to his work. Although in earlier years he had been intrigued by the disparate views of Malcolm X and Booker T. Washington, Thomas gradually settled into a view that advocated self-reliance, criticized the civil rights movement's focus on extreme integration, and opposed affirmative action.

Ronald Reagan found these views compatible, and only one year later, in May of 1982, named Thomas chair of the Equal Employment Opportunity Commission (EEOC). During his seven years as the head of that agency, Thomas developed and applied the philosophy that civil rights should be individual, and that group-based approaches such as quotas and timetables, and even the use of statistical proof of discrimination, were wrong. Thomas began to identify himself consistently with the more conservative wing of his party, becoming an active speaker before Republican and conservative audiences. In these speeches, Thomas shared his developing views on race and civil rights and endorsed conservative positions on a variety of other issues. One speech before the Heritage Foundation, for example, was entitled, "Why Black Americans Should Look to Conservative Policies." In his speeches and writings, Thomas argued against affirmative action ("Affirmative Action Goals and Timetables: Too Tough? Not Tough Enough," 5 *Yale Law & Policy Review* 402 [1987]; "Colorblindness," Letter to the Editor, *Wall Street Journal*, February 20, 1987, at 21; "The Equal Employment Opportunity Commission: Reflections on a New Philosophy," 15 *Stetson Law Review* 29 [1985]). He also began to advocate looking to natural law as a source of guidance in constitutional interpretation, criticizing conservatives for rejecting the notion that "higher law," although not spelled out in the Constitution, is part of the "inalienable rights" protected by the Constitution, as well as the Declaration of Independence ("The Higher Law Background of the Privileges and Immunities Clause of the Fourteenth Amendment," 12 *Harvard Journal of Law and Public Policy* 63 [1989]; "Toward a 'Plain Reading' of the Constitution—The Declaration of Independence in Constitutional Interpretation," 30 *Howard Law Journal* 983 [1985]). In his speech to the Heritage Foundation, Thomas made one comment that was to receive considerable notice during his judicial confirmation hearings: he praised as "a splendid example of applying natural law" an article by Lewis Lehrman that condemned the Supreme Court's decision in *Roe* v. *Wade* partially on the basis that a "child-about-to-be-born" has an "inalienable right to life" (Lehrman, "The Declaration of Independence and the Right to Life," 21 *The American Spectator* [April 1987]).

During his tenure at the EEOC, Thomas' views became increasingly inconsistent with the case and statutory law governing his agency. He disagreed with the Supreme Court on the view of affirmative action expressed in *Regents of the University of California* v. *Bakke*, 438 U.S. 265 (1978), and also on its acceptance of statistical proof as a means of establishing discrimination (see *Griggs* v. *Duke Power Co.*, 401 U.S. 424 [1971]). Thomas was unsympathetic to group-based claims, preferring individual actions, and unsympathetic to claims of discrimination not based on race. Under his leadership, the EEOC allowed some 10,000 age-discrimination claims to lapse, although they were clearly covered by applicable statutory law; Congress later reinstated those claims.

In 1989, George Bush nominated Thomas, then forty-three years old, to the seat on the United States Court of Appeals for the District of Columbia Circuit vacated by Robert Bork, whose conservative philosophy and restrictive view of the judicial role had led to the Senate's refusal in 1987 to confirm him for appointment to the Supreme Court. (The vote on Bork, fifty-eight to forty-two, was the largest vote against any Supreme Court nominee in history.) Thomas' confirmation hearings went as smoothly as his confirmation hearings for the position at the EEOC, and Thomas joined the D.C. court of appeals in the spring of 1990. He spent barely a year on that court before

President Bush announced that he was nominating Thomas to succeed Thurgood Marshall, who had just announced his retirement from the Supreme Court. Again, Thomas was stalked by the question of whether he was an affirmative action candidate; President Bush responded by declaring, to widespread skepticism, that Thomas' race had not influenced the selection process, but that Thomas was simply the best man for the job.

Unlike the perfunctory hearing on Thomas' appointment to the D.C. Circuit, Thomas' Supreme Court confirmation hearing exploded into the most controversial, most intensely publicized, most widely debated, and most divisive in history. Because of these hearings, Clarence Thomas' name came to evoke a complex of issues about race, gender, and the confirmation process itself.

The five-day hearing before the Senate Judiciary Committee began tamely enough as the senators explored the issue of whether Thomas was in fact the best candidate for the job. Thomas' relative lack of judicial experience and scholarly credentials posed an issue for some senators. Other senators wanted to question the extent to which Thomas' clearly formulated public views on subjects such as affirmative action and natural law would determine his judicial approach. But questioning Thomas about his views on issues such as affirmative action and abortion proved both controversial and difficult. Both the Senate and the administration had learned from the Senate's refusal to confirm Robert Bork, whose conservative judicial philosophy, expressed in numerous law review articles and speeches, seemed to prefigure how he would decide any given case. An equally important lesson could be gleaned from the Senate's ninety-to-nine vote to confirm the most recent appointee, David Souter, who had never expressed views on controversial issues such as abortion or affirmative action and who declined to answer questions about his views of controversies likely to be raised before the Court.

The administration argued that the critical question before the Senate was Thomas' character, not his views on particular issues. Thomas attempted to deflect controversy by insisting that he had formed no opinions that would accompany him to the Supreme Court. On issues on which he had not previously expressed a public position, like the fate of *Roe* v. *Wade*, 410 U.S. 113 (1973), he maintained that he had not developed any views and had not discussed the issue. (He made light of his endorsement of Lehrman's views on abortion, claiming that this did not represent a thought-out position on abortion, but merely a general interest in natural law philosophy.) Like Souter, Thomas declined to answer questions on the merits of various constitutional questions on the ground that it would be inappropriate to prejudge issues that might come before the Court. On issues on which he had publicly expressed views, such as affirmative action, Thomas declared that his statements had been only contextual. He described some of his speeches criticizing civil rights litigators and the Justice he was to replace, Thurgood Marshall, as opportunistic political speeches made to political audiences. Thomas even averred that some of his speeches and writings had been drafted by others, and that he did not necessarily agree with all of the implications of the views expressed.

The articles in which Thomas espoused natural law as a source of constitutional interpretation drew particular attention because Thomas' views on the sources and content of natural law were so vague. This attraction to the idea of natural law seemed to indicate that, unlike Bork, Thomas would be willing to find unenumerated rights in the Constitution. It was not clear whether Thomas' version of unenumerated rights would resemble those rights the Court had already inferred, such as the right to privacy, or rights the Court had declined to recognize, such as a right to fetal life. The committee never successfully questioned Thomas on his understanding of natural law, or on many of the other topics discussed in his previous writing. Avoiding the fate of Robert Bork, Thomas avowed that nothing he had said previously could be taken as a reflection of what his judicial philosophy might be, because he entered the judiciary "stripped down like a runner."

Thomas convinced only half of the Judiciary Committee to endorse him. On September 27, the committee voted, splitting seven to seven on whether to endorse him, and sent his nomination to the floor without recommendation. Nevertheless, with the support of John Danforth and the sentiment of many liberal senators that it would be futile to reject Thomas because the next nominee would be just as conservative, Thomas appeared to be headed for a smooth and certain confirmation.

Exactly how and why Anita Hill's statements were elicited and later leaked to the press was a subject of considerable debate. Hill, a law professor at the University of Oklahoma Law School, had submitted an affidavit alleging that Thomas, who had been her employer at the Department of Education and then at the EEOC, had repeatedly sexually harassed her. In her affidavit and later in her live testimony, she described conversations where Thomas had paid her unwanted attention, reveled in sexual innuendo, and forced her to listen to detailed descriptions of pornographic films he had seen. The members of the Judiciary Committee were provided with Hill's affidavit, but decided not to call Hill as a witness. Chairman Joseph Biden later cited Hill's reluctance to give up her privacy as one of his reasons for not holding hearings on these allegations. Thomas submitted an affidavit completely denying the truth of Hill's allegations. After the Judiciary Committee vote but before the nomination went to the floor of the Senate, Hill's affidavit was leaked to the press.

The sensational publication of Hill's allegations provoked an avalanche of reactions. Constituents, including an unusually large number of women, besieged their senators by telephone and telegram; the media besieged Hill; women members of the House of Representatives were photographed marching up the steps of the Capitol to confront the Senate with the demand that Hill's charges be given serious attention. As a result of the public outcry, the

Senate decided to postpone the floor debate on Thomas' nomination and to give the Judiciary Committee the task of reopening their hearings in order to investigate Hill's allegations. From October 11 to October 13, 1991, the Committee held these supplementary hearings, with minimal advance preparation and maximum publicity. The hearings, widely broadcast on radio and television, riveted the nation as an audience of millions tried to decide who was telling the truth.

There was little ground for compromise. Hill's account of what had occurred and Thomas' flat denial that the events she described had taken place could not be reconciled. One of them, either Thomas or Hill, was lying. It seemed to be the political skills of Thomas and his advisers that, once again, led Thomas to survive this phase of the confirmation process. The committee decided to let Thomas speak first. He used the opportunity to reestablish his image as a dignified, upright citizen, to excoriate the confirmation process as "Kafkaesque" for the upheaval it had caused in his life, to portray himself as the victim of the process, and to inject the specter of racism by referring to the process as a "lynching." Thomas tried to circumscribe the scope of the hearings by declaring that he would not provide the rope for his own lynching by submitting to questions about intimate aspects of his private life. In his later statement to the committee, Thomas sharpened his allusion to racism, referring to the hearings as "a high-tech lynching for uppity blacks."

Democratic Judiciary Committee chairman Joseph Biden also aided Thomas' cause by declaring that even though the proceeding was not a trial, Thomas was entitled to a presumption of innocence. By the time Anita Hill testified, most observers seemed inclined to doubt her testimony, having already given Thomas the benefit of the doubt. Hill was a surprise, however. Calm and dignified, she told her story in a detailed and matter-of-fact manner that convinced many who would have preferred to dismiss her charges outright that the charges should be seriously considered. The Republican senators on the committee, having had little time to investigate Hill or her allegations, flailed wildly trying to find a basis for attacking her credibility. Hill was accused alternately of being vengeful, jealous, mentally unbalanced, or an erotomaniac. She was accused of plagiarizing parts of her testimony from a judicial opinion and other parts from the popular novel *The Exorcist*. The most telling criticisms seemed to be that the alleged incidents had taken place ten years earlier and that Hill had not reported or tried to litigate her claim of sexual harassment at the time, but had continued to work for Thomas and had maintained, as shown by his office telephone log, cordial relations with him even after she left his employ.

Other witnesses were rapidly dredged up—women who had worked with Thomas who testified to his character, friends of Hill's who tried to rebut suggestions that Hill's statements were a recent fabrication by testifying that she had told them of these events contemporaneously, and even a man who had met Hill at a party who testified that he thought Hill had sexual fantasies about him and therefore probably had fantasies about Thomas as well. The haste with which the hearings were convened meant that decisions about what testimony would be heard were made without much deliberation. A second woman who claimed that she had been sexually harassed by Thomas was not called as a witness; no experts on the subject of sexual harassment were called to inform the senators as to whether Hill's failure to report these incidents earlier and her failure to leave her job with Thomas were unusual or typical reactions in incidents of this sort. Thus, the committee members tried to develop theories about sexual harassment and Hill's credibility on the basis of information hastily compiled by their staffs or on the lay opinions of anyone who happened to be a witness. Whether or not Thomas would be confirmed seemed now to depend on whether the public believed Thomas or Hill, and that credibility assessment seemed to hinge on a range of factors, some quite subtle. Some observers theorized, for example, that the timing of the hearings, combined with the unusual degree of public interest, meant that whatever testimony was heard during prime time would be most influential with the public, so that the order of testimony became critical. Others thought that Biden's injunction to give Thomas the benefit of the doubt was decisive.

Discussions about who was telling the truth and about the nature of sexual harassment were ubiquitous. The constituent reaction this time favored Thomas. More people reported believing Thomas than Hill. Southern blacks, who held key votes in some states, sympathized with Thomas' suggestion that the treatment he was receiving during the hearings was tinged with racism. Deluged by calls and telegrams from their constituents and with scant time to reflect on the complex issues raised, on October 15 the Senate held its floor debate and vote. As senator after senator expressed views about Anita Hill's testimony, or about Thomas' record, suspense mounted as the pro and con votes remained evenly balanced. After the last senator spoke, Thomas was confirmed by a vote of fifty-two to forty-eight, the narrowest margin for confirmation of any Justice since 1881. Thomas was sworn in on November 1, 1991, joining a Court that had already begun the work of the term several weeks earlier.

After the ravages of the confirmation hearings, there was widespread speculation about how Thomas' views on issues like the rights of women or the rights of the accused might be affected by the crucible of the hearings. One immediate impact of the intense publicity was that after the hearings, Thomas guarded his privacy. He made no public appearances and rarely spoke at oral argument. But he did not maintain a low profile in his written work on the Court.

By custom, the first opinion Thomas wrote was for a unanimous Court in a relatively noncontroversial area. The unremarkable opinion in *Molzof* v. *United States*, 112 S. Ct. 711 (1992), announced January 14, 1992, concerned the scope of the definition of the punitive damages prohibited by the Federal Tort Claims Act. The next day, however, Thomas released a second opinion far more revealing of the judicial role he would play during his first term: to advocate that precedent be stretched to conform to original premises, to seek bright-line rules, to favor the government, and to undervalue consensus.

In the case of *White* v. *Illinois*, 112 S. Ct. 736 (1992), the defendant had been prosecuted for sexually assaulting a four-year-old girl who was not called as a witness at trial. Her hearsay statements to her baby-sitter, mother, an investigating officer, an emergency-room nurse, and a doctor were all admitted at trial under exceptions to the hearsay rule (as spontaneous declarations or as statements made in the course of securing medical treatment). Writing for a unanimous Court, Justice Rehnquist declared that the Confrontation Clause did not require the declarant to have been produced or found unavailable before the hearsay could be introduced.

The United States, in an amicus curiae brief, had proposed a much broader basis for rejecting the defendant's claim, namely that the Confrontation Clause was only intended to redress the old English practice of prosecution on the basis of ex parte affidavits and therefore should not be construed to cover hearsay evidence at all. Rehnquist and six other members of the Court rejected this claim, finding the proposed narrow reading of the clause foreclosed by prior Supreme Court case law dating from 1895 to 1990. Rehnquist described the Court's Confrontation Clause jurisprudence, focusing on whether hearsay evidence has an adequate guarantee of reliability to allow dispensing with cross-examination, as a compromise between the extreme positions of disallowing all hearsay or allowing all hearsay.

Although the Court was unanimous as to the result in *White*, Thomas, joined by Scalia, wrote a concurring opinion to suggest that the Court had unnecessarily rejected in dicta the government's argument. Thomas' opinion invoked plain-language and original-intent arguments reminiscent of Scalia's approach to constitutional interpretation, but at the same time Thomas' desire to take account of all possible bases of interpretation, including precedent, left his opinion logically inconsistent. At the end of the opinion, Thomas proposed a novel interpretation of the Confrontation Clause that represented a compromise between the government's position and the Court's prior case law, but it was a compromise not grounded in the linguistic or historical analysis in the earlier part of his opinion.

Thomas began from the position that "our" Confrontation Clause jurisprudence had evolved in a manner that was "perhaps inconsistent with the text and history of the Clause itself." The view of the Confrontation Clause Thomas advocated was not based on the intent of the framers of the Constitution since, as Thomas acknowledged, there is little evidence as to what the framers intended the Confrontation Clause to mean. Like Scalia, Thomas turned first to the text, considering what the Confrontation Clause might mean by guaranteeing a defendant the right to confront the "witnesses against him." Wigmore (and Scalia in dicta in his dissent in *Maryland* v. *Craig*, 497 U.S. 836 [1990]) had interpreted these words as referring to witnesses at trial, and Thomas agreed that the plain meaning of the text supported this interpretation. However, Thomas went on to suggest that this pure reading might not be historically correct because of the evolution of the preconstitutional common law *and* because of the Court's own jurisprudence. Thomas described the common-law right of confrontation as developing in response to abuses such as pretrial interrogations of witnesses by magistrates outside of the defendant's presence, and use at trial of proof by deposition, letter, or accomplices' confessions (as in the infamous trial of Sir Walter Raleigh). He was less clear about whether he thought that the Confrontation Clause itself was intended to incorporate the common-law right, citing Justice Story as believing that it did, and citing some of the Court's earlier cases as indicating that the primary purpose of the clause was to prevent depositions or prosecution on the basis of ex parte affidavits, as the United States had argued. As Thomas had acknowledged earlier, he found no satisfactory evidence of how the framers intended the clause to relate to these historical developments, so any views about whether the Confrontation Clause incorporates common law must be, according to his view, based on inadequate evidence. As to the issue of hearsay, Thomas concluded that the Supreme Court had never adequately analyzed whether hearsay rule exceptions were understood at common law to be limited by a right of confrontation. But Thomas did not offer his own analysis of the common-law approach to hearsay. At this point of the argument, he returned to the text, explaining that there seems no good reason to apply the Confrontation Clause to hearsay. Concerns about reliability of evidence, according to Thomas, are not Sixth Amendment concerns, but due process concerns.

Up to this point, the opinion is a wash. The language, which Wigmore found plain, Thomas believed to be modified by a common-law right whose scope is uncertain and which may or may not have been incorporated by the Confrontation Clause. Nevertheless, Thomas forged ahead and declared that the suggestion of the United States that the Confrontation Clause should be interpreted not to apply to hearsay "is in some ways more consistent with the text and history of the Clause than our current jurisprudence." Since Thomas himself had believed that the text does not reveal a plain meaning, that the intent of the framers is unclear, and that more historical research is necessary before even the scope of the common-law right of confrontation can be defined, it is surprising that he felt able to draw any conclusions. He might have ended the opinion at this point, merely observing that the issue should be considered open to resolution in a future opinion. But Thomas wanted to resolve the question of how the Confrontation Clause should be interpreted, even though resolution was not necessary to the Court's decision in the instant case or even to his concurrence. Having voiced his attraction to the government's position, Thomas then expressed his own concern that the government's proposed definition was too vague. The government's proposal was to apply the clause to persons who provide in-court testimony or the "functional equivalent," such as affidavits, depositions, or confessions that are made in contemplation of legal proceedings. Because the "functional equivalent" language is ambiguous, Thomas proposed narrowing even the government's proposed standard in the interests of simplicity: the right of confrontation should apply to any witness who actually testifies at trial, and is implicated by extrajudicial statements "only insofar as they are contained in formalized testimonial materials, such as affidavits, depositions, prior testimony, or confessions." Thomas defended his compromise as a simple, easy-to-follow means of respecting the government's version of history as well as the results of the "vast majority" of the Court's earlier cases.

This is reckless constitutional renovation. This first flight shows that, even with Scalia's company, Thomas was not ready to solo in Scalia's specialty of using plain language and history to correct the Supreme Court's course. The logical inconsistencies in this opinion may have been due to Thomas' attempt to honor too many bases of constitutional interpretation. Had he adhered to the text in the absolutist manner Scalia had laid out in *Maryland* v. *Craig*, the approach of interpreting "witnesses against him" as referring only to witnesses at trial would have been logically defensible on a purist plain-meaning theory. Thomas' attention to history and precedent drew him to a broader interpretation. The broader interpretation he derived was not based on his account of history, which stopped before ascertaining whether the common-law right of confrontation indeed limited the use of hearsay. Alternatively, had Thomas adhered to the government's narrow explication of history, interpreting the Confrontation Clause as governed by only one clear purpose—preventing a particular English abuse—the government's proposed standard would be defensible. Thomas' broader, if not historically supported, view of the purposes of the clause and his desire to accommodate at least some of the Court's precedents, however, should have led him to conclude that the government's proposal was inappropriate or at least premature. Thomas' decision to narrow even the government's proposed standard in the interest of simplicity is also logically indefensible. If the text has no acceptable plain meaning, if the intent of the framers in adopting the clause is unknown, if the scope of the common-law right on which the clause might be based is unclear, and if even the limiting definition forged from the government's narrow view of the purposes of the clause must be shrunk before it is sufficiently practical, why is Thomas' stinting view of the clause preferable to the Court's previous compromise? Furthermore, why should any member of the Court abandon stare decisis to revise the Confrontation Clause in the ad hoc manner proposed? Thomas' approach lacks the presumably objective referents Scalia typically proffers as an alternative to stare decisis—it is not an interpretation based on the plain meaning of the text and it is not any recognizable version of originalism. Scalia's approach of binding himself to dictionary definitions and *Blackstone's* is one form of judicial conservatism; Thomas' selective use of language and history is, as his attraction to natural law philosophy prefigured, radically subjective.

Thomas' first constitutional law opinion reveals a number of assumptions underlying his constitutional interpretation, all of which surface in later opinions. First, it is clear that stare decisis is not a dominant value, although Thomas does attempt to accommodate the Court's previous holdings to a greater extent than Scalia has in many of his opinions. Second, it is equally clear that bright line rules attract him, and that he finds ambiguity a good enough reason to reject what otherwise might be a persuasive constitutional interpretation. That Thomas was willing on the basis of inconclusive text and history to shrink the Confrontation Clause, despite stare decisis, also shows an inclination to be grudging about the scope of constitutional protections, either because of an inclination to allow the government more leeway, particularly in criminal cases, or because of a desire to define a modest role for the courts, perhaps particularly the federal courts. Thomas shows no interest at all in a functional analysis of the Confrontation Clause. He is uninterested in the role the right of confrontation plays at trial and, other than relegating concerns about reliability to the Due Process Clause, shows no awareness of the interests of criminal defendants in confronting and cross-examining declarants. Thomas' view of the Confrontation Clause focuses on the manner in which the Clause might limit the government in its prosecutorial role, and not on the clause as a guarantor of individual rights. All of these assumptions continued to govern and to grow more apparent in Thomas' later constitutional opinions.

In *Hudson* v. *McMillian*, 112 S. Ct. 995 (1992), for example, Thomas wrote his first dissent in a constitutional case to express his view that, contrary to the Court's recent case law, the Eighth Amendment's ban on cruel and unusual punishment should not be found applicable to issues involving the treatment of prisoners. As he did in *White*, Thomas looked to a truncated version of history (mostly borrowed from the Court's previous opinions) to establish the proper scope of a Bill of Rights provision. As in *White*, ancient history was of greater import than the recent past. The fact that the Court's recognition of a prisoner's right not to be abused while in prison was relatively recent was, to Thomas, damning. Without the full-scale historical analysis that Scalia would have provided (compare *Payne* v. *Tennessee*, 111 S. Ct. 2597 [1991]; *Harmelin* v. *Michigan*, 111 S. Ct. 2680 [1991]; *California* v. *Hodari D.*, 111 S. Ct. 1547 [1991]), Thomas concluded that the Eighth Amendment has been fatally misinterpreted. Also as in *White*, he urged that the historical understanding of the clause be used as a rationale for narrowly interpreting the Court's role. In *White*, history was used as a reason to revise the Court's preexisting case law; in *Hudson*, Thomas interprets prior case law to be consistent with the result he would reach, despite the fact that his novel interpretation of the cases is squarely rejected by seven other Justices.

At issue in *Hudson* was a prisoner's Section 1983 claim that he had been beaten by prison guards while shackled and handcuffed. The court of appeals had dismissed Hudson's claim on the ground that he had not suffered any significant injury. The Supreme Court, in an opinion by O'Connor, held that a prisoner need not establish a serious physical injury in order to sustain an Eighth Amendment claim based on excessive use of force. The Court held that the applicable standard, derived from the case of *Whitley* v. *Albers*, 475 U.S. 312 (1986), was whether an excessive use of force constitutes an "unnecessary and wanton infliction of pain." In rejecting the idea that any previous Supreme Court case had required prisoners to prove extensive injuries as a general prerequisite to relief, O'Connor commented that to borrow the objective standard discussed in some earlier cases challenging the constitutionality of prison conditions would be to deny that there is a difference between punching a prisoner in the face and serving him unappetizing food.

Thomas' reading of the previous cases indeed denied that there was any constitutionally relevant difference between those two situations. In Thomas' view, the Court's earlier cases had established that prisoners must prove both an objective component (that an alleged injury is serious) and a subjective component (that prison officials were deliberately indifferent to the prisoner's needs) to make out an Eighth Amendment claim in any case. Thomas was unpersuaded by the argument that any references to an objective requirement were confined to prison condition cases factually distinguishable from *Hudson*. "Why," he asked, "should an objectively serious deprivation be required [in a case contending that prison overcrowding was cruel and unusual] and not here?" He was unpersuaded by the majority's answer, namely, that an attack on a prisoner unrelated to a prison's legitimate attempt to maintain order is by definition wanton and malicious.

Because the Eighth Amendment is defined with reference to society's "evolving standards of decency," Thomas offered his own personal evaluation of society's concerns with respect to prisoners. First, he contended that harsh prison conditions over a period of time would be of greater concern to society than a deprivation, or beating, inflicted on one occasion. He offered no authority for this opinion, and did not acknowledge that seven members of the Court, members of society themselves, clearly were more troubled by brutality than by unpleasant prison conditions. Additionally, Thomas asserted that society has no expectation that prisoners will have " 'unqualified' freedom from force, since forcibly keeping prisoners in detention is what prisons are all about." This observation, again not supported by reference to any authority, fails to distinguish between lawful and excessive uses of force.

At the same time that Thomas was relying on the Court's generalizations and dicta in previous cases to argue that a general objective component had been established for all cases and was now being dishonored, Thomas argued that the Court's generalizations and dicta in earlier cases concerning the subjective requirement were irrelevant, and that the Court was unwisely creating new law by applying a difficult "wanton and malicious" subjective standard to this case. Thomas asserted that most instances of prison brutality are not committed wantonly or maliciously, so that prisoners would not be able to meet what he described as a heightened subjective standard. Thomas believed that the standard was a new and difficult one because of his refusal to credit any difference between prison conditions and brutality actions. The standard he found less stringent, the "deliberate indifference" standard, had been applied to prison conditions, denials of medical treatment, and failure to protect prisoners from harm. The standard O'Connor applied in this brutality action, the "wanton and malicious" standard, was the standard applied in *Whitley* v. *Albers,* a previous brutality case where prison guards justified the level of force they had used as necessary to quell a prison riot. The standards are worded differently not because one is more difficult than the other, but because it makes no more sense to ask whether a guard who is beating a prisoner is being "deliberately indifferent" to the prisoner's needs than it would to ask whether a prison superintendent who has decided to double-bunk an overcrowded facility is being "wanton and malicious." Prison superintendents may be forced to preside over deplorable conditions because they have been allotted insufficient funds; prison guards who beat prisoners when there is no justification for using force are, as O'Connor asserts, by definition malicious. Having refused to distinguish the conditions cases and the brutality cases with respect to the question of whether an objective component should be required, Thomas was also willing to try to ask the same subjective question in both contexts.

Thomas' interpretation of the earlier cases is so procrustean, and his refusal to distinguish between prison conditions and torture so obdurate, that they can only be explained as interpretations in the service of some overriding principle. Thomas introduces his guiding principle later in the opinion: that it is the responsibility of the states to prevent brutal conduct toward prisoners and that the Eighth Amendment should not be "turned into a National Code of Prison Regulation." Because keeping all prison cases, whether they concern conditions or brutality, out of federal court is equally important to Thomas, he is unwilling to perceive any relevant differences among the cases. That Thomas is willing to extend these views to other prisoners' rights cases is demonstrated by the last paragraph of his dissent where he urges that, as in the area of habeas corpus, the Court should be inquiring only whether prisoners have been afforded due process under state law. If a prisoner's claims could be raised in state court, Thomas is willing to interpret the Eighth Amendment to require the federal courts to remain uninvolved. The Rehnquist Court's compromise, agreeing to hear the most egregious claims of prison brutality or inhumane conditions, but cutting back on the scope of the federal court relief afforded prisoners during the 1970's, had become acceptable to all of the Justices except Scalia and now Thomas.

In *Hudson* as in *White,* Thomas discusses only one point of view. Even the most conservative appointees on the federal bench had discovered that to leave prisoners' rights claims to the states was often to leave prisoners with-out any meaningful recourse for their complaints of increasingly intolerable prison conditions. Because prisoners are politically powerless, because state legislators are unwilling to adequately fund their ever expanding prisons, and because most state court judges are elected, the federal judiciary has re-mained the only realistic prospect of ensuring that treatment of prisoners is not cruel and unusual. Thomas had nothing to say about the need that im-pelled the federal judiciary to accept the unpopular task of guaranteeing minimal rights to a despised population. The members of the Court have certainly differed about how prisoners' interests should be balanced against the interests of federalism and the needs of prison administrators. But Thomas does not even mention the other side of the balance. As he interprets the Constitution, the federal courts should be alert to society's concerns about the treatment of prisoners and not to the prisoners' own concerns. More than one journalist, in reporting Thomas' opinion in *Hudson*, ironically recalled an empathetic comment that Thomas had made during his confirmation hear-ings: that as he watched prisoners being led outside his office window, he had thought that but for the grace of God, he might have been one of them.

Another feature of *Hudson* that was to become unfortunately familiar was the contentious tone of both O'Connor's and Thomas' opinions. In *White*, Rehnquist's majority opinion did not address Thomas' concurrence except by clearly rejecting the government position Thomas was championing. In *Hud-son*, Thomas' invocation of the Court's own precedents as a basis for narrow-ing the Court's approach led O'Connor to spend a section (section IIB) of her otherwise fairly short opinion responding to Thomas, describing his opinion as misapplying precedent, ignoring the body of the Court's Eighth Amend-ment jurisprudence, and resting on unfounded arguments. Thomas, in turn, refers to the majority's opinion as expanding the ban on cruel and unusual punishment "beyond all bounds of history and precedent" in service of the "pervasive view that the Federal Constitution must address all ills in our society." Thomas does not allow for the possibility that reasonable people might differ about how to interpret prior case law—he sees interpretation questions as a matter of right or wrong. The self-righteous tone of Thomas' and O'Connor's disputes about the meaning of case law was to become shrill by the end of the term.

Thomas' general affinity with Scalia lasted throughout his first term on the Court. He agreed with Scalia in over 85 per cent of cases; on those cases where they voted on the same side, Thomas almost always joined the same opinion as Scalia. This placed Thomas and Scalia in a fairly extreme right-wing position on the Court, often in the company of Chief Justice Rehnquist, and sometimes with various other fairly conservative members of the Court. Out of twenty-three opinions Thomas wrote during his first term, he wrote for the majority nine times, dissented six times, and concurred eight times.

However, Thomas did disagree with Scalia in several important cases, providing a deciding vote on issues involving criminal procedure, habeas corpus, and federal jurisdiction. Thomas wrote most of his opinions in constitutional criminal procedure cases, where he continued to construe criminal defendants' rights narrowly. In *Doggett* v. *United States*, 112 S. Ct. 2686 (1992), for example, Thomas wrote a dissent from a five-to-four decision finding that Doggett could raise a speedy trial claim based on the government's failure to try him for eight and one-half years, without having to prove that he had been prejudiced by the delay. Once again, Thomas invoked common-law history to support his claim that the speedy trial guarantee was not intended to prevent the type of harm suffered by the defendant in this case. Once again, Thomas rejected the Court's recent jurisprudence as too much of a compromise between two potential extreme interpretations of the text, advocating the substitution of a new compromise. Once again, Thomas selectively used dicta from some of the Court's precedents as a basis for arguing that positions taken in other cases should not be followed. And once again, the argument Thomas accepted, in the face of case law that at least five members of the Court found clearly dispositive, was an argument made by the United States.

The Court had already limited the scope of application of the speedy trial guarantee by finding that speedy trial claims could not be raised by "accused" who were arrested but not yet indicted (see *United States* v. *Marion*, 404 U.S. 307 [1971]), and that claims by those eligible would be evaluated according to a four-factor test, considering length of the delay, reason for the delay, whether the defendant had asserted his right to a speedy trial, and whether the delay had prejudiced the defendant's ability to defend himself (see *Barker* v. *Wingo*, 407 U.S. 514 [1972]). Doggett had been indicted, so *Marion* did not apply; the lower courts held that the government had been negligent in prosecuting him and that the *Barker* factors had been met, except that the lower courts disagreed about whether Doggett had shown sufficiently that the delay had prejudiced his ability to defend himself. The United States argued that, despite *Barker*'s dicta about the relevance of prejudice, the speedy trial guarantee should not be understood to protect the defendant's interest in fair adjudication, precisely because cases like *Marion* had held that interest not in itself a sufficient basis to allow defendants who had not yet been indicted to raise speedy trial claims. Justice Souter's opinion found the issue of the sufficiency of the presumptive prejudice Doggett suffered a somewhat difficult question, but easily found the government's argument about the meaning of the speedy trial guarantee to be foreclosed by *Barker*, noting that the dicta the government quoted from cases like *Marion* only addressed whether pre-indictment delay came within the scope of the speedy trial guarantee.

Thomas' dissent, joined by Scalia and Rehnquist, prefers the out-of-context dicta in *Marion* to the explicit ruling of *Barker* v. *Wingo* that impairment of a defendant's ability to present a defense, so long as the defendant suffered that impairment after he had been charged, is cognizable under the speedy trial guarantee. Thomas again looked to the Due Process Clause (and the statute of limitations) as the appropriate locus of any concern about fairness to defendants, and therefore did not discuss the defendant's interest in fair adjudication at all. Unlike *White*, Thomas did not attempt a plain-language argument here; the plain language of the speedy trial guarantee would seem to cut the other way. Doggett plainly was accused for eight and one-half years before he was tried, regardless of whether or not he knew he had been accused. What bothered Thomas was that Doggett was unaware of the accusation against him and therefore was not suffering the anxiety that the speedy trial guarantee was intended to prevent. The government in *White* had promoted the notion that each clause has one overriding purpose, and for Thomas, if the defendant was not anxious and if fairness concerns are relegated to the Due Process Clause, the speedy trial guarantee becomes irrelevant, unless the defendant has a right of repose independent of either of those concerns. This is the only issue on which Thomas offers a bit of common-law history, concluding that whatever right to repose defendants might have had at common law is adequately protected by statutes of limitations.

At the end of his opinion in *Doggett*, Thomas set out a credo already foreshadowed by his opinions in *White* and *Hudson*: "Our constitutional law has become ever more complex in recent decades. That is, in itself, a regrettable development, for the law draws force from the clarity of its command and the certainty of its application." Thomas expressed his belief that complex constitutional law, like the multifactor balancing test of *Barker*, "obscures . . . foundational principles" and generates new law in a way that threatens to "transform the courts of the land into boards of law enforcement supervision." But again, Thomas is unwilling to follow his critique of this expanded judicial role as far as Scalia might. He did not question *Barker*'s approach, he said, but only its scope.

Thomas' technique of acknowledging most of precedent and relocating all of the considerations of fairness he has drained from the Sixth Amendment to the Due Process Clause does not augur a limited judicial role. The Court will still have to decide most of the same issues, but on the basis of a vaguer guarantee whose history and language are less instructive. With due process as the ultimate and ubiquitous issue, judges still must make subjective choices among values competing for judicial protection.

It was only a matter of months before Thomas found a value that he believed the Constitution protected even in the absence of specific language or history, that warranted expansive judicial review, and that caused him to vote against Scalia: the prevention of prosecutorial overreaching. Thomas had asserted in *Doggett* that it is not the Court's role to "slap the Government on the wrist for sloppy work or misplaced priorities." But two federal criminal cases, *Jacobson* v. *United States*, 112 S. Ct. 1535 (1992), and *Williams* v. *United States*, 112 S. Ct. 1735 (1992), involving what Thomas seemed to view as prosecutorial misconduct, presented a different situation. Jacobson, a Nebraska farmer, had ordered child pornography through the mail and defended himself on the ground that he had been entrapped. Customs officials had spent over two years sending Jacobson mailings from fictitious organizations purporting to survey his literary tastes, expressing the view that people have the right to read what they want without interference by the government and inviting him to order a variety of sexually explicit materials. A dissenting opinion, written by Justice O'Connor and joined by Kennedy, Rehnquist, and Scalia, found sufficient evidence that Jacobson was predisposed to receive illegal pornography to uphold the jury's verdict. Thomas cast the deciding vote to overturn Jacobson's conviction, joining Justice White's opinion, which held that the government had gone too far in creating Jacobson's predisposition, without adding any comments of his own.

One month later, Thomas again voted in favor of expanding judicial control over possible prosecutorial misfeasance, although this time he joined a four-Justice minority dissenting from Scalia's majority opinion (*Williams* v. *United States*). The issue in this federal prosecution was whether a prosecutor had any obligation to present to a grand jury substantial exculpatory information within its possession. Scalia argued that to impose such an obligation on prosecutors would be inconsistent with history, turning the grand jury from an accusatory to an adjudicatory body, and would also overinvolve the courts with the work of the grand jury. Although the grand jury is technically an arm of the court, Scalia observed that the relationship had always been "at arm's length" and should continue to be so in order to promote grand jury independence. Justice Stevens' dissent, which Thomas joined, argued on the basis of the Court's recent case law that the courts do have a responsibility to prevent "unrestrained prosecutorial misconduct" in the grand jury, such as failing to present substantial exculpatory evidence, or knowingly relying on perjured testimony. Stevens did not discuss the history of the Fifth Amendment's grand jury provision, the language of that provision (which does not suggest any particular relationship of grand jury, prosecutor, and court), or common-law practices. His hoariest cite was to a 1919 case characterizing the federal grand jury as a part of the judicial branch.

The prosecutorial misconduct cases confirmed what Thomas' own opinions in *White* and *Doggett* had suggested, that despite their general affinity, Thomas was intent on preserving his independence both from Scalia's positions in particular cases and from Scalia's extreme but consistent version of originalism. Thomas' vote could be won by defendants even where Scalia's reading of history, text, and concern about the judicial role would have led to support for the government's position. Although Thomas was attracted to Scalia's lodestars of plain language and historical meaning in the interpretation of any individual constitutional guarantee, he clearly was also attracted to some conflicting principle of the judicial role in protecting defendants against unfair prosecutions—perhaps a view more rooted in the Due Process

Clause than in individual Bill of Rights provisions, like the jurisprudence of John Marshall Harlan. To serve whatever interests Thomas saw reflected in such ambiguous guarantees as the Due Process Clause (and perhaps natural law), Thomas was willing to cut himself loose from the moorings of Scalia's objective referents. And although Thomas was prepared to jettison much of the Court's recent case law if he believed it to be incorrect, his greater respect for stare decisis led him to seek compromises between what he regarded as an ideal constitutional interpretation and what he interpreted as current law. His echoing of Scalia's excoriations of judicial activism in any form rang hollow in light of his endorsement of the Court's role in protection of some rights not explicitly articulated in the Constitution. Because Thomas did not write opinions in any of the cases in which he voted in favor of defendants, it is impossible to tell how he would have rationalized his positions. Throughout the remainder of his first term, it also proved impossible to identify the principles by which Thomas chose nonexplicit, non–historically dictated rights to defend, or the principles by which he decided how closely to adhere to stare decisis.

Because Thomas' prodefendant votes came in federal criminal prosecutions, one possible explanation was that Thomas' view of federalism had led him to differentiate the responsibilities of the Court in federal and in state cases. Indeed, Thomas voted in favor of the state in all of the state criminal cases the Court reviewed during his first term. This support for the state included all of the capital cases the Court considered during his first term. In one capital case, Thomas joined Scalia's dissent from a six-Justice opinion holding that capital defendants have a right to ask potential jurors on voir dire whether they would automatically impose the death penalty once they had voted to convict, or whether they would be willing to consider mitigating circumstances (*Morgan* v. *Illinois*, 112 S. Ct. 2222 [1992]). In another, he joined Rehnquist and White in an opinion finding harmless an Eighth Amendment error (use of an impermissible capital sentencing factor) that a majority of the Court found to provide a basis for vacating and remanding a capital sentence (*Sochor* v. *Florida*, 112 S. Ct. 2114 [1992]). In the latter case, Thomas did not associate himself with Scalia's dissent, reiterating his previously expressed view that the Court's capital punishment jurisprudence was inconsistent and could best be corrected by overruling cases requiring capital sentencers to consider mitigating evidence (see *Walton* v. *Arizona*, 497 U.S. 639 [1990]).

The first capital case in which Thomas wrote an opinion was *Dawson* v. *Delaware*, 112 S. Ct. 1093 (1992), where he was the only Justice to support the state's position. Justice Rehnquist's majority opinion held that the First and Fourteenth Amendments prohibited the introduction of a capital defendant's membership in an organization called the Aryan Brotherhood at a capital sentencing proceeding where membership in the group was not relevant to the crime. Thomas believed that the evidence of the defendant's membership in a white supremacist organization was relevant to sentencing because it reflected the defendant's character and thus rebutted positive character evidence the defendant had introduced. Thomas came close to endorsing Scalia's position in *Walton* by complaining that the Court's jurisprudence set a double standard, allowing defendants to introduce mitigating evidence, such as group associations, but not allowing the prosecution to introduce membership in less benign groups.

More interesting than any disagreement about the relevance of the evidence, however, was Thomas' bold assertion that if the Court believed that relevance was a significant inquiry, invoking the First Amendment added nothing to the analysis. As in his earlier opinions in criminal cases, Thomas defined the issue presented as coming within the purview of the Due Process Clause rather than the particular constitutional provision invoked. He accused the majority of "incorrectly" citing *Schware* v. *Board of Bar Examiners of New Mexico*, 353 U.S. 232 (1957), for the proposition that the First Amendment prohibited consideration of an applicant's membership in the Communist party with respect to the issue of the applicant's moral character. Thomas denied that *Schware* implicated the First Amendment, describing the Court as having decided that Communist party membership was not relevant to fitness for admission to the bar and then having found that the applicant had been denied due process because, without the evidence of Communist party membership, there was no evidence of poor moral character sufficient to exclude the applicant. Thomas seems unconcerned, once again, that his expansive vision of the Due Process Clause would require the courts, including the Supreme Court, to evaluate whether any piece of evidence in any proceeding, state or federal, criminal, civil, or administrative, is sufficiently relevant or unduly prejudicial. Thomas is equally untroubled by the fact that his constricted view of the applicability of the First Amendment is at odds with the view of eight members of the Court, including Antonin Scalia. As in earlier cases, his position is made possible because the majority's view represents a compromise between two pure but extreme positions. Rehnquist discusses the Court's freedom of association cases as generally preventing the state from imposing a penalty on group membership, but as not precluding all possibility of a prosecutor introducing such evidence in a criminal prosecution where the group membership is highly relevant to what is being proved (perhaps the intent element in a bias-crime prosecution, for example). Thomas prefers to find the First Amendment irrelevant rather than choose whether to honor the Court's previous cases precluding adverse use of an individual's associations, or whether to live with a First Amendment theory—that a high degree of relevance might justify introduction of a defendant's associations—unconstrained by a bright line.

The other state criminal prosecutions considered during the 1991 term included a trio of cases concerning the intersection of mental illness or incompetence and the state's criminal authority. Thomas voted to allow a state to impose the burden of proof of incompetence on a capital defendant (*Medina v. California*, 112 S. Ct. 2572 [1992]); to allow a state to require a defendant found not guilty by reason of insanity to prove that he is not dangerous as well as that he is no longer mentally ill as a precondition for release (*Foucha v. Louisiana*, 112 S. Ct. 1780 [1992]); and to uphold the conviction of a defendant tried while under the influence of antipsychotic medication (*Riggins* v. *Nevada*, 112 S. Ct. 1810 [1992]). In *Medina*, Thomas' vote put him in a seven-to-two majority; in *Foucha*, in a four-vote minority; in *Riggins*, in a two-vote minority. In both *Foucha* and *Riggins*, Thomas wrote his own dissents. His opinion in *Foucha*, joined by Rehnquist and Scalia, selectively used the Court's precedents to argue that this new decision was not consistent with prior case law. Thomas continued to show great interest in recharacterizing the claims raised. While White's majority opinion addressed the problem as one of procedural due process, Thomas preferred to recast the problem as one of equal protection (whether those found not guilty by reason of insanity, once sane, may be treated differently from the civilly committed). This new analysis does not seem to make any difference, since what is at stake is procedure. In addressing the substantive due process claim, Thomas admonished the Court for not stating whether or not a fundamental right is at stake that would entitle Foucha to strict scrutiny of the state practice. Refining his approach to the Due Process Clause, Thomas advocated as a standard of review that the state practice here should be found to be unconstitutional only if it denies due process by "offending some principle of justice so rooted in the traditions and conscience of our people as to be ranked as fundamental" (*Snyder* v. *Massachusetts*, 291 U.S. 97, at 105 [1934]). As evidence that the right of a person found not guilty by reason of insanity to be free from indefinite commitment is not fundamental, Thomas asserted that a procedure similar to Louisiana's is embodied in the American Law Institute's Model Penal Code, adopted by eleven states.

Thomas' description of the state legislation drew a response from Justice O'Connor who, in a concurring opinion, sharply distinguished away seven of the eleven state laws Thomas had cited and criticized the breadth of the dissenters' position. (She concurred with the majority, but also agreed with the dissent that those found not guilty by reason of insanity had much in common with convicted defendants, and that a state might be allowed to continue to confine them if the nature and duration of their confinement were tailored to reflect society's concern with dangerousness.)

O'Connor and Thomas disagreed even more vehemently about both the law and the facts in *Riggins*, decided the same day as *Foucha*. O'Connor's majority opinion found that Riggins had been denied rights under the Sixth Amendment by being compelled to take antipsychotic medication during his trial. In a painfully limited opinion, O'Connor declined to address Riggins' argument that medicating him against his will in order to render him competent to stand trial violated his Eighth Amendment rights. O'Connor also did not decide whether Riggins had a due process right to refuse unwanted antipsychotic drugs, finding that the state might, at least in some circumstances, have a sufficiently strong countervailing interest in trying otherwise incompetent defendants. Finding that there was a risk in this case that Riggins' right to a fair trial had been compromised because the jury could not observe his natural demeanor, O'Connor also declined to find that such prejudice constitutes a denial of Sixth or Fourteenth Amendment rights because she thought that trial prejudice in some cases might be justified by the state's interest in bringing an otherwise incompetent defendant to trial. Avoiding all of these ultimate questions, O'Connor fell back on the procedural point that the trial court had not determined whether the amount of antipsychotic drugs prescribed in this case had in fact been medically necessary to render Riggins competent and remanded the case for additional proceedings.

O'Connor's cautious approach was joined by five other members of the Court who were willing to defer the larger questions presented and by Justice Kennedy, who concurred in the judgment. Thomas' dissent was joined only by Justice Scalia, and only in part. In the section of the dissent that Scalia disavowed, Thomas concluded that the factual record did not support Riggins' claim that he had been compelled to take the medication involuntarily. Continuing the theme he had raised in *Foucha*, Thomas also attacked what he characterized as the majority's strict scrutiny of the procedures necessary (a charge O'Connor disputed in her opinion), again selectively relying on the Court's precedents to argue about whether the Court was expanding precedent. Thomas concluded that Riggins did have a fair trial and therefore had no due process claim in that respect. He also discounted Riggins' claim of a substantive due process right to refuse unwanted medication, finding that the claim had not been properly raised below, and that the only appropriate remedy for that claim would have been an injunction against continuation of the drugs, not reversal of Riggins' conviction. With a greater majority agreeing with her conclusions, O'Connor spent little time addressing Thomas' different interpretations of the record and the law.

Thomas' disagreements with O'Connor in these state criminal cases were notable in part because O'Connor had become identified with a strong stance on federalism, a concern Thomas also valued. She tended to support states' claims of a right to operate in their own sphere of influence. In *New York* v. *United States*, 112 S. Ct. 2408 (1992), for example, O'Connor found unconstitutional legislation based on an interstate agreement where Congress had claimed the right to instruct a state to legislate under certain circumstances. (Under the act, a state could be required to take title to radioactive waste if the state did not meet its obligations to cooperate in regional or individual state disposal of those wastes.) Thomas joined O'Connor's opinion, which contained the seeds of a broader view of the Tenth Amendment than the Court had espoused since it had overruled the case of *National League of Cities* v. *Usery*, 426 U.S. 833 (1976), in *Garcia* v. *San Antonio Metropolitan Transit Au-*

thority, 469 U.S. 528 (1985). In some instances, Thomas found federalism issues even where O'Connor did not. His concern for federalism led him to write a dissent in a case that he regarded as an unwarranted expansion of federal criminal jurisdiction. In *Evans* v. *United States,* 112 S. Ct. 1881 (1992), for example, he stridently accused the majority (Stevens, writing for six members of the Court) of misapprehending and disregarding history and violating every known principle of statutory construction.

O'Connor's concern for federalism was mitigated by her concern for countervailing individual rights, as shown in *Foucha* and *Riggins,* and as shown even more dramatically in the Court's habeas corpus jurisprudence. In a series of cases, the Supreme Court, frequently led by O'Connor, had been narrowing the circumstances under which the federal courts would hear state prisoners' challenges to their convictions (see, for example, *Teague* v. *Lane,* 489 U.S. 288 [1989]). Several cases during Thomas' first term tested how broadly the Court would define its limiting doctrines. In each case, Thomas disagreed with O'Connor's assessment of how to balance the interests of federalism and finality against the interests of individuals in freedom from unconstitutionally obtained convictions, and in each case he voted in favor of further restrictions on habeas corpus. In *Stringer* v. *Black,* 112 S. Ct. 1130 (1992), a six-person majority including O'Connor held that a capital defendant's Eighth Amendment claim was not a new claim within the meaning of *Teague* v. *Lane* and therefore could be raised on habeas corpus. Thomas and Scalia joined Justice Souter in dissent. Thomas provided the deciding vote in *Keeney* v. *Tamayo-Reyes,* 112 S. Ct. 1715 (1992), which required a habeas petitioner to show "cause and prejudice" before obtaining an evidentiary hearing on a claim for which he had failed to develop a factual record in the state courts. O'Connor, joined by three other Justices, dissented, finding the majority's decision irreconcilable with the Court's precedents and with the will of Congress. But Thomas' differences with O'Connor reached a peak in *Wright* v. *West,* 112 S. Ct. 2482 (1992), despite the fact that both agreed on the disposition of the case before the Court. The question in that case was whether a federal habeas corpus court evaluating evidence at a petitioner's state trial to determine whether the evidence was so insufficient as to constitute a denial of due process should use a de novo standard of review, or a standard more deferential to the state courts on an issue involving mixed questions of law and facts. Because the Court unanimously agreed that the evidence in the case at bar was sufficient under either standard, the Court did not need to reach the issue of standard of review.

Thomas, writing an opinion for what might have been a unanimous Court, wrote an opinion that only Scalia and Rehnquist signed. With four separate concurring opinions, Justice O'Connor's opinion for three Justices was written "only to express disagreement with certain statements in Justice Thomas' extended discussion . . . of this Court's habeas corpus jurisprudence." Thomas' account of the Court's habeas case law, repeatedly attacked bluntly by O'Connor as incorrect, described the earlier cases, particularly the recent cases on retroactivity, as having already called into question the standard of de novo review. Consuming almost as much space as Thomas' opinion itself are seven lengthy footnotes in which Thomas defends his opinion against O'Connor's charges of inaccuracy. This pitched battle, over an issue not necessary to the decision of the case, suggests that by June, Thomas was steeled against compromise. Another way to account for O'Connor's criticisms would have been to rewrite Thomas' opinion in a way that would have permitted it to represent a consensus of the Court's views on the issue presented by the case. But as his early opinions had begun to show, Thomas was too anxious to revise the law, too dismissive of the value of consensus, or simply too arrogant to write a new draft of his opinion that would have provoked less disagreement on unnecessary case law exegesis. The combative stance of *Wright* v. *West* and even the harsh language of Thomas' dissent in *Evans* suggested that the Court's much awaited decisions in the abortion and school prayer cases, not yet released at this date, would reflect a sharply divided Court.

In nonconstitutional cases, Thomas' votes also quickly revealed patterns. Thomas regularly voted to limit federal jurisdiction and remedies in a variety of ways. He dissented from a ruling that an immunity defense was unavailable to certain private defendants in civil rights actions (*Wyatt* v. *Cole*, 112 S. Ct. 1827 [1992]); dissented from a decision allowing original Supreme Court jurisdiction, voicing a concern about opening the floodgates of original jurisdiction (*Wyoming* v. *Oklahoma*, 112 S. Ct. 789 [1992]); voted with a majority of the Court to deny standing to members of an environmental group who wished to challenge federal agency policy (*Lujan* v. *Defenders of Wildlife*, 112 S. Ct. 2130 [1992]); voted with a majority to find that the Adoption Assistance Act does not create a private right of action (*Suter* v. *Artist M*, 112 S. Ct. 1360 [1992]); and voted with a majority to allow district courts expansive powers to dismiss pro se actions found to be frivolous (*Denton* v. *Hernandez*, 112 S. Ct. 1728 [1992]). Given the positions that Thomas had taken as the head of the EEOC, it was not surprising that he would dissent from a decision expansively interpreting the availability of a damages remedy in Title VII harassment actions (*Franklin* v. *Gwinnett*, 112 S. Ct. 1028 [1992]). It was more surprising that the former head of a federal agency showed a marked reluctance to support agency authority or to defer to agencies' interpretations of their statutory mandates (see *Lechmere* v. *National Labor Relations Board*, 112 S. Ct. 841 [1992], where Thomas' majority opinion limiting federal agency power drew a dissent from White, Blackmun, and Stevens, who advocated greater deference to the agency; *National Railroad Passenger Corporation* v. *Boston & Maine Corporation*, 112 S. Ct. 1394 [1992], where Thomas dissented from a finding that the Interstate Commerce Commission had reasonably interpreted the governing statute, contending that the agency's reasoning was actually a post hoc rationalization; and *Federal Trade Commission* v. *Ticor Title Co.*, 112 S.

Ct. 2169 [1992], where Thomas dissented from a finding giving primacy to the Federal Trade Commission rather than immunities created by state law, on the ground that the states should be allowed flexibility and not be burdened by federal intervention). Despite his abiding concerns for curtailing federal court and agency jurisdiction, however, Thomas was willing to cast his vote in opposition to these interests in some cases where his interpretation of the governing statutes led him to that result. In *American National Red Cross* v. *S. G.*, 112 S. Ct. 2465 (1992), for example, Thomas provided the deciding vote in a five-to-four decision holding, over a dissent written by Scalia, that the Red Cross charter confers original federal jurisdiction over suits against the Red Cross. Thomas also supported federal preemption in instances where he believed that the relevant federal legislation required that result (see *Morales* v. *Trans World Airlines*, 112 S. Ct. 2031 [1992], where Thomas was the deciding vote; and *Cipollone* v. *Liggett Group, Inc.*, 112 S. Ct. 2608 [1992], where he dissented in part from a decision holding that federal law did not preempt certain state law actions against cigarette manufacturers). But he opposed findings of preemption under other statutes (see *Gade* v. *National Solid Wastes Management Association*, 112 S. Ct. 2374 (1992), where he dissented from a finding of preemption in a five-to-four decision where Scalia voted with the majority).

There were too few civil procedure or evidence cases to evaluate Thomas' views in those areas, although in *United States* v. *Salerno*, 112 S. Ct. 2503 (1992), Thomas wrote an opinion for an eight-Justice majority holding that former testimony may not be introduced under Rule 804(b)(1) without a showing of "similar motive." It was clear that Thomas' eclectic approach to statutory interpretation, the chief feature of which was apparent total self-confidence, would continue to develop as applied to other statutes and rules.

Given Thomas' background, it is noteworthy that the only cases during his first term that Thomas seemed to find difficult, the only cases in which he expressed any significant doubt about which result was the most desirable, were cases involving race. There were no cases raising questions about affirmative action during Thomas' first term on the Court, so his views on that subject were not put to the test. Thomas had joined the Court after the argument in *Freeman* v. *Pitts*, 112 S. Ct. 1430 (1992), an important case concerning the extent of the federal courts' continuing supervisory role in school desegregation cases, so he did not participate in that opinion. Another case in which Thomas did participate raised issues about continuing segregation at the college level in Mississippi. In *United States* v. *Fordice*, 112 S. Ct. 2727 (1992), an almost unanimous Court (Scalia dissented in part) held that Mississippi had not met its obligation to dismantle its formerly segregated university school system, and remanded the case for fuller exploration of state practices that might be contributing to continued de facto segregation, including an examination of the state's policy of funding three historically black schools. Thomas wrote a concurring opinion expressing, for the first time on the Court, his concerns about the radical integrationist policies he had opposed before joining the Court. His concurring opinion suggested that the standards for judging state efforts to desegregate schools at the university level should differ from the standards used to judge the desegregation of lower schools. Most significantly, Thomas wrote to declare that the Court's opinion should not be taken to foreclose the possibility that a sound educational justification might exist for maintaining the black colleges *"as such"* (emphasis in original). Thomas wrote eloquently of the black colleges as a symbol of the highest attainments of black culture, and expressed his hope that the black colleges, which had sustained black students during segregation, would not be "themselves destroyed in an effort to combat its vestiges." The opinion leaves open the possibility that Thomas might not concur with the colorblind approach to race advocated by some members of the Court, including Scalia.

The other opinion in which Thomas identified himself with an issue concerning race was *Georgia* v. *McCollum*, 112 S. Ct. 2348 (1992). The state criminal defendants in that case were a white couple who, charged with assaulting two blacks, had used their peremptory challenges during jury selection to exclude blacks from the jury. The Court had held during the previous term, in *Edmonson* v. *Leesville Concrete Co.*, 111 S. Ct. 2077 (1991), that peremptory challenges by parties in a civil action involve sufficient state action to preclude their use in a racially discriminatory fashion. Only Justice O'Connor thought that the result in *McCollum* was not dictated by *Edmonson*, because she believed that criminal defendants should have greater leeway in jury selection. Scalia dissented on the ground that he believed *Edmonson* was wrongly decided and should be overturned. Rehnquist concurred, stating that although he believed *Edmonson* had been wrong, he felt bound by stare decisis. Thomas came down in between Rehnquist and Scalia. He declared that "as a matter of first impression" he thought that he would have agreed with the dissent, but that he considered himself bound by *Edmonson* for the formal reason that the respondents had not challenged that decision. Thomas' concurring opinion goes on to express dissatisfaction with the Court's jurisprudence limiting the use of peremptory challenges, sharing O'Connor's concern that what began as an attempt to prevent the prosecution from disadvantaging a black defendant by excusing all black prospective jurors had now been perverted to value the rights of jurors over the rights of defendants. Unlike Thurgood Marshall, who in a concurring opinion in *Batson* v. *Kentucky*, 476 U.S. 79 (1986), had advocated that the peremptory challenge system be found unconstitutional, Thomas predicted that black defendants would rue the day when the Court started down the path that he saw as inevitably leading to the disallowance of peremptory challenges. Marshall had viewed the peremptory challenge as a shield for racial discrimination; Thomas viewed it as a sword for defendants to use in their attempt to select an unbiased jury. Where Marshall saw a way in which the courts could aid the antidiscrimination effort by invalidating the peremptory challege system, Thomas saw in peremptory challenges, as he had seen in the black colleges in Mississippi, an opportunity for self-help.

Unusually, Thomas' opinion in *McCollum* does not present any alternative and does not attempt to identify precisely where, or even whether, the Court went wrong. The tone of this opinion is reflective rather than argumentative and exudes ambivalence. It is clear from these two opinions that race remains and is likely to remain a troubling issue for Thomas, but one on which he feels himself to have a unique perspective on the Court. Although unlikely to express his concerns about race in the same manner in which Marshall expressed his, Thomas clearly was willing to identify himself as having a special concern with these issues.

The most controversial cases on the Court's docket during the 1991 term—First Amendment cases involving freedom of expression and of religion, and a major case on abortion rights—were not decided until late June. In the free expression case, *R. A. V. v. City of St. Paul*, 112 S. Ct. 2538 (1992), a unanimous Court declared unconstitutional an ordinance prohibiting hate crimes. Thomas cast the deciding vote giving a majority to those who endorsed Scalia's opinion finding a First Amendment violation based on a broad rationale (that the ordinance punished on the basis of the content of one's expressions) rather than the narrower basis urged by four members of the Court (that the ordinance was overbroad). The expansiveness of the Court's opinion cast doubt on the constitutionality of hate-crime legislation throughout the country, rather than focusing only on the language of the ordinance at issue. Here again, Thomas preferred to declare a far-reaching rule of constitutional law rather than to adopt a more conservative one-step-at-a-time approach.

In a pair of freedom of expression cases, *International Society for Krishna Consciousness, Inc. v. Lee*, 112 S. Ct. 2701 (1992), and *Lee v. International Society for Krishna Consciousness, Inc.*, 112 S. Ct. 2709 (1992), Thomas voted with the majority to find that airports are not a public forum and that a reasonable ban on a religious group's solicitation at airports was therefore constitutional, but then joined Scalia, Rehnquist, and White in dissenting from a holding that a ban on dissemination of literature did violate the First Amendment. While Thomas had not yet personally written on the First Amendment, it seemed apparent that the approach to constitutional adjudication he had derived in the criminal cases would carry over and lead him to a narrow interpretation of the limitations the First Amendment imposes on the states.

The alliance of Thomas, Scalia, Rehnquist, and White on constitutional interpretation came close to overturning the Supreme Court's prevailing approach in the two most closely watched cases of the term, *Lee v. Weisman*, 112 S. Ct. 2649 (1992), and *Planned Parenthood of Southeastern Pennsylvania v. Casey*, 112 S. Ct. 2791 (1992). *Weisman* considered the contention that including a prayer by clergy at a public school graduation violated the Establishment Clause. Petitioners and the United States as amicus curiae invited the Court to reformulate the test it applied in Establishment Clause cases, derived from *Lemon v. Kurtzman*, 403 U.S. 602 (1971), in favor of a test that would allow the states more leeway to allow opportunities for religious observance that the state did not consider coercive. Justice Kennedy's majority declined the invitation, stating, with purposeful obtuseness, that it was unnecessary to reconsider *Lemon* because the law was not unclear. The law under *Lemon* dictated the result in this case. Concurring opinions by Justices Blackmun and Souter addressed the government's position more directly, arguing that there was no good reason to reconsider *Lemon*. Scalia's dissent, joined by Rehnquist, White, and Thomas, pointed out that the majority's opinions were "conspicuously bereft of history," by which of course he meant something other than the history of the Court's case law. The dissenters, at considerable length, disagreed with the Court's approach to Establishment Clause cases (the application of the *Lemon* test), and even disagreed that the Court was applying the *Lemon* test. Underlying this discussion was Scalia's credo: "our Nation's protection, that fortress which is our Constitution, cannot possibly rest upon the changeable philosophical predilections of the Justices of this Court, but must have deeper foundations in the historic practices of our people."

This historical approach led the same group of four dissenters to vote to overrule *Roe v. Wade*, 410 U.S. 113 (1973), the case in which the Supreme Court had declared women to have a constitutionally protected right to choose to have an abortion. In *Planned Parenthood of Southeastern Pennsylvania v. Casey*, the last opinion of Thomas' first term, Thomas joined dissents written by both Rehnquist and Scalia which declared *Roe v. Wade* to have been mistaken as a matter of history, judicial philosophy, and social policy. The holding in *Roe v. Wade* had been under continuous assault for close to twenty years as Supreme Court nominees had been grilled by Republican presidents and a Democratic Senate about their views on abortion. Some nominees, like Thomas and Souter, had denied having formed any opinion that would affect them as judges, but were believed, because of their conservative judicial philosophies, to be likely to vote to overturn the decision. Others had actually expressed some antipathy toward abortion rights, although prudently declining to prejudge cases while speaking with the Senate Judiciary Committee or the press. To the surprise of many, five members of the Court nevertheless refused to join Scalia, Rehnquist, Thomas, and White, and voted to retain "the essential holding" of *Roe v. Wade*.

The issue on which the Court was most deeply divided, as the work of the term had shown, was the significance of stare decisis. Justice O'Connor, writing for a bare majority, noted the reservations of some members of the Court who might not have voted with the majority in *Roe v. Wade*. But because *Roe v. Wade* had been decided, her opinion asks a different question:

under what circumstances should the Court be willing to overrule a previously decided case? O'Connor sets forth her own credo, her own analysis of the manner in which the course of the Court's previous decisions provides a momentum and a protection against judicial subjectivity, and her description of the circumstances under which a Justice is warranted in fighting the current of previous case law and changing direction. After the *Casey* opinion, O'Connor, Kennedy, and Souter were hailed as the new moderately conservative center of the Court. Souter had voted to uphold *Roe* v. *Wade* and still had not revealed whether he agreed with that decision. Thomas, on the other hand, made clear his agreement with Scalia that being correct is more important than being consistent and he disagreed with the holding of *Roe* v. *Wade*.

More important than the agreement or disagreement with the results in particular cases was the willingness of four members of the Court to radically reconstruct constitutional law by adopting Scalia's principle of the use of history as judicial stabilizer rather than O'Connor's principle of respecting stare decisis. With one more vote, the Supreme Court seemed likely to change the face of constitutional law dramatically.

At the beginning of Clarence Thomas' second term on the Court, a Democratic president, Bill Clinton, was elected and Court watchers speculated that the momentum toward radical change on the Court, in which Thomas was playing a significant part, had died. The next appointment might determine whether Thomas was likely to remain in a dissenting corner with Scalia and Rehnquist, or whether his views would more often command a majority. As long as the composition of the Court remained the same, radical change seemed unlikely, particularly because during the 1992 term the Court seemed inclined to avoid cases that might provide an occasion for an overhaul of the Constitution. Thomas played a significant role in shaping the Court's docket, too. In the opening months of his second term, for example, Thomas deserted his fellow dissenters in *Planned Parenthood* to vote against granting certiorari in *Ada* v. *Guam Society of Obstetricians and Gynecologists*, 113 S. Ct. (missing page no.) (1992), a case in which the Ninth Circuit had relied on *Planned Parenthood* to find the Guam abortion law unconstitutional. Thomas' respect for stare decisis (or perhaps his views about futility) had led him to refuse to provide the necessary vote for the Court to revisit the issue of abortion.

In less than one term, Thomas' role on the Court had become clear. He was precisely who he had appeared to be during his confirmation hearings—a fairly radical conservative, but a conservative who retained his racial identity. The minor surprises were to be found between the lines of Thomas' growing body of opinions. The Scalia disciple had an independent streak; the judicial conservative was willing to entertain highly subjective exceptions to a presumptively originalist philosophy. The Justice who was quiet at argument had rapidly developed a self-confident and bold, if not always meticulous or modulated, judicial voice. The questions to be answered in later terms concerned how Thomas would define the principles that drew him away from

Scalia's philosophy—when to depart from history, when to refuse to overrule a result one would not have reached, and when to promote activism on a typically conservative Court.

SELECTED BIBLIOGRAPHY

Biographical material on Clarence Thomas and discussion of some of his views may be found in *Clarence Thomas: Confronting the Future, Selections from the senate Confirmation Hearings and Prior Speeches* (L. Gordon Crovitz, ed., Washington, D.C.: Regnery Gateway, 1992) and Timothy M. Phelps and Helen Winternitz, *Capitol Games* (New York: Hyperion, 1992). Additional discussion of the Thomas confirmation hearings and the confirmation hearing process in general may be found in Paul Simon, *Advice & Consent: Clarence Thomas, Robert Bork and the Intriguing History of the Supreme Court's Nomination Battles* (Washington, D.C.: National Press Books, 1992), in a symposium in volume 65 of the *Southern California Law Review* (1992), and in Toni Morrison, ed., *Race-ing Justice, En-gendering Power: Essays on Anita Hill, Clarence Thomas, and the Construction of Social Reality* (New York: Pantheon, 1992).

The following articles by Thomas were published before he was nominated to the Court. "Affirmative Action Goals and Timetables: Too Tough? Not Tough Enough!," 5 *Yale Law and Policy Review* 402 (Spring/Summer 1987); "Current Litigation Trends and Goals at the Equal Opportunity Employment Commission," 34 *Labor Law Journal* 208 (April 1983); "The Equal Opportunity Employment Commission: Reflections on a New Philosophy," 15 *Stetson Law Review* 29 (Fall 1985); "The Higher Law Background of the Privileges and Immunities Clause of the Fourteenth Amendment," 12 *Harvard Journal of Law and Public Policy* 63 (Winter 1989); "No Room at the Inn: The Loneliness of the Black Conservative," 58 *Policy Review* 72 (Fall 1991); "Pay Equity and Comparable Worth," 34 *Labor Law Journal* 3 (January 1983); "Toward a 'Plain Reading' of the Constitution—The Declaration of Independence in Constitutional Interpretation," 30 *Howard Law Journal* 983 (1987).

Ruth Bader Ginsburg

☆ 1933– ☆

APPOINTED BY BILL CLINTON

YEARS ON COURT
1993–

by
CHRISTOPHER HENRY

Ruth Bader Ginsburg became only the second woman to be nominated to the United States Supreme Court when newly elected President Bill Clinton picked her to serve as a Justice in 1993. Her appointment came a dozen years after the first woman, Sandra Day O'Connor, was chosen by President Ronald Reagan to join the Court.

Justice O'Connor, like Reagan, was conservative in both personal beliefs and judicial philosophy. Her stance on abortion rights was particularly troubling to many national women's organizations. She believed that *Roe* v. *Wade*, 410 U.S. 113 (1973), had been wrongly decided, and she voted repeatedly in the many challenges to that decision to either curtail or eliminate entirely the rights of reproductive choice that had been established by *Roe*. In addition, Justice O'Connor examined all challenged affirmative action policies with a skeptical eye, finding them permissible only in exceptional and well-documented circumstances. Sandra Day O'Connor was generally conservative in other areas as well, including criminal procedure and the death penalty.

Ruth Bader Ginsburg, on the other hand, was a longtime believer in gender equality and women's rights. A leading pioneer in the attempt to establish the unconstitutionality of state-sponsored gender discrimination, she argued a series of winning cases before the Supreme Court that radically altered the American lifestyle and psyche. There was no doubt in anyone's mind where Ginsburg stood politically; she had been aligned with the fashionable but not radical left for decades. Her service with the American Civil Liberties Union (ACLU) was extensive, including seven years as its general counsel (1973–80) and eight years as counsel to the ACLU's Women's Rights Project (1972–80), which she organized.

President Clinton did not nominate Ginsburg to the Supreme Court without political risk. He had pledged to nominate many women to high federal positions when he was campaigning for the White House. Yet he was forced to sacrifice his first two female nominees for U.S. attorney general after it emerged that immigration and tax law improprieties had spotted their records. (The president then nominated another woman, Janet Reno, who ultimately became the attorney general.)

It was widely assumed that Clinton would select a woman for the Court when an opening arose for a Justice, but Ginsburg was not nominated primarily because of her gender. Her qualifications were extraordinary by any standard. As an attorney, social activist, legal scholar, noted author, professor, litigator, and federal Court of Appeals judge with more than thirty years of experience and an enviable record of Supreme Court advocacy that resulted in several historic decisions, Ginsburg was more qualified than many of the 105 men who had been appointed to the Court during the previous 204 years.

The retirement of 76-year-old Justice Byron White had created an opening on the Court a short time after Clinton had assumed the presidency. Appointed to the Court by President John F. Kennedy in 1962, White had begun his judicial career as a moderate, but as time wore on he sided with the centrist conservative faction of Justices led by Chief Justice William H. Rehnquist. Of particular significance to American feminists was White's vehement opposition to *Roe* v. *Wade* and to virtually all of the protections that decision had established in 1973. He had voted against the fundamental principles of *Roe* in almost every challenge to the case in the ensuing two decades. Then, in 1992, he and Justices O'Connor and David Souter authored a joint opinion in *Planned Parenthood* v. *Casey* that purported to uphold *Roe* v. *Wade* while at the same time stripping most of its original meaning. Clearly, abortion rights were threatened by the makeup of the sitting Court, with Justices Antonin Scalia, Anthony Kennedy, Clarence Thomas, and Rehnquist committed to overturning *Roe* in its entirety.

Because Justice White's retirement came in the first year of the Clinton presidency rather than in the final year of George Bush's tenure as president, the life expectancy of *Roe* v. *Wade* increased vastly; for White's retirement permitted Clinton to choose a Justice who could cast a decisive vote in any future challenge to *Roe*. The selection of Ruth Bader Ginsburg enabled Clinton to satisfy two groups who were underrepresented on the Court, women and Jews, and allowed him to save face after the near disaster that occurred when he tried to appoint the nation's first female attorney general.

Justice Ginsburg was born Ruth Bader to Nathan and Celia Bader on March 15, 1933, in the Brooklyn borough of New York City. She grew up in the ethnically mixed neighborhood of Flatbush, where she regularly came into contact with families that had emigrated from Italy, Ireland, and Eastern Europe.

Like most Jews who lived in New York City during the Great Depression, Ruth Bader was no stranger to the sting of anti-Semitism. She was aware from a very early age that she was Jewish and that being a Jew meant a responsibility to achieve her full potential and to serve society. Her identity as a Jew was based far less on religious dogma and cultural rituals than on the intrinsic value of human life and a person's right to be treated with fairness and dignity. Long before she ever thought of becoming a lawyer or a judge, Ruth Bader was a believer in human rights.

The Baders were neither wealthy nor upper-middle class, but they did not live in poverty. Nathan Bader was a merchant who tried his hand at a number of ventures, including the furrier and retail clothing businesses. Celia Bader was Ruth's intellectual mentor and inspirational force. If there was one thing Celia wanted from life, it was an education for Ruth. Celia had been denied an education by her own father, who did not believe in schooling for women. Having already lost a young daughter to disease, Celia became nearly fanatical in her insistence that her surviving daughter receive an education.

Sadly, Celia Bader did not live to see her dream fulfilled; she died of cancer the night before Ruth graduated from James Madison High School in Brooklyn. Yet the tragedy of Celia's death became combined with the love of education she had instilled in her daughter to further infuse Ruth with an unquenchable thirst for achievement and knowledge and a burning desire to honor the memory of her mother.

In the late summer of 1950, Ruth Bader began her undergraduate studies at Cornell University. There she met Martin David Ginsburg, a fellow student who came from a middle-class Jewish family on Long Island. They were married in June, 1954, a few weeks after Ruth received her bachelor's degree from Cornell. She was a Phi Beta Kappa graduate and was ranked first among the women in her class.

Martin was a student at Harvard Law School at the time of their marriage. But then the army drafted him and stationed him at Fort Sill, Oklahoma. Ruth followed him west, and the newlyweds remained in Oklahoma for the next two years.

The Ginsburgs' first child, Jane Carol (now a professor at the Columbia University School of Law), was born in July, 1955. To help support her growing family, Ruth went looking for work. She found a government job as a typist and counted the months until her husband's stint in the army was over.

In 1956, the Ginsburgs returned to the East Coast. Martin resumed his studies at Harvard Law School, and Ruth also enrolled in the school. When her husband graduated in 1958 and received a job offer in New York City, she was faced with a major decision: Should she remain at Harvard without her husband for a year and obtain her law degree from the prestigious school or follow him to New York?

Her decision to accompany him to New York and complete her studies at Columbia Law School—which at that time did not have quite the same reputation that Harvard enjoyed—is crucial to understanding the personality and values of Ruth Bader Ginsburg. She has always been a very traditional, family-oriented person. Although her professional career has been built largely upon challenges to societal gender discrimination, and although she has been driven by personal ambition to far greater levels of achievement in the field of law than all but a handful of men, there has never been anything at all radical or even nonconformist about Ginsburg's personal life.

Ginsburg proved to be an exceptional student at law school and was selected for membership on both the Harvard and Columbia law reviews. She also received a number of academic honors, including being named a Kent Scholar at Columbia.

After receiving an LL.B. degree from Columbia in 1959, Ginsburg spent the following two years clerking for the Honorable Edmund L. Palmieri, a United States District Court judge for the Southern District of New York. When her clerkship ended in 1961, she returned to Columbia and worked for the next two years on the law school's Project on International Procedure, serving as its associate director.

In 1962, Ginsburg published her first law review article. She would, over the next three decades, become a legal scholar of prolific proportions, authoring several books and writing scores of law review articles, speeches, and academic papers. An expert in Swedish law, she even coauthored two books on the subject, *Civil Procedure in Sweden* (1965) and *Swedish Code of Judicial Procedure* (1968), and wrote several law review articles on Scandinavian legal issues.

In 1963 Ginsburg began her legal teaching career as an assistant professor at the Rutgers University School of Law. She was promoted twice within six years, then assumed a full professorship at Rutgers in 1969 and another at Columbia in 1972, where she remained on the faculty until 1980. Ginsburg's choice to pursue a career in academia reflected not only her interest and ability but the social reality of 1960's America, for no law firm was willing to hire her. She may have been an exceptional law student, but it did not escape the notice of potential employers that she was a married woman, a mother, and Jewish.

During her professorships, Ginsburg was an active and well-known litigant before the United States Supreme Court—indeed, no more than a handful of Justices have possessed as much experience in litigation before the Court as Ginsburg accumulated during her second decade of legal practice. She argued the merits of six cases before the Supreme Court and prepared briefs for three others as counsel; in addition, she submitted amicus briefs, petitions for certiorari, briefs in opposition to certiorari, jurisdictional statements, and other documents in regard to more than two dozen matters that came before the Court in the 1970's.

In September, 1965, Justice Ginsburg's second child, James Steven, was born. During that same year the Supreme Court handed down its decision in *Griswold* v. *Connecticut*, 381 U.S. 479 (1965), written by Justice William O. Douglas. Although several other Court decisions had mentioned an amorphous "right to privacy" that usually emanated from the Ninth or Fourteenth amendments, Douglas' opinion in *Griswold* first articulated the right in a manner that could be construed as affording a general liberty in the domain of personal sexuality. A challenge to Connecticut's anticontraceptive laws, *Griswold* became a vehicle for defining the constitutional boundaries of state intervention into various areas of private conduct, including birth control, sex acts between consenting adults, and abortion. In addition, *Griswold* also helped to set the stage for the challenges to gender-specific laws applying to education, employment, and public benefits that would be made by Ginsburg and other feminist attorneys (many of them associated with the ACLU's Women's Rights Project) in the 1970's.

While Ginsburg's idealism certainly motivated her decision to work for the ACLU, her success as an advocate before the Supreme Court was due more to what in her father's field was called sales instinct. Winning a case concerning the illegality of gender-based discrimination required first that the (usually male) judges or Justices who heard such cases acknowledge that the claimed discrimination actually existed. At the time, obtaining such acknowledgment was much more easily said than done; male judges tended to take such challenges personally, especially the more benevolent ones who believed that women needed to be protected from the harsh realities of the world. Ginsburg soon showed an exceptional ability to find cases that would change history and "sell" to the predominantly male judiciary. To an extent, Ginsburg left her idealism at home when she chose cases to present to the Supreme Court. She was not interested in symbolic gestures or lost causes; she wanted to win, to firmly establish precedents that would slowly but surely create gender equality in the law.

Ginsburg's first contact with the Supreme Court was in connection with the case of *Reed* v. *Reed*, 404 U.S. 71 (1971), when she collaborated with several other attorneys to write the appellant's briefs. *Reed* was a challenge to the Idaho laws that mandated a preference for men when persons otherwise similarly entitled applied to the court for appointment as administrator of a decedent's estate. According to the appellant, Idaho's provision impermissibly violated the Equal Protection Clause of the Fourteenth Amendment.

The facts of the case were the sort that would evoke both personal sympathy and skepticism about the law—exactly the type of facts that Ginsburg sought in choosing a case. Richard Reed, a minor, had died intestate in Idaho in 1967. Reed's adoptive parents had separated prior to his death, and each sought court appointment as his administrator. The Idaho probate court, following state laws, awarded the office of administrator to Reed's adoptive father, despite the fact that there was absolutely no suggestion that Reed's adoptive mother was unfit or less fit to serve as the estate's administrator. Indeed, no such investigation into relative fitness was deemed necessary by the Idaho law, which was absolute in its terms.

Reed proved an astounding victory for Ginsburg and the other attorneys for the appellant, forcing the Court (thanks to the inflexibility of the Idaho statute) to address the constitutionality of gender-specific state laws. Chief

Justice Warren Burger, the supposedly conservative Nixon appointee who would ultimately become a reliable vote on issues of gender discrimination and abortion rights, wrote in the opinion of the unanimous Court,

> To give a mandatory preference to members of either sex over members of the other, merely to accomplish the elimination of hearings on the merits, is to make the very kind of arbitrary legislative choice forbidden by the Equal Protection Clause of the Fourteenth Amendment; and whatever may be said as to the positive values of avoiding intrafamily controversy, the choice in this context may not lawfully be mandated solely on the basis of sex.

Ginsburg's first oral argument before the Supreme Court came less than fifteen months later, in the case of *Frontiero* v. *Richardson*, 411 U.S. 677 (1973), an amicus appearance for the ACLU. Once again, Ginsburg chose a case in which the issues were both sharply defined and contemporarily relevant. Sharron Frontiero, an officer in the United States Air Force, had attempted to claim her civilian husband as a dependent in order to obtain better housing and medical benefits. Such benefits were granted automatically to male air force officers claiming their wives as dependents, but the air force required that Frontiero prove that her husband was dependent upon her for more than one-half of his support.

Ginsburg gained another victory, for the air force's requirements were held as unconstitutional. Eight of the nine Justices either joined the opinion or concurred in the judgment, which held the requirements to be in violation of the Due Process Clause of the Fifth Amendment. The lone dissent in the case was filed by the recently appointed Justice William H. Rehnquist.

A year later, in February, 1974, Ginsburg argued her only losing case before the Supreme Court, *Kahn* v. *Shevin*, 416 U.S. 351 (1974). Notably, the case was not actually chosen by Ginsburg but was merely argued by her at the request of the ACLU. The case challenged Florida's policy of granting a tax exemption to widows but not to widowers regardless of individual financial circumstances. In defending its policy, Florida pointed to statistics that demonstrated a general disparity between the earnings of men and women who were employed on a full-time basis in the Florida workforce. These statistics did not offer a detailed perspective comparing the earnings of men and women in identical occupations, nor did they compare the incomes of widows and widowers.

The majority opinion, written by Justice William O. Douglas, upheld the Florida statute because it had a "fair and substantial relation to the object of the legislation." The opinion only addressed the status of Florida's widows as a group compared with the state's widowers as a group and did not question the fundamental right of the state to treat individuals differently based upon their gender. Florida's statistics, which the state claimed showed a vast disparity between the median earnings of men and women, were enough to satisfy Justices Douglas, Burger, Stewart, Blackmun, Powell, and Rehnquist of the state's rectitude. Justices Brennan, Marshall, and White dissented, and Justice White's opinion stated in part:

I perceive no purpose served by the exemption other than to alleviate current economic necessity, but the State extends the exemption to widows who do not need the help and denies it to widowers who do. It may be administratively inconvenient to make individual determinations of entitlement and to extend the exemption to needy men as well as needy women, but administrative efficiency is not an adequate justification for discrimination based purely on sex.

To modern observers the majority opinion in *Kahn* may appear factually problematic and ill-reasoned, and the case vividly demonstrates how difficult it was (and is) for advocates of gender equality to find winnable and precedent-setting cases to bring before the Supreme Court. Unlike in *Reed* or *Frontiero*, in *Kahn* maintaining the status quo obviously appealed to the sympathies of the Justices, and the majority of the Justices were obviously reluctant to take away the widows' benefits bestowed by the state of Florida regardless of the larger and necessarily more abstract issue of equality at stake.

A case like *Kahn* demonstrates how very exceptional Ginsburg's understanding of the intricacies of advocacy and her skill in choosing and presenting cases was. Instead of presenting gender-equality cases as situations in which injustices aimed specifically against women had to be rectified (perhaps at the expense of men), Ginsburg chose to present gender equality as a more comprehensive struggle, a popular cause that pitted powerless women *and* men against egregious, capricious, and arbitrary acts of their own government. Her method of presentation is reflected in the fact that the majority of the statutes she challenged before the Supreme Court were found in violation of the Due Process Clause of the Fifth Amendment rather than the Equal Protection Clause of the Fourteenth Amendment. Ginsburg well understood that, as far as gender equality was concerned, the path of least resistance was to seek justice for all rather than justice for women alone.

Less than a year later, Ginsburg once again appeared before the Supreme Court, this time to argue for the appellee, Stephen Wiesenfeld, in the case of *Weinberger* v. *Wiesenfeld*, 420 U.S. 636 (1975). Again the case involved gender-based discrimination that adversely affected the rights of a widower to receive benefits ensuing from his spousal relationship. At issue were provisions of the Social Security Act, which granted survivor's benefits to widows not equally granted to widowers.

Although *Weinberger* superficially resembled *Kahn*, the facts of the case were quite different—and practically ensured sympathy for the appellee. Wiesenfeld's former wife, Paula, was a schoolteacher who had been the family's chief source of financial support and had died in childbirth while delivering their firstborn infant. After her death, Wiesenfeld applied to the Social Security Administration for survivors' benefits for himself and his infant son. The baby's benefits were granted pro forma, but Wiesenfeld was informed that he was ineligible for benefits solely because of his gender. Another major difference between *Weinberger* and *Kahn* was that the former case forced the

Court to examine the constitutionality of the portion of the Social Security Act that denied benefits to widowers. Justice William Brennan delivered the unanimous opinion of the Court, holding that the controlling sections of the Social Security Act were unconstitutional for they violated the Due Process Clause of the Fifth Amendment.

Ginsburg also argued *Califano* v. *Goldfarb*, 430 U.S. 199 (1977), which, like *Weinberger*, resulted from a challenge to certain gender-specific provisions of the Social Security Act. As was typical for Ginsburg's cases, *Califano* was both a women's rights and men's rights case because the provisions of law that were disputed regulated the payment of survivors' benefits to husbands who had outlived their wives.

Hannah Goldfarb was a secretary employed by the New York City Board of Education for a quarter of a century before she died in 1968. During that period of time, the normal Social Security taxes were withheld from her paycheck. When Goldfarb's husband, Leon, retired and became eligible for Social Security, he was denied a widower's benefit because, according to the Social Security Administration, at the time of his wife's death he had not been receiving at least half of his support from her.

This regulation was challenged not as much on the claim that it discriminated against widowers (as in *Weinberger*) as on the basis that it unfairly discriminated against female workers by depriving them of the protection and support for their surviving spouse that they had purchased, at the same rates as male workers, through their Social Security taxes. *Califano* proved to be a much more difficult case to win than *Weinberger* had been, partly because the regulations challenged by Califano did appear to have some rational basis and partly because the regulations were not entirely inflexible—widowers who could demonstrate that they had been dependent upon their wives for at least half of their support qualified for the benefits; therefore, there was an individualized determination of eligibility.

Nonetheless, Ginsburg once again emerged victorious. Although oral arguments before the Supreme Court often seem to have little bearing on the outcome of the case, Ginsburg by all accounts outdid herself—and *Califano*, a five-to-four decision, could not have been closer. Justice Brennan's majority opinion (joined by Justices White, Marshall, and Powell) held that the gender-based distinctions of the Social Security Act violated the Due Process Clause of the Fifth Amendment by denying equal treatment to female workers. Justice Stevens filed an opinion concurring in the judgment that went even further, addressing the discrimination against surviving husbands and recognizing their claim to equal treatment. Justice Rehnquist wrote the dissent and was joined by Chief Justice Burger (usually a dependable vote against any gender bias) and Justices Stewart and Blackmun.

Ginsburg's last appearance before the Supreme Court as a litigant came in 1978, when she joined in the arguments for the petitioner in the case of *Duren* v. *Missouri*, 439 U.S. 357 (1979). Unlike all her other Supreme Court cases, which challenged gender discrimination in regard to government benefits of some sort, *Duren* was a criminal procedure case. The petitioner was also unlike Ginsburg's usual upstanding and sympathy-evoking clients: convicted of murder and robbery in the state of Missouri, Duren contested his conviction based upon the fact that the jury had not contained a sufficient number of women, who presumably would form a more sympathetic audience.

Although Duren's logic was perhaps shaky, the facts of the case were fairly straightforward—at least they were to the Supreme Court of 1979, although today the case quite possibly would have turned out differently. (It is interesting to speculate as to how Justice Ginsburg would vote if confronted with the facts of *Duren*. An ardent advocate, she proved to be a skeptical and reserved judge.) The state of Missouri allowed women an exemption from jury duty solely at their request. Consequently, where fifty-four per cent of the adult population in Duren's convicting jurisdiction were women, the average number of women on juries in that jurisdiction was only about fifteen per cent, and the jury that convicted Duren was comprised entirely of men. Duren easily won his case, garnering a total of eight of the nine Justices in his favor (Justice Rehnquist dissented). The majority ruled that the Missouri laws allowing women to exempt themselves from juries were unconstitutional because they violated the Sixth Amendment, which states in part: "In all criminal prosecutions, the accused shall enjoy the right to a speedy and public trial, by an impartial jury of the State and district wherein the crime shall have been committed."

In 1980, Ruth Bader Ginsburg was appointed a Circuit judge of the United States Court of Appeals for the District of Columbia Circuit by President Jimmy Carter, ending a career in advocacy that has been favorably compared to the renowned Thurgood Marshall's. She immediately plunged into controversy with the case of *Wright* v. *Regan*, 656 F.2d 820 (1981), an action brought against Secretary of the Treasury Donald Regan charging the Internal Revenue Service (IRS) with unlawfully granting tax-exempt status to private schools with racially discriminatory admissions policies. The United States District Court had dismissed the action, which was taken by the parents of black children, finding that the plaintiffs lacked standing and that the matter was nonjusticiable because both the Congress and the IRS had already promulgated regulations in regard to the matter that mandated the court's deference.

Joined by another member of the three-judge panel, Judge Ginsburg reversed the district court's decision, holding that the plaintiffs did have standing and that any acts of Congress curtailing new IRS regulations did not preclude federal court intervention. Considering the facts of the case, Judge Ginsburg's grant of standing was somewhat indulgent. The complaint, filed as a class action, was brought by parents who had never attempted nor planned to attempt to enroll their children in any of the private schools whose tax exemptions they challenged. Their complaint was based on the allegation that the IRS would somehow hinder desegregation of schools in general and contribute to the eventual decline of educational opportunities for minority children such as theirs by granting tax-exempt status to such schools. This assertion was nebulous at best, and the nexus between the governmental action that was challenged and the anticipated harm that the plaintiffs claimed would result was hazy, if not invisible.

Nonetheless, Judge Ginsburg was not satisfied with the district court's logic; her reversal of its finding, however, was based on legal precedent rather than political sympathies. Citing a series of previous cases, Judge Ginsburg found a basis for standing when the state had aided private racial discrimination in situations where the Constitution commanded that government steer clear of such action. In addition, Judge Ginsburg found no basis for the district court's finding of nonjusticiability, stating:

> In amendments to the Treasury Appropriations Act for fiscal year 1980, Congress twice prohibited the Internal Revenue Service from using appropriated funds to formulate or carry out new guidelines which would cause any private school to lose tax-exempt status. . . .
>
> Read to extend to a federal court's remedial authority, plaintiffs assert, the riders could not withstand constitutional review. The plaintiffs invoke both separation of powers doctrine and the proscription of government support for race discrimination.
>
> Our starting point is a proposition not disputed in this litigation or in conflict with the appropriations riders: racially discriminatory institutions are ineligible for tax-exempt status under section 501(c) (3) of the Internal Revenue Code.

The dissenting member of the panel, Judge Tamm, acerbically opined:

> Under cover of selecting between conflicting lines of Supreme Court precedent, the court today boldly creates new law on the jurisdiction of federal courts. Under cover of selecting the most comfortable precedent, the court in fact oversteps well-established limits upon the power of the judiciary. We are not required, as the majority suggests, to choose among Supreme Court precedent as we would footwear—selecting that which "best fits the case before us." Instead, we need only examine carefully the law of standing as it presently exists and properly apply that law to the case before us.

Judge Ginsburg's opinion in *Wright* placed her firmly in the camp of the judicial activists; one of the hallmarks of such judges is an extremely permissive view to the question of standing, especially when the actions of government agencies or large business entities are challenged. Controversies over standing loomed large over many of the crucial constitutional cases of the 1960's and 1970's (such as *Roe* v. *Wade*), and liberal Justices—Ginsburg included—often granted standing to marginally entitled plaintiffs in order to address the social conflicts underlying their cases.

Another issue that often split the judiciary during the 1970's and 1980's was the right of federal officials to withhold information from other governmental authorities and from the public. Ginsburg was prominently involved in one of the more infamous cases, *Senate of Puerto Rico* v. *U.S. Department of*

Justice, 823 F.2d 574 (1987). In this case, the Senate of Puerto Rico was attempting to obtain investigative records from the Department of Justice concerning the 1978 killings of two *Independentistas* (advocates of Puerto Rican sovereignty and self-determination) in Puerto Rico. The request was founded largely on the provisions of the Freedom of Information Act, but the Department of Justice claimed that the requested documents were exempt from disclosure because of a number of factors, including an ongoing investigation. The Senate disputed the exemptions, and the United States District Court ruled in favor of the Department of Justice on every exemption.

The appellate court overruled the district court almost entirely, allowing for only a small number of exemptions for records that would constitute an unwarranted invasion of personal privacy if disclosed. The majority opinion, written by Ginsburg, eloquently reiterates the facts of the case, including an account of the murder under investigation:

> On July 25, 1978, two Puerto Rican political activists, Arnaldo Rosado and Carlos Soto, were killed by Puerto Rican police officers at Cerro Maravilla, a remote mountain location some distance from San Juan. The incident soon generated fierce controversy as conflicting accounts of the day's events emerged. The official explanation—that Rosado and Soto had arrived at Cerro Maravilla intending to blow up a nearby television transmission tower and had fired on the officers, who retaliated in self-defense—was contradicted by several eyewitnesses to the shooting; both the taxi driver, who had transported Rosado, Soto, and a third individual (later identified as a government undercover agent) to the scene, and a technician working at the transmission station, claimed that Rosado and Soto surrendered without a struggle and had been taken, unharmed, into custody before the fatal shots were fired.

Judge Ginsburg then recounted the painstakingly slow progress of the investigation into the killings that the Puerto Rican Senate's Judiciary Committee launched in 1981 and detailed how the United States Department of Justice had consistently failed to cooperate with the investigation, even when directed to do so by the United States District Court.

Although the force of the appellate court order was simply to remand the case to the district court, Judge Ginsburg's lengthy and exactingly detailed opinion left little doubt as to her feelings concerning the conduct of the Department of Justice in this case. While no longer officially an advocate, Ginsburg's opinions, commitments, and ideals still deeply and overtly influence her decision making.

Judge Ginsburg was far from a liberal ideologue during her time on the appellate court, however. Her measured approach to governmental restrictions on freedom of speech is aptly illustrated by her decision in *Action for Children's Television* v. *FCC,* 852 F.2d 1332 (1988). The Federal Communications Commission (FCC) had decided upon a rather vague definition of "indecent" material and had promulgated regulations that such material could be broadcast only between the hours of midnight and 6:00 A.M. in order to protect children who might be listening to the radio or watching television.

The agency had previously circumscribed indecent broadcasts to the hours between 10:00 P.M. and 6:00 A.M. but raised the earlier time limitation to an hour it considered a more reasonable delineation point. A number of broadcasters, journalists, and public interest groups challenged the FCC regulations, alleging that the agency's definition of indecency was impermissibly vague and that the agency's proposed broadcast limitations were unconstitutional.

Judge Ginsburg split the difference in her opinion, agreeing with the plaintiffs that "the FCC failed to adduce evidence of cause, particularly in view of the first amendment interest involved, sufficient to support its hours restraint," but upholding the FCC's method of defining indecency. Ginsburg reasoned:

> The [FCC] now measures broadcast material against the generic definition of indecency, while formerly "no action was taken unless material involved the repeated use, for shock value, similar or identical to those satirized in the [comedian George] Carlin 'Filthy Words' monologue." . . .
>
> The explanation offered by the Commission, in its Reconsideration Order, is that it found the deliberately-repeated-use-of-dirty-words policy unduly narrow as a matter of law. . . . The former approach permitted the unregulated broadcast of any material that did not contain Carlin's "filthy words," no matter how the material might affect children exposed to it. It made no legal or policy sense, the FCC said, to regulate the Carlin monologue but not "material that portrayed sexual or excretory activities or organs in as patently offensive a manner . . . simply because it avoided certain words." . . .
>
> We find the FCC's explanation adequate. Short of the thesis that only the seven dirty words are properly designated indecent—an argument petitioners disavow—some more expansive definition must be attempted. The FCC rationally determined that its former policy could yield anomalous, even arbitrary, results. No reasonable formulation tighter than the one the Commission has announced has been suggested in this review proceeding.

Certainly in this opinion Judge Ginsburg avoids any knee-jerk defense of the First Amendment as some sort of holy grail; instead, she allows considerable discretion to a federal agency's placement of limitations on both commercial and noncommercial speech.

After her nomination to the Supreme Court by President Clinton, many legal scholars found it difficult to categorize Ginsburg as either a liberal or a conservative. Even the Justice herself has seemed stymied by this question for most of her professional career. She discusses her sometimes ironic observations about the liberal/conservative divide in two law review articles printed in the 1980's. One article, written for 15 *Georgia Law Review* 539 (1981) and entitled "Inviting Judicial Activism: A 'Liberal' or 'Conservative' Technique?" displays both her independence of thought and her willingness to question the stereotypes of both conservatism and liberalism. In her article she points out:

> The judiciary has been the forum of ultimate resort for individuals and organizations representing almost every position on the political spectrum. Civil right groups hold no

monopoly position among those discontent with legislative or executive action who seek the aid of the courts. As Professor Maurice Rosenberg remarked, Americans nowadays troop to court with "distresses, anxieties, and wounds they once regarded as the slings and arrows of outrageous fortune."

Ginsburg goes on to discuss how liberal and conservative groups readily forget their differences and form temporary political alliances when a common interest is at stake; as an example she describes how the far-right American Independent Party (organized by Alabama governor and presidential candidate George Wallace) allied itself with the Socialist Labor Party in order to challenge Ohio electoral regulations that made it virtually impossible for minor party candidates to get onto the ballot in that state. She also points out that despite the fact that most First Amendment cases are brought by liberals, conservative business entities have also brought a number of commercial speech actions before the courts, and she claims that "it may be fair to conclude that, in the American legal system, calls for judicial intervention, for activist review of legislative and executive decisions, depend less upon the challenger's 'liberal' or 'conservative' ideology, and more on the pragmatic question, whose ox is being gored."

Ginsburg's own practical concerns with the role of the judiciary are strongly addressed in her article, and she readily forms a practical alliance with a far more conservative Justice. Although in her career as an advocate Ginsburg often found herself at odds with then Associate Justice Rehnquist, she finds common ground with him in her article and twice quotes him favorably on the various frustrations that beset federal judges.

Ginsburg's personal political independence is paralleled in her article by her strong devotion to preserving the political independence of the federal judiciary. She refers to an organization called the United Families of America that had appeared before the Senate Committee on the Judiciary to express concern about the attitudes of federal judges in regard to certain social issues and to propose a long list of questions—hypothetical in nature but dealing with contemporary and controversial political issues—that might be asked of judicial nominees. To Ginsburg, such political methods of choosing Justices would virtually destroy the essential role of the courts in this country. She observes,

The federal bench in the United States enjoys and merits a position high in public esteem. In large part, that high esteem reflects the independence and integrity of the people who serve on the federal bench. In my view, the suggested attitude test for federal judicial nominees is a frightening prospect.

Although no longer an advocate, Ginsburg remains unapologetically a feminist, which may cause some observers to pigeonhole her as an unthinking, politically correct liberal. Ginsburg herself, however, rejects any rigid link between a commitment to gender equality and liberal politics in another article of hers, "Interpretations of the Equal Protection Clause" (9 *Harvard Journal of Law and Public Policy* 41 [1986]). This article is a thought-provoking study that suggests (in opposition to much liberal dogma) that the causes of feminism and gender equality are not necessarily inextricably linked with other leftist or liberal social and political movements. Ginsburg maintains that advances in these other movements (such as civil rights or labor) have not always helped the cause of women; she points out that after the ratification of the Fourteenth Amendment, with its Equal Protection Clause, "every woman who came before the Supreme Court with a gender equality plea in the next one hundred years lost her case."

Ginsburg sums up her feelings on liberalism and conservatism by championing political independence among the federal judiciary:

> Its greatest figures—Learned Hand perhaps is the best example in this century—have not been born once or reborn later liberals or conservatives. They have been independent-thinking individuals with open, but not drafty, minds, individuals willing to listen and, throughout their days, to learn. They have been notably skeptical of all party lines; above all, they have exhibited a readiness to reexamine their own premises, liberal or conservative, as thoroughly as those of others. They set a model I strive to follow.

SELECTED BIBLIOGRAPHY

Justice Ginsburg has written a number of books and articles on domestic and foreign judicial issues, including "The Burger Court's Grapplings with Sex Discrimination" in Vincent Blasi, ed. *The Burger Court: The Counter-Revolution That Wasn't* (New Haven, Conn.: Yale University Press, 1983); "Some Thoughts on Autonomy and Equality in Relation to *Roe v. Wade*," 63 *North Carolina Law Review* 375 (1985); and "Sex, Equality and the Constitution: The State of the Art," 4 *Women's Rights Law Reporter* 143 (1978). Ginsburg's appointment was widely covered by the press. An introduction to Ginsburg's feminist background and thinking can be found in Jeffrey Rosen, "The Book of Ruth," 209 *The New Republic* 19 (2 August 1993), while a critique of her Senate hearings can be found in Michael Comiskey, "The Usefulness of Senate Confirmation Hearings for Judicial Nominees: The Case of Ruth Bader Ginsburg," 27 *PS* 224 (1994).

Stephen G. Breyer

☆ 1938– ☆

APPOINTED BY BILL CLINTON

YEARS ON COURT
1994–

by
LEON FRIEDMAN

It is rare for a President to have two chances to select a Supreme Court Justice in the space of one year. It is rarer still for a candidate to be passed over for a seat on the Court on his or her first chance and then to be selected the second time around. Yet that is precisely what happened in 1994, when President Bill Clinton picked Judge Stephen G. Breyer of the First Circuit Court of Appeals to be the nominee for the Supreme Court seat being vacated because of the retirement of Justice Harry A. Blackmun.

A year earlier, after Justice Byron White resigned, Judge Breyer became the leading candidate on the final short list for the Court. He was invited for a get-acquainted lunch with the President on the Friday before his selection was to be announced. But over the weekend, President Clinton decided instead to nominate Circuit Judge Ruth Bader Ginsburg to the Court. Judge Breyer congratulated his colleague on her selection with generous words of praise, attended her swearing-in ceremony, and generally handled his disappointment in not being chosen with such style and grace that he created a reservoir of goodwill with the White House.

When Justice Blackmun stepped down from the Court in 1994, Judge Breyer again found himself on the final list of potential nominees, this time after Senator George Mitchell, the early favorite, declined the position. Most observers thought that Judge Breyer's inclusion on the list was simply window dressing, repayment for his civilized behavior a year earlier, and that the real fight was between Circuit Judge Richard Arnold of Arkansas and Secretary of the Interior Bruce Babbitt. But when the final announcement was made on May 13, 1994, Judge Breyer was the nominee.

He was everyone's second choice, said the commentators, a moderate judge and the person least likely to prompt a strenuous Senate debate over his confirmation. President Clinton did not want to provoke any fights in Congress, where he was having trouble with his legislative program, and he was seeking a candidate who would sail through the confirmation process. Judge Breyer had friends on both sides of the political aisle based on his former service as chief counsel to the Senate Judiciary Committee and his moderate record as a judge. He would serve, very well, the President's purpose of avoiding a legislative fight.

Of course, the persons who derided the choice as a political compromise were paying Judge Breyer a significant compliment. That so many senators admired his talent and that he had impressed them favorably when he worked as a legislative aide in Congress were not irrelevant factors. His academic specialties were in the fields of administrative agencies, economic regulation, and the legislative process. There were few candidates for the Court in recent years who had any legislative experience—Justice Sandra Day O'Connor was the only person on the Court who had ever served as an elected representative. There were many good reasons why no opposition developed to his candidacy—his distinguished academic career, the careful opinions he wrote as a Circuit Court judge, and his extracurricular activities, including his service on the United States Sentencing Commission—all of which indicated that he would bring considerable intellectual powers and a breadth of practical experience to the Court. When the final Senate vote was taken on his nomination in August of 1994, only nine votes (all from conservative Republicans) were recorded against him.

Stephen G. Breyer was born in San Francisco, California, on August 15, 1938. The son of Irving Breyer, a lawyer for the local school board, he attended Lowell High School in San Francisco. Among his schoolmates was Edmund G. "Jerry" Brown, Jr., who later became governor of California.

A star debater, Breyer was voted most likely to succeed by his high school class in 1955. He then attended Stanford University, graduating as a Phi Beta Kappa honoree in 1959. Winning a Marshall Scholarship subsequently enabled Breyer to attend Oxford University for two years. There he studied philosophy, politics, and economics, and in the process became an Anglophile: he favors conservative British-style clothing, talks with a slight English accent, and is married to Joanna Hare—the daughter of Lord John Blankenham, the former leader of the Conservative party—whom he wedded in 1967, after meeting her while they were both working in Washington, D.C. They have two daughters and a son.

Breyer returned to the United States in 1961 to enroll at Harvard Law School. After being selected for the Harvard Law Review and graduating with high honors in 1964, he obtained a position as a Supreme Court clerk for Justice Arthur Goldberg, who had been appointed in 1962 to replace Justice Felix Frankfurter. The 1964–65 term in which Breyer clerked was Goldberg's last; he would resign in July of 1965 to become the American delegate to the United Nations. But that Supreme Court term was one of the high-water marks of the Warren Court. Along with Justice Goldberg there were four other solid votes generally in favor of an activist position: Chief Justice Earl Warren, Justice Hugo L. Black, Justice William O. Douglas, and Justice

William J. Brennan. Four moderate Justices also sat on the Court: John M. Harlan, Potter Stewart, Tom C. Clark, and Byron White.

In the year in which Judge Breyer served as his clerk, Justice Goldberg often voted with one or more of his liberal brethren to establish important constitutional landmarks for the future. Thus he wrote an important concurring opinion in *Griswold* v. *Connecticut*, 381 U.S. 479 (1965), invalidating a Connecticut birth-control law that prohibited even married couples from obtaining contraceptives and establishing that the right to privacy was protected by the Constitution.

The majority decision by Justice Douglas was short on legal analysis. It concluded that the right to privacy was based upon "penumbras" and "emanations" from other specific provisions of the Bill of Rights. Justice Goldberg went further in his concurrence. He explicitly stated that the concept of "liberty" contained in the due process clause was not restricted to the specific terms of the first eight amendments. There were unenumerated rights not designated in the Bill of Rights that were also constitutionally protected. He based his analysis on the Ninth Amendment, a rarely invoked provision that reads, "The enumeration in the Constitution, of certain rights, shall not be construed to deny or disparage others retained by the People." Justice Goldberg concluded that the words and history of this amendment indicated that "there are additional fundamental rights, protected from government infringement, which exist alongside those fundamental rights specifically mentioned in the first eight constitutional amendments" (385 U.S. 488). Among those rights was the right to marital privacy, which was invaded by the Connecticut birth-control law.

The concurring opinion in *Griswold* helped to expand the definition of the right to privacy, eventually leading to the decision in *Roe* v. *Wade,* 410 U.S. 113 (1973). Years later Judge Breyer was questioned by the Senate Judiciary Committee about his involvement in the *Griswold* case. Senator Howell Heflin asked him if it was true, as reported in scholarly studies of the decision, that "you wrote the first part of Justice Goldberg's concurrence in *Griswold*." Judge Breyer insisted that "if you worked for Justice Goldberg . . . you would be fully aware that Justice Goldberg's drafts are Justice Goldberg's." Nevertheless, Breyer's involvement in that case was comforting for those Senators supporting the right to an abortion, who believed that a commitment to the principles of *Roe* v. *Wade* was an important prerequisite for a Justice in the 1990's.

Among the other significant cases decided in the 1964-65 term was *United States* v. *Brown,* 381 U.S. 437 (1965), in which the Court held by a five-to-four vote that a section of the National Labor Relations Act disqualifying a Communist from being an official in a labor union was an unconstitutional bill of attainder. Years later, when Breyer became a Court of Appeals judge, he wrote a similar decision in *Ozonoff* v. *Berzak,* 744 F. 2d 224 (1st Cir. 1984), in which he held unconstitutional an executive order requiring that applicants for a position with the World Health Organization must undergo a loyalty check before they could join the organization. The Court held that the order was overbroad and violated the First Amendment rights of such applicants.

The Supreme Court also decided a series of important civil rights cases in 1964–65. The Court upheld the constitutionality of Title II (public accommodations) of the Civil Rights Act of 1964 against an attack that it exceeded Congress' power under the Fourteenth Amendment (*Heart of Atlanta Motel, Inc.* v. *United States*, 379 U.S. 241 [1964]). In addition, Justice Goldberg wrote the Court's opinion in *Cox* v. *Louisiana*, 379 U.S. 536 (1965), overturning the convictions of certain protesting civil rights workers in Baton Rouge, Louisiana. That decision established an important precedent in favor of public demonstrations.

Once again, these decisions, handed down when he was a Supreme Court clerk, may have influenced Judge Breyer's later judicial career. He wrote the First Circuit's decision in *NAACP* v. *Secretary, HUD*, 817 F. 2d 149 (1st Cir. 1989), in which the Court held that federal courts have broad power to oversee HUD's policies under Title VIII of the Fair Housing Law. He also wrote the Court's opinion in *Boston Chapter, NAACP* v. *Beecher*, 749 F. 2d 102 (1st Cir. 1984), refusing to reconsider prior orders establishing specific quotas for minority policemen in the Boston police force and prohibiting any reduction in the percentage of minority officers. And in *Gallagher* v. *Wilton Enterprises*, 962 F. 2d 120 (1st Cir. 1992), he joined a per curiam decision broadly upholding the right to jury trials in employment discrimination cases brought under state law.

Justice Goldberg also dissented in two important cases in the 1964–65 term. In *Swain* v. *Alabama*, 380 U.S. 202 (1965), the Court held that it was not a violation of the equal protection clause for a prosecutor to use all his peremptory strikes to eliminate prospective black jurors. Justice Goldberg dissented, anticipating the Supreme Court's later decision in *Batson* v. *Kentucky*, 476 U.S. 79 (1986), which overruled *Swain*. In *Zemel* v. *Rusk*, 381 U.S. 1 (1965), the Court upheld restrictions on travel to Cuba, holding that Congress had authorized those restrictions in the Passport Act. Justice Goldberg did not believe that Congress had authorized the State Department to impose area restrictions on travel in time of peace. Years later Judge Breyer came to the same conclusion in a case he decided as a circuit judge, *Wald* v. *Regan*, 708 F. 2d 794 (1st Cir. 1983), when he held that the Trading with the Enemy Act did not authorize the State Department to prohibit the payment of a traveler's expenses to Cuba. However, the Supreme Court reversed his decision (468 U.S. 222 [1984]).

Breyer later wrote about his year as a Supreme Court clerk, commenting that from Justice Goldberg he "learned a highly practical view of the Constitution. [The Justice] saw the Constitution as protecting basic liberties in a practical way, a way that permitted achieving the ideal without unduly interfering with the workings of government."

After his tour as a Supreme Court clerk ended, Breyer joined the Justice Department for the next two years, from 1965 to 1967, working as a special assistant to the assistant attorney general in charge of antitrust enforcement. It was then that Breyer met his future wife, Joanna Hare, who was working as a journalist in Washington, D.C.

Like so many other brilliant graduates of the time, Breyer returned to Boston and Harvard Law School (in 1967) as an assistant professor of law and taught there on and off for the next 24 years. His specialty was administrative law and antitrust. In 1973 he was appointed to the Watergate Special Prosecution staff by his Harvard Law School colleague Archibald Cox. From 1974 to 1975 he served as the special counsel to the Administrative Practices Committee of the Senate Judiciary Committee, acting as staff director for the investigation of the Civil Aeronautics Board. After returning to Harvard to teach in 1975, he came back to Washington, D.C., in 1979, at the urging of Senator Edward Kennedy, then the chairman of the Senate Judiciary Committee, and became special counsel for the Senate Judiciary Subcommittee on Administrative Practices. A year later Breyer became chief counsel to the Senate Judiciary Committee. Among his tasks was working on the revision of the federal criminal code, the FBI Charter, revision of the fair housing law, and legislation to deregulate the airline and trucking industry.

In the fall of 1980 President Jimmy Carter nominated Judge Breyer to be a Circuit Court judge. When Ronald Reagan was elected President in November 1980, all the judicial nominations previously sent to the Senate by Carter were withdrawn, with one exception: that of Stephen G. Breyer. The Republican senators on the Judiciary Committee with whom he had worked— Strom Thurmond, Orrin Hatch, and Paul Laxalt—recommended that Judge Breyer be confirmed. Two other senators—Democratic senator Robert Morgan of North Carolina and Republican senator Gordon Humphrey of New Hampshire—objected and mounted a filibuster to stop the nomination. Morgan was angry because one of his nominees for a federal judgeship—his former campaign manager—had previously been turned down by the committee, and he blamed Breyer for that rejection. Humphrey objected to any Democrat being selected for a judgeship after Reagan's victory. But Kennedy pressed Breyer's nomination, and in a series of compromises at the end of the legislative session and with the help of the leading Republicans on the committee, the filibuster was broken by a sixty-eight-to-twenty-eight vote. Breyer was quickly confirmed by a vote of eighty to ten.

He immediately began a fourteen-year productive period as a Circuit Court judge. In 1980 the First Circuit was the smallest of the federal courts of appeal, with only four judges sitting on cases and rotating in three judge panels. (Later, in 1984, an additional judge was added to the panel, and in 1986 another judge was added, for a total of six.) It says much for Judge Breyer that he had excellent relations with all of his colleagues, and they spoke highly of his ability when he was later nominated for the Court.

The Almanac of the Federal Judiciary, which recounts the leading cases of each federal judge, listed as Judge Breyer's most important cases three opinions in which he was later reversed by the Supreme Court. In each of those cases, he had voted for a more liberal position than the Court later accepted.

Thus, in *Wald* v. *Regan* he struck down certain regulations that restricted travel to Cuba. But the Supreme Court reversed the decision and upheld the regulations (468 U.S. 222 [1984]).

In *Keeton* v. *Hustler Magazine*, 682 F. 2d 33 (1st Cir. 1982), Judge Breyer held for his court that a magazine with minimal circulation in New Hampshire could not be sued for libel in that state by a nonresident, because the plaintiff was only trying to take advantage of a longer statute of limitations in that state and had no real contacts there. The Supreme Court reversed the decision, holding that the "minimum contacts" rule required to allow long-arm jurisdiction under the due process clause could not be interpreted in a more restrictive manner when the First Amendment was implicated in a libel suit. The small circulation of the offending magazine was sufficient to allow New Hampshire courts to consider the case.

In *Lydon* v. *Justices of the Boston Municipal Court*, 698 F. 2d 1 (1st Cir. 1982), Judge Breyer held that the double jeopardy clause of the Fifth Amendment was implicated by a Massachusetts two-tier procedure under which a judge makes an initial determination of whether a defendant is guilty or not, and then the defendant can be tried de novo in a full jury trial thereafter. Breyer believed that if there was insufficient evidence to convict at the first-tier bench trial, then a second de novo trial could not be held because it would violate the Fifth Amendment. The Supreme Court reversed that determination, 466 U.S. 294 (1984), holding that the double jeopardy clause could not be invoked if the verdict in the first-tier trial only involved the insufficiency of evidence and was not an outright acquittal. Another important case in which the Supreme Court disagreed with Judge Breyer was *Commonwealth of Massachusetts* v. *Secretary of Health and Human Services* (899 F. 2d 53 [1st Cir. 1990]). Breyer wrote a decision refusing to uphold an HHS regulation that prohibited a public health clinic that received federal funds for family planning from advising a patient on abortion services. The First Circuit held that the regulation was not authorized by the underlying legislation (Title X). That interpretation of the law was later rejected by the Supreme Court in *Rust* v. *Sullivan* (500 U.S. 193 [1991]). However, Congress later overruled the Court's decision by amending the legislation to eliminate the prohibition on counseling.

On the other hand, the Supreme Court upheld Judge Breyer's dissent in *Associated Builders and Contractors* v. *Massachusetts Water Resources Authority* (935 F. 2d 345 [1st Cir. 1991]). The panel decision had held that the state could not require contractors working on large state construction projects to belong to a union, maintaining that such a requirement violated the National Labor Relations Act (NLRA). Judge Breyer disagreed, noting that the state agency was attempting to secure labor peace in return for union membership and that private contractors could enter into similar arrangements without violating the NLRA. The Supreme Court agreed with his analysis and reversed the panel decision (113 S. Ct. 1190 [1993]).

On the basis of these few decisions, it would appear that Judge Breyer was following the activist approach that he had learned under Justice Goldberg. Indeed, he wrote a number of decisions upholding the constitutional rights of citizens and striking down governmental action that he felt violated those rights. He wrote the court's opinion in *Shannon* v. *Telco Communications*, 824 F. 2d 150 (1st Cir. 1987), striking down a Massachusetts law that restricted a professional solicitor's compensation for charitable purposes. Such a law interfered with the charity's rights of free speech. He upheld a requirement that favored minority applicants for the rank of sergeant in the Boston police department even after the Supreme Court decision in *City of Richmond* v. *J. A. Croson Co.* (488 U.S. 469 [1989]). Judge Breyer concluded that the requirement met the strict scrutiny standards established by *Croson.* (See *Stuart* v. *Roache*, 951 F. 2d 446 [1st Cir. 1991]). He also wrote a series of decisions dealing with the rights of public employees (mostly from Puerto Rico) not to be fired for political reasons. (See *Hernandez-Tirado* v. *Artau*, 874 F. 2d 866 [1st Cir. 1989] and *Caro* v. *Aponte-Roque*, 878 F. 2d 1 [1st Cir. 1989]).

Judge Breyer was also punctilious about proper procedures being followed in criminal cases. Thus, he wrote the opinion for his court reversing a criminal conviction because an improper charge was given on reasonable doubt, *United States* v. *Colon-Pagan* (1 F. 3d 80 [1st Cir. 1993]). In *United States* v. *Noone*, 938 F. 2d 334 (1st Cir. 1991), he interpreted a federal fugitive law narrowly and reversed a conviction when a person was accused of crossing state lines to avoid federal prosecution rather than a state crime. In *United States* v. *Santa-Manzano*, 842 F. 2d 1 (1st Cir. 1988), he carefully scrutinized the words of an indictment and reversed the conviction when he found a variance between the offenses charged and the crimes proved. In *United States* v. *Underwood*, 880 F. 2d 612 (1st Cir. 1989), he reduced a three-year sentence for contempt to six months.

However, in the criminal law field, Judge Breyer generally upheld the government's position. Thus in *United States* v. *Gillies*, 851 F. 2d 492 (1st Cir. 1988), he upheld a prosecution for firearms possession by an ex-felon against a claim that the law violated the ex post facto clause of the Constitution because the gun in question had moved in commerce before the law went into effect. He upheld a conviction of a demonstrator inside a court building against a claim that the law was overbroad and violated the demonstrator's First Amendment rights, *United States* v. *Bader* (698 F. 2d 553 [1st Cir. 1983]). He wrote the court's opinion in *United States* v. *Gendron*, 18 F. 3d 955 (1st Cir. 1994), upholding a conviction under the child pornography law and rejecting a claim of entrapment. He dissented in a Fourth Amendment case, *United States* v. *Guarino*, 729 F. 2d 864 (1st Cir. 1984), when the panel reversed a conviction because the other judges thought the FBI had exceeded the scope of a magistrate's order to seize certain pornographic material. Judge Breyer did not believe that the order had been violated. He also rejected a Fourth Amendment claim in *United States* v. *Navedo-Colon,* 996 F. 2d 1337 (1st Cir. 1993), holding that the defendant had consented to a search of their luggage at the airport.

One major activity that occupied much of Judge Breyer's time and attention was his service on the United States Sentencing Commission. In 1984 Congress enacted a new sentencing law that was designed to promote uniformity in punishment and promote "honesty in sentencing." One problem that the law was meant to solve was the wide disparity in sentencing imposed by federal judges for essentially the same offenses. For example, a person convicted of armed robbery might receive a three-year term by one judge, but another person convicted of armed robbery and possessing the same criminal law background as the other armed robber might receive a 20-year term by another judge. In addition, a parole board might release a person after he or she served one third of the sentence, so a 12-year term might actually mean four years in prison.

Congress established a seven-person Sentencing Commission to determine the median range of punishment for all the offenses covered by the federal criminal law. The commission established certain guidelines for federal judges to apply that focused on the offense, the defendant's background, and other characteristics of his or her behavior—for example, whether the offender cooperated with the government or whether the offender was regularly engaged in criminal activity. The commission worked continuously from October, 1985, to April, 1987, to meet Congress' deadline for establishing the necessary guidelines. It studied 10,000 cases to determine the average sentence for every federal crime and then established standards that would follow typical past practice.

The guidelines set a narrow range of sentencing for each judge, based upon certain specified characteristics of the crime and the criminal, which were supposed to track the past practice. The maximum and minimum sentence allowed under the guidelines were only twenty-five per cent apart. Judges could "depart" from the guidelines, but if they did they would have to give written reasons for such departure, and the opposing party could appeal the sentence to a higher court. Judge Breyer explained the background to the guidelines in a later article, "The Federal Sentencing Guidelines and the Key Compromises upon Which They Rest" (17 *Hofstra Law Review* 1 [1988]).

Federal trial judges generally hated the new system. It took away what they considered to be their prerogative to sentence and required them to apply certain rigid criteria and then to defend any departure. Judge Breyer had the dubious honor of having to explain the new guidelines to federal judges around the country, which he did with considerable understanding and tact. Gradually the new guidelines took hold. Judge Breyer himself wrote a number of decisions applying the guidelines, which generally gave trial judges more leeway to act. (See *United States* v. *Flowers*, 995 F. 2d 315 [1st Cir. 1993], upholding consecutive sentence issued under guidelines; *United States* v. *Beasley*, 12 F. 3d 280 [1st Cir. 1993], holding that prior state convictions could be used for enhancement purposes under the guidelines; *United States* v. *McFadden*, 13 F. 3d 463 [1st Cir. 1994, Breyer dissenting], opinion concluding that enhancement not called for under guidelines for possession of gun if not used in connection with drug crime; *United States* v. *Mendez-Colon*, 15 F. 3d 188 [1st Cir. 1994], upholding upward departure for sentence but remanding for explanation of extent of increased sentence; and *United States* v. *Doe*, 18 F. 3d 41 [1st Cir. 1994], upholding upward departure under guidelines.)

Judge Breyer's decisions in other areas were generally within the mainstream of American constitutional law. In an abortion case, *Planned Parenthood League of Massachusetts* v. *Bellotti*, 868 F. 2d 459 (1st Cir. 1989), he dissented when the majority remanded a case attacking the constitutionality of a parental consent law involving the approval of an abortion for minors. Although the majority remanded the case for trial, Judge Breyer believed that the Massachusetts law complied with constitutional requirements and a remand was not necessary.

In a First Amendment free-exercise case, *New Life Baptist Church Academy* v. *Town of East Longmeadow*, 885 F. 2d 940 (1st Cir. 1989), Judge Breyer held, in one of his few freedom of religion cases, that a town school committee could make minimal investigation into a religious school's secular program in order to insure that the school was complying with state educational requirements. There was no invasion of the school's religious freedom in such an inquiry. In *Lamphere* v. *Brown University*, 875 F. 2d 916 (1st Cir. 1989), he upheld a lower court decision that the university did not discriminate in refusing to grant tenure to a female candidate in sociology.

Judge Breyer's interest in antitrust continued when he was on the bench. He wrote a leading case on the Sherman Act, *Town of Concord, Mass.* v. *Boston Edison*, 915 F. 2d 17 (1st Cir. 1990), holding that a large utility could not be found guilty of antitrust violations when the electrical prices complained of by the municipal purchaser were the result of regulatory requirements of the state power commission. He also held that the utility had no monopoly position because power was available to the municipalities through other sources.

Judge Breyer wrote the court's opinion in *Barry-Wright Corp.* v. *I.T.T.-Grinnell Corp.*, 724 F. 2d 227 (1st Cir. 1983), rejecting an antitrust challenge to certain supply agreements with a large manufacturer. And he rejected an antitrust claim brought in *Kartell* v. *Blue Shield*, 749 F. 2d 922 (1st Cir. 1984), dealing with doctors' billing practices. He upheld a municipality's immunity for antitrust violations in *Fisichelli* v. *The Town of Methuen* (956 F. 2d 12 [1st Cir. 1992]). He also rejected a claim of differential price setting under the

Robinson-Patman Act in *Caribe BMW, Inc.* v. *Bayerische Motoren Werke Aktiengesellschaft* (19 F. 3d 745 [1st Cir. 1994]).

Later, during Breyer's confirmation hearing, Ralph Nader and certain liberal senators complained that he never voted in favor of an antitrust plaintiff or claim. Judge Breyer responded that he decided each case on the merits, and he concluded in each case no antitrust violation had been made out.

Judge Breyer wrote a number of decisions in the environmental field and was generally praised by environmental interest groups. He has been described as "demonstrat[ing] an unusual interest in and grasp of environmental issues. . . . Judge Breyer takes environmental issues, and the environmental responsibilities of administrators and judges, very seriously" (Stephen Kass and Michael Gerrard, "The Record of Judge Breyer," *New York Law Journal*, May 27, 1994, p. 4). Thus, he upheld a preliminary injunction prohibiting the Department of the Interior from auctioning rights to drill for oil in the Georges Bank, a rich fishing area. He found that the department had not made a complete environmental study of the impact of oil drilling as it was required to do by the National Environmental Protection Act (*Commonwealth of Massachusetts* v. *Watt*, 716 F. 2d 946 [1st Cir. 1983]). He wrote the court's opinion prohibiting any further sewer hookups discharging waste into Boston harbor until sufficient landfill sites had been acquired to alleviate the problem of dumping into the harbor (*United States* v. *Metropolitan District Commission*, 930 F. 2d 132 [1st Cir. 1991]). He voted to impose cleanup costs against a parent company whose subsidiary had created a hazardous waste site (*United States* v. *Kayser-Roth*, 910 F. 2d 24 [1st Cir. 1990]). In *United States* v. *Ottati & Goss, Inc.*, 900 F. 2d 429 (1st Cir. 1990), Judge Breyer wrote a careful opinion assessing the costs of further cleanup of a superfund site and concluded that the EPA had supported its claims for costs as to some pollutants but not as to others and therefore further additional impositions on the company were not justified by the record in the case. He also wrote an important decision upholding the federal government's sovereign immunity in a suit for cleanup costs brought by the State of Maine (*State of Maine* v. *Department of the Navy*, 973 F. 2d 1007 [1st Cir. 1992]). And he voted in favor of a broad plan to protect the National Seashore dunes on Cape Cod (*Conservation Law Foundation of New England* v. *Secretary of the Interior*, 864 F. 2d 954 [1st Cir. 1989]).

However, despite Judge Breyer's good record in this area, critics later complained that he should have disqualified himself from a number of these cases because he owned stock in certain pharmaceutical and chemical companies and held an undisclosed interest in an insurance company that might have affected his judgment. It turns out that Judge Breyer was a "name" behind Lloyd's of London; that is, a personal guarantor of certain reinsurance policies issued by the British insured for American companies. It was conceivable, said his critics, that some of the superfund cleanup cases upon which he sat could impact upon his investment in Lloyd's. The defendant company in one of those cases might have been ordered to reimburse the government for millions after the cleanup of an environmentally dangerous area. It might have its costs reimbursed by an American insurance company that was in turn insured by Lloyd's, which would then look to its "names" for further reimbursement. Senator Howard Metzenbaum commented that Judge Breyer's decision in the *Ottati* case "might set a precedent, might set certain standards of the law, that could affect your investment" in Lloyd's. The Senator noted "that as a practical matter, the *Ottati* case does make it more difficult for EPA to pressure polluters into speedy hazardous waste removal under stringent cleanup standards."

Other witnesses who testified before the Senate Judiciary Committee thought that this possibility was too remote to require disqualification. In any event, there certainly was no pattern of Judge Breyer voting to minimize superfund cleanup costs in order to protect his investment.

While he served as a Court of Appeals judge, Breyer continued an active role as teacher, lecturer, and author. He wrote a number of articles and books in his chosen fields, administrative law and antitrust. (See Breyer, "Reforming Regulation," 59 *Tulane Law Review* 4 [1984], and "The Legacy of the New Deal: Problems and Possibilities in the Administrative State," 92 *Yale Law Journal* 1614 [1983].) He is the coauthor of a leading casebook on administrative law.

In 1993 Breyer published a study of governmental economic control, "Breaking the Vicious Circle," in which he argued that government regulation did not rationally allocate its resources to deal with health and safety matters. There was too much concern with public opinion and not enough concern with scientific risk assessment, according to Breyer. The government might spend millions to deal with a highly visible health problem (such as asbestos), which eliminated only a small risk to the public. But it would then refuse to spend a smaller amount on preventive policies that would have much more long-lasting effects.

Breyer also wrote an article placing him on the opposite pole to Justice Antonin Scalia on the issue of the interpretation of statutes, "On the Uses of Legislative History in Interpreting Statutes" (65 *Southern California Law Review* [1992]). He continued to teach at the Harvard Law School while he served as a Court of Appeals judge in Boston and often lectured to other federal judges through the auspices of the Federal Judicial Center.

After Breyer was nominated to the Supreme Court, there was little opposition in the Senate. He had made a good record on issues such as abortion, the First Amendment, and crime. Ralph Nader criticized him because of his lack of enthusiasm for government regulation of business. Senator Metzenbaum was concerned because Breyer seemed to vote with big business in virtually any antitrust case that came before his court. The senator urged Judge Breyer to remember the questions asked of him before the Judiciary Committee and hoped that he would allow "the milk of human kindness" to run through him, instead of applying technical rules on antitrust. "I guarantee I will remember," Judge Breyer assured the senator.

The other senators were generally satisfied with Breyer's judicial decisions and were not interested in pressing him on difficult matters. He convinced the committee that his record was that of a moderate, centrist judge. He noted that the constitutionality of the death penalty had been upheld. He described *Roe* v. *Wade* as the law of the land. He avoided answering questions on issues that might come before him. The hearings were almost a lovefest and lasted only a week.

By the middle of August of 1994—that is, in record time—Stephen G. Breyer was confirmed and sworn in as the 108th Justice of the United States Supreme Court.

SELECTED BIBLIOGRAPHY

Justice Breyer has written three books, all concerning governmental regulations: *Energy Regulation by the Federal Power Commission* (with Paul W. Macavoy; Washington, D.C.: The Brookings Institution, 1974); *Regulation and Its Reform* (Cambridge: Harvard University Press, 1982); and *Breaking the Vicious Circle: Towards Effective Risk Regulation* (Cambridge: Harvard University Press, 1993). His latest book was widely reviewed, most critically in Sheila Jasonoff, "The Dilemmas of Risk Regulation," 10 *Issues in Science and Technology* 79 (1994). Other writings by Breyer include "Analyzing Regulatory Failure: Mismatches, Less Restrictive Alternatives, and Reform," 92 *Harvard Law Review* 549 (1979); a memorial to Paul M. Bator, president of the *Harvard Law Review*, 102 *Harvard Law Review* 1737, 1741 (1989); and his contribution, "A U.S. Perspective," to "The Appropriate Level of Regulation in Europe: Local, National or Community-Wide? A Roundtable Discussion" in 4 *Economic Policy* 467, 476 (1989).

The Statistics

ON THE SUPREME COURT

by ROY M. MERSKY

WHEN STEPHEN G. BREYER took the oath of office in 1994 as an Associate Justice of the Supreme Court of the United States, he was participating in the 108th swearing-in ceremony in the history of the nation's highest tribunal. Yet Mr. Justice Breyer was the 103rd, rather than the 108th, jurist elevated to the Supreme Court. True, the figures of sixteen Chief Justices and ninety-one Associate Justices add up to the requisite 108th. But five members of the Court were sworn in twice: first as Associate Justices and subsequently as Chief Justices of the United States.

Who were these five members of the Supreme Court? Who were the other eleven Chief Justices and the other ninety-two Associate Justices? How long did each of them serve? Why did they leave the bench? The answers to these and other similar questions are essential both as an introduction to and as a summary of the biographies of the Justices in these volumes.

Some of the answers are listed on the charts which accompany this statistical summary. But before one can understand these charts and put the statistics into perspective, it is essential to take an excursion into history.

The first Judiciary Act provided for a six-member Supreme Court. And these first six Justices— numbered (1) to (6) on Chart I— were among the ten appointed by President Washington. Note also that the seats they occupied are likewise numbered [1] to [6] on Chart II, the seat of the Chief Justice being designated as [1]. Thomas Johnson (7), the seventh Justice appointed to the Court, was the occupant of Seat [2].

The Court was increased to seven members in 1807, with Thomas Todd (16), the sixteenth Justice, as the first occupant of the seventh seat. In 1837, the Court membership was increased to nine. John Catron (26) was the first Justice appointed to Seat [8] and John McKinley (27) was the first Justice appointed to Seat [9]. Save for the period 1863 to 1869, the size of the Court has remained nine.

However Stephen J. Field (38), who served on the Court from 1863 to 1897, was undoubtedly the tenth Justice at the time of his appointment. His successor, Joseph McKenna (57), can be designated as the occupant of either Seat [8] or Seat [10].

Only one number has been assigned to each of the five jurists who have served both as Chief Justice and as an Associate Justice: it is the number assigned on a chronological basis to their first appointments as Associate Justices.

THE CHIEF JUSTICES

Sixteen men have occupied Seat [1] as Chief Justice of the United States. The five who had previously served as Associate Justices were John Rutledge (2), Edward D. White (55), Charles E. Hughes (62), Harlan F. Stone (73), and William H. Rehnquist (100). White, Stone, and Rehnquist were all promoted while on the bench. White was an Associate Justice from 1894 to 1910 and Chief Justice from 1910 to 1921. Stone served as an Associate Justice from 1925 to 1941 and then as Chief Justice until 1946. Rehnquist served as Associate Justice from 1971 to 1986 and as Chief Justice from 1986 to the present (1994).

The second man appointed to the Supreme Court later became its second Chief Justice. John Rutledge was officially designated an Associate Justice from 1789 to 1791, but he actually resigned without ever sitting to accept the Chief Justiceship of South Carolina in the latter year. He was in Seat [1] only in 1795, under an unconfirmed recess appointment. Hughes, who was Chief Justice from 1930 to 1941, had been an Associate Justice from 1910 to 1916 when he resigned to run for the presidency.

Holding the longest tenure as a Chief Justice was John Marshall, who served thirty-four years from his appointment at age forty-five to his death at seventy-nine. The first Chief Justice was even younger at the date of his appointment: John Jay was only forty-four, but he held the post for only five years prior to his resignation at age forty-nine. His distinguished post-judicial career continued until his death at age eighty-three. Oldest when they were sworn in as Chief Justice were Stone and Hughes, sixty-eight and sixty-seven respectively. Other Chief Justices appointed after their sixtieth birthdays were White at sixty-five, William H. Taft at sixty-three, Earl Warren at sixty-two, and Warren Burger and William H. Rehnquist at sixty-one.

Three of the sixteen Chief Justices were from New York and three others were from Ohio. The New Yorkers were Jay, Hughes, and Stone, and the Ohioans Salmon P. Chase, Morrison R. Waite, and Taft. The other ten represent ten other states.

LENGTH OF SERVICE

The longest term of service on the Supreme Court was by William O. Douglas (79), who served for thirty-six years and seven months. Stephen J. Field was a Justice for thirty-four years and nine months, followed by John Marshall, who served for thirty-four years and five months. Nine other Justices were on the Court for thirty or more years. Hugo L. Black, the seventy-sixth Justice, was appointed in 1937 and served until his retirement in 1971 for a total of thirty-four years of service. John Marshall Harlan, Sr., the forty-fourth Justice, Joseph Story, the eighteenth Justice, and William J. Brennan (90) all served thirty-three years. James M. Wayne (23) was on the Court for thirty-two years; John McLean (21) and Byron R. White (93) each served a total of thirty-one years. In office for just over thirty years were Bushrod Washington (11) and William Johnson (14). Oliver Wendell Holmes (58) was appointed in 1902 and resigned in 1932, with a term of service just under thirty years.

Length of service is also reflected in the number of Justices who have held each of the ten seats in the history of the Court. Sixteen Justices have occupied Seat [4], as well as sixteen in Seat [1] (the post of Chief Justice) as compared to twelve in Seats [5] and [6]. Coincidentally, there have been thirteen Justices in Seats [2], [3], and [7]. And there have been ten Justices who have occupied Seat [9], including Sandra Day O'Connor, the first woman to be appointed to the Supreme Court. Only eight Justices have occupied Seats [8] and [10] together.

The shortest terms of office, next to that of John Rutledge as Chief Justice, were those of Thomas Johnson (7), who served for fourteen months in 1791–1793, and James F. Byrnes (81), who was on the Court for just under sixteen months in 1941–1942.

DATA ON AGE

Statistical data on the ages of the 108 Justices can be broken down under three categories: (a) age at taking office; (b) age at terminating service on the court; and (c) length of service.

It is difficult to find any pattern in the analysis of these age data—except to note that those who served on the Supreme Court are distinguished by their longevity. Every era of Supreme Court history has had its quota of Justices considered unusually young, of average age, or somewhat above average age at the time of their appointment.

Only four Justices were named to the Court prior to their fortieth birthdays: William Johnson (14) and Story (18) were thirty-two; Bushrod Washington (11) was thirty-six and James Iredell (6) was thirty-eight. True, these four represent only the early history of the Court. However, McLean (21), who served from 1829 to 1861, was forty-four at the time he took his oath of office in 1877 and Hughes (62) was forty-eight when he became an Associate Justice in 1910.

William O. Douglas (79) was just forty when he joined the Court in 1939. Potter Stewart (92) and Clarence Thomas (106) were both forty-three when appointed in 1958 and 1991 respectively, and Byron R. White (93) was forty-four when appointed in 1962.

Oldest at the time they took their oaths of office were Chief Justice Stone at sixty-eight and Chief Justice Hughes at sixty-seven—but in each case it was their second appointment to the Court. Chief Justice White was sixty-five, as was

Associate Justice Horace H. Lurton (61). Associate Justice Lewis F. Powell (99) was sixty-four when sworn in, and Chief Justice Taft was sixty-three years old. Sworn in at age sixty-two were Chief Justice Earl Warren (88) and Associate Justices Ward Hunt (42), Samuel Blatchford (48), Lucius Q. Lamar (49), and James F. Byrnes (81). Both appointed at the age of sixty-one were Chief Justices Warren Burger (97) and William H. Rehnquist (100), Rehnquist being sworn in previously as an Associate Justice at age forty-seven in 1971. Also sworn in at age sixty-one were Associate Justices William Strong (40), Oliver Wendell Holmes (58), Benjamin Cardozo (75), and Harry A. Blackmun (98).

Resignation, retirement, or death terminated the service of most Justices in their sixties and seventies. And twelve Justices left the Court in their fifties. This is to be expected. But what is unusual is that five Justices left the Court prior to age fifty and that eleven have served past their eightieth birthdays, including Holmes (58), who did not retire until he was ninety.

Chief Justice Taney died in office at age eighty-seven. Harry A. Blackmun (98) and Hugo L. Black (76) both retired at the age of eighty-five, and William J. Brennan (90) served until the age of eighty-four. Justices Louis D. Brandeis (67), Thurgood Marshall (96), and Gabriel Duvall (17) stepped down at eighty-two, while Justices McKenna (57) and Field (38) retired at eighty-one. Additionally, Samuel Nelson (29) retired at age eighty.

Iredell (6) died in office at only forty-eight. The other four men who left the Court in their forties all resigned: Curtis (32) at forty-seven, Moore (12) at forty-eight, and Chief Justice Jay (1) and Justice Campbell (33) at forty-nine.

Iredell was the only member of the Court to die prior to his fiftieth birthday and only six died in their fifties. More unusual is the fact that thirty Justices have lived past eighty, five of them living past the age of ninety. Stanley F. Reed (77) died at ninety-five, and Holmes (58) died at ninety-three. George Shiras, Jr. (53) and James F. Byrnes (81) died at ninety-two, and Duvall (17) died at ninety-one.

APPOINTED BY PRESIDENT

Since five members of the Supreme Court each received two presidential appointments—first as an Associate Justice and later as Chief Justice—there have been one hundred and thirteen nominations for the one hundred and eight Justices who have served on the nation's highest tribunal. But the number of actual presidential appointments to the Supreme Court has exceeded that figure, for twenty-six nominees failed to obtain Senate approval. Only one of these twenty-six, Chief Justice John Rutledge, served on the Court under an unconfirmed recess appointment.

Here is what happened to the twenty-six nominees who failed to obtain Senate approval under the Constitution's "advice and consent" clause. Twelve were rejected by Senate vote and eleven were not acted on by the Senate (in effect, rejections). Three nominations were withdrawn: two by President Grant due to the public protest their names drew, and one by Justice nominee Douglas

Ginsburg himself. Roger Taney in 1835 and Stanley Matthews in 1881 failed in getting Senate approval but later were renominated and confirmed. Only six appointees since 1900 have failed to receive Senate approval: John J. Parker, whom President Herbert Hoover nominated in 1930 but who was rejected by the Senate, and Abe Fortas, nominated as Chief Justice in 1968 but whose nomination was never acted upon because of a Senate filibuster. President Nixon nominated Clement F. Haynsworth, Jr. in 1969 and G. Harrold Carswell in 1970, both of whom were rejected by the Senate. In addition to Douglas Ginsburg's withdrawal, President Reagan failed to appoint Robert Bork with Senate approval.

The number in parenthesis following the name of each Justice on the charts provides a guide to the data on presidential appointments. Since these numbers have been assigned chronologically—based on dates of appointment to the Court—they also indicate the era of American history in which each of the 108 Justices played their roles.

President George Washington made the first eleven appointments, twice nominating Rutledge. Abraham Lincoln appointed Justices 35 to 39. And the first Justice nominated in the twentieth century was Holmes (58), the first of the three appointed by President Theodore Roosevelt.

Of the nine appointments made by President Franklin D. Roosevelt, eight were for Associate Justices 76 to 83 (from Black in 1937 to Rutledge in 1943), and the ninth was the promotion of Chief Justice Stone (73) in 1941; Stone was originally appointed to the Court by President Calvin Coolidge in 1925. Edward D. White (55) was appointed an Associate Justice in 1894 in the second term of Grover Cleveland, and promoted to the Chief Justiceship by President William H. Taft in 1910. And Taft himself became the sixty-ninth Justice when President Warren G. Harding named him to Seat [1] in 1921. Hughes was named as the sixty-second Justice in 1910 by President Taft and as the eleventh Chief Justice in 1930 by President Herbert Hoover.

The retirement of Byron R. White (93) in 1993 marked the end of service by President Kennedy's appointees, and Thurgood Marshall's (96) retirement in 1991 marked the end of service by President Johnson's appointees. Of President Nixon's four nominees, only William H. Rehnquist (100) remains. Meanwhile all appointees by President Ford, Stevens (101); President Reagan, O'Connor (102), Scalia (103), Anthony Kennedy (104) and the promotion of William Rehnquist (100) to Chief Justice; President Bush, Souter (105) and Thomas (106); and President Clinton, Ginsburg (107) and Breyer (108), are still serving.

Only four presidents failed to make appointments to the Supreme Court: William H. Harrison, Zachary Taylor, Andrew Johnson, and Jimmy Carter. President Washington made eleven appointments (counting Rutledge twice) and President Franklin D. Roosevelt made nine. Presidents Jackson (1829–1837) and Taft (1909–1913) made six appointments; and five each were selected by Lincoln (1861–1865) and Eisenhower (1953–1961).

Seven presidents made four appointments: Grant (1869–1877), Benjamin Harrison (1889–1893), Harding (1921–1923), Truman (1945–1953), Grover Cleveland (1885–1889 and 1893–1897), Nixon (1969–1974), and Reagan (1981–1989).

Thus thirteen presidents made seventy of the 113 Supreme Court appointments (including Chief Justice appointments). Twenty-four presidents chose the other forty-three appointees: five selected three Justices, nine selected two, and ten have selected one.

THE PRESIDENTS, THE JUSTICES, AND THEIR POLITICS

Of the thirty-seven presidents who made Supreme Court appointments, seventeen were Republicans and twelve were Democrats. There were four Democrat-Republicans, two Federalists, and two Whigs. Federalist presidents George Washington and John Adams made fourteen appointments together—and all their appointments were Federalists. The last of these was John Marshall, named to the Court in the final days of the Adams administration. Chief Justice Marshall remained in office for thirty-four years and six months until his death in 1835 during the second term of President Andrew Jackson.

The four Democrat-Republican presidents likewise confined their appointments to members of their own political party. President Thomas Jefferson named William Johnson, Brockholst Livingston, and Thomas Todd; President James Madison selected Gabriel Duvall and Joseph Story; President James Madison chose Smith Thompson; and President John Quincy Adams appointed Robert Trimble. Justice Story was on the Court longer than any other member of his party, remaining on the bench until 1845, more than fifteen years after the last Democrat-Republican president left office.

Whig president John Tyler appointed a Democrat to the Supreme Court: Samuel Nelson, the twenty-ninth Justice, who served from 1845 to 1872. However, the other Whig president, Millard Fillmore, appointed another Whig. He was Benjamin R. Curtis (32) and was on the Court from 1851 to 1857.

Although the statistics show that seventeen Republican presidents made fifty-two judicial appointments, the number of Republicans selected totaled only forty-six. On the other hand, while the twelve Democratic presidents made thirty-eight judicial appointments, the number of appointees from the Democratic party was forty-four. One Justice has not been classified above: President Jackson's first nominee, John McLean (21), who served from 1829 to 1861, was first a Democrat and later a Republican.

As a general rule, Republican presidents appointed Republican Justices and Democratic presidents likewise selected members of their own party for posts on the Supreme Court. But there have been notable exceptions.

Republican Abraham Lincoln named Democrat Stephen J. Field (38) as one of his five appointees; Republican Benjamin Harrison named Democrat Howell E. Jackson (54) as one of his four nominees; Republican Warren G. Harding selected Democrat Pierce Butler (71) as one of his four choices; Republican Dwight D. Eisenhower named Democrat William J. Brennan, Jr. (90) among his five nominees; and Republican Herbert Hoover named Democrat Benjamin N. Cardozo (75) as one of his three choices. More interesting, Republican Taft elevated White (55), a Democrat, to Chief Justice and appointed two other Democrats to the Court, Horace H. Lurton (61) and Joseph R. Lamar (64).

Conversely, Democratic presidents Franklin D. Roosevelt and Harry S. Truman each appointed one Republican. Roosevelt promoted Republican Harlan E. Stone to the Chief Justiceship, and Truman named Republican Harold H. Burton (84) as the first of his four Supreme Court appointees.

GEOGRAPHICAL BACKGROUND

America's 108 Justices represent only thirty-one of the fifty states, and ten states have had only one Justice on the Court. On the other hand, fourteen Justices were former residents of New York.

States in addition to New York that have sent four or more Justices to the Supreme Court include the following: Ohio, ten; Massachusetts, nine; Virginia, seven; Pennsylvania and Tennessee, six; Kentucky, five; Georgia, Maryland, New Jersey, California, and Illinois, four. The three states that have had three Justices are Minnesota, South Carolina, and Alabama. There have been two Justices each from North Carolina, Connecticut, New Hampshire, Arizona, Iowa, and Michigan. The ten states with one representative each are Wyoming, Utah, Texas, Missouri, Colorado, Maine, Kansas, Louisiana, Mississippi, and Indiana.

The fourteen from New York include Chief Justices Jay, Hughes, and Stone, and Associate Justices Livingston (15), Smith Thompson (19), Nelson (29), Hunt (42), Blatchford (48), Peckham (56), Cardozo (75), Robert H. Jackson (82), the second Harlan (89), Marshall (96), and Ruth Bader Ginsburg (107).

The geographical breakdown on the 1994 Supreme Court includes two from Arizona, Chief Justice Rehnquist and O'Connor, Stevens from Illinois, Scalia from Virginia, Kennedy from California, Souter from New Hampshire, Thomas from Georgia, Ginsburg from New York, and Breyer from Massachusetts.

Perhaps the most interesting geographical fact about the Supreme Court's 108 Justices is that six of them were born abroad. Four of the six were born in the British Isles. Both James Iredell (6), who served from 1790 to 1799, and George Sutherland (70), who served from 1922 to 1938, were born in England; James Wilson (4) was born in Scotland and William Patterson (8) was born in Ireland. The others were David Brewer (51), who was on the Court from 1890 to 1910, and Felix Frankfurter (78), who served from 1939 to 1962. Brewer was born in Turkey in 1837 and Frankfurter was born in Austria in 1882.

BACKGROUND: IN GENERAL

Thus the statistics show, for example:

That Justice Oliver Wendell Holmes, Jr., was born in 1841 and died in 1935 at age ninety-three, having lived longer than any previous fellow Supreme Court Justice up to that time. Also that he was a Massachusetts Republican, named by President Theodore Roosevelt as the fifty-eighth appointee to the Court. And also that he served from 1902–1932, with the ninth longest period of service at that time in the history of the Court, retiring at age ninety, the oldest of any Justice.

That Chief Justice Salmon Portland Chase was born in 1808 and died in 1873 in his sixty-fifth year. Also that he took his oath of office as the thirty-ninth Justice in 1864 at age fifty-six, and served for less than nine years, dying in office in 1873. And also that he was an Ohio Republican, appointed by President Lincoln.

But such data fail to reveal the nature of the men behind the statistics. They do not tell the story of the Boston aristocrat—an Oliver and Wendell, as well as a Holmes—who was the son of a Harvard medical professor and a leading American man of letters. Nor do the statistics tell of the Chase boy whose father died when he was only nine. They say nothing about Holmes, the legal scholar—the law professor and author of law books who became the Chief Justice of the Massachusetts Supreme Court before his United States Supreme Court appointment. Nor do they explain Chase, the fighting lawyer who became known as "the attorney general of fugitive slaves"; Chase, a power in politics, who served in the United States Senate, who served as Ohio's governor and who served in Lincoln's Cabinet as Secretary of the Treasury.

Nor do these statistics reveal the fact that Holmes married his "friend" Fanny when they were both over thirty and were childless—while Chase sired two daughters in his three marriages.

There are, however, statistical data that do explain much about the backgrounds of those who served on the Supreme Court—in addition to figures on age, length of service, geography, and political affiliations, plus the names of which presidents made which appointments.

These *background* statistics on the 108 Supreme Court Justices fall into three categories:

(a) Family data: ancestry, religion, marital status and parental status;
(b) Education;
(c) Occupational experience prior to appointment.

FAMILY DATA

While the bench of the Supreme Court has had its quota of "rags to riches" stories, a surprisingly large number of Justices were born to the law. Twelve Justices were the sons of judges and fifteen others were otherwise related to prominent jurists.

Judge's sons included Cushing (3), Moore (12), Waite (43), Lucius Q. C. Lamar (49), Edward D. White (55), Peckham (56), Day (59), Pitney (65), John H. Clarke (68), Taft (69), Cardozo (75), and Stewart (92).

Those who were otherwise related to members of the bench included Marshall (13), Livingston (15), Todd (16), Thompson (19), Barbour (25), Campbell (33), Harlan (44), Gray (47), Fuller (50), Brewer (51), Shiras (53), Holmes (58), Moody (60), Joseph R. Lamar (64), and Harlan (89).

Only eight Catholics and seven Jews have served on the Court. The first non-Protestant named to the high bench was a Catholic, Chief Justice Roger B. Taney, the twenty-fourth Justice, appointed by Jackson in 1836. The second Catholic was Edward D. White (55), appointed as an Associate Justice by President Taft in 1910. Justice Joseph McKenna (57) was the third Catholic on the Court, nominated by President McKinley in 1898.

The first of the seven Jewish Justices was Louis D. Brandeis (67), named by President Wilson in 1916.   Pierce Butler (71), the fourth Catholic, joined Brandeis on the bench as a Harding appointee in 1922. And both were joined by the second Jew on the Court, Benjamin N. Cardozo (75), named by President Hoover in 1932.

President Franklin D. Roosevelt named the third Jew and the fifth Catholic to the Court: Felix Frankfurter (78) in 1939 and Frank Murphy (80) in 1940. And Roman Catholic William J. Brennan, Jr. (90) was named by President Eisenhower in 1956. The fourth and fifth Jews on the Court were Arthur J. Goldberg (94), an appointee of President Kennedy, who served from 1962–1965, and his replacement on the bench, Abe Fortas (95), who was nominated by President Lyndon Johnson. Antonin Scalia (103) and Anthony Kennedy (104), both Catholics, were appointed by President Reagan.   President Clinton appointed the sixth and seventh Jewish Justices: Ruth Bader Ginsburg (107) and Stephen Breyer (108).

Perhaps the most interesting—and certainly the most surprising—statistics on the Supreme Court are those which tell the story of the Justices and their roles as parents. Only six of the 108 Justices remained single and the other 102 married a total of 138 times. One of the Justices, Douglas, married four times. Three Justices married three times and twenty-seven Justices married twice.

The bachelors were Moody (60), McReynolds (66), Clarke (68), Cardozo (75), Murphy (80), and Souter (105).

The Justices thrice married were Livingston (15), Curtis (32), and Salmon P. Chase (39).

Even more surprising is the number of offspring of the Justices. At least one-fourth of them had five or more children. Justice Curtis (32) had twelve children, and Justice Livingston (15) had eleven. Five Justices had ten children, two had nine, five had eight, and seven Justices had seven offspring. The sixteen Chief Justices had the amazing total of seventy-three children. The tabulation is as follows:

Jay	6	Waite	5	Vinson	2
Rutledge	10	Fuller	10	Warren	5
Ellsworth	2	White	0	Burger	2
Marshall	10	Taft	3	Rehnquist	3
Taney	7	Hughes	4		
Chase	2	Stone	2	Total	73

In addition to Chief Justices Rutledge, Marshall, and Fuller, two Associate Justices had ten children: Robert Trimble (20) and Stanley Matthews (46). Antonin Scalia (103) has nine children, as did Samuel Chase (9). Thomas Johnson (7), William Johnson (14), Thomas Todd (16), John McLean (21), and Pierce Butler (71) each had eight children. Chief Justice Taney had seven children; the five associate Justices who had seven children include Story (18), Thompson (19), Barbour (25), Strong (40), Bradley (41), and Howell Jackson (54). The first John Marshall Harlan (44), as well as Associate Justices Wilson (4), Clifford (34), and Chief Justice Jay (1), each had a family of six.

Sandra Day O'Connor (102) and Ruth Bader Ginsburg (107) are respectively the first and second mothers to serve on the Supreme Court.

LEGAL EDUCATION

It was not until 1957 that the Supreme Court, for the first time in its history, had a bench composed entirely of law school graduates. This happened when Charles E. Whittaker was sworn in as the ninety-first Justice, replacing Stanley F. Reed, the seventy-seventh Justice. For although he had at one time attended the law schools of both Columbia and the University of Virginia, Reed, like the vast majority of his fellow Justices, had never received a law degree.

Since that time, however, every member of the Court has had either an LL.B. or its equivalent, the J.D. degree.

Yet this should come as no surprise. "[T]here were no law schools, as we now view law schools, in the first seventy years of the Republic's existence." (Evans, "Political Influences in the Selection of Federal Judges," 1948 *Wisconsin Law Review* 330, 346.) And even after the establishment of the LL.B. degree, the overwhelming majority of the bar was trained under the apprenticeship system until after World War I. Washington, the eleventh Justice, studied law in the office of Wilson, the fourth Justice, with all expenses paid by the student's uncle, President Washington.

Because the nature of legal education, even at the great universities, changed so radically in the late nineteenth century, the statistical data on law schools were compiled only for members of the Court appointed after 1900.

Of this group Holmes (58) was the first to have received an LL.B., having earned his degree from Harvard in 1866 and his judicial appointment in 1902. Lurton (61), who was appointed in 1909, was the second LL.B., having been awarded his law degree by Cumberland University in 1867. Other early recipients of law degrees include Harvard alumni Brandeis (67), who graduated in 1877, and Sanford (72), who graduated in 1889. Taft (69) and Van Devanter (63) both obtained their law degrees from Cincinnati Law School, the former in 1880 and the latter a year later. And McReynolds (66) was awarded an LL.B. by the University of Virginia Law School in 1884.

The modern era of law school graduates on the Supreme Court began with the appointment of Stone (73) in 1925. There have been only four Justices since that date who did not have law degrees, and three of those four had some law school training. Following Stone's nomination, the next appointee to the Court was Chief Justice Hughes (62), who was joining the bench for the second time. Hughes graduated from Columbia Law School in 1884. Cardozo (75) and Reed (77) had both attended Columbia without obtaining degrees. And Jackson (82), named in 1941 as the last appointee without a law degree, attended Albany Law School. Of this group only Byrnes (81) obtained his legal education without formal training. Byrnes left school at the age of fourteen and became a Court reporter, studying law at the same time. Here is the education data on the last thirty-five Supreme Court appointments, in inverse order:

108	Breyer	Harvard	1964
107	Ginsburg	Columbia	1959
106	Thomas	Yale	1974
105	Souter	Harvard	1966
104	Kennedy	Harvard	1961
103	Scalia	Harvard	1960
102	O'Connor	Stanford	1952
101	Stevens	Northwestern	1947
100	Rehnquist	Stanford	1952
99	Powell	Wash. & Lee	1931
		Harvard (LL.M.)	1932
98	Blackmun	Harvard	1932
97	Burger	St. Paul	1931
96	Marshall	Howard	1933
95	Fortas	Yale	1933
94	Goldberg	Northwestern	1930
93	White	Yale	1946
92	Stewart	Yale	1941
91	Whittaker	U. Kansas City	1924
90	Brennan	Harvard	1931
89	Harlan	N.Y. Law Sch.	1924
88	Warren	U. of Calif.	1914
87	Minton	Ind.(LL.B.)	1915
		Yale (LL.M.)	1916
86	Clark	U. of Texas	1922
85	Vinson	Centre College	1911
84	Burton	Harvard	1912
83	Rutledge	U. of Colorado	1922
82	Jackson	Albany	attnd
81	Byrnes	-	-
80	Murphy	U. of Mich.	1914
79	Douglas	Columbia	1925
78	Frankfurter	Harvard	1906
77	Reed	U. of Va.	
		Columbia	attnd
76	Black	U. of Ala.	1906
75	Cardozo	Columbia	attnd
74	Roberts	U. of Pa.	1898
73	Stone	Columbia	1898

Harvard, Yale, and Columbia have had the greatest number of alumni on the Supreme Court bench. Fourteen past and present Justices were law students at Harvard: Holmes (58), Moody (60), Brandeis (67), Sanford (72), Frankfurter (78), Burton (84), Brennan (90), Blackmun (98), Powell (99), Scalia (103), Kennedy (104), Souter (105), and Breyer (108).

Of the six Justices who attended Columbia, four were awarded degrees: Hughes (62), Douglas (79), Stone (73), and Ginsburg (107). Those who were students but did not graduate were Cardozo (75) and Reed (77).

One of the five Yale alumni received an LL.M., Minton (87), having previously obtained his LL.B. from Indiana. Of the four Justices who were awarded the Yale LL.B., three were on the Court together in 1968. They were Stewart (92), White (93), and Fortas (95). The fourth, Thomas (106), was appointed to the Court in 1991.

But while only a small percentage of the members of the Supreme Court were law school graduates, a surprisingly large number of those graduates were law school professors. When Iowa's Law School Dean Wiley B. Rutledge was named to the Court in 1943, there were six ex–law professors on the bench at the same time: Stone (73), Roberts (74), Frankfurter (78), Douglas (79), Murphy (80), and Rutledge (83).

At least sixteen Justices were law school professors for significant periods of their lives, and for approximately a dozen of them, teaching law was their principal occupation. Five Justices were law school deans.

Frankfurter (78) certainly gained his reputation as a Harvard Law School professor; Stone (73) was best known for his years as dean of Columbia Law School; and Douglas (79) spent most of his pre-judicial career as a law professor, first at Columbia and then at Yale.

Lurton (61) was dean of the law school at Vanderbilt; Taft (69) was dean of law at Cincinnati Law School and was later a law professor at Yale between his term as president and his appointment as Chief Justice; Roberts (74) was a professor of law at the University of Pennsylvania before his selection to the Court and was named dean after leaving the bench; and Rutledge (83) held the deanship at the law school of Washington University in St. Louis before becoming dean at Iowa.

Strong (40) taught law at Columbia College (later George Washington University); Lamar (49) taught law at the University of Mississippi; Brown (52) taught at the University of Michigan; Hughes (62) was a Cornell Law School professor for two years; McReynolds (66) was once a professor of law at Vanderbilt; Murphy (80) spent a few years teaching law at the University of Detroit College of Law; and Fortas (95) followed Taft and Douglas as the third of the Justices to serve as a Yale Law School professor. Blackmun taught at William Mitchell College of Law and at the University of Minnesota prior to his appointment, and Antonin Scalia taught at the University of Virginia School of Law before becoming a Supreme Court Justice. Both John Paul Stevens (101) and Anthony Kennedy (104) taught on a part-time basis while practicing law, Stevens at the Northwestern University and University of Chicago law schools, and Kennedy at the

McGeorge School of Law. Ruth Bader Ginsburg (107) taught at Rutgers University School of Law and Columbia Law School, and Stephen Breyer (108) was a professor at Harvard Law School.

And the remarkable Mr. Justice Story (18), the youngest appointee in the history of the Supreme Court, served as the first professor of law at Harvard College *during* his service on the bench from 1811 to 1845.

OCCUPATIONAL BACKGROUNDS

Whether prior judicial experience should be a prerequisite to Supreme Court service has long been a matter of debate among members of the legal profession. President Eisenhower was convinced that such experience was essential. And, after his appointment of California governor Earl Warren as Chief Justice, his next four nominees were lower court judges. Brennan (90) was a long-time member of the New Jersey Supreme Court. But Eisenhower appointed Harlan (89), Whittaker (91), and Stewart (92) to the lower federal bench before advancing them to the U.S. Supreme Court.

Generally speaking, the more conservative members of the bar have been the strongest advocates of prior judicial experience. For during the Roosevelt New Deal administration it was argued that the Court's liberal opinions were the result of too many ivory-towered law professors on the bench. It is true that five of F.D.R.'s nine appointees were former law teachers, but Frankfurter (78) was the only Justice to go directly from the classroom to the court—and Frankfurter was hardly an exponent of extreme liberalism. Of the other four ex–law professors, Chief Justice Stone (73) was already an experienced Associate Justice, and the other three were likewise far from their old law schools. At the time of their appointments Douglas (79) was chairman of the Securities and Exchange Commission, Murphy (80) was U.S. Attorney General, and Rutledge (83) was a federal judge.

Nor has prior judicial experience been any guide to Supreme Court performance. At the time of his appointment, Chief Justice Cardozo of the New York Court of Appeals was, undoubtedly, the nation's most distinguished state jurist. Yet his career on the Supreme Court bench was far less distinguished than that of the hard-bitten practitioner Brandeis or of Professor Frankfurter. And the most distinguished of the Chief Justices—Marshall, Taney, and Warren—had never had judicial experience until their Supreme Court appointments.

Of the nation's 108 Supreme Court Justices, forty-eight were judges at the time of their appointment; twenty-two state judicial officers and twenty-six federal judges. Here is the breakdown on the other sixty:

U.S. Attorney General	7
Deputy U.S. Attorney General	2
U.S. Solicitor General	2
Other Cabinet posts	7
U.S. Senate	6

U.S. House of Representatives	2
State Governors	3
Private practice of law	25
Professors of law	2
Miscellaneous	4
TOTAL	60

The four in the miscellaneous category include Douglas (79), chairman of the S.E.C.; Duvall (17), U.S. comptroller of the treasury; Jay (1), secretary of foreign affairs under the Articles of the Confederation; and Iredell (6), a state employee of North Carolina with the title of "Digester" of statutes. It was Iredell's responsibility to organize the state laws and make appropriate revisions. Prior to that time he had been both a state judge and a state attorney general.

In addition to Iredell and the forty-eight Justices who were judges at the time of their appointments, at least a dozen other Supreme Court Justices had prior judicial experience. Chief Justice Taft was a Yale law professor at the time of his selection; but he had formerly served as a federal judge as well as having been president of the United States. And both Chief Justice Vinson (85) and McKenna (57) were likewise former federal judges. Chief Justice Hughes (62) was governor of New York before his appointment as Associate Justice, but he was a judge of the Permanent Court of International Justice before being named Chief Justice.

Thompson (19) was a former Chief Justice of the New York Supreme Court and Catron (26) was at one time Chief Justice of the Supreme Court of Tennessee. Other former state supreme court justices include McLean (21) of Ohio, Strong (40) of Pennsylvania, and Chief Justice White (55) of Louisiana. Ex-Superior Court judges were Ellsworth (10), Wayne (23), Woodbury (30), and Matthews (46).

POST-JUDICIAL ACTIVITIES

So prestigious is an appointment to the Supreme Court—and so important and interesting is the work—that few Justices have voluntarily left the bench while still capable of judicial service. Quite the contrary, there has sometimes been the problem of getting a Justice to resign after he was no longer able to perform his judicial duties. (See Fairman, "The Retirement of Federal Judges," 51 *Harvard Law Review* 397 [1938].)

Forty-eight of the 108 Justices died in office; and there are, of course, nine incumbents. This totals fifty-seven. Of the remaining fifty-one, the vast majority resigned or retired in their advanced years and survived only a short time thereafter.

There were, however, a number of Justices who resigned while still in their active years to take other important positions. The first Chief Justice, John Jay, left the Court to become governor of New York and the second Chief Justice, Oliver Ellsworth, resigned to become United States commissioner to France. David

Davis (37), administrator to the estate of President Lincoln, resigned in 1877 to accept a Senate seat.

Benjamin R. Curtis (32) served from only 1851 to 1857, from ages forty-one to forty-seven, leaving the Court to return to private practice in Massachusetts. He became the chief counsel for President Andrew Johnson during the latter's impeachment trial and was a leader of the American bar during the seventeen years between his retirement and death. John A. Campbell (33) was also appointed to the Court at age forty-one, served a short period (eight years), and was likewise a leader of the bar. Justice Campbell, who was born in Georgia and practiced in Alabama, resigned to join the Confederate government. After the war he had a large practice in New Orleans.

Owen J. Roberts (74) became the dean of the University of Pennsylvania Law School following his resignation in 1945 at age seventy.

After serving for less than sixteen months in 1941–42, James F. Byrnes (81) resigned to assume the post as chairman of the newly created Economic Stabilization Board. He was later secretary of state under President Truman and governor of South Carolina. And Arthur J. Goldberg (94) resigned after three years on the Court from 1962 to 1965 to become United States ambassador to the United Nations.

Other Justices left the Supreme Court to enjoy the leisure pursuits of retirement. George Shiras, Jr. (53) retired in 1903 at age seventy-one after ten years of service to devote himself to such activities as fishing. He did not die until 1924 in his ninety-second year. And John H. Clarke (68) resigned in 1922 at age sixty-five, saying this: "For a long time I have promised what I think as my better self that at that age I would free myself as much as possible from imperative duties that I may have time to read many books which I have not had time to read in a busy life; to travel and to serve my neighbors and some public causes." He died twenty-three years later in 1945.

Editor's note. This statistical essay was originally prepared by Roy M. Mersky and Albert P. Blaustein for the first edition of The Justices of the United States Supreme Court 1789–1969. *I would like to thank those at the Jamail Center for Legal Research at the University of Texas School of Law whose efforts made this update possible: Gary Hartman, who coordinated the project; Jutta Gebauer, who provided technical support; and to Steve Bromberg, Mark Giangrande, and Vicki Howard, whose skill and diligence were essential to the quality of the final product.*

Chart I

INFORMATIONAL TABLE

ON THE JUSTICES

Justice Name	Number	Age upon Appointment	Year Oath Taken	Year Service Terminated	Number of Years Served	Age upon Termination	Reason for Termination
Appointed by President Washington, Federalist, from Virginia, 1789–1797							
Jay, John	1	44	1789	1795	6	49	Resigned
Rutledge, John	2	50	1790	1791	1	51	Resigned
Cushing, William	3	57	1790	1810	20	78	Death
Wilson, James	4	47	1789	1798	9	55	Death
Blair, John	5	58	1790	1796	6	64	Resigned
Iredell, James	6	38	1790	1799	9	48	Death
Johnson, Thomas	7	59	1792	1793	1	60	Resigned
Paterson, William	8	47	1793	1806	13	60	Death
Rutledge, John	2	55	1795	1795	0.5	56	Rejected
Chase, Samuel	9	54	1796	1811	15	70	Death
Ellsworth, Oliver	10	50	1796	1800	4	55	Resigned
Appointed by President Adams, Federalist, from Massachusetts, 1797–1801							
Washington, Bushrod	11	36	1799	1829	31	67	Death
Moore, Alfred	12	45	1800	1804	4	48	Resigned
Marshall, John	13	45	1801	1835	34	79	Death
Appointed by President Jefferson, Democrat-Republican, from Virginia, 1801–1809							
Johnson, William	14	32	1804	1834	30	62	Death
Livingston, Brockholst	15	49	1807	1823	16	65	Death
Todd, Thomas	16	42	1807	1826	19	61	Death
Appointed by President Madison, Democrat-Republican, from Virginia, 1809–1817							
Duvall, Gabriel	17	58	1811	1835	23	82	Resigned
Story, Joseph	18	32	1812	1845	34	65	Death
Appointed by President Monroe, Democrat-Republican, from Virginia, 1817–1825							
Thompson, Smith	19	55	1823	1843	20	75	Death
Appointed by President Adams, Democrat-Republican, from Massachusetts, 1825–1829							
Trimble, Robert	20	49	1826	1828	2	51	Death
Appointed by President Jackson, Democrat, from Tennessee, 1829–1837							
McLean, John	21	44	1830	1861	32	76	Death
Baldwin, Henry	22	50	1830	1844	14	64	Death
Wayne, James M.	23	45	1835	1867	32	77	Death
Taney, Roger B.	24	59	1836	1864	28	87	Death
Barbour, Philip P.	25	52	1836	1841	5	57	Death
Catron, John	26	51	1837	1865	28	79	Death
Appointed by President Van Buren, Democrat, from New York, 1837–1841							
McKinley, John	27	57	1838	1852	15	72	Death
Daniel, Peter V.	28	57	1842	1860	18	76	Death
Appointed by President Tyler, Whig, from Virginia, 1841–1845							
Nelson, Samuel	29	52	1845	1872	27	80	Retired

Political Party	Position Previously Held	Year of Death	Age upon Death	Home State	Justice Name
Federalist	Secretary of Foreign Affairs	1829	83	NY	**Jay, John**
Federalist	State Judge	1800	60	SC	Rutledge, John
Federalist	State Judge	1810	78	MA	Cushing, William
Federalist	Private Practice	1798	55	PA	Wilson, James
Federalist	State Judge	1800	68	VA	Blair, John
Federalist	State Employee	1799	48	NC	Iredell, James
Federalist	State Judge	1819	86	MD	Johnson, Thomas
Federalist	New Jersey State Governor	1806	60	NJ	Paterson, William
Federalist	State Judge	1800	60	SC	**Rutledge, John**
Federalist	State Judge	1811	70	MD	Chase, Samuel
Federalist	U.S. Senate	1807	62	CT	**Ellsworth, Oliver**

Political Party	Position Previously Held	Year of Death	Age upon Death	Home State	Justice Name
Federalist	Private Practice	1829	67	VA	Washington, Bushrod
Federalist	State Judge	1810	55	NC	Moore, Alfred
Federalist	U.S. Secretary of State	1835	79	VA	**Marshall, John**

Political Party	Position Previously Held	Year of Death	Age upon Death	Home State	Justice Name
Dem.-Rep.	State Judge	1834	62	SC	Johnson, William
Dem.-Rep.	State Judge	1823	65	NY	Livingston, Brockholst
Dem.-Rep.	State Judge	1826	61	KY	Todd, Thomas

Political Party	Position Previously Held	Year of Death	Age upon Death	Home State	Justice Name
Dem.-Rep.	U.S. Comptroller of Treasury	1844	91	MD	Duvall, Gabriel
Dem.-Rep.	Private Practice	1845	65	MA	Story, Joseph

Political Party	Position Previously Held	Year of Death	Age upon Death	Home State	Justice Name
Dem.-Rep.	U.S. Secretary of Navy	1843	75	NY	Thompson, Smith

Political Party	Position Previously Held	Year of Death	Age upon Death	Home State	Justice Name
Dem.-Rep.	Federal Judge	1828	51	KY	Trimble, Robert

Political Party	Position Previously Held	Year of Death	Age upon Death	Home State	Justice Name
Dem. then Rep.	U.S. Postmaster-General	1861	76	OH	McLean, John
Democrat	Private Practice	1844	64	PA	Baldwin, Henry
Democrat	U.S. House of Representatives	1867	77	GA	Wayne, James M.
Democrat	Private Practice	1864	87	MD	**Taney, Roger B.**
Democrat	Federal Judge	1841	57	VA	Barbour, Philip P.
Democrat	Private Practice	1865	79	TN	Catron, John

Political Party	Position Previously Held	Year of Death	Age upon Death	Home State	Justice Name
Democrat	U.S. House of Representatives	1852	72	AL	McKinley, John
Democrat	Federal Judge	1860	76	VA	Daniel, Peter V.

Political Party	Position Previously Held	Year of Death	Age upon Death	Home State	Justice Name
Democrat	State Judge	1873	81	NY	Nelson, Samuel

Justice Name	Number	Age upon Appointment	Year Oath Taken	Year Service Terminated	Number of Years Served	Age upon Termination	Reason for Termination
Appointed by President Polk, Democrat, from Tennessee, 1845–1849							
Woodbury, Levi	30	55	1845	1851	5	61	Death
Grier, Robert C.	31	52	1846	1870	23	75	Retired
Appointed by President Fillmore, Whig, from New York, 1850–1853							
Curtis, Benjamin R.	32	41	1851	1857	5	47	Resigned
Appointed by President Pierce, Democrat, from New Hampshire, 1853–1857							
Campbell, John A.	33	41	1853	1861	8	49	Resigned
Appointed by President Buchanan, Democrat, from Pennsylvania, 1857–1861							
Clifford, Nathan	34	54	1858	1881	23	77	Death
Appointed by President Lincoln, Republican, from Illinois, 1861–1865							
Swayne, Noah H.	35	57	1862	1881	19	76	Retired
Miller, Samuel F.	36	46	1862	1890	28	74	Death
Davis, David	37	47	1862	1877	14	61	Resigned
Field, Stephen J.	38	46	1863	1897	34	81	Retired
Chase, Salmon P.	39	56	1864	1873	8	65	Death
Appointed by President Grant, Republican, from Ohio, 1869–1877							
Strong, William	40	61	1870	1880	10	72	Retired
Bradley, Joseph P.	41	57	1870	1892	21	78	Death
Hunt, Ward	42	62	1873	1882	9	71	Disabled
Waite, Morrison R.	43	57	1874	1888	14	71	Death
Appointed by President Hayes, Republican, Ohio, 1877–1881							
Harlan I, John M.	44	44	1877	1911	34	78	Death
Woods, William B.	45	56	1881	1887	6	62	Death
Appointed by President Garfield, Republican, from Ohio, March–September 1881							
Matthews, Stanley	46	56	1881	1887	7	62	Death
Appointed by President Arthur, Republican, from New York, 1881–1885							
Gray, Horace	47	53	1882	1902	20	74	Death
Blatchford, Samuel	48	62	1882	1893	11	73	Death
Appointed by President Cleveland, Democrat, from New York, 1885–1889							
Lamar, Lucius Q.C.	49	62	1888	1893	5	67	Death
Fuller, Melville W.	50	55	1888	1910	22	77	Death
Appointed by President Harrison, Republican, from Indiana, 1889–1893							
Brewer, David J.	51	52	1890	1910	20	72	Death
Brown, Henry B.	52	54	1891	1906	15	70	Retired
Shiras, Jr., George	53	60	1892	1903	10	71	Retired
Jackson, Howell E.	54	60	1893	1895	2	63	Death

Political Party	Position Previously Held	Year of Death	Age upon Death	Home State	Justice Name
Democrat	U.S. Senate	1851	61	NH	Woodbury, Levi
Democrat	State Judge	1870	76	PA	Grier, Robert C.
Whig	Private Practice	1874	64	MA	Curtis, Benjamin R.
Democrat	Private Practice	1889	77	AL	Campbell, John A.
Democrat	Private Practice	1881	77	ME	Clifford, Nathan
Republican	Private Practice	1884	79	OH	Swayne, Noah H.
Republican	Private Practice	1890	74	IA	Miller, Samuel F.
Republican	State Judge	1886	71	IL	Davis, David
Democrat	State Judge	1899	82	CA	Field, Stephen J.
Republican	U.S. Secretary of Treasury	1873	65	OH	**Chase, Salmon P.**
Republican	Private Practice	1895	87	PA	Strong, William
Republican	Private Practice	1892	78	NJ	Bradley, Joseph P.
Republican	State Judge	1886	75	NY	Hunt, Ward
Republican	Private Practice	1888	71	OH	**Waite, Morrison R.**
Republican	Private Practice	1911	78	KY	Harlan I, John M.
Republican	Federal Judge	1887	62	GA	Woods, William B.
Republican	Private Practice	1889	64	OH	Matthews, Stanley
Republican	State Judge	1902	74	MA	Gray, Horace
Republican	Federal Judge	1893	73	NY	Blatchford, Samuel
Democrat	U.S. Secretary of Interior	1893	67	MS	Lamar, Lucius Q.C.
Democrat	Private Practice	1910	77	IL	**Fuller, Melville W.**
Republican	Federal Judge	1910	72	KS	Brewer, David J.
Republican	Federal Judge	1913	77	MI	Brown, Henry B.
Republican	Private Practice	1924	92	PA	Shiras, Jr., George
Democrat	Federal Judge	1895	63	TN	Jackson, Howell E.

1907

Justice Name	Number	Age upon Appointment	Year Oath Taken	Year Service Terminated	Number of Years Served	Age upon Termination	Reason for Termination
Appointed by President Cleveland, Democrat, from New York, 1893–1897							
White, Edward D.	55	48	1894	1910	17	65	Promoted
Peckham, Rufus W.	56	57	1896	1909	13	70	Death
Appointed by President McKinley, Republican, from New York, 1897–1901							
McKenna, Joseph	57	54	1898	1925	26	81	Retired
Appointed by President Roosevelt, Republican, from New York, 1901–1909							
Holmes, Oliver W.	58	61	1902	1932	29	90	Retired
Day, William R.	59	53	1903	1922	19	73	Retired
Moody, William H.	60	52	1906	1910	3	56	Disabled
Appointed by President Taft, Republican, from Ohio, 1909–1913							
Lurton, Horace H.	61	65	1910	1914	4	70	Death
Hughes, Charles E.	62	48	1910	1916	6	54	Resigned
White, Edward D.	55	65	1910	1921	10	75	Death
Van Devanter, Willis	63	51	1911	1937	26	78	Retired
Lamar, Joseph R.	64	53	1911	1916	5	58	Death
Pitney, Mahlon	65	54	1912	1922	10	64	Disabled
Appointed by President Wilson, Democrat, from New Jersey, 1913–1921							
McReynolds, James C.	66	52	1914	1941	26	78	Retired
Brandeis, Louis D.	67	59	1916	1939	22	82	Retired
Clarke, John H.	68	59	1916	1922	6	65	Resigned
Appointed by President Harding, Republican, from Ohio, 1921–1923							
Taft, William H.	69	63	1921	1930	8	72	Retired
Sutherland, George	70	60	1922	1938	15	75	Retired
Butler, Pierce	71	56	1923	1939	17	73	Death
Sanford, Edward T.	72	57	1923	1930	7	64	Death
Appointed by President Coolidge, Republican, from Massachusetts, 1923–1929							
Stone, Harlan F.	73	52	1925	1941	16	68	Promoted
Appointed by President Hoover, Republican, from California, 1929–1933							
Hughes, Charles E.	62	67	1930	1941	11	79	Retired
Roberts, Owen J.	74	55	1930	1945	15	70	Resigned
Cardozo, Benjamin N.	75	61	1932	1938	6	68	Death
Appointed by President Roosevelt, Democrat, from New York, 1933–1945							
Black, Hugo L.	76	51	1937	1971	34	85	Retired
Reed, Stanley F.	77	53	1938	1957	19	72	Retired
Frankfurter, Felix	78	56	1939	1962	23	79	Retired
Douglas, William O.	79	40	1939	1975	36	77	Retired
Murphy, Frank	80	49	1940	1949	9	59	Death
Byrnes, James F.	81	62	1941	1942	1	63	Resigned
Stone, Harlan F.	73	68	1941	1946	5	73	Death
Jackson, Robert H.	82	49	1941	1954	13	62	Death
Rutledge, Wiley B.	83	48	1943	1949	6	55	Death

Political Party	Position Previously Held	Year of Death	Age upon Death	Home State	Justice Name
Democrat	U.S. Senate	1921	75	LA	White, Edward D.
Democrat	State Judge	1909	70	NY	Peckham, Rufus W.
Republican	U.S. Attorney General	1926	83	CA	McKenna, Joseph
Republican	State Judge	1935	93	MA	Holmes, Oliver W.
Republican	Federal Judge	1923	74	OH	Day, William R.
Republican	U.S. Attorney General	1917	63	MA	Moody, William H.
Democrat	Federal Judge	1914	70	TN	Lurton, Horace H.
Republican	N.Y. Governor	1948	86	NY	Hughes, Charles E.
Democrat	Supreme Ct. Assoc. Justice	1921	75	LA	**White, Edward D.**
Republican	Federal Judge	1941	81	WY	Van Devanter, Willis
Democrat	Private Practice	1916	58	GA	Lamar, Joseph R.
Republican	State Judge	1924	66	NJ	Pitney, Mahlon
Democrat	U.S. Attorney General	1946	84	TN	McReynolds, James C.
Democrat	Private Practice	1941	84	MA	Brandeis, Louis D.
Democrat	Federal Judge	1945	87	OH	Clarke, John H.
Republican	Law Professor	1930	72	OH	**Taft, William H.**
Republican	Private Practice	1942	80	UT	Sutherland, George
Democrat	Private Practice	1939	73	MN	Butler, Pierce
Republican	Federal Judge	1930	64	TN	Sanford, Edward T.
Republican	U.S. Attorney General	1946	73	NY	Stone, Harlan F.
Republican	Judge–Intnl. Court of Justice	1948	86	NY	**Hughes, Charles E.**
Republican	Private Practice	1955	80	PA	Roberts, Owen J.
Democrat	State Judge	1938	68	NY	Cardozo, Benjamin N.
Democrat	U.S. Senate	1971	85	AL	Black, Hugo L.
Democrat	U.S. Solicitor General	1980	95	KY	Reed, Stanley F.
Democrat	Law Professor	1965	82	MA	Frankfurter, Felix
Democrat	Chair, SEC	1980	81	CT	Douglas, William O.
Democrat	U.S. Attorney General	1949	59	MI	Murphy, Frank
Democrat	U.S. Senate	1972	92	SC	Byrnes, James F.
Republican	Supreme Ct. Assoc. Justice	1946	73	NY	**Stone, Harlan F.**
Democrat	U.S. Attorney General	1954	62	NY	Jackson, Robert H.
Democrat	Federal Judge	1949	55	IA	Rutledge, Wiley B.

Justice Name	Number	Age upon Appointment	Year Oath Taken	Year Service Terminated	Number of Years Served	Age upon Termination	Reason for Termination
Appointed by President Truman, Democrat, from Missouri, 1945–1953							
Burton, Harold H.	84	57	1945	1958	13	70	Retired
Vinson, Fred M.	85	56	1946	1953	7	63	Death
Clark, Tom C.	86	49	1949	1967	17	67	Retired
Minton, Sherman	87	58	1949	1956	7	65	Retired
Appointed by President Eisenhower, Republican, from Kansas, 1953–1961							
Warren, Earl	88	62	1953	1969	15	78	Retired
Harlan II, John M.	89	55	1955	1971	16	72	Retired
Brennan, Jr., William J.	90	50	1956	1990	33	84	Retired
Whittaker, Charles E.	91	56	1957	1962	5	61	Disabled
Stewart, Potter	92	43	1958	1981	23	66	Retired
Appointed by President Kennedy, Democrat, from Massachusetts, 1961–1963							
White, Byron R.	93	44	1962	1993	31	75	Retired
Goldberg, Arthur J.	94	54	1962	1965	2	56	Resigned
Appointed by President Johnson, Democrat, from Texas, 1963–1969							
Fortas, Abe	95	55	1965	1969	3	58	Resigned
Marshall, Thurgood	96	59	1967	1991	23	82	Retired
Appointed by President Nixon, Republican, from New York, 1969–1974							
Burger, Warren E.	97	61	1969	1986	17	79	Resigned
Blackmun, Harry A.	98	61	1970	1994	24	85	Retired
Powell, Jr., Lewis F.	99	64	1972	1987	15	79	Retired
Rehnquist, William H.	100	47	1972	1986	14	61	Promoted
Appointed by President Ford, Republican, from Michigan, 1974–1977							
Stevens, John Paul	101	55	1975				
Appointed by President Reagan, Republican, from California, 1981–1989							
O'Connor, Sandra Day	102	51	1981				
Rehnquist, William	100	61	1986				
Scalia, Antonin	103	50	1986				
Kennedy, Anthony M.	104	51	1988				
Appointed by President Bush, Republican, from Texas, 1989–1993							
Souter, David H.	105	51	1990				
Thomas, Clarence	106	43	1991				
Appointed by President Clinton, Democrat, from Arkansas, 1993–							
Ginsburg, Ruth B.	107	60	1993				
Breyer, Stephen G.	108	55	1994				

Political Party	Position Previously Held	Year of Death	Age upon Death	Home State	Justice Name
Republican	U.S. Senate	1964	76	OH	Burton, Harold H.
Democrat	U.S. Secretary Treasury	1953	63	KY	**Vinson, Fred M.**
Democrat	U.S. Attorney General	1977	77	TX	Clark, Tom C.
Democrat	Federal Judge	1965	74	IN	Minton, Sherman
Republican	California Governor	1974	83	CA	**Warren, Earl**
Republican	Federal Judge	1971	72	NY	Harlan II, John M.
Democrat	State Judge			NJ	Brennan, Jr., William J.
Republican	Federal Judge	1973	72	MO	Whittaker, Charles E.
Republican	Federal Judge	1985	70	OH	Stewart, Potter
Democrat	U.S. Deputy Attorney General			CO	White, Byron R.
Democrat	U.S. Secretary of Labor	1990	81	IL	Goldberg, Arthur J.
Democrat	Private Practice	1982	71	TN	Fortas, Abe
Democrat	U.S. Solicitor General	1993	84	NY	Marshall, Thurgood
Republican	Federal Judge			MN	**Burger, Warren E.**
Republican	Federal Judge			MN	Blackmun, Harry A.
Republican	Private Practice			VA	Powell, Jr., Lewis F.
Republican	U.S. Asst. Attorney General			AZ	Rehnquist, William H.
Republican	Federal Judge			IL	Stevens, John Paul
Republican	State Judge			AZ	O'Connor, Sandra Day
Republican	Supreme Ct. Assoc. Justice			AZ	**Rehnquist, William**
Republican	Federal Judge			VA	Scalia, Antonin
Republican	Federal Judge			CA	Kennedy, Anthony M.
Republican	State Judge			NH	Souter, David H.
Republican	Federal Judge			GA	Thomas, Clarence
Democrat	Federal Judge			NY	Ginsburg, Ruth B.
Democrat	Federal Judge			MA	Breyer, Stephen G.

Chart II

SEAT CHART

The following chart shows the successive occupants of each seat on the Court. By reading vertically, one can trace the line of succession of each seat on the court. Seat 3, for example, was the New England seat on the Court, being occupied by Cushing (MA), Story (MA), Woodbury (NH), Curtis (MA), Clifford (ME), Gray (ME), and Holmes (MA). When Oliver Wendell Holmes resigned in 1935, his place was taken by Benjamin Cardozo of New York, an outstanding scholar and philosopher of the law, who was thought to be a worthy successor of Story, Gray, and Holmes. Cardozo was succeeded by Felix Frankfurter, a Massachusetts resident, who was also a great legal scholar. Since Cardozo and Frankfurter were Jews, the seat became the Jewish seat on the court, with Arthur Goldburg and Abe Fortas succeeding Frankfurter. Seat 2 has had five residents of New York, Seat 4, four Pennsylvanians, and Seat 6, five southerners.

The court increased from six members (1789–1807) to seven (1807–1837) to nine (1837–1863). In 1863, a tenth seat was added but when John Catron died in 1865, he was never replaced and Seat 8 merged with Seat 10 thereafter. For clarity, they are kept separate on the chart. From 1869 on, the court has had nine members.

To determine individual members of the Court at any given time, the chart should be read horizontally. For example, reading across in the year 1880 and tracing each seat upwards untill a name appears, one finds the following members on the Court: Waite, Hunt, Clifford, Strong, Miller, Bradley, Swayne, Harlan, and Field. In some cases there is a gap between the death of one Justice and the appointment of a successor. After Justice Wayne died in 1867, it was three years before Bradley was appointed to succeed him.

The following information appears with the name of each Justice on the chart: appointing president, birth and death dates, and length of service on the Court.

1913

DATE	CHIEF JUSTICE	SEAT 2	SEAT 3	SEAT 4	SEAT 5
1789 (Supreme Court of six justices established in 1789)	John Jay (NY) WASHINGTON (1745–1829) (<u>1789</u>–1795)	John Rutledge (SC) WASHINGTON (1739–1800) (<u>1790</u>–1791)	William Cushing (MA) WASHINGTON (1732–1810) (<u>1790</u>–1810)	James Wilson (PA) WASHINGTON (1742–1798) (<u>1789</u>–1798)	John Blair (VA) WASHINGTON (1732–1800) (<u>1790</u>–1796)
		Thomas Johnson (MD) WASHINGTON (1732–1819 (<u>1792</u>–1793)			
		William Paterson (NJ) WASHINGTON (1745–1806) (<u>1793</u>–1806)			
1795	John Rutledge (SC) WASHINGTON (1739–1800) (<u>1795</u>)				
	Oliver Ellsworth (CT) WASHINGTON (1745–1807) (<u>1796</u>–1800)				Samuel Chase (MD) WASHINGTON (1741–1811) (<u>1796</u>–1811)
				Bushrod Washington (VA) ADAMS (1762–1829) (<u>1799</u>–1829)	
1800					

DATE	SEAT 6	SEAT 7	SEAT 8	SEAT 9	SEAT 10
1789					
	James Iredell (NC) WASHINGTON (1751–1799) (1790–1799)				
1795					
1800					

1915

DATE	CHIEF JUSTICE	SEAT 2	SEAT 3	SEAT 4	SEAT 5
1800	Oliver Ellsworth (CT) WASHINGTON (1745–1807) (1796–1800)	William Paterson (NJ) WASHINGTON (1745–1806) (1793–1806)	William Cushing (MA) WASHINGTON (1732–1810) (1790–1810)	Bushrod Washington (VA) ADAMS (1762–1829) (1799–1829)	Samuel Chase (MD) WASHINGTON (1741–1811) (1796–1811)
	John Marshall (VA) ADAMS (1755–1835) (1801–1835)				
1805					
1807 (one seat added making a total of seven)		Brockholst Livingston (NY) JEFFERSON (1757–1823) (1807–1823)			
1810					

DATE	SEAT 6	SEAT 7	SEAT 8	SEAT 9	SEAT 10
1800	Alfred Moore (NC) ADAMS (1755–1810) (1800–1804)				
1805	William Johnson (SC) JEFFERSON (1771–1834) (1804–1834)				
		Thomas Todd (KY) JEFFERSON (1765–1826) (1807–1826)			
1810					

1917

DATE	CHIEF JUSTICE	SEAT 2	SEAT 3	SEAT 4	SEAT 5
1810	John Marshall (VA) ADAMS (1755–1835) (1801–1835)	Brockholst Livingston (NY) JEFFERSON (1757–1823) (1807–1823)	William Cushing (MA) WASHINGTON (1732–1810) (1790–1810)	Bushrod Washington (VA) ADAMS (1762–1829) (1799–1829)	Samuel Chase (MD) WASHINGTON (1741–1811) (1796–1811)
					Gabriel Duvall (MD) MADISON (1752–1844) (1811–1835)
			Joseph Story (MA) MADISON (1779–1845) (1812–1845)		
1815					
1820					

1918

DATE	SEAT 6	SEAT 7	SEAT 8	SEAT 9	SEAT 10
1810	William Johnson (SC) JEFFERSON (1771–1834) (1804–1834)	Thomas Todd (KY) JEFFERSON (1765–1826) (1807–1826)			
1815					
1820					

1919

DATE	CHIEF JUSTICE	SEAT 2	SEAT 3	SEAT 4	SEAT 5
1820	John Marshall (VA) ADAMS (1755–1835) (<u>1801</u>–1835)	Brockholst Livingston (NY) JEFFERSON (1757–1823) (<u>1807</u>–1823)	Joseph Story (MA) MADISON (1779–1845) (<u>1812</u>–1845)	Bushrod Washington (VA) ADAMS (1762–1829) (<u>1799</u>–1829)	Gabriel Duvall (MD) MADISON (1752–1844) (<u>1811</u>–1835)
1825		Smith Thompson (NY) MONROE (1768–1843) (<u>1823</u>–1843)			
1830				Henry Baldwin (PA) JACKSON (1780–1844) (<u>1830</u>–1844)	

1920

DATE	SEAT 6	SEAT 7	SEAT 8	SEAT 9	SEAT 10
1820	William Johnson (SC) JEFFERSON (1771–1834) (<u>1804</u>–1834)	Thomas Todd (KY) JEFFERSON (1765–1826) (<u>1807</u>–1826)			
1825		Robert Trimble (KY) ADAMS (1776–1828) (<u>1826</u>–1828)			
1830		John McLean (OH) JACKSON (1785–1861) (<u>1830</u>–1861)			

1921

DATE	CHIEF JUSTICE	SEAT 2	SEAT 3	SEAT 4	SEAT 5
1830	John Marshall (VA) ADAMS (1755–1835) (1801–1835)	Smith Thompson (NY) MONROE (1768–1843) (1823–1843)	Joseph Story (MA) MADISON (1779–1845) (1812–1845)	Henry Baldwin (PA) JACKSON (1780–1844) (1830–1844)	Gabriel Duvall (MD) MADISON (1752–1844) (1811–1835)
1835	Roger B. Taney (MD) JACKSON (1777–1864) (1836–1864)				Phillip B. Barbour (VA) JACKSON (1783–1841) (1836–1841)
1837 (two seats added making a total of 9)					
1840					

1922

DATE	SEAT 6	SEAT 7	SEAT 8	SEAT 9	SEAT 10
1830	William Johnson (SC) JEFFERSON (1771–1834) (<u>1804</u>–1834)	John McLean (OH) JACKSON (1785–1861) (<u>1830</u>–1861)			
1835	James M. Wayne (GA) JACKSON (1790–1867) (<u>1835</u>–1867)				
1837 (two seats added making a total of 9)			John Catron (TN) JACKSON (1786–1865) (<u>1837</u>–1865)	John McKinley (AL) VAN BUREN (1780–1852) (<u>1838</u>–1852)	
1840					

DATE	CHIEF JUSTICE	SEAT 2	SEAT 3	SEAT 4	SEAT 5
1840	Roger B. Taney (MD) JACKSON (1777–1864) (1836–1864)	Smith Thompson (NY) MONROE (1768–1843) (1823–1843)	Joseph Story (MA) MADISON (1779–1845) (1812–1845)	Henry Baldwin (PA) JACKSON (1780–1844) (1830–1844)	Phillip B. Barbour (VA) JACKSON (1783–1841) (1836–1841)
					Peter V. Daniel (VA) VAN BUREN 1784–1860) (1842–1860)
1845		Samuel Nelson (NY) TYLER (1792–1873) (1845–1872	Levi Woodbury (NH) POLK (1789–1851) (1845–1851)	Robert C. Grier (PA) POLK (1794–1870) (1846–1870)	
1850					

1924

DATE	SEAT 6	SEAT 7	SEAT 8	SEAT 9	SEAT 10
1840	James M. Wayne (GA) JACKSON (1790–1867) (<u>1835</u>–1867)	John McLean (OH) JACKSON (1785–1861) (<u>1830</u>–1861)	John Catron (TN) JACKSON (1786–1865) (<u>1837</u>–1865)	John McKinley (AL) VAN BUREN (1780–1852) (<u>1838</u>–1852)	
1845					
1850					

1925

DATE	CHIEF JUSTICE	SEAT 2	SEAT 3	SEAT 4	SEAT 5
1850	Roger B. Taney (MD) JACKSON (1777–1864) (1836–1864)	Samuel Nelson (NY) TYLER (1792–1873) (1845–1872)	Levi Woodbury (NH) POLK (1789–1851) (1845–1851)	Robert C. Grier (PA) POLK (1794–1870) (1846–1870)	Peter V. Daniel (VA) VAN BUREN (1784–1860) (1842–1860)
			Benjamin R. Curtis (MA) FILLMORE (1809–1874) (1851–1857)		
1855					
			Nathan Clifford (ME) BUCHANAN (1803–1881) (1858–1881)		
1860					

1926

DATE	SEAT 6	SEAT 7	SEAT 8	SEAT 9	SEAT 10
1850	James M. Wayne (GA) JACKSON (1790–1867) (<u>1835</u>–1867)	John McLean (OH) JACKSON (1785–1861) (<u>1830</u>–1861)	John Catron (TN) JACKSON (1786–1865) (<u>1837</u>–1865)	John McKinley (AL) VAN BUREN (1780–1852) (<u>1838</u>–1852)	
				John A. Campbell (AL) PIERCE (1811–1889) (<u>1853</u>–1861)	
1855					
1860					

1927

DATE	CHIEF JUSTICE	SEAT 2	SEAT 3	SEAT 4	SEAT 5
1860	Roger B. Taney (MD) JACKSON (1777–1864) (<u>1836</u>–1864)	Samuel Nelson (NY) TYLER (1792–1873) (<u>1845</u>–1872)	Nathan Clifford (ME) BUCHANAN (1803–1881) (<u>1858</u>–1881)	Robert C. Grier (PA) POLK (1794–1870) (<u>1846</u>–1870)	Peter V. Daniel (VA) VAN BUREN (1784–1860) (<u>1842</u>–1860)
1863 (one seat added making a total of ten)	Salmon P. Chase (OH) LINCOLN (1808–1873) (<u>1864</u>–1873)				Samuel F. Miller (IA) LINCOLN (1816–1890) (<u>1862</u>–1890)
1865					
1869 (court fixed at 9 members)					
1870				William Strong (PA) GRANT (1808–1895) (<u>1870</u>–1880)	

DATE	SEAT 6	SEAT 7	SEAT 8	SEAT 9	SEAT 10
1860	James M. Wayne (GA) JACKSON (1790–1867) (<u>1835</u>–1867)	John McLean (OH) JACKSON (1785–1861) (<u>1830</u>–1861)	John Catron (TN) JACKSON (1786–1865) (<u>1837</u>–1865)	John A. Campbell (AL) PIERCE (1811–1889) (<u>1853</u>–1861)	
1863 (one seat added making a total of ten)		Noah H. Swayne (OH) LINCOLN (1804–1884) (<u>1862</u>–1881)		David Davis (IL) LINCOLN (1815–1886) (<u>1862</u>–1877)	Stephen J. Field (CA) LINCOLN (1816–1899) (<u>1863</u>–1897)
1865			John Catron died 1865— no new appointment		
1869 (court fixed at 9 members)					
1870	Joseph P. Bradley (NJ) GRANT (1813–1892) (<u>1870</u>–1892)				

DATE	CHIEF JUSTICE	SEAT 2	SEAT 3	SEAT 4	SEAT 5
1870	Salmon P. Chase (OH) LINCOLN (1808–1873) (1864–1873)	Samuel Nelson (NY) TYLER (1792–1873) (1845–1872)	Nathan Clifford (ME) BUCHANAN (1803–1881) (1858–1881)	William Strong (PA) GRANT (1808–1895) (1870–1880)	Samuel F. Miller (IA) LINCOLN (1816–1890) (1862–1890)
		Ward Hunt (NY) GRANT (1810–1886) (1873–1882)			
1875	Morrison R. Waite (OH) GRANT (1816–1888) (1874–1888)				
1880					

1930

DATE	SEAT 6	SEAT 7	SEAT 8	SEAT 9	SEAT 10
1870	Joseph P. Bradley (NJ) GRANT (1813–1892) (1870–1892)	Noah H. Swayne (OH) LINCOLN (1804–1884) (1862–1881)		David Davis (IL) LINCOLN (1815–1886) (1862–1877)	Stephen J. Field (CA) LINCOLN (1816–1899) (1863–1897)
1875					
				John Marshall Harlan (KY) HAYES (1833–1911) (1877–1911)	
1880					

DATE	CHIEF JUSTICE	SEAT 2	SEAT 3	SEAT 4	SEAT 5
1880	Morrison R. Waite (OH) GRANT (1816–1888) (<u>1874</u>–1888)	Ward Hunt (NY) GRANT (1810–1886) (<u>1873</u>–1882)	Nathan Clifford (ME) BUCHANAN (1803–1881) (<u>1858</u>–1881)	William Strong (PA) GRANT (1808–1895) (<u>1870</u>–1880)	Samuel F. Miller (IA) LINCOLN (1816–1890) (<u>1862</u>–1890)
		Samuel Blatchford (NY) ARTHUR (1820–1893) (<u>1882</u>–1893)	Horace Gray (MA) ARTHUR (1828–1902) (<u>1882</u>–1902)	William B. Woods (GA) HAYES (1824–1887) (<u>1881</u>–1887)	
1885					
	Melville W. Fuller (IL) CLEVELAND (1833–1910) (<u>1888</u>–1910)			Lucius Q. C. Lamar (MS) CLEVELAND (1825–1893) (<u>1888</u>–1893)	
1890					

1932

DATE	SEAT 6	SEAT 7	SEAT 8	SEAT 9	SEAT 10
1880	Joseph P. Bradley (NJ) GRANT (1813–1892) (1870–1892)	Noah H. Swayne (OH) LINCOLN (1804–1884) (1862–1881)		John Marshall Harlan (KY) HAYES (1833–1911) (1877–1911)	Stephen J. Field (CA) LINCOLN (1816–1899) (1863–1897)
		Stanley Matthews (OH) GARFIELD (1824–1889) (1881–1889)			
1885					
1890		David J. Brewer (KS) HARRISON (1837–1910) (1890–1910)			

1933

DATE	CHIEF JUSTICE	SEAT 2	SEAT 3	SEAT 4	SEAT 5
1890	Melville W. Fuller (IL) CLEVELAND (1833–1910) (1888–1910)	Samuel Blatchford (NY) ARTHUR (1820–1893) (1882–1893)	Horace Gray (MA) ARTHUR (1828–1902) (1882–1902)	Lucius Q.C. Lamar (MS) CLEVELAND (1825–1893) (1888–1893)	Samuel F. Miller (IA) LINCOLN (1816–1890) (1862–1890)
					Henry B. Brown (MI) HARRISON (1836–1913) (1891–1906)
				Howell E. Jackson (TN) HARRISON (1832–1895) (1893–1895)	
1895		Edward D. White (LA) CLEVELAND (1845–1921) (1894–1910)			
				Rufus W. Peckham (NY) CLEVELAND (1838–1909) (1896–1909)	
1900					
1934					

DATE	SEAT 6	SEAT 7	SEAT 8	SEAT 9	SEAT 10
1890	Joseph P. Bradley (NJ) GRANT (1813–1892) (<u>1870</u>–1892)	David J. Brewer (KS) HARRISON (1837–1910) (<u>1890</u>–1910)		John Marshall Harlan (KY) HAYES (1833–1911) (<u>1877</u>–1911)	Stephen J. Field (CA) LINCOLN (1816–1899) (<u>1863</u>–1897)
	George Shiras (PA) HARRISON (1832–1924) (<u>1892</u>–1903)				
1895					
					Joseph McKenna (CA) MCKINLEY (1843–1926) (<u>1898</u>–1925)
1900					

1935

DATE	CHIEF JUSTICE	SEAT 2	SEAT 3	SEAT 4	SEAT 5
1900	Melville W. Fuller (IL) CLEVELAND (1833–1910) (<u>1888</u>–1910)	Edward D. White (LA) CLEVELAND (1845–1921) (<u>1894</u>–1910)	Horace Gray (MA) ARTHUR (1828–1902) (<u>1882</u>–1902)	Rufus W. Peckham (NY) CLEVELAND (1838–1909) (<u>1896</u>–1909)	Henry B. Brown (MI) HARRISON (1836–1913) (<u>1891</u>–1906)
			Oliver W. Holmes (MA) ROOSEVELT (1841–1935) (<u>1902</u>–1932)		
1905					
					William H. Moody (MA) ROOSEVELT (1853–1917) (<u>1906</u>–1910)
1910	Edward D. White (LA) CLEVELAND (1845–1921) (<u>1910</u>–1921)			Horace H. Lurton (TN) TAFT (1844–1914) (<u>1910</u>–1914)	

1936

DATE	SEAT 6	SEAT 7	SEAT 8	SEAT 9	SEAT 10
1900	George Shiras (PA) HARRISON (1832–1924) (<u>1892</u>–1903)	David J. Brewer (KS) HARRISON (1837–1910) (<u>1890</u>–1910)		John Marshall Harlan (KY) HAYES (1833–1911) (<u>1877</u>–1911)	Joseph McKenna (CA) MCKINLEY (1843–1926) (<u>1898</u>–1925)
	William R. Day (OH) ROOSEVELT (1849–1923) (<u>1903</u>–1922)				
1905					
1910		Charles E. Hughes (NY) TAFT (1862–1948) (<u>1910</u>–1916)			

1937

DATE	CHIEF JUSTICE	SEAT 2	SEAT 3	SEAT 4	SEAT 5
1910	Edward D. White (LA) TAFT (1845–1921) (1910–1921)	Willis Van Devanter (WY) TAFT (1859–1941) (1911–1937)	Oliver W. Holmes (MA) ROOSEVELT (1841–1935) (1902–1932)	Horace H. Lurton (TN) TAFT (1844–1914) (1910–1914)	Joseph R. Lamar (GA) TAFT (1857–1916) (1911–1916)
1915				James C. McReynolds (TN) WILSON (1862–1946) (1914–1941)	
1920					Louis D. Brandeis (MA) WILSON (1856–1941) (1916–1939)

1938

DATE	SEAT 6	SEAT 7	SEAT 8	SEAT 9	SEAT 10
1910	William R. Day (OH) ROOSEVELT (1849–1923) (<u>1903</u>–1922)	Charles E. Hughes (NY) TAFT (1862–1948) (<u>1910</u>–1916)		John Marshall Harlan (KY) HAYES (1833–1911) (<u>1877</u>–1911)	Joseph McKenna (CA) MCKINLEY (1843–1926) (<u>1898</u>–1925)
				Mahlon Pitney (NJ) TAFT (1858–1924) (<u>1912</u>–1922)	
1915					
		John H. Clarke (OH) WILSON (1857–1945) (<u>1916</u>–1922)			
1920					

1939

DATE	CHIEF JUSTICE	SEAT 2	SEAT 3	SEAT 4	SEAT 5
1920	Edward D. White (LA) TAFT (1845–1921) (1910–1921)	Willis Van Devanter (WY) TAFT (1859–1941) (1911–1937)	Oliver W. Holmes (MA) ROOSEVELT (1841–1935) (1902–1932)	James C. McReynolds (TN) WILSON (1862–1946) (1914–1941)	Louis D. Brandeis (MA) WILSON (1856–1941) (1916–1939)
	William H. Taft (OH) HARDING (1857–1930) (1921–1930)				
1925					
1930	Charles E. Hughes (NY) HOOVER (1862–1948) (1930–1941)				

1940

DATE	SEAT 6	SEAT 7	SEAT 8	SEAT 9	SEAT 10
1920	William R. Day (OH) ROOSEVELT (1849–1923) (1903–1922)	John H. Clarke (OH) WILSON (1857–1945) (1916–1922)		Mahon Pitney (NJ) TAFT (1858–1924) (1912–1922)	Joseph McKenna (CA) MCKINLEY (1843–1926) (1898–1925)
	Pierce Butler (MN) HARDING (1866–1939) (1923–1939)	George Sutherland (UT) HARDING (1862–1942) (1922–1938)		Edward T. Sanford (TN) HARDING (1865–1930) (1923–1930)	
1925					Harlan F. Stone (NY) COOLIDGE (1872–1946) (1925–1941)
1930				Owen J. Roberts (PA) HOOVER (1875–1955) (1930–1945)	

1941

DATE	CHIEF JUSTICE	SEAT 2	SEAT 3	SEAT 4	SEAT 5
1930	Charles E. Hughes (NY) HOOVER (1862–1948) (1930–1941)	Willis Van Devanter (WY) TAFT (1859–1941) (1911–1937)	Oliver W. Holmes (MA) ROOSEVELT (1841–1935) (1902–1932)	James C. McReynolds (TN) WILSON (1862–1946) (1914–1941)	Louis D. Brandeis (MA) WILSON (1856–1941) (1916–1939)
			Benjamin Cardozo (NY) HOOVER (1870–1938) (1932–1938)		
1935					
		Hugo L. Black (AL) ROOSEVELT (1886–1971) (1937–1971)			
			Felix Frankfurter (MA) ROOSEVELT (1882–1965) (1939–1962)		William O. Douglas (CT) ROOSEVELT (1898–1980) (1939–1975)
1940					

1942

DATE	SEAT 6	SEAT 7	SEAT 8	SEAT 9	SEAT 10
1930	Pierce Butler (MN) HARDING (1866–1939) (1923–1939)	George Sutherland (UT) HARDING (1862–1942) (1922–1938)		Owen J. Roberts (PA) HOOVER (1875–1955) (1930–1945)	Harlan F. Stone (NY) COOLIDGE (1872–1946) (1925–1941)
1935		Stanley F. Reed (KY) ROOSEVELT (1884–1980) (1938–1957)			
1940	Frank Murphy (MI) ROOSEVELT (1890–1949) (1940–1949)				

1943

DATE	CHIEF JUSTICE	SEAT 2	SEAT 3	SEAT 4	SEAT 5
1940	Charles E. Hughes (NY) HOOVER (1862–1948) (<u>1930</u>–1941)	Hugo L. Black (AL) ROOSEVELT (1886–1971) (<u>1937</u>–1971)	Felix Frankfurter (MA) ROOSEVELT (1882–1965) (<u>1939</u>–1962)	James C. McReynolds (TN) WILSON (1862–1946) (<u>1914</u>–1941)	William O. Douglas (CN) ROOSEVELT (1898–1980) (<u>1939</u>–1975)
	Harlan F. Stone (NY) ROOSEVELT (1872–1946) (<u>1941</u>–1946)			James F. Byrnes (SC) ROOSEVELT (1879–1972) (<u>1941</u>–1942)	
				Wiley B. Rutledge (IA) ROOSEVELT (1894–1949) (<u>1943</u>–1949)	
1945					
	Fred M. Vinson (KY) TRUMAN (1890–1953) (<u>1946</u>–1953)				
				Sherman Minton (IN) TRUMAN (1890–1965) (<u>1949</u>–1956)	
1950					

1944

DATE	SEAT 6	SEAT 7	SEAT 8	SEAT 9	SEAT 10
1940	Frank Murphy (MI) ROOSEVELT (1890–1949) (<u>1940</u>–1949)	Stanley F. Reed (KY) ROOSEVELT (1884–1980) (<u>1938</u>–1957)		Owen J. Roberts (PA) HOOVER (1875–1955) (<u>1930</u>–1945)	Harlan F. Stone (NY) COOLIDGE (1872–1946) (<u>1925</u>–1941)
					Robert H. Jackson (NY) ROOSEVELT (1892–1954) (<u>1941</u>–1954)
1945				Harold H. Burton (OH) TRUMAN (1888–1964) (<u>1945</u>–1958)	
	Tom C. Clark (TX) TRUMAN (1899–1977) (<u>1949</u>–1967)				
1950					

1945

DATE	CHIEF JUSTICE	SEAT 2	SEAT 3	SEAT 4	SEAT 5
1950	Fred M. Vinson (KY) TRUMAN (1890–1953) (<u>1946</u>–1953)	Hugo L. Black (AL) ROOSEVELT (1886–1971) (<u>1937</u>–1971)	Felix Frankfurter (MA) ROOSEVELT (1882–1965) (<u>1939</u>–1962)	Sherman Minton (IN) TRUMAN (1890–1965) (<u>1949</u>–1956)	William O. Douglas (CN) ROOSEVELT (1898–1980) (<u>1939</u>–1975)
	Earl Warren (CA) EISENHOWER (1891–1974) (<u>1953</u>–1969)				
1955					
				William J. Brennan, Jr. (NJ) EISENHOWER (1906–) (<u>1956</u>–1990)	
1960					

1946

DATE	SEAT 6	SEAT 7	SEAT 8	SEAT 9	SEAT 10
1950	Tom C. Clark (TX) TRUMAN (1899–1977) (1949–1967)	Stanley F. Reed (KY) ROOSEVELT (1884–1980) (1938–1957)		Harold H. Burton (OH) TRUMAN (1888–1964) (1945–1958)	Robert H. Jackson (NY) ROOSEVELT (1892–1954) (1941–1954)
1955					John Marshall Harlan (NY) EISENHOWER (1899–1971) (1955–1971)
		Charles Whittaker (MO) EISENHOWER (1901–1973) (1957–1962)		Potter Stewart (OH) EISENHOWER (1915–1985) (1958–1981)	
1960					

1947

DATE	CHIEF JUSTICE	SEAT 2	SEAT 3	SEAT 4	SEAT 5
1960	Earl Warren (CA) EISENHOWER (1891–1974) (<u>1953</u>–1969)	Hugo L. Black (AL) ROOSEVELT (1886–1971) (<u>1937</u>–1971)	Felix Frankfurter (MA) ROOSEVELT (1882–1965) (<u>1939</u>–1962)	William J. Brennan, Jr. (NJ) EISENHOWER (1906–) (<u>1956</u>–1990)	William O. Douglas (CN) ROOSEVELT (1898–1980) (<u>1939</u>–1975)
			ArthurJ. Goldberg (IL) KENNEDY (1908–1990) (<u>1962</u>–1965)		
1965			Abe Fortas (TN) JOHNSON (1910–1982) (<u>1965</u>–1969)		
	Warren E. Burger (MN) NIXON (1907–1986) (<u>1969</u>–1986)				
1970			Harry A. Blackmun (MN) NIXON (1908–) (<u>1970</u>–1994)		

1948

DATE	SEAT 6	SEAT 7	SEAT 8	SEAT 9	SEAT 10
1960	Tom C. Clark (TX) TRUMAN (1899–1977) (<u>1949</u>–1967)	Charles Whittaker (MO) EISENHOWER (1901–1973) (<u>1957</u>–1962)		Potter Stewart (OH) EISENHOWER (1915–1985) (<u>1958</u>–1981)	John Marshall Harlan (NY) EISENHOWER (1899–1971) (<u>1955</u>–1971)
		Byron R. White (CO) KENNEDY (1917–) (<u>1962</u>–1993)			
1965					
	Thurgood Marshall (NY) JOHNSON (1908–1993) (<u>1967</u>–1991)				
1970					

1949

DATE	CHIEF JUSTICE	SEAT 2	SEAT 3	SEAT 4	SEAT 5
1970	Warren E. Burger (MN) NIXON (1907–) (<u>1969</u>–1986)	Hugo L. Black (AL) ROOSEVELT (1886–1971) (<u>1937</u>–1971)	Harry A. Blackmun (MN) NIXON (1908–) (<u>1970</u>–1994)	William J. Brennan, Jr. (NJ) EISENHOWER (1906–) (<u>1956</u>–1990)	William O. Douglas (CN) ROOSEVELT (1898–1980) (<u>1939</u>–1975)
		Louis F. Powell, Jr. (VA) NIXON (1907–) (<u>1972</u>–1987)			
1975					John Paul Stevens (IL) FORD (1920–) (<u>1975</u>–)
1980					

1950

DATE	SEAT 6	SEAT 7	SEAT 8	SEAT 9	SEAT 10
1970	Thurgood Marshall (NY) JOHNSON (1908–1993) (<u>1967</u>–1991)	Byron R. White (CO) KENNEDY (1917–) (<u>1962</u>–1993)		Potter Stewart (OH) EISENHOWER (1915–1985) (<u>1958</u>–1981)	John Marshall Harlan (NY) EISENHOWER (1899–1971) (<u>1955</u>–1971)
					William H. Rehnquist (AZ) NIXON (1924–) (<u>1972</u>–1986)
1975					
1980					

1951

DATE	CHIEF JUSTICE	SEAT 2	SEAT 3	SEAT 4	SEAT 5
1980	Warren E. Burger (MN) NIXON (1907–) (1969–1986)	Louis F. Powell, Jr. (VA) NIXON (1907–) (1972–1987)	Harry A. Blackmun (MN) NIXON (1908–) (1970–1994)	William J. Brennan, Jr. (NJ) EISENHOWER (1906–) (1956–1990)	John Paul Stevens (IL) FORD (1920–) (1975–)
1985					
	William H. Rehnquist (AZ) REAGAN (1924–) (1986–)				
		Anthony M. Kennedy (CA) REAGAN (1936–) (1988–)			
1990				David H. Souter (NH) BUSH (1939–) (1990–)	

1952

DATE	SEAT 6	SEAT 7	SEAT 8	SEAT 9	SEAT 10
1980	Thurgood Marshall (NY) JOHNSON (1908–1993) (<u>1967</u>–1991)	Byron R. White (CO) KENNEDY (1917–) (<u>1962</u>–1993)		Potter Stewart (OH) EISENHOWER (1915–1985) (<u>1958</u>–1981)	William H. Rehnquist (AZ) REAGAN (1924–) (<u>1972</u>–1986)
				Sandra Day O'Connor (AZ) REAGAN (1930–) (<u>1981</u>–)	
1985					
					Antonin Scalia (VA) REAGAN (1936–) (<u>1986</u>–)
1990					

1953

DATE	CHIEF JUSTICE	SEAT 2	SEAT 3	SEAT 4	SEAT 5
1990	William H. Rehnquist (AZ) REAGAN (1924–) (<u>1986</u>–)	Anthony M. Kennedy (CA) REAGAN (1936–) (<u>1988</u>–)	Harry A. Blackmun (MN) NIXON (1908–) (<u>1970</u>–1994)	David H. Souter (NH) BUSH (1939–) (<u>1990</u>–)	John Paul Stevens (IL) FORD (1920–) (<u>1975</u>–)
			Stephen G. Breyer (MA) CLINTON (1938–) (<u>1994</u>–)		
1995					
2000					

1954

DATE	SEAT 6	SEAT 7	SEAT 8	SEAT 9	SEAT 10
1990	Thurgood Marshall (NY) JOHNSON (1908–1993) (1967–1991)	Byron R. White (CO) KENNEDY (1917–) (1962–1993)		Sandra Day O'Connor (AZ) REAGAN (1930–) (1981–)	Antonin Scalia (VA) REAGAN (1936–) (1986–)
	Clarence Thomas (GA) BUSH (1948–) (1991–)	Ruth Bader Ginsburg (NY) CLINTON (1930–) (1993–)			
1995					
2000					

1955

Chart III

ALPHABETICAL CHART
OF THE JUSTICES OF THE SUPREME COURT

Those who served as Chief Justice are shown in **boldface** type

NAME OF JUSTICE	APPOINTMENT NUMBER	SEAT NUMBER	APPOINTING PRESIDENT	POLITICAL PARTY	STATE
Baldwin, Henry	22	4	Jackson	Democrat	PA
Barbour, Philip P.	25	5	Jackson	Democrat	VA
Black, Hugo L.	76	2	F. Roosevelt	Democrat	AL
Blackmun, Harry A.	98	3	Nixon	Republican	MN
Blair, John	05	5	Washington	Federalist	VA
Blatchford, Samuel	48	2	Arthur	Republican	NY
Bradley, Joseph P.	41	6	Grant	Republican	NJ
Brandeis, Louis D.	67	5	Wilson	Democrat	MA
Brennan, William J.	90	4	Eisenhower	Democrat	NJ
Brewer, David J.	51	7	Harrison	Republican	KS
Breyer, Stephen G.	108	3	Clinton	Democrat	MA
Brown, Henry B.	52	5	Harrison	Republican	MI
Burger, Warren E.	97	1	Nixon	Republican	MN
Burton, Harold H.	84	9	Truman	Republican	OH
Butler, Pierce	71	6	Harding	Democrat	MN
Byrnes, James F.	81	4	F. Roosevelt	Democrat	SC
Campbell, John A.	33	9	Pierce	Democrat	AL
Cardozo, Benjamin N.	75	3	Hoover	Democrat	NY
Catron, John	26	8 or 10	Jackson	Democrat	TN
Chase, Salmon P.	39	1	Lincoln	Republican	OH
Chase, Samuel	09	5	Washington	Federalist	MD
Clark, Tom C.	86	6	Truman	Democrat	TX
Clarke, John H.	68	7	Wilson	Democrat	OH
Clifford, Nathan	34	3	Buchanan	Democrat	ME
Curtis, Benjamin R.	32	3	Fillmore	Whig	MA
Cushing, William	03	3	Washington	Federalist	MA

NAME OF JUSTICE	APPOINTMENT NUMBER	SEAT NUMBER	APPOINTING PRESIDENT	POLITICAL PARTY	STATE
Daniel, Peter V.	28	5	Van Buren	Democrat	VA
Davis, David	37	9	Lincoln	Republican	IL
Day, William R.	59	6	T. Roosevelt	Republican	OH
Douglas, William O.	79	5	F. Roosevelt	Democrat	CT
Duvall, Gabriel	17	5	Madison	Dem.-Rep.	MD
Ellsworth, Oliver	10	1	Washington	Federalist	CT
Field, Stephen J.	38	8 or 10	Lincoln	Democrat	CA
Fortas, Abe	95	3	Johnson	Democrat	TN
Frankfurter, Felix	78	3	F. Roosevelt	Democrat	MA
Fuller, Melville W.	50	1	Cleveland	Democrat	IL
Ginsburg, Ruth B.	107	7	Clinton	Democrat	NY
Goldberg, Arthur J.	94	3	Kennedy	Democrat	IL
Gray, Horace	47	3	Arthur	Republican	MA
Grier, Robert C.	31	4	Polk	Democrat	PA
Harlan, John M., I	44	9	Hayes	Republican	KY
Harlan, John M., II	89	8 or 10	Eisenhower	Republican	NY
Holmes, Oliver W.	58	3	T. Roosevelt	Republican	MA
Hughes, Charles E.	62	7 & 1	Taft & Hoover	Republican	NY
Hunt, Ward	42	2	Grant	Republican	NY
Iredell, James	06	6	Washington	Federalist	NC
Jackson, Howell E.	54	4	Harrison	Democrat	TN
Jackson, Robert H.	82	8 or 10	F. Roosevelt	Democrat	NY
Jay, John	01	1	Washington	Federalist	NY
Johnson, Thomas	07	2	Washington	Federalist	MD
Johnson, William	14	6	Jefferson	Dem.-Rep.	SC
Kennedy, Anthony	104	2	Reagan	Republican	CA
Lamar, Joseph R.	64	5	Taft	Democrat	GA
Lamar, Lucius Q.C.	49	4	Cleveland	Democrat	MS
Livingston, Brockholst	15	2	Jefferson	Dem.-Rep.	NY
Lurton, Horace H.	61	4	Taft	Democrat	TN
McKenna, Joseph	57	8 or 10	McKinley	Republican	CA
McKinley, John	27	9	Van Buren	Democrat	AL
McLean, John	21	7	Jackson	Whig, Dem., Rep.	OH
McReynolds, James C.	66	4	Wilson	Democrat	TN
Marshall, John	13	1	Adams	Federalist	VA
Marshall, Thurgood	96	6	Johnson	Democrat	NY
Matthews, Stanley	46	7	Garfield	Republican	OH
Miller, Samuel F.	36	5	Lincoln	Republican	IA
Minton, Sherman	87	4	Truman	Democrat	IN
Moody, William H.	60	5	T. Roosevelt	Republican	MA
Moore, Alfred	12	6	Adams	Federalist	NC
Murphy, Frank	80	6	F. Roosevelt	Democrat	MI

NAME OF JUSTICE	APPOINTMENT NUMBER	SEAT NUMBER	APPOINTING PRESIDENT	POLITICAL PARTY	STATE
Nelson, Samuel	29	2	Tyler	Democrat	NY
O'Connor, Sandra Day	102	9	Reagan	Republican	AZ
Paterson, William	08	2	Washington	Federalist	NJ
Peckham, Rufus W.	56	4	Cleveland	Democrat	NY
Pitney, Mahlon	65	9	Taft	Republican	NJ
Powell, Louis F., Jr.	99	2	Nixon	Republican	VA
Reed, Stanley F.	77	7	F. Roosevelt	Democrat	KY
Rehnquist, William	100	10 & 1	Nixon & Reagan	Republican	AZ
Roberts, Owen J.	74	9	Hoover	Republican	PA
Rutledge, John	02	2 & 1	Washington	Federalist	SC
Rutledge, Wiley B.	83	4	F. Roosevelt	Democrat	IA
Sanford, Edward T.	72	9	Harding	Republican	TN
Scalia, Antonin	103	10	Reagan	Republican	VA
Shiras, George	53	6	Harrison	Republican	PA
Souter, David H.	105	4	Bush	Republican	NH
Stevens, John Paul	101	5	Ford	Republican	IL
Stewart, Potter	92	9	Eisenhower	Republican	OH
Stone, Harlan F.	73	8 or 10 & 1	Coolidge & F. Roosevelt	Republican	NY
Story, Joseph	18	3	Madison	Dem.-Rep.	MA
Strong, William	40	4	Grant	Republican	PA
Sutherland, George	70	7	Harding	Republican	UT
Swayne, Noah H.	35	7	Lincoln	Republican	OH
Taft, William H.	69	1	Harding	Republican	OH
Taney, Roger B.	24	1	Jackson	Democrat	MD
Thomas, Clarence	106	6	Bush	Republican	GA
Thompson, Smith	19	2	Monroe	Dem.-Rep.	NY
Todd, Thomas	16	7	Jefferson	Dem.-Rep.	KY
Trimble, Robert	20	7	Adams	Dem.-Rep.	KY
Van Devanter, Willis	63	2	Taft	Republican	WY
Vinson, Fred M.	85	1	Truman	Democrat	KY
Waite, Morrison R.	43	1	Grant	Republican	OH
Warren, Earl	88	1	Eisenhower	Republican	CA
Washington, Bushrod	11	4	Adams	Federalist	VA
Wayne, James M.	23	6	Jackson	Democrat	GA
White, Byron R.	93	7	Kennedy	Democrat	CO
White, Edward D.	55	2 & 1	Cleveland & Taft	Democrat	LA
Whittaker, Charles E.	91	7	Eisenhower	Republican	MO
Wilson, James	04	4	Washington	Federalist	PA
Woodbury, Levi	30	3	Polk	Democrat	NH
Woods, William B.	45	4	Hayes	Republican	GA

Table I

ACTS OF CONGRESS HELD
UNCONSTITUTIONAL
IN WHOLE OR IN PART
BY THE SUPREME COURT
OF
THE UNITED STATES

1. Act of September 24, 1789 (1 Stat. 81, §13, in part).

    Provision that "… [the Supreme Court] shall have power to issue writs of mandamus, in cases warranted by the principles and usages of law, to any … persons holding office, under authority of the United States" as applied to the issue of mandamus to the secretary of state, requiring him to deliver to plaintiff a commission (duly signed by the president) as Justice of the Peace in the District of Columbia *held* an attempt to enlarge the original jurisdiction of the Supreme Court, fixed by Article III, § 2.

    Marbury v. Madison, 5 U.S. (1 Cranch) 137 (1803)

2. Act of February 20, 1812 (2 Stat. 677).

    Provisions establishing board of revision to annul titles conferred many years previously by governors of the Northwest Territory *held* violative of the Due Process Clause of the Fifth Amendment.

    Reichart v. Felps, 73 U.S. (6 Wall.) 160 (1868)

3. Act of March 6, 1820 (3 Stat. 548, § 8, proviso).

    The Missouri Compromise, prohibiting slavery within the Louisiana Territory north of 36° 30', except Missouri, *held* not warranted as a regulation of territory belonging to the United States under Article IV, § 3, clause 2 (and *see* Fifth Amendment).

    Scott v. Sandford, 60 U.S. (19 How.) 393 (1857)

4. Act of February 25, 1862 (12 Stat. 345, § 1); July 11, 1862 (12 Stat. 532, § 1); March 3, 1863 (12 Stat. 711, § 3), each in part only.

"Legal tender cases," making noninterest-bearing United States notes legal tender in payment of "all debts, public and private," so far as applied to debts contracted before passage of the act, *held* not within express or implied powers of Congress under Article I, § 8, and inconsistent with Article I, § 10, and the Fifth Amendment.

Hepburn v. Griswold, 75 U.S. (8 Wall.) 603 (1870); overruled in *Knox v. Lee* (*Legal Tender Cases*), 79 U.S. (12 Wall.) 457 (1871)

5. Act of May 20, 1862 (§ 35, 12 Stat.); Act of May 21, 1862 (12 Stat. 407); Act of June 25, 1864 (13 Stat. 187); Act of July 23, 1866 (14 Stat. 216); Revised Statutes Relating to the District of Columbia, Act of June 22, 1874 (§§ 281, 282, 294, 304, 18 Stat. pt. 2).

Provisions of law requiring, or construed to require, racial separation in the schools of the District of Columbia, *held* to violate the equal protection component of the Due Process Clause of the Fifth Amendment.

Bolling v. Sharpe, 347 U.S. 497 (1954)

6. Act of March 3, 1863 (12 Stat. 756, § 5).

"So much of the fifth section ... as provides for the removal of a judgment in a State court, and in which the cause was tried by a jury to the circuit court of the United States for a retrial on the facts and law, is not in pursuance of the Constitution, and is void" under the Seventh Amendment.

The Justices v. Murray, 76 U.S. (9 Wall.) 274 (1870)

7. Act of March 3, 1863 (12 Stat. 766, § 5).

Provision for an appeal from the Court of Claims to the Supreme Court—there being, at the time, a further provision (§ 14) requiring an estimate by the secretary of the treasury before payment of final judgment, *held* to contravene the judicial finality intended by the Constitution, Article III.

Gordon v. United States, 69 U.S. (2 Wall.) 561 (1865) (Case was dismissed without opinion; the grounds upon which this decision was made were stated in a posthumous opinion by Chief Justice Taney printed in the appendix to volume 117 U.S. 697.)

8. Act of June 30, 1864 (13 Stat. 311, § 13).

Provision that "any prize cause now pending in any circuit court shall, on the application of all parties in interest ... be transferred by that court to the Supreme Court ...," as applied in a case where no action had been taken in the Circuit Court on the appeal from the District Court, *held* to propose an appeal procedure not within Article III, § 2.

The Alicia, 74 U.S. (7 Wall.) 571 (1869)

9. Act of January 24, 1865 (13 Stat. 424).

    Requirement of a test oath (disavowing actions in hostility to the United States) before admission to appear as attorney in a Federal Court by virtue of any previous admission, *held* invalid as applied to an attorney who had been pardoned by the president for all offenses during the Rebellion—as *ex post facto* (Article I, § 9, clause 3) and an interference with the pardoning power (Article II, § 2, clause 1).
    Ex parte Garland, 71 U.S. (4 Wall.) 333 (1867)

10. Act of March 2, 1867 (14 Stat. 484, § 29).

    General prohibition on sale of naphtha, etc., for illuminating purposes, if inflammable at less temperature than 110°F, *held* invalid "except so far as the section named operates within the United States, but without the limits of any State," as being a mere police regulation.
    United States v. Dewitt, 78 U.S. (9 Wall.) 41 (1870)

11. Act of May 31, 1870 (16 Stat. 140, §§ 3, 4).

    Provisions penalizing (1) refusal of local election official to permit voting by persons offering to qualify under state laws, applicable to any citizens; and (2) hindering of any person from qualifying or voting, *held* invalid under Fifteenth Amendment.
    United States v. Reese, 92 U.S. 214 (1876)

12. Act of July 12, 1870 (16 Stat. 235).

    Provision making presidential pardons inadmissible in evidence in Court of Claims, prohibiting their use by that court in deciding claims or appeals, and requiring dismissal of appeals by the Supreme Court in cases where proof of loyalty had been made otherwise than as prescribed by law, *held* an interference with judicial power under Article III, § 1, and with the pardoning power under Article II, § 2, clause 1.
    United States v. Klein, 80 U.S. (13 Wall.) 128 (1872)

13. Act of June 22, 1874 (18 Stat. 1878, § 4).

    Provision authorizing federal courts, in suits for forfeitures under revenue and custom laws, to require production of documents, with allegations expected to be proved therein to be taken as proved on failure to produce such documents, was *held* violative of the search and seizure provision of the Fourth Amendment and the self-incrimination clause of the Fifth Amendment.
    Boyd v. United States, 116 U.S. 616 (1886)

14. Revised Statutes 1977 (Act of May 31, 1870, 16 Stat. 144).

    Provision that "all persons within the jurisdiction of the United States shall have the same right in every State and Territory to make and enforce contracts ... as is enjoyed by white citizens ...," *held* invalid under the Thirteenth Amendment.

Hodges v. *United States,* 203 U.S. 1 (1906)

15. Revised Statutes 4937–4947 (Act of July 8, 1870, 16 Stat. 210), and Act of August 14, 1876 (19 Stat. 141).

Original trademark law, applying to marks "for exclusive use within the United States," and a penal act designed solely for the protection of rights defined in the earlier measure, *held* not supportable by Article I, § 8, clause 8 (copyright clause), nor Article I, § 8, clause 3, by reason of its application to intrastate as well as interstate commerce.

Trade-Mark Cases, 100 U.S. 82 (1879)

16. Revised Statutes 5132, subdivision 9 (Act of March 2, 1867, 14 Stat. 539).

Provision penalizing "any person respecting whom bankruptcy proceedings are commenced ... who, within 3 months before the commencement of proceedings in bankruptcy, under the false color and pretense of carrying on business and dealing in the ordinary course of trade, obtains on credit from any person any goods or chattels with intent to defraud ...," *held* a police regulation not within the bankruptcy power (Article I, § 4, clause 4).

United States v. *Fox,* 95 U.S. 670 (1878)

17. Revised Statutes 5507 (Act of May 31, 1870, 16 Stat. 141, § 4).

Provision penalizing "every person who prevents, hinders, controls, or intimidates another from exercising ... the right of suffrage, to whom that right is guaranteed by the Fifteenth Amendment to the Constitution of the United States, by means of bribery ...," *held* not authorized by the Fifteenth Amendment.

James v. *Bowman,* 190 U.S. 127 (1903)

18. Revised Statutes 5519 (Act of April 20, 1871, 17 Stat. 13, § 2).

Section providing punishment in case "two or more persons in any State ... conspire ... for the purpose of depriving ... any person ... of the equal protection of the laws ... or for the purpose of preventing or hindering the constituted authorities of any State ... from giving or securing to all persons within such State ... the equal protection of the laws ...," *held* invalid as not being directed at state action proscribed by the Fourteenth Amendment.

United States v. *Harris,* 106 U.S. 629 (1883)

19. Revised Statutes of the District of Columbia, § 1064 (Act of June 17, 1870, 16 Stat. 154, § 3).

Provision that "prosecutions in the police court [of the District of Columbia] shall be by information under oath, without indictment by grand jury or trial by petit jury," as applied to punishment for conspiracy, *held* to contravene Article III, § 2, clause 3, requiring jury trial of all crimes.

Callan v. Wilson, 127 U.S. 540 (1888)

20. Act of March 1, 1875 (18 Stat. 336, §§ 1, 2).

Provision that "all persons within the jurisdiction of the United States shall be entitled to the full and equal enjoyment of the accommodation ... of inns, public conveyances on land or water, theaters, and other places of public amusement; subject only to the conditions and limitations established by law, and applicable alike to citizens of every race and color, regardless of any previous condition of servitude"— subject to penalty, *held* not to be supported by the Thirteenth or Fourteenth Amendments.

Civil Rights Cases, 109 U.S. 3 (1883)

21. Act of March 3, 1875 (18 Stat. 479, § 2).

Provision that "if the party [i.e., a person stealing property from the United States] has been convicted, then the judgment against him shall be conclusive evidence in the prosecution against [the] receiver that the property of the United States therein described has been embezzled, stolen, or purloined," *held* to contravene the Sixth Amendment.

Kirby v. United States, 174 U.S. 47 (1899)

22. Act of July 12, 1876 (19 Stat. 80, sec. 6, in part).

Provision that "postmasters of the first, second, and third classes ... may be removed by the President by and with the advice and consent of the Senate," *held* to infringe the executive power under Article II, § 1, clause 1.

Myers v. United States, 272 U.S. 52 (1926)

23. Act of August 11, 1888 (25 Stat. 411).

Clause, in a provision for the purchase or condemnation of a certain lock and dam in the Monongahela River, that "... in estimating the sum to be paid by the United States, the franchise of said corporation to collect tolls shall not be considered or estimated ...," *held* to contravene the Fifth Amendment.

Monongahela Navigation Co. v. United States, 148 U.S. 312 (1893)

24. Act of May 5, 1892 (27 Stat. 25, § 4).

Provision of a Chinese exclusion act, that Chinese persons "convicted and adjudged to be not lawfully entitled to be or remain in the United States shall be imprisoned at hard labor for a period not exceeding 1 year and thereafter removed from the United States ..." (such conviction and judgment being had before a justice, judge, or commissioner upon a summary hearing), *held* to contravene the Fifth and Sixth Amendments.

Wong Wing v. *United States,* 163 U.S. 228 (1896)

25. Joint Resolution of August 4, 1894 (28 Stat. 1018, No. 41).

Provision authorizing the secretary of the interior to approve a second lease of certain land by an Indian chief in Minnesota (granted to lessor's ancestor by Art. 9 of a treaty with the Chippewa Indians), *held* an interference with judicial interpretation of treaties under Article III, § 2, clause 1 (and repugnant to the Fifth Amendment).

Jones v. *Meehan,* 175 U.S. 1 (1899)

26. Act of August 27, 1894 (28 Stat. 553–560, §§ 27–37).

Income tax provisions of the tariff act of 1894. "The tax imposed by §§ 27 and 37, inclusive … so far as it falls on the income of real estate and of personal property, being a direct tax within the meaning of the Constitution, and, therefore, unconstitutional and void because not apportioned according to representation [Article I, § 2, clause 3], all those sections, constituting one entire scheme of taxation, are necessarily invalid" (158 U.S. 601, 637).

Pollock v. *Farmers' Loan & Trust Co.,* 157 U.S. 429 (1895), and rehearing, 158 U.S. 601 (1895)

27. Act of January 30, 1897 (29 Stat. 506).

Prohibition on sale of liquor "… to any Indian to whom allotment of land has been made while the title to the same shall be held in trust by the Government …," *held* a price regulation infringing state powers, and not warranted by the Commerce Clause, Article I, § 8, clause 3.

In re Heff, 197 U.S. 488 (1905)

28. Act of June 1, 1898 (30 Stat. 428).

Section 10, penalizing "any employer subject to the provisions of this act" who should "threaten any employee with loss of employment … because of his membership in … a labor corporation, association, or organization" (the act being applicable "to any common carrier … engaged in the transportation of passengers or property … from one State … to another State …," etc.), *held* an infringement of the Fifth Amendment and not supported by the Commerce Clause.

Adair v. *United States,* 208 U.S. 161 (1908)

29. Act of June 13, 1898 (30 Stat. 448, 459).

Stamp tax on foreign bills of lading, *held* a tax on exports in violation of Article I, § 9.

Fairbank v. *United States,* 181 U.S. 283 (1901)

30. Same (30 Stat. 448, 460).

Tax on charter parties, as applied to shipments exclusively from ports in United States to foreign ports, *held* a tax on exports in violation of Article I, § 9.

United States v. Hvoslef, 237 U.S. 1 (1915)

31. Same (30 Stat. 448, 461).

Stamp tax on policies of marine insurance on exports, *held* a tax on exports in violation of Article I, § 9.

Thames & Mersey Marine Ins. Co. v. United States, 237 U.S. 19 (1915)

32. Act of June 6, 1900 (31 Stat. 359, § 171).

Section of the Alaska Code providing for a six-person jury in trials for misdemeanors, *held* repugnant to the Sixth Amendment, requiring "jury" trial of crimes.

Rassmussen v. United States, 197 U.S. 516 (1905)

33. Act of March 3, 1901 (31 Stat. 1341, § 935).

Section of the District of Columbia Code granting the same right of appeal, in criminal cases, to the United States or the District of Columbia as to the defendant, but providing that a verdict was not to be set aside for error found in rulings during trial, *held* an attempt to take an advisory opinion, contrary to Article III, § 2.

United States v. Evans, 213 U.S. 297 (1909)

34. Act of June 11, 1906 (34 Stat. 232).

Act providing that "every common carrier engaged in trade or commerce in the District of Columbia ... or between the several States ... shall be liable to any of its employees ... for all damages which may result from the negligence of any of its officers ... or by reason of any defect ... due to its negligence in its cars, engines ... roadbed," etc., *held* not supportable under Article I, § 8, clause 3, because it extended to intrastate as well as interstate commercial activities.

Employers' Liability Cases, 207 U.S. 463 (1908)

35. Act of June 16, 1906 (34 Stat. 269, § 2).

Provision of Oklahoma Enabling Act restricting relocation of the state capital prior to 1913, *held* not supportable by Article IV, § 3, authorizing admission of new states.

Coyle v. Smith, 221 U.S. 559 (1911)

36. Act of February 20, 1907 (34 Stat. 889, § 3).

Provision in the Immigration Act of 1907 penalizing "whoever ... shall keep, maintain, control, support, or harbor in any house or other place for the purpose of prostitution ... any alien woman or girl, within 3 years after she shall have entered the United States," *held* an exercise of police power not within the control of Congress over immigration (whether drawn from the Commerce Clause or based on inherent sovereignty).

Keller v. *United States,* 213 U.S. 138 (1909)

37. Act of March 1, 1907 (34 Stat. 1028).

Provisions authorizing certain Indians "to institute their suits in the Court of Claims to determine the validity of any acts of Congress passed since ... 1902, insofar as said acts ... attempt to increase or extend the restrictions upon alienation ... of allotments of lands of Cherokee citizens ...," and giving a right of appeal to the Supreme Court, *held* an attempt to enlarge the judicial power restricted by Article III, § 2, to cases and controversies.

Muskrat v. *United States,* 219 U.S. 346 (1911)

38. Act of May 27, 1908 (35 Stat. 313, § 4).

Provision making locally taxable "all land [of Indians of the Five Civilized Tribes] from which restrictions have been or shall be removed," *held* a violation of the Fifth Amendment, in view of the Atoka Agreement, embodied in the Curtis Act of June 28, 1898, providing tax exemption for allotted lands while title in original allottee, not exceeding 21 years.

Choate v. *Trapp,* 224 U.S. 665 (1912)

39. Act of February 9, 1909, § 2, 35 Stat. 614, as amended.

Provision of Narcotic Drugs Import and Export Act creating a presumption that possessor of cocaine knew of its illegal importation into the United States *held*, in light of the fact that more cocaine is produced domestically than is brought into the country and in absence of any showing that defendant could have known his cocaine was imported, if it was, inapplicable to support conviction from mere possession of cocaine.

Turner v. *United States,* 396 U.S. 398 (1970)

40. Act of August 19, 1911 (37 Stat. 28).

A proviso in §8 of the Federal Corrupt Practices Act fixing a maximum authorized expenditure by a candidate for senator "in any campaign for his nomination and election," as applied to a primary election, *held* not supported by Article I, § 4, giving Congress power to regulate the manner of holding elections for senators and representatives.

Newberry v. *United States,* 256 U.S. 232 (1921), overruled in *United States* v. *Classic,* 313 U.S. 299 (1941)

41. Act of June 18, 1912 (37 Stat. 136, § 8).

Part of § 8 giving Juvenile Court of the District of Columbia (proceeding upon information) concurrent jurisdiction of desertion cases (which were, by law, punishable by fine or imprisonment in the workhouse at hard labor for 1 year), *held* invalid under the Fifth Amendment which gives right to presentment by a grand jury in case of infamous crimes.

United States v. *Moreland*, 258 U.S. 433 (1922)

42. Act of March 4, 1913 (37 Stat. 988, part of par. 64).

   Provision of the District of Columbia Public Utility Commission Act authorizing appeal to the United States Supreme Court from decrees of the District of Columbia Court Appeals modifying valuation decisions of the Utilities Commission, *held* an attempt to extend the appellate jurisdiction of the Supreme Court to cases not strictly judicial within the meaning of Article III, § 2.

Keller v. *Potomac Electric Power Co.*, 261 U.S. 428 (1923)

43. Act of September 1, 1916 (39 Stat. 675).

   The original Child Labor Law, providing "that no producer … shall ship … in interstate commerce … any article or commodity the product of any mill … in which within 30 days prior to the removal of such product therefrom children under the age of 14 years have been employed or permitted to work more than 8 hours in any day or more than 6 days in any week, …," *held* not within the commerce power of Congress.

Hammer v. *Dagenhart*, 247 U.S. 251 (1918)

44. Act of September 8, 1916 (39 Stat. 757, § 2(a), in part).

   Provision of the income tax law of 1916, that a "stock dividend shall be considered income, to the amount of its cash value," *held* invalid (in spite of the Sixteenth Amendment) as an attempt to tax something not actually income, without regard to apportionment under Article I, § 2, clause 3.

Eisner v. *Macomber*, 256 U.S. 170 (1921)

45. Act of October 6, 1917 (40 Stat. 395).

   The amendment of §§ 24 and 256 of the Judicial code (which prescribe in jurisdiction of district courts) "saving … to claimants the rights and remedies under the workmen's compensation law of any State," *held* an attempt to transfer federal legislative powers to the States—the Constitution, by Article III, § 2, and Article I, § 8, having adopted rules of general maritime law.

Knickerbocker Ice Co. v. *Stewart*, 253 U.S. 149 (1920)

46. Act of September 19, 1918 (40 Stat. 960).

   Specifically, that part of the Minimum Wage Law of the District of Columbia which authorized the Wage Board "to ascertain and declare … Standards of minimum wages for women in any occupation within the District of Columbia, and what wages are inadequate to supply the necessary cost of living to any such women workers to maintain them in good health and to protect their morals ...," *held* to interfere with freedom of contract under the Fifth Amendment.

Adkins v. *Children's Hospital* v. *District of Columbia*, 261 U.S. 525 (1923) overruled in *West Coast Hotel Co.* v. *Parrish*, 300 U.S. 379 (1937)

47. Act of February 24, 1919 (40 Stat. 1065, § 213, in part).

That part of § 213 of the Revenue Act of 1919 which provided that "... for the purposes of the title ... the term 'gross income' ... includes gains, profits, and income derived from salaries, wages, or compensation for personal service (including in the case of ... judges of the Supreme and inferior courts of the United States ... the compensation received as such) ..." as applied to a judge in office when the act was passed, *held* a violation of the guaranty of judges' salaries, in Article III, § 1.

Evans v. *Gore*, 253 U.S. 245 (1920)
Miles v. *Graham*, 268 U.S. 501 (1925)

48. Act of February 24, 1919 (40 Stat. 1097, § 402[c]).

That part of the estate tax law providing that "gross estate" of a decedent should include value of all property "to the extent of any interest therein of which the decedent has at any time made a transfer or with respect to which he had at any time created a trust, in contemplation of or intended to take effect in possession or enjoyment at or after his death (whether such transfer or trust is made or created before or after the passage of this act), except in case of a *bona fide* sale ..." as applied to a transfer of property made prior to the act and intended to take effect "in possession or enjoyment" at death of grantor, but not in fact testamentary or designed to evade taxation, *held* confiscatory, contrary to Fifth Amendment.

Nicholds v. *Coolidge*, 274 U.S. 531 (1927)

49. Act of February 24, 1919, title XII (40 Stat. 1138, entire title).

The Child Labor Tax Act, providing that "every person ... operating ... any ... factory ... in which children under the age of 14 years have been employed or permitted to work ... shall pay ... in addition to all other taxes imposed by law, an excise tax equivalent to 10 percent of the entire net profits received ... for such year from the sale ... of the product of such ... factory ...," *held* beyond the taxing power under Article I, § 8, clause 1, and an infringement of state authority.

Child Labor Tax Case, 259 U.S. 20 (1922)

50. Act of October 22, 1919 (41 Stat. 298, § 2), amending Act of August 10, 1917 (40 Stat. 277, § 4).

(a) § 4 of the Lever Act, providing in part "that it is hereby made unlawful for any person willfully ... to make any unjust or unreasonable rate or charge in handling or dealing in or with any necessaries ... and fixing a penalty, *held* invalid to support an indictment for charging an unreasonable price on sale—as not setting up an ascertainable standard of guilt within the requirement of the Sixth Amendment.

> *United States v. L. Cohen Grocery Co.,* 255 U.S. 81 (1921)

(b) That provision of § 4 making it unlawful "to conspire, combine, agree, or arrange with any other person to ... exact excessive prices for any necessaries" and fixing a penalty, *held* invalid to support an indictment, on the reasoning of the *Cohen Grocery* case.

> *Weeds, Inc. v. United States,* 255 U.S. 109 (1921)
> Concurring: Chief Justice White, and Justices McKenna, Holmes, Van Devanter, McReynolds, and Clarke.
> Concurring specially: Justices Pitney and Brandeis.

51. Act of August 24, 1921 (42 Stat. 187, Future Trading Act).

(a) § 4 (and interwoven regulations) providing a "tax of 20 cents a bushel on every bushel involved therein, upon each contract of sale of grain for future delivery, except ... where such contracts are made by or through a member of a board of trade which has been designated by the Secretary of Agriculture as a 'contract market' ...," *held* not within the taxing power under Article I, § 8.

> *Hill v. Wallace,* 259 U.S. 44 (1922)

(b) § 3, providing "that in addition to the taxes now imposed by law there is hereby levied a tax amounting to 20 cents per bushel on each bushel involved therein, whether the actual commodity is intended to be delivered or only nominally referred to, upon each ... option for a contract either of purchase or sale of grain ...," *held* invalid on the same reasoning.

> *Trusler v. Crooks,* 269 U.S. 475 (1926)

52. Act of November 23, 1921 (42 Stat. 261, § 245, in part).

Provision of Revenue Act of 1921 abating the deduction (4 per cent of mean reserves) allowed from taxable income of life insurance companies in general by the amount of interest on their tax exempts, and so according no relative advantage to the owners of the tax-exempt securities, *held* to destroy a guaranteed exemption.

> *National Life Ins. v. United States,* 277 U.S. 508 (1928)

53. Act of June 10, 1922 (42 Stat. 634).

A second attempt to amend §§ 24 and 256 of the Judicial Code, relating to jurisdiction of District Courts, by saving "to claimants for compensation for injuries to or death of persons other than the master or members of the crew of a vessel, their rights and remedies under the workmen's compensation law of any State ..." *held* invalid on authority of *Knickerbocker Ice Co.* v. *Stewart.*

> *Washington v. W.C. Dawson & Co.,* 264 U.S. 219 (1924)

54. Act of June 2, 1924 (43 Stat. 313).

> The gift tax provisions of the Revenue Act of 1924, applicable to gifts made during the calendar year, were *held* invalid under the Fifth Amendment insofar as they applied to gifts made before passage of the act.
>
> *Untermeyer* v. *Anderson,* 276 U.S. 440 (1928)

55. Act of February 26, 1926 (44 Stat. 70, § 302, in part).

> Stipulation creating a conclusive presumption that gifts made within two years prior to the death of the donor were made in contemplation of death of donor and requiring the value thereof to be included in computing the death transfer tax on decedent's estate was *held* to effect an invalid deprivation of property without due process.
>
> *Heiner* v. *Donnan,* 258 U.S. 312 (1932)

56. Act of February 26, 1926 (44 Stat. 95, § 701).

> Provision imposing a special excise tax of $1,000 on liquor dealers operating in states where such business is illegal, was *held* a penalty, without constitutional support following repeal of the Eighteenth Amendment.
>
> *United States* v. *Constantine,* 296 U.S. 287 (1935)

57. Act of March 20, 1933 (48 Stat. 11, § 17, in part).

> Clause in the Economy Act of 1933 providing "… all laws granting or pertaining to yearly renewable term war risk insurance are hereby repealed," *held* invalid to abrogate an outstanding contract of insurance, which is a vested right protected by the Fifth Amendment.
>
> *Lynch* v. *United States,* 292 U.S. 571 (1934)

58. Act of May 12, 1933 (48 Stat. 31).

> Agricultural Adjustment Act providing for processing taxes on agricultural commodities and benefit payments therefore to farmers, *held* not within the taxing power under Article I, § 8, clause 1.
>
> *United States* v. *Butler,* 297 U.S. 1 (1936)

59. Act of Joint Resolution of June 5, 1933 (48 Stat. 113, § 1).

> Abrogation of gold clause in government obligations, *held* a repudiation of the pledge implicit in the power to borrow money (Article I, § 8, clause 2), and within the prohibition of the Fourteenth Amendment, against questioning the validity of the public debt. (The majority of the Court, however, held plaintiff not entitled to recover under the circumstances.)
>
> *Perry* v. *United States,* 294 U.S. 330 (1935)

60. Act of June 16, 1933 (48 Stat. 195, the National Industrial Recovery Act).

> (a) Title I, except § 9.
>
> Provisions relating to codes of fair competition, authorized to be approved by the president in his discretion "to effectuate the policy" of

the act, *held* invalid as a delegation of legislative power (Article I, § 1) and not within the commerce power (Article I, § 8, clause 3).

A.L.A. Schechter Poultry Corp. v. United States, 295 U.S. 495 (1935)

(b) § 9 (c).

Clause of the oil regulation section authorizing the president "to prohibit the transportation in interstate ... commerce of petroleum ... produced or withdrawn from storage in excess of the amount permitted ... by any State law ..." and prescribing a penalty for violation of orders issued thereunder, *held* invalid as a delegation of legislative power.

Panama Refining Co. v. Ryan, 293 U.S. 388 (1935)

61. Act of June 16, 1933 (48 Stat. 307, § 13).

Temporary reduction of 15 per cent in retired pay of judges, retired from service by subject to performance of judicial duties under the Act of March 1, 1929 (45 Stat. 1422), was *held* a violation of the guaranty of judges' salaries in Article III, § 1.

Booth v. United States, 291 U.S. 339 (1934)

62. Act of April 27, 1934 (48 Stat. 646, § 6), amending § 5(i) of Home Owners' Loan Act of 1933.

Provision for conversion of state building and loan associations into federal associations, upon vote of 51 per cent of the votes cast at a meeting of stockholders called to consider such action, *held* an encroachment on reserved powers of State.

Hopkins Federal Sav. & Loan Assoc. v. Cleary, 296 U.S. 315 (1935)

63. Act of May 24, 1934 (48 Stat. 798).

Provision for readjustment of municipal indebtedness, though "adequately related" to the bankruptcy power, was *held* invalid as an interference with state sovereignty.

Ashton v. Cameron County Water Improv. Dist., 298 U.S. 513 (1936)

64. Act of June 27, 1934 (48 Stat. 1283).

The Railroad Retirement Act, establishing a detailed compulsory retirement system for employees of carriers subject to the Interstate Commerce Act, *held* not a regulation of commerce within the meaning of Article I, § 8, clause 3, and violative of the Due Process Clause (Fifth Amendment).

Railroad Retirement Bd. v. Alton R. Co., 295 U.S. 330 (1935)

65. Act of June 28, 1934 (48 Stat. 1289, ch. 869).

The Frazier-Lemke Act, adding subsection (s) to § 75 of the Bankruptcy Act, designed to preserve to mortgagors the ownership and enjoyment of their farm property and providing specifically, in paragraph 7, that a bankrupt left in possession has the option at any time within 5 years of buying at the appraised value—subject meanwhile to no monetary obligation other than payment of reasonable rental, *held* a violation of property rights, under the Fifth Amendment.

Louisville Joint Stock Land Bank v. *Radford*, 295 U.S. 555 (1935)

66. Act of August 24, 1935 (48 Stat. 750).

Amendments of Agricultural Adjustment Act *held* not within the taxing power.

Rickert Rice Mills, Inc. v. *Fontenot*, 297 U.S. 110 (1936)

67. Act of August 30, 1935 (49 Stat. 991).

Bituminous Coal Conservation Act of 1935, *held* to impose not a tax within Article I, § 8, but a penalty not sustained by the commerce clause (Article I, § 8, clause 3).

Carter v. *Carter Coal Co.*, 298 U.S. 238 (1936)

68. Act of June 25, 1938 (52 Stat. 1040).

Federal Food, Drug, and Cosmetic Act of 1938, § 301(f), prohibiting the refusal to permit entry or inspection of premises by federal officers *held* void for vagueness and as violative of the Due Process Clause of the Fifth Amendment.

United States v. *Cardiff*, 344 U.S. 174 (1952)

69. Act of June 30, 1938 (52 Stat. 1251).

Federal Firearms Act, § 2(f) establishing a presumption of guilt based on a prior conviction and present possession of a firearm, *held* to violate the test of due process under the Fifth Amendment.

Tot v. *United States*, 319 U.S. 463 (1943)

70. Act of August 10, 1939 (§ 201[d], 53 Stat. 1362, as amended, 42 U.S.C. § 402[g]).

Provision of Social Security Act that grants survivors' benefits based on the earnings of a deceased husband and father covered by the Act to his widow and to the couple's children in her care but that grants benefits based on the earnings of a covered deceased wife and mother only to the minor children and not to the widower *held* violative of the right to equal protection secured by the Fifth Amendment's Due Process Clause, since it unjustifiably discriminates against female wage earners required to pay social security taxes by affording them less protection for their survivors than is provided for male wage earners.

Weinberger v. *Wiesenfeld*, 420 U.S. 636 (1975)

71. Act of October 14, 1940 (54 Stat. 1169 § 401[g]); as amended by Act of January 20, 1944 (58 Stat. 4, § 1).

Provision of Aliens and Nationality Code (8 U.S.C. § 1481[a][8]), derived from the Nationality Act of 1940, as amended, that citizenship shall be lost upon conviction by court martial and dishonorable discharge for deserting the armed services in time of war, *held* invalid as imposing a cruel and unusual punishment barred by the Eighth Amendment and not authorized by the war powers conferred by Article I, § 8, clauses 11 to 14.

Trop v. *Dulles,* 356 U.S. 86 (1958)

72. Act of November 15, 1943 (57 Stat. 450).

Urgent Deficiency Appropriation Act of 1943, § 304, providing that no salary should be paid to certain named federal employees out of moneys appropriated, *held* to violate Article I, § 9, clause 3, forbidding enactment of bill of attainder or *ex post facto* law.

United States v. *Lovett,* 328 U.S. 303 (1946)

73. Act of September 27, 1944 (58 Stat. 746, § 401[J]); and Act of June 27, 1952 (66 Stat. 163, 267–268, § 349[a][10]).

§ 401(J) of Immigration and Nationality Act of 1940, added in 1944, and § 49(a)(10) of the Immigration and Nationality Act of 1952 depriving one of citizenship, without the procedural safeguards guaranteed by the Fifth and Sixth Amendments, for the offense of leaving or remaining outside the country, in time of war or national emergency, to evade military service *held* invalid.

Kennedy v. *Mendoza-Martinez,* 372 U.S. 144 (1963)

74. Act of July 31, 1946 (ch. 707, § 7, 60 Stat. 719).

District court decision *holding* invalid under First and Fifth Amendments statute prohibiting parades or assemblages on United States Capitol grounds is summarily affirmed.

Chief of Capitol Police v. *Jeanette Rankin Brigade,* 409 U.S. 972 (1972)

75. Act of June 25, 1948 (62 Stat. 760).

Provision of Lindberg Kidnapping Act which provided for the imposition of the death penalty only if recommended by the jury *held* unconstitutional inasmuch as it penalized the assertion of a defendant's Sixth Amendment right to jury trial.

United States v. *Jackson,* 390 U.S. 570 (1968)

76. Act of August 18, 1949 (63 Stat. 617, 40 U.S.C. § 13k).

Provision, insofar as it applies to the public sidewalks surrounding the Supreme Court building, which bars the display of any flag, banner, or device designed to bring into public notice any party, organization, or movement *held* violative of the Free Speech Clause of the First Amendment.

United States v. *Grace,* 461 U.S. 171 (1983)

77. Act of May 5, 1950 (64 Stat. 107).

Article 3(a) of the Uniform Code of Military Justice subjecting civilian ex-servicemen to court martial for crime committed while in military service *held* to violate Article III, § 2, and the Fifth and Sixth Amendments.

Toth v. *Quarles,* 350 U.S. 11 (1955)

78. Act of May 5, 1950 (64 Stat. 107).

Insofar as Article 2(11) of the Uniform Code of Military Justice subjects civilian dependents accompanying members of the armed forces overseas in time of peace to trial, in capital cases, by court martial, it is violative of Article III, § 2, and the Fifth and Sixth Amendments.

Reid v. *Covert,* 354 U.S. 1 (1957)

Insofar as the aforementioned provision is invoked in time of peace for the trial of noncapital offenses committed on land bases overseas by employees of the armed forces who have not been inducted or who have not voluntarily enlisted therein, it is violative of the Sixth Amendment.

McElroy v. *United States,* 361 U.S. 281 (1960)

Insofar as the aforementioned provision is invoked in time of peace for the trial of noncapital offenses committed by civilian dependents accompanying members of the armed forces overseas, it is violative of Article III, § 2, and the Fifth and Sixth Amendments.

Kinsella v. *United States,* 361 U.S. 234 (1960)

Insofar as the aforementioned provision is invoked in time of peace for the trial of a capital offense committed by a civilian employee of the armed forces overseas, it is violative of Article III, § 2, and the Fifth and Sixth Amendments.

Grisham v. *Hagan,* 361 U.S. 278 (1960)

79. Act of August 16, 1950 (64 Stat. 451, as amended).

Statutory scheme authorizing the Postmaster General to close the mails to distributors of obscene materials *held* unconstitutional in the absence of procedural provisions which would assure prompt judicial determination that protected materials were not being restrained.

Blount v. *Rizzi,* 400 U.S. 410 (1971)

80. Act of August 28, 1950 (§ 202[c][1][D], 64 Stat. 483, 42 U.S.C. § 402[c][1][C]).

District Court decision *holding* invalid as a violation of the equal protection component of the Fifth Amendment's Due Process Clause a Social Security provision entitling a husband to insurance benefits through his wife's benefits, provided he received at least one-half of his support from her at the time she became entitled, but requiring no such showing of support for the wife to qualify for benefits through her husband, is summarily affirmed.

Califano v. *Silbowitz,* 430 U.S. 934 (1977)

81. Act of August 28, 1950 (§ 202[f][1][E], 64 Stat. 485, 42 U.S.C. § 402[f][1][D]).
Social Security Act provision awarding survivor's benefits based on earnings of a deceased wife to widower only if he was receiving at least half of his support from her at the time of her death, whereas widow received benefits regardless of dependency, *held* violative of equal protection element of Fifth Amendment's Due Process Clause because of its impermissible sex classification.
Califano v. Goldfarb, 430 U.S. 199 (1977)

82. Act of September 23, 1950 (Title I, § 5, 64 Stat. 992).
Provision of Subversive Activities Control Act making it unlawful for member of Communist front organization to work in a defense plant *held* to be an overbroad infringement of the right of association protected by the First Amendment.
United States v. Robel, 389 U.S. 258 (1967)

83. Act of September 23, 1950 (64 Stat. 993, § 6).
Subversive Activities Control Act of 1950, § 6, providing that any member of a Communist organization, which has registered or has been ordered to register, commits a crime if he attempts to obtain or use a passport, *held* violative of due process under the Fifth Amendment.
Aptheker v. Secretary of State, 378 U.S. 500 (1964)

84. Act of September 28, 1950 (Title I, § 7, 64 Stat. 993).
Provisions of Subversive Activities Control Act of 1950 requiring in lieu of registration by the Communist party registration by party members may not be applied to compel registration or to prosecute for refusal to register of alleged members who have asserted their privilege against self-incrimination inasmuch as registration would expose such persons to criminal prosecution under other laws.
Albertson v. Subversive Activities Control Board, 382 U.S. 70 (1965)

85. Act of October 30, 1951 (§ 5[f][ii], 65 Stat. 683, 45 U.S.C. § 231a[c][3][ii]).
Provision of Railroad Retirement Act similar to section voided in *Goldfarb* (ns. 81).
Railroad Retirement Bd. v. Kalina, 431 U.S. 909 (1977)

86. Act of June 27, 1952 (Title III, § 349, 66 Stat. 267).
Provision of Immigration and Nationality Act of 1952 providing for revocation of United States citizenship of one who votes in a foreign election *held* unconstitutional under § 1 of the Fourteenth Amendment.
Afroyim v. Rusk, 387 U.S. 253 (1967)

87. Act of June 27, 1952 (66 Stat. 163, 269, § 352[a][1]).
§ 352(a)(1) of the Immigration and Nationality Act of 1952 depriving a naturalized person of citizenship for "having a continuous residence

for three years" in state of his birth or prior nationality *held* violative of the Due Process Clause of the Fifth Amendment.

Schneider v. *Rusk,* 377 U.S. 163 (1964)

88. Act of August 16, 1954 (68A Stat. 525, Int. Rev. Code of 1954, §§ 4401–4423).

Provisions of tax laws requiring gamblers to pay occupational and excise taxes may not be used over an assertion of one's privilege against self-incrimination either to compel extensive reporting of activities, leaving the registrant subject to prosecution under the laws of all the states with the possible exception of Nevada, or to prosecute for failure to register and report, because the scheme abridged the Fifth Amendment privilege.

Marchetti v. *United States,* 390 U.S. 39 (1968) and *Grosso* v. *United States,* 390 U.S. 62 (1968)

89. Act of August 16, 1954 (68A Stat. 560, Marijuana Tax Act, §§ 4741, 4744, 4751, 4753).

Provisions of tax laws requiring possessors of marijuana to register and to pay a transfer tax may not be used over an assertion of the privilege against self-incrimination to compel registration or to prosecute for failure to register.

Leary v. *United States,* 395 U.S. 6 (1969)

90. Act of August 16, 1954 (68A Stat. 728, Int. Rev. Code of 1954, §§ 5841, 5851).

Provisions of tax laws requiring the possessor of certain firearms, which are made illegal to receive or to possess, to register with the Treasury Department may not be used over an assertion of the privilege against self-incrimination to prosecute one for failure to register or for possession of an unregistered firearm since the statutory scheme abridges the Fifth Amendment privilege.

Haynes v. *United States,* 390 U.S. 85 (1968)

91. Act of August 16, 1954 (68A Stat. 867, Int. Rev. Code of 1954, § 7302).

Provision of tax laws providing for forfeiture of property used in violating internal revenue laws may not be constitutionally used in face of invocation of privilege against self-incrimination to condemn money in possession of gambler who had failed to comply with the registration and reporting scheme *held* void in *Marchetti* v. *United States,* 390 U.S. 39 (1968).

United States v. *United States Coin & Currency,* 401 U.S. 715 (1971)

92. Act of July 18, 1956 (§ 106, Stat. 570).

Provision of Narcotic Drugs Import and Export Act creating a presumption that possessor of marijuana knew of its illegal importation into the United States *held*, in absence of showing that all marijuana in

United States was of foreign origin and that domestic users could know that their marijuana was more likely than not of foreign origin, unconstitutional under the Due Process Clause of the Fifth Amendment.

Leary v. *United States,* 395 U.S. 6 (1969)

93. Act of August 10, 1956 (70A Stat. 65, Uniform Code of Military Justice, Articles 80, 130, 134).

Servicemen may not be charged under the Act and tried in military courts because of the commission on nonservice connected crimes committed off-post and off-duty which are subject to civilian court jurisdiction where the guarantees of the Bill of Rights are applicable.

O'Callahan v. *Parker,* 395 U.S. 258 (1969)

94. Act of August 10, 1956 (70A Stat. 35, § 772[f]).

Proviso of statute permitting the wearing of United States military apparel in theatrical production only if the portrayal does not tend to discredit the armed forces imposes an unconstitutional restraint upon First Amendment freedoms and precludes a prosecution under 18 U.S. C. § 702 for unauthorized wearing of uniform in a street skit disrespectful of the military.

Schacht v. *United States,* 398 U.S. 58 (1970)

95. Act of September 2, 1958 (§ 5601[b][1], 72 Stat. 1399).

Provision of Internal Revenue Code creating a presumption that one's presence at the site of an unregistered still shall be sufficient for conviction under a statute punishing possession, custody, or control of an unregistered still unless defendant otherwise explained his presence at the site to the jury *held* unconstitutional because the presumption is not a legitimate, rational, or reasonable inference that defendant was engaged in one of the specialized functions proscribed by the statute.

United States v. *Romano,* 382 U.S. 136 (1965)

96. Act of September 2, 1958 (§ 1[25][B], 72 Stat. 1446), and Act of September 7, 1962 (§ 401, 76 Stat. 469).

Federal statutes providing that spouses of female members of the armed forces must be dependent in fact in order to qualify for certain dependent's benefits, whereas spouses of male members are statutorily deemed dependent and automatically qualified for allowances, whatever their actual status, *held* an invalid sex classification under the equal protection principles of the Fifth Amendment's Due Process Clause.

Frontiero v. *Richardson,* 411 U.S. 677 (1973)

97. Act of September 14, 1959 (§ 504, 73 Stat. 536).

Provision of Labor-Management Reporting and Disclosure Act of 1959 making it a crime for a member of the Communist party to serve as an officer or, with the exception of clerical or custodial positions, as an employee of a labor union *held* to be a bill of attainder and unconstitutional.

> *United States* v. *Brown*, 381 U.S. 437 (1965)

98. Act of October 11, 1962 (§ 305, 76 Stat. 840).

Provision of Postal Services and Federal Employees Salary Act of 1962 authorizing the Post Office Department to detain material determined to be "communist political propaganda" and to forward it to the addressee only if he requested it after notification by the Department, the material to be destroyed otherwise, *held* to impose on the addressee an affirmative obligation which amounted to an abridgment of First Amendment rights.

> *Lamont* v. *Postmaster General*, 381 U.S. 301 (1965)

99. Act of October 15, 1962 (76 Stat. 914).

Provision of District of Columbia laws requiring that a person to be eligible to receive welfare assistance must have resided in the District for at least one year impermissibly classified persons on the basis of an assertion of the right to travel interstate and therefore *held* to violate the Due Process Clause of the Fifth Amendment.

> *Shapiro* v. *Thompson*, 394 U.S. 618 (1969)

100. Act of December 16, 1963 (77 Stat. 378, 20 U.S.C. § 754).

Provision of Higher Education Facilities Act of 1963 which in effect removed restriction against religious use of facilities constructed with federal funds after 20 years *held* to violate the Establishment Clause of the First Amendment inasmuch as the property will still be of considerable value at the end of the period and removal of the restriction would constitute a substantial governmental contribution to religion.

> *Tilton* v. *Richardson*, 403 U.S. 672 (1971)

101. Act of July 30, 1965 (§ 339, 79 Stat. 409).

Section of Social Security Act qualifying certain illegitimate children for disability insurance benefits by presuming dependence but disqualifying other illegitimate children, regardless of dependency, if the disabled wage earner parent did not contribute to the child's support before the onset of the disability or if the child did not live with the parent before the onset of disability *held* to deny latter class of children equal protection as guaranteed by the Due Process Clause of the Fifth Amendment.

> *Jimenez* v. *Weinberger*, 417 U.S. 628 (1974)

102. Act of September 3, 1966 (§ 102[b], 80 Stat. 831), and Act of April 8, 1974 (§§ 6[a][1] amending § 3[d] of Act, 6[a][2] amending 3[e][2][C], 6[a][5] amending § 3[s][5], and 6[a][6] amending § 3[x]).

Those sections of the Fair Labor Standards Act extending wage and hour coverage to the employees of state and local governments *held* invalid because Congress lacks the authority under the Commerce

Clause to regulate employee activities in areas of traditional governmental functions of the states.

National League of Cities v. *Usery,* 426 U.S. 833 (1976)

103. Act of January 2, 1968 (§ 163[a][2], 81 Stat. 872).

District Court decisions *holding* unconstitutional under Fifth Amendment's Due Process Clause section of Social Security Act that reduced, perhaps to zero, benefits coming to illegitimate children upon death of parent in order to satisfy the maximum payment due the wife and legitimate children are summarily affirmed.

Richardson v. *Davis,* 409 U.S. 1069 (1972)

104. Act of January 2, 1968 (§ 203, 81 Stat. 882).

Provision of Social Security Act extending benefits to families whose dependent children have been deprived of parental support because of the unemployment of the father but not giving benefits when the mother becomes unemployed *held* to impermissibly classify on the basis of sex and violate the Fifth Amendment's Due Process Clause.

Califano v. *Westcott,* 443 U.S. 76 (1979)

105. Act of June 22, 1970 (ch. III, 84 Stat. 318).

Provision of Voting Rights Act Amendments of 1970 which set a minimum voting age qualification of eighteen in state and local elections *held* to be unconstitutional because it is beyond the powers of Congress to legislate.

Oregon v. *Mitchell,* 400 U.S. 112 (1970)

106. Act of December 29, 1970 (§ 8[a], 84 Stat. 1598, 29 U.S.C. § 637[a]).

Provision of Occupational Safety and Health Act authorizing inspections of covered work places in industry without warrants *held* to violate Fourth Amendment.

Marshall v. *Barlow's, Inc.,* 436 U.S. 307 (1978)

107. Act of January 11, 1971 (§ 2, 84 Stat. 2048).

Provision of Food Stamp Act disqualifying from participation in program any household containing an individual unrelated by birth, marriage, or adoption to any other member of the household violates the Due Process Clause of the Fifth Amendment.

United States Dept. of Agriculture v. *Moreno,* 413 U.S. 528 (1973)

108. Act of January 11, 1971 (§ 4, 84 Stat. 2049).

Provision of Food Stamp Act disqualifying from participation in program any household containing a person eighteen years or older who had been claimed as a dependent child for income tax purposes in the present or preceding tax year by a taxpayer not a member of the household violates the Due Process Clause of the Fifth Amendment.

United States Dept. of Agriculture v. *Murray,* 413 U.S. 508 (1973)

109. Federal Election Campaign Act of February 7, 1972 (86 Stat. 3), as amended by the Federal Campaign Act Amendments of 1974 (88 Stat. 1263), adding or amending 18 U.S.C. §§ 608(a), 608(e), and 2 U.S.C. § 437c.

Provisions of election law that forbid a candidate or the members of his immediate family from expending personal funds in excess of specified amounts, that limit to $1,000 the independent expenditures of any person relative to an identified candidate, and that forbid expenditures by candidates for federal office in excess of specified amounts violate the First Amendment speech guarantees; provisions of the law creating a commission to oversee enforcement of the Act are an invalid infringement of constitutional separation of powers in that they devolve responsibilities upon a commission four of whose six members are appointed by Congress and all six of whom are confirmed by the House of Representatives as well as by the Senate, not in compliance with the Appointments Clause.

Buckley v. *Valeo*, 424 U.S. 1 (1986)

110. Act of October 1, 1976 (title II, 90 Stat. 1446); Act of October 12, 1979 (101[c], 93 Stat. 657).

Provisions of appropriations laws rolling back automatic pay increases for federal officers and employees is unconstitutional as to Article III Judges because, the increases having gone into effect, they violate the security of Compensation Clause of Article III, § 1.

United States v. *Will*, 449 U.S. 200 (1980)

111. Act of November 6, 1978 (§ 241[a], 92 Stat. 2668, 28 U.S.C. § 1471)

Assignment to Judges who do not have tenure and guarantee of compensation protections afforded Article III Judges of jurisdiction over all proceedings arising under or in the bankruptcy act and over all cases relating to proceedings under the bankruptcy act is invalid, inasmuch as Judges without Article III protection may not receive at least some of this jurisdiction.

Northern Pipeline Constr. Co. v. *Marathon Pipe Line Co.*, 458 U.S. 50 (1982)

112. Act of May 30, 1980 (94 Stat. 399, 45 U.S.C. § 1001 et seq.) as amended by the Act of October 14, 1980 (94 Stat. 1959).

Acts of Congress applying to bankruptcy reorganization of one railroad and guaranteeing employee benefits is repugnant to the requirement of Article I, § 8, cl. 4, that bankruptcy legislation be "uniform."

Railroad Labor Executives' Assoc. v. *Gibbons*, 455 U.S. 457 (1982)

113. Act of March 3, 1873 (ch. 258 § 2, 17 Stat. 599, recodified in 39 U.S.C. § 3001 [e][2]).

Comstock Act provision barring from the mails any unsolicited advertisement for contraceptives, as applied to circulars and flyers promoting prophylactics or containing information discussing the desirability and availability of prophylactics, violates the Free Speech Clause of the First Amendment.

Bolger v. *Youngs Drug Products Corp.,* 463 U.S. 60 (1983)

114. Act of February 15, 1938 (ch. 29, 52 Stat. 30).

District of Columbia Code §22–1115, prohibiting the display of any sign within 500 feet of a foreign embassy if the sign tends to bring the foreign government into "public odium" or "public disrepute," violates the First Amendment.

Boos v. *Borry,* 485 U.S. 312 (1988).

115. Act of June 27, 1952 (ch. 477, § 244[e][2], 66 Stat. 214, 8 U.S.C. § 1254 [c][2]).

Provision of the immigration law that permits either House of Congress to veto the decision of the attorney general to suspend the deportation of certain aliens violates the bicameralism and presentation requirements of lawmaking imposed upon Congress by Article I, §§1 and 7.

INS v. *Chadha,* 462 U.S. 919 (1983)

116. Act of September 2, 1958 (Pub. L. 85–921, § 1, 72 Stat. 1771, 18 U.S.C. § 504[1]).

Exemptions from ban on photographic reproduction of currency "for philatelic, numismatic, educational, historical, or newsworthy purposes" violates the First Amendment because it discriminates on the basis of the content of a publication.

Regan v. *Time, Inc.,* 468 U.S. 641 (1984)

117. Act of November 7, 1967 (Pub. L. 90–129, § 201[8], 81 Stat. 368), as amended by Act of August 13, 1981 (Pub. L. 97–35, § 1229, 95 Stat. 730, 47 U.S.C. § 399).

Communications Act provision banning noncommercial educational stations receiving grants from the Corporation for Public Broadcasting from engaging in editorializing violates the First Amendment.

FCC v. *League of Women Voters,* 468 U.S. 364 (1984)

118. Act of December 10, 1971 (Pub. L. 92–178, § 801, 85 Stat. 570, 26 U.S.C. § 9012[f]).

Provision of Presidential Election Campaign Fund Act limiting to $1,000 the amount that independent committees may expend to further the election of a presidential candidate financing his campaign with public funds is an impermissible limitation of freedom of speech and association protected by the First Amendment.

Federal Election Com. v. *National Conservative Political Action Committee,* 470 U.S. 480 (1985)

119. Act of May 11, 1976 (Pub. L. 92–225, § 316, 90 Stat. 490, 2 U.S.C. § 441[b]).

Provision of Federal Election Campaign Act requiring that independent corporate campaign expenditures be financed by voluntary contributions to a separate segregated fund violates the First Amendment as applied to a corporation organized to promote political ideas, having no stockholders, and not serving as a front for a business corporation or union.

Federal Election Com. v. Massachusetts Citizens for Life, Inc., 479 U.S. 238 (1986)

120. November 9, 1978 (Pub. L. 95–621, § 202[c][1], 92 Stat. 3372, 15 U.S.C. § 3342[c][1]).

Decision of Court of Appeals holding unconstitutional provision giving either House of Congress power to veto rules of Federal Energy Regulatory Commission on certain natural gas pricing matters is summarily affirmed on the authority of *Chadha.*

Process Gas Consumers Group v. Consumer Energy Council, 463 U.S. 1216 (1983)

121. Act of May 28, 1980 (Pub. L. 96–252, § 21[a], 94 Stat. 393, 15 U.S.C. § 57a–1[a]).

Decision of Court of Appeals holding unconstitutional provision of FTC Improvements Act giving Congress power by concurrent resolution to veto final rules of the FTC is summarily affirmed on the basis of *Chadha.*

United States Senate v. FTC, 463 U.S. 1216 (1983)

122. Act of January 12, 1983 (Pub. L. 97–459, § 207, 96 Stat. 2519, 25 U.S.C. § 2206).

Section of Indian Land Consolidation Act providing for escheat to tribe of fractionated interests in land representing less than 2 per cent of a tract's total acreage violates the Fifth Amendment's taking clause by completely abrogating rights of intestacy and devise.

Hodel v. Irving, 481 U.S. 704 (1987)

123. Act of December 12, 1985 (Pub. L. 99–177, § 251, 99 Stat. 1063, 2 U.S.C. § 901).

That portion of the Balanced Budget and Emergency Deficit Control Act which authorizes the comptroller general to determine the amount of spending reductions which must be accomplished each year to reach congressional targets and which authorizes him to report a figure to the president which the president must implement violates the constitutional separation of powers inasmuch as the comptroller general is subject to congressional control (removal) and cannot be given a role in the execution of the laws.

Bowsher v. Synar, 478 U.S. 714 (1986)

124. Act of April 28, 1988 (Pub. L. 100–297, § 6101, 102 Stat. 424, 47 U.S.C. § 223[b]).

Provision insofar as it bans indecent as well as obscene commercial interstate telephone messages violates the Speech Clause of the First Amendment.

Sable Communications of California, Inc. v. FCC, 492 U.S. 115 (1989)

125. Act of October 28, 1989 (Pub. L. 101–131, 103 Stat. 777, 18 U.S.C. §700)

Flag Protection Act of 1989, criminalizing burning and certain other forms of destruction of the United States flag, violates the First Amendment. Most of the prohibited acts involve disrespectful treatment of the flag and evidence a purpose to suppress expression out of concern for its likely communicative impact.

United States v. *Eichman,* 496 U.S. 310 (1990)

126. Act of January 15, 1986 (Pub. L. 99–240, 99 Stat. 1842, 42 U.S.C. §2021[b] et seq.).

Portion of the Low-Level Radiation Waste Policy Amendments Act of 1985 requiring states to take title to and possession of the low-level radioactive waste generated within their borders and to become liable for all damages waste generators suffer as a result of the states' failure to promptly do so held inconsistent with the Tenth Amendment's allocation of power between federal and state governments.

New York v. *United States et al.,* ___ U.S. ___, 112 S.Ct. 2408 (1992)

Sources: Entries through number 125 compiled from Library of Congress, The Constitution of the United States of America; Analysis and Interpretation, S. Doc. 99–16, 99th Cong. 1st sess. Johnny H. Killian, editor, Leland E. Beck, associate editor (1987 & supp 1990); Library of Congress, Congressional Research Service.

Table II

SUPREME COURT DECISIONS OVERRULED BY SUBSEQUENT DECISION

The Supreme Court has, of course, exercised its prerogative of changing its mind—but it has not always admitted having done so. And thus an exact list of *Supreme Court Decisions Overruled by Subsequent Decision* is not always easy to compile. Nor will the experts always agree on the cases which should make up such a list.

A basic list of 90 overruling cases was published in an article by Albert P. Blaustein and Andrew H. Field in 1958. See "Overruling Opinions in the Supreme Court," 57 *Michigan Law Review* 151, 184–194 (1958). This list was expanded to 133 in the first edition of "The Justices of the Supreme Court" by Friedman and Israel in 1969. The list has been updated once again for the present volume and brings the total number of cases to 202.

Overruling Case	*Overruled Case*
1. *Hudson v. Guestier*, 10 U.S. (6 Cranch) 281 (1810)	*Rose v. Himley*, 8 U.S. (4 Cr.) 241 (1808)
2. *Gordon v. Ogden*, 28 U.S. (3 Pet.) 33 (1830)	*Wilson v. Daniel*, 3 U.S. (3 Dall.) 401 (1798)
3. *Greene v. Lessee of Neal*, 31 U.S. (6 Pet.) 291 (1832)	*Patton v. Easton*, 14 U.S. (1 Wheat.) 476 (1816)
	Powell's Lessee v. Harmon, 27 U.S. (2 Pet.) 241 (1829)
4. *Louisville Railroad Co. v. Letson*, 43 U.S. (2 How.) 497 (1844)	*Commercial & Railroad Bank v. Slocomb*, 39 U.S. (14 Pet.) 60 (1840)
	Strawbridge v. Curtiss, 7 U.S. (3 Cranch) 267(1806); and qualifying,
	Bank of the United States v. Deveaux, 9 U.S. (5 Cranch) 61 (1809)
5. *The Genessee Chief v. Fitzhugh*, 53 U.S. (12 How.) 443 (1851)	*The Thomas Jefferson*, 23 U.S. (10 Wheat.) 428 (1825)
	The Orleans v. Phoebus, 36 U.S. (11 Pet.) 175 (1837)
6. *Gazzam v. Phillip's Lessee*, 61 U.S. (20 How.) 372 (1858)	*Brown's Lessee v. Clements*, 44 U.S. (3 How.) 650 (1845)

Overruling Case	*Overruled Case*
7. *Suydam v. Williamson*, 65 U.S. (24 How.) 427 (1861)	*Williamson v. Berry*, 49 U.S. (8 How.) 495 (1850); *Williamson v. Irish Presbyterian Congregation*, 49 U.S. (8 How.) 565 (1850); *Williamson v. Ball*, 49 U.S. (8 How.) 566 (1850)
8. *Mason v. Eldred*, 73 U.S. (6 Wall.) 231 (1868)	*Sheehy v. Mandeville & Jameson*, 10 U.S. (6 Cranch) 253 (1810)
9. *The Belfast*, 74 U.S. (7 Wall.) 624 (1869)	*Allen v. Newberry*, 62 U.S. (21 How.) 244 (1858) (in part)
10. *Knox v. Lee*, 79 U.S. (12 Wall.) 457 (1871)	*Hepburn v. Griswold*, 75 U.S. (8 Wall.) 603 (1870)
11. *Trebilcock v. Wilson*, 79 U.S. (12 Wall.) 687 (1871)	*Roosevelt v. Meyer*, 68 U.S. (1 Wall.) 512 (1863)
12. *Hornbuckle v. Toombs*, 85 U.S. (18 Wall.) 648 (1874)	*Noonan v. Lee*, 67 U.S. (2 Black) 499 (1863); *Orchard v. Hughes*, 68 U.S. (1 Wall.) 73 (1864)
13. *Union Pac. R. Co. v. McShane*, 89 U.S. (22 Wall.) 444 (1874)	*Dunphy v. Kleinsmith*, 78 U.S. (1 Wall.) 610 (1871)
14. *County of Cass v. Johnston*, 95 U.S. 360 (1877)	*Raliway Co. v. Prescott*, 83 U.S. (16 Wall.) 603 (1873) (in part)
15. *Fairfield v. County of Gallatin*, 100 U.S. 47 (1879)	*Harshman v. Bates County*, 92 U.S. 569 (1876)
16 *Tilghman v. Proctor*, 102 U.S. 707 (1881)	*Concord v. Portsmouth Sav. Bank*, 92 U.S. 625 (1876)
17. *Kilbourn v. Thompson*, 103 U.S. 168 (1881)	*Mitchell v. Tilghman*, 86 U.S. (19 Wall.) 287 (1874)
18. *United States v. Phelps*, 107 U.S. 320 (1883)	*Anderson v. Dunn*, 19 U.S. (6 Wheat.) 204 (1821)
19. *Kountze v. Omaha Hotel Co.*, 107 U.S. 378 (1883)	*Shelton v. Collector*, 72 U.S. (5 Wall.) 113 (1867)
20. *Morgan v. United States*, 113 U.S. 476 (1885)	*Stafford v. Union Bank of Louisiana*, 57 U.S. (16 How.) 135 (1853)
21. *Wabash, S. L. & P. R. Co. v. People*, 118 U.S. 557 (1886)	*Texas v. White*, 74 U.S. (7 Wall.) 700 (1869)
22. *Philadelphia & Southern Mail S.S. Co. v. Pennsylvania*, 122 U.S. 326 (1887)	*Peik v. Chicago & N. W. R. Co.*, 94 U.S. 164 (1877) ("substantially though not expressly overruled")
23. *In re Ayers*, 123 U.S. 443 (1887)	*State Tax on Railway Gross Receipts*, 82 U.S. (15 Wall.) 284 (1873) ("basic grounds of decision repudiated")
24. *Leloup v. Port of Mobile*, 127 U.S. 640 (1888)	*Osborne v. President, Directors & Co. of Bank of the United States*, 22 U.S. (9 Wheat.) 738 (1824) *Osborne v. Mobile*, 83 U.S. (16 Wall.) 479 (1873)
25. *Leisy v. Hardin*, 135 U.S. 100 (1890)	*Pierce v. New Hampshire*, 46 U.S. (5 How.) 504 (1847)
26. *Brenham v. German-American Bank*, 144 U.S. 173 (1892)	*Rogers v. Burlington*, 10 U.S. (3 Wall.) 654 (1866);

Overruling Case	Overruled Case
	Mitchell v. Burlington, 71 U.S. (4 Wall.) 270 (1867)
27. Roberts v. Lewis, 153 U.S. 367 (1894)	Giles v. Little, 104 U.S. 291 (1881)
28. Pollock v. Farmers' Loan & Trust Co., 158 U.S. 601 (1895)	Hylton v. United States, 3 U.S. (3 Dall.) 171 (1796)
29. Garland v. Washington, 232 U.S. 642 (1914)	Crain v. United States, 162 U.S. 625 (1896)
30. United States v. Nice, 241 U.S. 591 601 (1916)	In re Heff, 197 U.S. 488 (1905)
31. Pennsylvania R. Co. v. Towers, 245 U.S. 6 (1917)	Lake Shore & M.S. R. Co. v. Smith, 173 U.S. 684 (1899)
32. Rosen v. United States, 245 U.S. 467 (1918)	United States v. Reid, 53 U.S. (12 How.) 361 (1851)
33. Boston Store of Chicago v. American Graphophone Co., 246 U.S. 8 (1918) and Motion Picture Patents Co. v. Universal Film Mfg. Co., 243 U.S. 502 (1917)	Henry v. A. B. Dick Co., 224 U.S. 1 (1912)
34. Terrel v. Burke Constr. Co., 257 U.S. 653 (1923)	Doyle v. Continental Ins. Co., 94 U.S. 535 (1877); Security Mut. Life Ins. Co. v. Prewitt, 202 U.S. 246 (1906)
35. Lee v. Chesapeake & O. R. Co., 260 U.S. 653 (1923)	Ex parte Wisner, 203 U.S. 449 (1906); and qualifying, In re Moore 209 U.S. 490 (1908)
36. Alpha Portland Cement Co. v. Massachusetts, 268 U.S. 203 (1925)	Baltic Mining Co. v. Massachusetts, 231 U.S. 68 (1913)
37. Chesapeake & O. R. Co. v. Leitch, 276 U.S. 429 (1928)	Chesapeake & O. R. Co. v. Leitch, 275 U.S. 507 (1927)
38. Gleason v. Seaborad A. L. R. Co., 278 U.S. 349 (1929)	Friedlander v. Texas & P.R. Co., 130 U.S. 416 (1889)
39. Farmers Loan & Trust Co. v. Minnesota, 280 U.S. 204 (1930)	Blackstone v. Miller, 188 U.S. 189 (1903)
40. East Ohio Gas Co. v. Tax Com. of Ohio, 283 U.S. 465 (1931)	Pennsylvania Gas Co. v. Public Service Com., 252 U.S. 23 (1920)
41. Chicago & E.I.R. Co. v. Industrial Com. of Illinois, 284 U.S. 296 (1932)	Erie R. Co. v. Collins, 253 U.S. 77 (1920); Erie R. Co. v. Szary, 253 U.S. 86 (1920)
42. Fox Film Corp. v. Doyal, 286 U.S. 123 (1932)	Long v. Rockwood, 277 U.S. 142 (1928)
43. New York ex rel. Northern Finance Corp. v. Lynch, 290 U.S. 601 (1933) See also: United States v. Detroit, 355 U.S. 466 (1958)	Macallen Co. v. Massachusetts, 279 U.S. 620 (1929)
44. Funk v. United States, 290 U.S. 371 (1933) See also: Hawkins v. United States, 358 U.S. 74 (1958)	Stein v. Bowman, 38 U.S. (13 Pet.) 209 (1839) (in part); Hendrix v. United States, 219 U.S. 79 (1911);

Overruling Case	Overruled Case
	Logan v. United States, 144 U.S. 263 (1892); Jin Fuey Moy v. United States, 254 U.S. 189 (1920)
45. West Coast Hotel Co. v. Parrish, 300 U.S. 379 (1937)	Adkins v. Children's Hospital of District of Columbia, 261 U.S. 525 (1923) Morehead v. New York , 298 U.S. 587 (1936)
46. Railroad Com. of California v. Pacific Gas & Electric Co., 302 U.S. 388 (1938)	Railroad Com. v. Pacific Gas & E. Co., 301 U.S. 669 (1937)
47. Helvering v. Mountain Producers Corp., 303 U.S. 376 (1938)	Gillespie v. Oklahoma, 257 U.S. 501 (1922); Burnet v. Coronado Oil & Gas Co., 285 U.S. 393 (1932)
48. Erie R. Co. v. Tompkins, 304 U.S. 64 (1938)	Swift v. Tyson, 41 U.S. (16 Pet.) 1 (1842)
49. Graves v. New York, 306 U.S. 466 (1939)	Dobbins v. Commissioners of Erie County, 41 U.S. (16 Pet.) 435 (1842); Collector v. Day, 78 U.S. (11 Wall.) 113 (1871); Bengzon v. Secretary of Justice, 299 U.S. 410 (1937); Brush v. Commissioners, 300 U.S. 352 (1937)
50. Rochester Tel. Corp. v. United States, 307 U.S. 125 (1939)	Procter & Gamble v. United States, 225 U.S. 282 (1912)
51. O'Malley v. Woodrough, 307 U.S. 277 (1939)	Evans v. Gore, 253 U.S. 245 (1920) Miles v. Graham, 268 U.S. 501 (1925)
52. Madden v. Kentucky, 309 U.S. 83 (1940)	Colgate v. Harvey, 296 U.S. 404 (1935)
53. Helvering v. Hallock, 309 U.S. 106 (1940)	Helvering v. St. Louis Union Trust Co., 296 U.S. 39 (1935); Becker v. St. Louis Union Trust Co., 296 U.S. 48 (1935);
54. Tigner v. Texas, 310 U.S. 141 (1940)	Connolly v. Union Sewer Pipe Co., 184 U.S. 540 (1902)
55. United States v. Darby, 312 U.S. 100 (1941)	Hammer v. Dagenhart, 247 U.S. 251 (1918); Carter v. Carter Coal Co., 298 U.S. 238 (1936)
56. United States v. Chicago M. S. P. & P.R. Co., 312 U.S. 592 (1941)	United States v. Lynah, 188 U.S. 445 (1903); United States v. Heyward, 250 U.S. 633 (1919)
57. Nye v. United States, 313 U.S. 33 (1941)	Toledo Newspaper Co. v. United States 247 U.S. 402 (1918)
58. California v. Thompson, 313 U.S. 109 (1941)	Di Santo v. Pennsylvania, 273 U.S. 34 (1927)
59. United States v. Classic, 313 U.S. 299 (1941)	Newberry v. United States, 256 U.S. 232 (1921)

Overruling Case	Overruled Case
60. *Olsen v. Nebraska*, 313 U.S. 236 (1941)	*Ribnik v. McBride*, 277 U.S. 350 (1928)
61. *Alabama v. King & Boozer*, 314 U.S. 1 (1941)	*Panhandle Oil Co. v. Knox*, 277 U.S. 218 (1928); *Graves v. Texas Company*, 298 U.S. 393 (1936)
62. *Toucey v. New York Life Ins. Co.*, 314 U.S. 118 (1941)	*Supreme Tribe of Ben-Hur v. Cauble*, 255 U.S. 356 (1921)
63. *Edwards v. California*, 314 U.S. 160 (1941)	*City of New York v. Miln*, 36 U.S. (11 Pet.) 102 (1837)
64. *State Tax Com. v. Aldrich*, 316 U.S. 174 (1942)	*First Nat. Bank v. Maine*, 284 U.S. 312 (1932)
65. *Williams v. North Carolina*, 317 U.S. 575 (1943)	*Haddock v. Haddock*, 201 U.S. 562 (1906)
66. *Brady v. Roosevelt S.S. Co.*, 317 U.S. 575 (1943)	*Johnson v. U.S. Shipping Board Emergency Fleet Corporation*, 280 U.S. 320 (1930)
67. *Jones v. Opelika*, 319 U.S. 103 (1943); *Murdock v. Pennsylvania*, 319 U.S. 105 (1943)	*Jones v. Opelika*, 316 U.S. 584 (1942)
68. *Oklahoma Tax Com. v. United States*, 319 U.S. 598 (1943)	*Childers v. Beaver*, 270 U.S. 555 (1926)
69. *West Virginia State Bd. of Education v. Barnette*, 319 U.S. 624 (1943)	*Minersville School Dist. v. Gobitis*, 310 U.S. 586 (1940)
70. *Federal Power Com. v. Hope Natural Gas Co.*, 320 U.S. 591 (1944)	*United R. & Electric Co. v. West*, 280 U.S. 234 (1930)
71. *Mercoid Corp. v. Mid-Continent Invest Co.*, 320 U.S. 661 (1944)	*Leeds & Catlin Co. v. Victor Talking Machine Co.*, 213 U.S. 325 (1909)
72. *Mahnich v. Southern S.S. Co.*, 321 U.S. 96 (1944)	*Plamals v. S.S. Pinar Del Rio*, 277 U.S. 151 (1928)
73. *Smith v. Allwright*, 321 U.S. 649 (1944)	*Grovey v. Townsend*, 295 U.S. 45 (1935)
74. *United States v. Southeastern Underwriters Assoc.*, 322 U.S. 533 (1944)	*Paul v. Virginia*, 75 U.S. (8 Wall.) 168 (1869)
75. *Girouard v. United States*, 328 U.S. 61 (1946)	*United States v. Schwimmer*, 279 U.S. 644 (1929); *United States v. Macintosh*, 283 U.S. 605 (1931); *United States v. Bland*, 283 U.S. 636 (1931)
76. *Halliburton Co. v. Walker*, 329 U.S. 1 (1946)	*Halliburton Oil Well Cementing Co. v. Walker*, 326 U.S. 696 (1946)
77. *MacGregor v. Westinghouse Electric & Mfg. Co.*, 329 U.S. 402 (1947)	*MacGregor v. Westinghouse Electric & Mfg. Co.*, 327 U.S. 758 (1946)
78. *Angel v. Bullington*, 330 U.S. 183 (1947)	*David Lupton's Sons Co. v. Automobile Club of America*, 225 U.S. 489 (1912)
79. *Zap v. United States*, 330 U.S. 800 (1947)	*Zap v. United States*, 328 U.S. 624 (1946)

Overruling Case	Overruled Case
80. *Thibaut* v. *Car & General Insurance Corp.*, 332 U.S. 828 (1947)	*Thibaut* v. *Car & General Ins. Corp.*, 332 U.S. 751 (1947)
81. *Sherrer* v. *Sherrer*, 334 U.S. 343 (1948)	*Andrews* v. *Andrews*, 188 U.S. 14 (1903)
82. *Lincoln Federal Labor Union* v. *Northwestern Iron & Metal Co.*, 335 U.S. 525 (1949);	*Adair* v. *United States*, 208 U.S. 161 (1908)
See also:	
Phelps Dodge Corp. v. *NLRB*, 313 U.S. 177 (1941)	*Coppage* v. *Kansas*, 236 U.S. 1 (1915)
83. *Commissioner* v. *Estate of Church*, 335 U.S. 632 (1949)	*May* v. *Heiner*, 281 U.S. 238 (1930)
84. *Ott* v. *Mississippi Barge Line Co.*, 336 U.S. 169 (1949)	*St. Louis* v. *Ferry Company*, 78 U.S. (11 Wall.) 423 (1870); *Old Dominian S. S. Co.* v. *Virginia*, 198 U.S. 299 (1905); *Ayer & Lord Tie Co.* v. *Kentucky*, 202 U.S. 409 (1906)
85. *Oklahoma Tax Com.* v. *Texas Co.*, 336 U.S. 342 (1949)	*Choctaw , O. & G. R. Co.* v. *Harrison*, 235 U.S. 292 (1914); *Indian Territory Illuminating Oil Co.* v. *Oklahoma*, 240 U.S. 522 (1916); *Howard* v. *Gipsy Oil Co.*, 247 U.S. 503 (1918); *Large Oil Co.* v. *Howard*, 248 U.S. 549 (1919); *Oklahoma ex rel. Oklahoma Tax Com.* v. *Barnsdall Refineries, Inc.*, 296 U.S. 521 (1936)
86. *Cosmopolitan Shipping Co.* v. *McAllister*, 337 U.S. 783 (1949)	*Hust* v. *Moore-McCormack Lines*, 328 U.S. 707 (1946)
87. *United States* v. *Rabinowitz*, 339 U.S. 56 (1950)	*Trupiano* v. *United States*, 334 U.S. 699 (1948); *McDonald* v. *United States*, 335 U.S. 451 (1948)
88. *Joseph Burstyn, Inc.* v. *Wilson*, 343 U.S. 495 (1952)	*Mutual Film Corp.* v. *Industrial Com. of Ohio*, 236 U.S. 230 (1915)
89. *Brown* v. *Board of Education*, 347 U.S. 483 (1954)	*Cumming* v. *Richmond County Board of Education*, 175 U.S. 528 (1899); *Gong Lum* v. *Rice*, 275 U.S. 78 (1927)
90. *Disbarment of Isserman*, 348 U.S. 1 (1954)	*In re Isserman*, 345 U.S. 286 (1953)
91. *Gayle* v. *Browder*, 352 U.S. 903 (1956)	*Plessy* v. *Ferguson*, 163 U.S. 537 (1896)
92. *Reid* v. *Covert*, 354 U.S. 1 (1957)	*Kinsella* v. *Krueger*, 351 U.S. 470 (1956); *Reid* v. *Covert*, 351 U.S. 470 (1956)
93. *Vanderbilt* v. *Vanderbilt*, 354 U.S. 416, 419 (1957);	*Thompson* v. *Thompson*, 226 U.S. 551 (1913)
See also:	
Armstrong v. *Armstrong*, 350 U.S. 568, 581 (1956)	

Overruling Case	*Overruled Case*
94. *Ladner* v. *United States*, 358 U.S. 169 (1958)	*Ladner* v. *United States*, 355 U.S. 282 (1958)
95. *United States* v. *Raines*, 362 U.S. 1727 (1960)	*United States* v. *Reese*, 92 U.S. 214 (1876)
96. *Elkins* v. *United States*, 364 U.S. 206 (1960); *Rios* v. *United States*, 364 U.S. 253 (1960)	*Weeks* v. *United States*, 232 U.S. 383 (1914); *Center* v. *United States*, 267 U.S. 575 (1925); *Byars* v. *United States*, 273 U.S. 28 (1927); *Feldman* v. *United States*, 322 U.S. 487 (1944)
97. *James* v. *United States*, 366 U.S. 213 (1961)	*Commissioner* v. *Wilcox*, 327 U.S. 404 (1946)
98. *Mapp* v. *Ohio*, 367 U.S. 643 (1961); See also: *Ker* v. *California*, 374 U.S. 23, (1963)	*Wolf* v. *Colorado*, 338 U.S. 25 (1949) *Irvine* v. *California*, 347 U.S. 128 (1954)
99. *Baker* v. *Carr*, 369 U.S. 186 (1962)	*Colegrove* v. *Green*, 328 U.S. 549 (1946)
100. *Wesberry* v. *Sanders*, 376 U.S. 1 (1964)	*Colegrove* v. *Barrett*, 330 U.S. 804 (1947)
101. *Smith* v. *Evening News Assoc.*, 371 U.S. 195 (1962); See also: *General Drivers, W.&H.* v. *Riss & Co., Union* v. *Riss & Co.*, 372 U.S. 517 (1963)	*Association of Westinghouse Salaried Employees* v. *Westinghouse Electric Corp.*, 348 U.S. 437 (1955)
102. *Construction & General Laborers' Union* v. *Curry*, 371 U.S. 542 (1963)	*Montgomery Bldg. & Constr. Trades Council* v. *Ledbetter Erection Co.*, 344 U.S. 178 (1952)
103. *Gideon* v. *Wainwright*, 372 U.S. 335 (1963)	*Betts* v. *Brady*, 316 U.S. 455 (1942)
104. *Gray* v. *Sanders*, 372 U.S. 368 (1963)	*Turman* v. *Duckworth*, 329 U.S. 675 (1946); *South* v. *Peters*, 339 U.S. 959 (1950); *Cox* v. *Peters*, 342 U.S. 936 (1952); *Hartsfield* v. *Sloan*, 357 U.S. 916 (1958)
105. *Fay* v. *Noia*, 372 U.S. 391 (1963)	*Darr* v. *Burford*, 339 U.S. 200 (1950)
106. *Ferguson* v. *Skrupa*, 372 U.S. 726 (1963)	*Adams* v. *Tanner*, 244 U.S. 590 (1917)
107. *Schneider* v. *Rusk*, 377 U.S. 163 (1964)	*Mackenzie* v. *Hare*, 239 U.S. 299 (1915)
108. *Malloy* v. *Hogan*, 378 U.S. 1 (1964)	*Twining* v. *New Jersey*, 211 U.S. 78 (1908); *Adamson* v. *California*, 332 U.S. 46 (1947)
109. *Murphy* v. *Waterfront Com. of New York Harbor*, 378 U.S. 52 (1964)	*Jack* v. *Kansas*, 199 U.S. 372 (1905); *United States* v. *Murdock*, 284 U.S. 141 (1931);

Overruling Case	Overruled Case
	Feldman v. United States, 322 U.S. 487 (1944); Knapp v. Schweitzer, 357 U.S. 371 (1958); Mills v. Louisiana, 360 U.S. 230 (1959)
110. Jackson v. Denno, 379 U.S. 368, 391 (1964)	Stein v. New York, 346 U.S. 156 (1953)
111. Escobedo v. Illinois, 378 U.S. 478 (1964)	Crooker v. California, 357 U.S. 433 (1958); Cicenia v. LaGay, 357 U.S. 504 (1958)
112. Pointer v. Texas, 380 U.S. 400 (1965)	West v. Louisiana, 194 U.S. 258 (1904)
113. Gold v. Di Carlo, 380 U.S. 520 (1965)	Tyson & Bro. v. Banton, 273 U.S. 418 (1927)
114. Swift & Co. v. Wickham, 382 U.S. 111 (1965)	Kesler v. Dept. of Public Safety, 369 U.S. 153 (1962)
115. Harris v. United States, 382 U.S. 162 (1965)	Brown v. United States, 359 U.S. 41 (1959)
116. Harper v. Virginia State Board of Elections, 383 U.S. 663 (1966)	Breedlove v. Suttles, 302 U.S. 277 (1937); Butler v. Thompson, 341 U.S. 937 (1951)
117. Spevak v. Klein, 385 U.S. 511 (1967)	Cohen v. Hurley, 366 U.S. 117 (1961)
118. Keyishian v. Board of Regents, 385 U.S. 589 (1967)	Adler v. Board of Education, 342 U.S. 485 (1952)
119. Afroyim v. Rusk, 387 U.S. 253 (1967)	Perez v. Brownell, 356 U.S. 44 (1958)
120. Warden, Maryland Penitentiary v. Hayden, 387 U.S. 294 (1967)	Gouled v. United States, 255 U.S. 298 (1921)
121. Camara v. Municipal Court of San Francisco 387 U.S. 523 (1967)	Frank v. Maryland, 359 U.S. 360 (1959)
122. Berger v. New York, 388 U.S. 41 (1967)	Olmstead v. United States, 277 U.S. 438 (1928) (in part)
123. Katz v. United States, 389 U.S. 347 (1967)	Olmstead v. United States, 277 U.S. 438 (1928)
124. Peyton v. Rowe, 391 U.S. 54 (1968)	McNally v. Hill, 293 U.S. 131 (1934)
125. Bruton v. United States, 391 U.S. 123 (1968)	Delli Paoli v. United States, 352 U.S. 232 (1957)
126. Duncan v. Louisiana, 391 U.S. 145 (1968)	Maxwell v. Dow, 176 U.S. 581 (1900)
127. Carafas v. LaVallee, 391 U.S. 234 (1968)	Parker v. Ellis, 362 U.S. 574 (1960)
128. Lee v. Florida, 392 U.S. 378 (1968)	Schwartz v. Texas, 344 U.S. 199 (1952)
129. Jones v. Alfred H. Mayer Co., 392 U.S. 409 (1968)	Hodges v. United States, 203 U.S. 1 (1906)
130. Moore v. Ogilvie, 394 U.S. 814 (1969)	MacDougall v. Green, 335 U.S. 281 (1948)
131. Brandenburg v. Ohio, 395 U.S. 444 (1969)	Whitney v. California, 274 U.S. 357 (1927)
132. Chimel v. California, 395 U.S. 752 (1969)	Harris v. United States, 331 U.S. 145 (1947); United States v. Rabinowitz, 339 U.S. 56 (1950)

Overruling Case	*Overruled Case*
133. *Benton v. Maryland*, 395 U.S. 784 (1969)	*Palko v. Connecticut*, 302 U.S. 319 (1937)
134. *Ashe v. Swenson*, 397 U.S. 436 (1970)	*Hoag v. New Jersey*, 356 U.S. 464 (1958)
135. *Boys Markets, Inc. v. Retail Clerks Union*, 398 U.S. 235 (1970)	*Sinclair Refining Co. v. Atkinson*, 370 U.S. 195 (1962)
136. *Price v. Georgia*, 398 U.S. 323 (1970)	*Brantley v. Georgia*, 217 U.S. 284 (1910)
137. *Moragne v. States Marine Lines*, 398 U.S. 375 (1970)	*The Harrisburg*, 119 U.S. 199 (1886)
138. *Williams v. Florida*, 399 U.S. 78 (1970)	*Thompson v. Utah*, 170 U.S. 343 (1898) (in part); *Rassmussen v. United States*, 197 U.S. 516 (1905) (in part)
139. *Blonder-Tongue Laboratories, Inc. v. Univ. of Ill. Foundation*, 402 U.S. 313 (1971)	*Triplett v. Lowell*, 297 U.S. 638 (1936)
140. *Perez v. Campbell*, 402 U.S. 637 (1971)	*Kesler v. Dept. of Public Safety*, 369 U.S. 153 (1962)
141. *Griffin v. Breckenridge*, 403 U.S. 88 (1971)	*Collins v. Hardyman*, 341 U.S. 651 (1951) (in part)
142. *Dunn v. Blumstein*, 405 U.S. 330 (1972)	*Pope v. Williams*, 193 U.S. 621 (1904)
143. *Andrews v. Louisville & N.R. Co.*, 406 U.S. 320 (1972)	*Moore v. Illinois C. R. Co.*, 312 U.S. 630 (1941)
144. *Lehnhausen v. Lake Shore Auto Parts Co.*, 410 U.S. 356 (1973)	*Quaker City Cab Co. v. Pennsylvania*, 277 U.S. 389 (1928)
145. *Braden v. 30th Judicial Circuit Court*, 410 U.S. 484 (1973)	*Ahrens v. Clark*, 335 U.S. 188 (1948)
146. *Miller v. California*, 413 U.S. 15 (1973)	*A book named "John Cleland's Memoirs of a Woman of Pleasure" v. Attorney General of Massachusetts*, 383 U.S. 413 (1966)
147. *North Dakota State Board of Pharmacy v. Snyder's Drug Stores, Inc.*, 414 U.S. 156 (1973)	*Louis K. Liggett Co. v. Baldridge*, 278 U.S. 105 (1929)
148. *Edelman v. Jordan*, 415 U.S. 651 (1974)	*Shapiro v. Thompson*, 394 U.S. 618 (1969) (in part); *State Dept. of Health & Rehabilitation Services v. Zarate*, 407 U.S. 918 (1972); *Sterrett v. Mothers' & Children's Rights Organization*, 409 U.S. 809 (1973)
149. *Mitchell v. W. T. Grant Co.*, 416 U.S. 600 (1974)	*Fuentes v. Shevin*, 407 U.S. 67 (1972) (in part)
150. *Taylor v. Louisiana*, 419 U.S. 522 (1975)	*Hoyt v. Florida*, 368 U.S. 57 (1961) (in effect)
151. *United States v. Reliable Transfer Co.*, 421 U.S. 397 (1975)	*Schooner Catherine v. Dickinson*, 58 U.S. (17 How.) 170 (1854)
152. *Michelin Tire Corp. v. Wages*, 423 U.S. 276 (1976)	*Low v. Austin*, 80 U.S. (13 Wall.) 29 (1871)
153. *Dove v. United States*, 423 U.S. 325 (1976)	*Durham v. United States*, 401 U.S. 481 (1971)

Overruling Case	Overruled Case
154. *Hudgens* v. *NLRB*, 424 U.S. 507 (1976)	*Amalgamated Food Employees Union* v. *Logan Valley Plaza*, 391 U.S. 308 (1968)
155. *Virginia State Board of Pharmacy* v. *Virginia Citizens Consumer Council*, 425 U.S. 748 (1976)	*Valentine* v. *Chrestensen*, 316 U.S. 52 (1942)
156. *National League of Cities* v. *Usery*, 426 U.S. 833 (1976)	*Maryland* v. *Wirtz*, 392 U.S. 183 (1968)
157. *Int. Assoc. of Machinists & Aerospace Workers* v. *Wisconsin Employment Relations Comm.*, 427 U.S. 132 (1976)	*International Union, U.A.W.A.* v. *Wisconsin Employment Relations*, 336 U.S. 245 (1949)
158. *New Orleans* v. *Dukes*, 427 U.S. 297 (1976)	*Morey* v. *Doud*, 354 U.S. 457 (1957)
159. *Gregg* v. *Georgia*, 428 U.S. 153, 195 n. 47 (1976)	*McGautha* v. *California*, 402 U.S. 183 (1971)
160. *Craig* v. *Boren*, 429 U.S. 190 (1976)	*Goesaert* v. *Cleary*, 335 U.S. 464 (1948)
161. *Oregon ex rel. State Land Bd.* v. *Corvalis Sand & Gravel Co.*, 429 U.S. 363 (1977)	*Bonelli Cattle Co.* v. *Arizona*, 414 U.S. 313 (1973)
162. *Complete Auto Transit* v. *Brady*, 430 U.S. 274 (1977)	*Spector Motor Service, Inc.* v. *O'Connor*, 340 U.S. 602 (1951)
163. *Continental T.V., Inc.* v. *GTE Sylvania*, 433 U.S. 36 (1977)	*United States* v. *Arnold, Schwinn & Co.*, 388 U.S. 365 (1967)
164. *Shaffer* v. *Heitner*, 433 U.S. 186 (1977)	*Pennoyer* v. *Neff*, 95 U.S. 714 (1878)
165. *Dept. of Revenue* v. *Association of Washington Stevedoring Cos.*, 435 U.S. 734 (1978)	*Puget Sound Stevedoring Co.* v. *State Tax Com.*, 302 U.S. 90 (1937); *Joseph* v. *Carter & Weekes Stevedoring Co.*, 330 U.S. 422 (1947)
166. *Monell* v. *Department of Social Services*, 436 U.S. 658 (1978)	*Monroe* v. *Pape*, 365 U.S. 167 (1961) (in part); *Kenosha* v. *Bruno*, 412 U.S. 507 (1973) (in part); *Moor* v. *County of Alameda*, 411 U.S. 693 (1973) (in part)
167. *Burks* v. *United States*, 437 U.S. 1 (1978)	*Bryan* v. *United States*, 338 U.S. 552 (1950) (in part); *Sapir* v. *United States*, 348 U.S. 373 (1955) (in part); *Yates* v. *United States*, 354 U.S. 298 (1957) (in part); *Forman* v. *United States*, 361 U.S. 416 (1960)
168. *United States* v. *Scott*, 437 U.S. 82 (1978)	*United States* v. *Jenkins*, 420 U.S. 358 (1975)
169. *Duren* v. *Missouri*, 439 U.S. 357 (1978)	*Hoyt* v. *Florida*, 368 U.S. 57 (1961)
170. *Hughes* v. *Oklahoma*, 441 U.S. 322 (1979)	*Geer* v. *Connecticut*, 161 U.S. 519 (1896)
171. *Trammel* v. *United States*, 445 U.S. 40 (1980)	*Hawkins* v. *United States*, 358 U.S. 74 (1958)

Overruling Case	*Overruled Case*
172. *United States* v. *Salvucci,* 448 U.S. 83 (1980)	*Jones* v. *United States,* 362 U.S. 257 (1960)
173. *Commonwealth Edison Co.* v. *Montana,* 453 U.S. 609 (1981)	*Heisler* v. *Thomas Colliery Co.,* 260 U.S. 245 (1922)
174. *United States* v. *Ross,* 456 U.S. 798 (1982)	*Robbins* v. *California,* 453 U.S. 420 (1981)
175. *Sporhase* v. *Nebraska,* 458 U.S. 941 (1982)	*Hudson County Water Co.* v. *McCarter,* 209 U.S. 349 (1908)
176. *Illinois* v. *Gates,* 462 U.S. 213 (1983)	*Aguilar* v. *Texas,* 378 U.S. 108 (1964); *Spinelli* v. *United States,* 393 U.S. 410 (1969)
177. *Pennhurst State School & Hospital* v. *Halderman,* 465 U.S. 89 (1984)	*Rolston* v. *Missouri Fund Comrs.,* 120 U.S. 390 (1887); *Siler* v. *Louisville & N. R. Co.,* 213 U.S. 175 (1909); *Atchison, T. & S. F. R. Co.* v. *O'Connor,* 223 U.S. 280 (1912); *Greene* v. *Louisville & I. R. Co.,* 244 U.S. 499 (1917); *Johnson* v. *Lankford;* 245 U.S. 541 (1918)
178. *United States* v. *One Assortment of 89 Firearms,* 465 U.S. 354 (1984)	*Coffey* v. *United States,* 116 U.S. 436 (1886)
179. *Limbach* v. *Hooven & Allison Co.,* 466 U.S. 353 (1984)	*Hooven & Allison Co.* v. *Evatt,* 324 U.S. 652 (1945)
180. *Cooperweld Corp.* v. *Independence Tube Corp.,* 467 U.S. 752 (1984)	*United States* v. *Yellow Cab Co.,* 332 U.S. 218 (1947); *Kiefer-Stewart Co.* v. *Joseph E. Seagram & Sons, Inc.,* 340 U.S. 211 (1951)
181. *Garcia* v. *San Antonio Metropolitan Transit Authority,* 469 U.S. 528 (1985)	*National League of Cities* v. *Usery,* 426 U.S. 833 (1976)
182. *United States* v. *Miller,* 471 U.S. 130 (1985)	*Ex parte Bain,* 121 U.S. 1 (1887)
183. *Daniels* v. *Williams,* 474 U.S. 327 (1986)	*Parratt* v. *Taylor,* 451 U.S. 527 (1981)
184. *United States* v. *Lane,* 474 U.S. 438 (1986)	*McElroy* v. *United States,* 164 U.S. 76 (1896)
185. *Batson* v. *Kentucky,* 476 U.S. 79 (1986)	*Swain* v. *Alabama,* 380 U.S. 202 (1965)
186. *Puerto Rico* v. *Branstad,* 483 U.S. 219 (1987)	*Kentucky* v. *Dennison,* 65 U.S. (24 How.) 66 (1861)
187. *Solorio* v. *United States,* 483 U.S. 435 (1987)	*O'Callahan* v. *Parker,* 395 U.S. 258 (1969)
188. *Welch* v. *Texas Dept. of Highways & Public Transp.,* 483 U.S. 468 (1987)	*Parden* v. *Terminal R.,* 377 U.S. 84 (1964)
189. *Gulfstream Aerospace Corp.* v. *Mayacamas Corp.,* 485 U.S. 271 (1988)	*Enelow* v. *New York Life Ins. Co.,* 293 U.S. 379 (1935)
190. *South Carolina* v. *Baker,* 485 U.S. 505 (1988)	*Pollock* v. *Farmers' Loan & Trust Co.,* 157 U.S. 429 (1895)

Overruling Case	Overruled Case
191. *Thornburgh* v. *Abbott*, 490 U.S. 401 (1989)	*Procunier* v. *Martinez*, 416 U.S. 396 (1974) (in part).
192. *Rodriguez de Quijas* v. *Shearson/ AmericanExpress*, 490 U.S. 477 (1989)	*Wilko* v. *Swann*, 346 U.S. 427 (1953)
193. *Alabama* v. *Smith*, 490 U.S. 794 (1989)	*Simpson* v. *Rice*, 395 U.S. 711 (1969)
194. *Healy* v. *Beer Institute*, 491 U.S. 324 (1989)	*Joseph E. Seagram & Sons* v. *Hostetter*, 384 U.S. 35 (1966)
195. *W.S. Kirkpatrick & Co.* v. *Environmental Tectronics Corp.*, 493 U.S. 400 (1990)	*American Banana Co.* v. *United Fruit Co.*, 213 U.S. 347 (1909)
196. *Collins* v. *Youngblood*, 497 U.S. 37 (1990)	*Kring* v. *Missouri*, 107 U.S. 221 (1883); *Thompson* v. *Utah*, 170 U.S. 343 (1898)
197. *California* v. *Acevedo*, 500 U.S. 565 (1991)	*Arkansas* v. *Sanders*, 442 U.S. 753 (1979) (in part)
198. *Exxon Corp.* v. *Central Gulf Lines, Inc.*, 500 U.S. 603 (1991)	*Minturn* v. *Maynard*, 58 U.S. (17 How.) 477 (1855)
199. *Payne* v. *Tennessee*, 501 U.S. 808 (1991)	*Booth* v. *Maryland*, 482 U.S. 496 (1987); *South Carolina* v. *Gathers*, 490 U.S. 805 (1989) (in part)
200. *Quill Corp.* v. *North Dakota* ___ U.S. ___, 112 S.Ct. 1904 (1992)	*National Bellas Hess, Inc.* v. *Department of Revenue*, 386 U.S. 753 (1967) (in part)
201. *United States* v. *Dixon* ___ U.S. ___, 113 S.Ct. 1849 (1993)	*Grady* v. *Corbin*, 495 U.S. 508 (1990) (in part)
202. *Nichols* v. *United States* ___ U.S. ___, 114 S.Ct. 1921 (1994)	*Baldasar* v. *Illinois*, 446 U.S. 222 (1980) (in part)

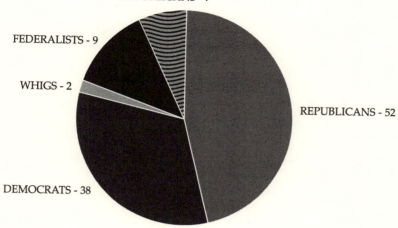

SUPREME COURT JUSTICES BY POLITICAL PARTY OF APPOINTING PRESIDENT

DEMOCRAT - REPUBLICANS - 7

FEDERALISTS - 9

WHIGS - 2

REPUBLICANS - 52

DEMOCRATS - 38

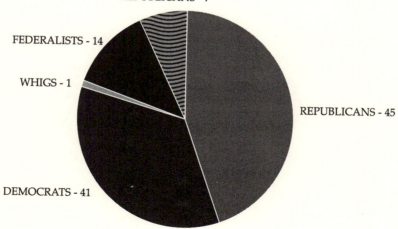

SUPREME COURT JUSTICES BY POLITICAL PARTY

DEMOCRAT - REPUBLICANS - 7

FEDERALISTS - 14

WHIGS - 1

REPUBLICANS - 45

DEMOCRATS - 41

1999

POSITIONS PREVIOUSLY HELD BY
SUPREME COURT JUSTICES

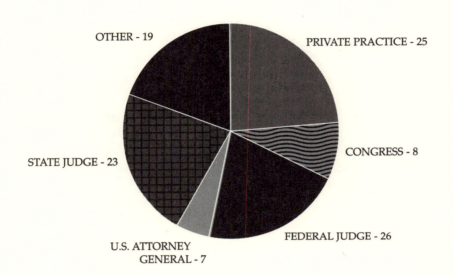

OTHER - 19

PRIVATE PRACTICE - 25

CONGRESS - 8

STATE JUDGE - 23

FEDERAL JUDGE - 26

U.S. ATTORNEY
GENERAL - 7

Index

A

B

Burger, Warren E. (*cont.*)
Federal Power Commission v. *Colorado Interstate Gas Company*
as counsel, 1469
Foley v. *Connelie*, 1476, 1488
Frigillana v. *United States*, 1470–71
Frontiero v. *Richardson*, 1489
Fullilove v. *Klutznick*, 1484
Furman v. *Georgia*, 1476
Geders v. *United States*, 1483
Geduldig v. *Aiello*, 1489
General Electric v. *Gilbert*, 1489
Gertz v. *Robert Welch, Inc.*, 1493
Giglio v. *United States*, 1483
Goldberg v. *Kelley*, 1490
Gooding v. *Wilson*, 1477
Goss v. *Lopez*, 1478
Gregg v. *Georgia*, 1476
Griffiths, In re, 1488, 1492
Hampton v. *Mow Sun Wong*, 1488
Harris v. *McRae*, 1624
Harris v. *New York*, 1481
Heller v. *New York*, 1480
Hishon v. *King & Spalding*, 1492
Holloway v. *Arkansas*, 1483
Hudgens v. *National Labor Relations Board*, 1479
Illinois v. *Gates*, 1481
I.N.S. v. *Chadha*, 1474
I.N.S. v. *Lopez-Mendoza*, 1481
Island Trees Board of Education v. *Pico*, 1477
Jimenez v. *Weinberger*, 1489
Johnson v. *Zerbst*, 1703
Kahn v. *Shevin*, 1865
Keyes v. *Denver School District No. 1*, 1486
Killough v. *United States*, 1471
Laird v. *Tatum*, 1487
Loper v. *Beto*, 1479
Lynch v. *Donnelly*, 1478, 1789–90
MacDonald v. *United States*, 1471
Maher v. *Roe*, 1483
Massachusetts Board of Retirement v. *Murgia*, 1490
Mathews v. *Lucas*, 1489
Mayberry v. *Pennsylvania*, 1492
Metromedia, Inc. v. *City of San Diego*, 1477
Miami Herald Publishing Co. v. *Tornillo*, 1484
Michael M. v. *Superior Court*, 1624
Michigan v. *Mosley*, 1481–82
Miller v. *California*, 1476, 1593
Milliken v. *Bradley*, 1486
Milliken v. *Bradley II*, 1486
Mississipi University for Women v. *Hogan*, 1771
Monell v. *Department of Social Services*, 1488
Monroe v. *Pape*, 1488
Moore v. *City of East Cleveland*, 1479
Morrissey v. *Brewer*, 1483
National League of Cities v. *Usery*, 1475
Nebraska Press Association v. *Stuart*, 1484

New Orleans v. *Dukes*, 1490
New York v. *Quarles*, 1482
New York Times v. *United States*, 1474
Nix v. *Whiteside*, 1492–93
Nix v. *Williams*, 1476
Nixon v. *Administrator of General Services*, 1475
Northern Pipeline Construction Co. v. *Marathon Pipeline Co.*, 1475
Nyquist v. *Mauclet*, 1476, 1488
Oregon v. *Elstad*, 1482
Oregon v. *Hass*, 1481
Oregon v. *Mathiason*, 1482
Papish v. *University of Missouri Curators*, 1477
Parham v. *J.R.*, 1478
Pasadena Board of Education v. *Spangler*, 1486
Patterson v. *New York*, 1700
Paul v. *Davis*, 1487
Peters v. *Hobby*
as counsel, 1469, 1470, 1473
Planned Parenthood of Central Missouri v. *Danforth*, 1483
Planned Parenthood of Southeastern Pennsylvania v. *Casey*, 1616
Plyler v. *Doe*, 1479
Poelker v. *Doe*, 1483
Powell v. *McCormack*, 1472
Procunier v. *Martinez*, 1474
Rawlings v. *Kentucky*, 1481
Reed v. *Reed*, 1474, 1489, 1624
Regents of the University of California v. *Bakke*, 1540–41
Rhode Island v. *Innis*, 1482
Richmond Newpapers, Inc. v. *Virginia*, 1484
Rizzo v. *Goode*, 1487
Roe v. *Wade*, 1474, 1483
San Antonio Independent School District v. *Rodriguez*, 1489–90
Santobello v. *New York*, 1483
Schad v. *Borough of Mount Ephraim*, 1478
Scheuer v. *Rhodes*, 1487
Schlesinger v. *Ballard*, 1489
Schlesinger v. *Reservists to Stop the War*, 1487
school busing, 1484–86
Snyder, In re, 1492
South Dakota v. *Opperman*, 1481
Stanton v. *Stanton*, 1489
Stone v. *Powell*, 1476, 1480, 1700
Sugarman v. *Dougall*, 1488
Supreme Court appointment, 1473
Supreme Court retirement, 1466
Swann v. *Charlotte-Mecklenburg Board of Education*, 1474, 1484–86
Thornburg v. *American College of Obstetricians and Gynecologists*, 1483–84
Trimble v. *Gordon*, 1489
United v. *Agurs*, 1700
United States v. *Binghamton Construction Co.*
as counsel, 1468

Burger, Warren E. (*cont.*)
United States v. Chadwick, 1481
United States v. Harris, 1480
United States v. Henry, 1492
United States v. Leon, 1476, 1481
United States v. Mandujano, 1482
United States v. Martinez-Fuerte, 1700
United States v. Miller, 1700
United States v. Nixon, 1474, 1493–94, 1535, 1536
United States v. Richardson, 1487
United States v. Salvucci, 1481
United States v. Washington, 1482, 1700
United States v. Wong, 1482
Virginia State Board of Pharmacy v. Virginia Citizens Consumer Council, 1474
Vlandis v. Kline, 1490
Wallace v. Jaffree, 1478, 1791
Warth v. Seldin, 1487
Watts v. United States, 1471
Weatherford v. Bursey, 1700
Weinburger v. Wiesenfeld, 1489
Winston-Salem/Forsyth County Board of Education v. Scott, 1485
Wisconsin v. Yoder, 1478
Wood v. Strickland, 1478
Young v. American Mini Theatres, 1479
Burger v. Kemp
Powell, Lewis F., Jr., 1642
Burgess v. Seligson
Bradley, Joseph P., 594
Burgett v. Texas
White, Byron R., 1582
Burnham v. Superior Court
Scalia, Antonin, 1726
Burns v. United States
Marshall, Thurgood, 1818
O'Connor, Sandra Day, 1818
Rehnquist, William H., 1818
Souter, David Hackett, 1818
White, Byron R., 1818
Burns Baking Co. v. Bryan
Brandeis, Louis D., 1028–29
Burr, Aaron, treason trial
Marshall, John, 196
Burson v. Freeman
Blackmun, Harry A., 1823
O'Connor, Sandra Day, 1823
Souter, David Hackett, 1823
Stevens, John Paul, 1711, 1823
Burstyn v. Wilson
Clark, Tom C., 1190
Reed, Stanley, 1190
Burton, Harold, 1322–33
Adler v. Board of Education of the City of New York, 1368
American Communications Assn. v. Douds, 1327
American Tobacco Co. v. United States, 1325

Anderson v. Mt. Clemens Pottery Co., 1325
Bailey v. Richardson, 1328
Beilan v. Board of Education, 1331
Betts v. Brady, 1273, 1276
Bowden v. Arkansas, 1273, 1276
Bridges v. California, 1273, 1276
Brown v. Board of Education, 1329
Bute v. Illinois, 1326
Carpenters and Joiners Union v. Ritter's Cafe, 1273, 1276
on civil liberties, 1325–32
on civil rights, 1329
Commissioner v. Wilcox, 1325
Dennis v. United States, 1327, 1330
Duncan v. Kahanamoku, 1325
Garner v. Board of Public Works, 1328
Garner v. Teamsters, Chauffeurs and Helpers, 1328
Georgia v. Evans, 1275, 1276
Glasser v. United States, 1273
Goldman v. United States, 1273
Haley v. Ohio, 1326
Harris v. South Carolina, 1326
Henderson v. United States, 1329
Hysler v. Florida, 1273, 1276
International Union, U.A.A. & A.I.W.U. v. Russell, 1331
Irvine v. California, 1384
Jencks v. United States, 1330
Jobin v. Arizona, 1273, 1276
Joint Anti-Fascist Refugee Committee v. McGrath, 1328
Jones v. Opelika, 1273
Kent v. Dulles, 1331
Kirschbaum v. Walling, 1275, 1276
Kraus & Bros. v. United States, 1325
labor law, 1330–31
Lerner v. Casey, 1331, 1355
Lichter v. United States, 1327
Lisenba v. California, 1273, 1276
Lorain Journal Co. v. United States, 1328
Louisiana ex rel Francis v. Resweber, 1326
McLaurin v. Oklahoma State Regents, 1329
Marsh v. Alabama, 1112, 1325
Morgan v. Virginia, 1325
Pennsylvania v. Nelson, 1330
Rochin v. California, 1384
Rowoldt v. Perfetto, 1331
Saia v. New York, 1327
Schulte v. Gangi, 1325
Slochower v. Board of Education, 1329–30
Supreme Court appointment, 1323, 1324
Supreme Court retirement, 1331
Sweatt v. Painter, 1329
Sweezy v. New Hamphire, 1330
Times-Mirror v. California, 1273, 1276
Trop v. Dulles, 1331
Tucker v. Texas, 1325
Turner v. Pennsylvania, 1326

Douglas, William O. (*cont.*)
  Adler v. Board of Education of the City of New York, 1368
  Afroyim v. Rusk, 1236
  Association of Data Processing Service Org. v. Camp, 1721
  Bailey v. Richardson, 1328
  Barenblatt v. United States, 1388
  Barsky v. Board of Regents, 1384
  Beauharnais v. Illinois, 1189
  Betts v. Brady, 1171, 1273, 1276
  Blau v. Lehman, 1225
  A Book Named "John Cleland's Memoirs of a Woman of Pleasure" v. Attorney General, 1236
  Bowden v. Arkansas, 1273, 1276
  Bridges v. California, 1273, 1276
  business, regulation of rates, 1228–29
  Carpenters and Joiners Union v. Ritter's Cafe, 1190, 1273, 1276
  Case v. Los Angeles Number Co., 1236
  on civil liberties, 1220, 1229–32, 1233–35, 1238
  Clearfield Trust Company v. United States, 1236
  Dennis v. United States, 1229–32, 1236
  Doe v. Bolton, 1614
  Edwards v. California, 1270
  Eisenstadt v. Baird, 1534
  Elfbrandt v. Russell, 1455
  Engel v. Vitale, 1237
  Everson v. Board of Education, 1237
  Federal Power Commission v. Hope Natural Gas Co., 1228–29, 1232
  Federal Power Commission v. Natural Gas Pipeline Co., 1228
  Feiner v. New York, 1367
  Galvan v. Press, 1383
  Garner v. Board of Public Works, 1351
  Georgia v. Evans, 1275, 1276
  Giles v. Maryland, 1459
  Glasser v. United States, 1273
  Goldman v. United States, 1273
  Green v. United States, 1427
  Griswold v. Connecticut, 1232–33, 1863, 1877
  Hartsfield v. Sloan, 1398
  Hysler v. Florida, 1273, 1276
  Irvine v. California, 1384
  Jencks v. United States, 1330
  Jobin v. Arizona, 1273, 1276
  Joint Anti-Fascist Refugee Committee v. McGrath, 1328
  Jones v. Opelika, 1273
  Kahn v. Shevin, 1865
  Keyishian v. The Board of Regents of the University of the State of New York, 1355
  Kirschbaum v. Walling, 1275, 1276
  Lehmann v. Carson, 1428

Lisenba v. California, 1273, 1276
Minersville School District v. Gobitis, 1111, 1236
Perez v. Brownell, 1236
Peters v. Hobby, 1385
Pierce v. United States, 1273
Poulos v. New Hampshire, 1191
Reitz v. Mealey, 1275, 1276
Rochin v. California, 1384
Roe v. Wade, 1535
Rogers v. Bellei, 1533
Saia v. New York, 1327
Securities and Exchange Commission, 1224–27
Shuman v. United States, 1273
Skinner v. Oklahoma, 1272
Stamler v. Willis, 1427
Supreme Court appointment, 1227
Supreme Court retirement, 1244
Terminiello v. Chicago, 1190
Times-Mirror v. California, 1273, 1276
United States v. Causby, 1235–36
United States v. Nixon, 1536
United States v. Pink, 1275, 1276
United States v. Powelson, 1236
United States v. Teamsters' Union, 1273
United Steelworkers of America v. United States, 1526
Utah v. Aldrich, 1275, 1276
vice-presidential possibilities, 1238–40
Watkins v. United States, 1388
West Virginia State Board of Education v. Barnette, 1111, 1170
Zorach v. Clauson, 1194
Douglas v. California
  Harlan, John M. (1899–1971), 1407–8, 1581
  Stewart, Potter, 1581
  White, Byron R., 1581
Dow v. Johnson
  Clifford, Nathan, 485
  Miller, Samuel, 511
  Swayne, Noah H., 498
Dowdell v. United States
  White, Edward Douglas, 823
Downes v. Bidwell
  Brown, Henry Billings, 736
  Fuller, Melville, 736
  Gray, Horace, 676
  Harlan, John M. (1833–1911), 638
  White, Edward Douglas, 822
Doyle v. Continental Insurance Co.
  Bradley, Joseph P., 596
Doyle v. Ohio
  Powell, Lewis F., Jr., 1636, 1643
  Stevens, John Paul, 1701
Draper v. United States
  Whittaker, Charles, 1429
Draper v. Washington
  Goldberg, Arthur J., 1447

E

F

G

H

Harlan, John M. (1833–1911) (cont.)
  United States ex rel Attorney General v.
    Delaware and Hudson Co., 633
  Virginia v. Rives, 623
  on voting rights, 639
Harlan, John M. (1899–1971), 1401–21
  Afroyim v. Rusk, 1408
  Avery v. Midland County, 1410
  Baker v. Carr, 1527
  Barenblatt v. United States, 1387–88, 1414,
    1417
  Beilan v. Board of Education 1331
  Brown v. Louisiana, 1416
  Brown Shoe Co. v. United States, 1405
  on civil liberties, 1412–14, 1416–17
  Cohen v. Beneficial Life Ins. Co.
    as counsel, 1403
  Cohen v. California, 1419, 1550
  Cole v. Young, 1415
  on criminal law, 1408, 1411–12
  Drombrowski v. Pfister, 1406
  Douglas v. California, 1407–8, 1581
  Duncan v. Louisiana, 1411
  Emspack v. United States, 1405
  Evans v. Newton, 1411
  Fay v. Noia, 1406
  federal government and state government,
    1409–10, 1413
  Federal Trade Commission v. Procter & Gamble
    Co., 1405
  Flast v. Cohen, 1406
  Flemming v. Nestor, 1415
  Garner v. Louisiana, 1416
  Gault, In re, 1411, 1417
  Gibson v. Florida Legislative Committee, 1581
  Gideon v. Wainright, 1407, 1408, 1411
  Ginzburg v. United States, 1412
  Giordenello v. United States, 1412
  Griffin v. Illinois, 1407–8
  Griswold v. Connecticut, 1416
  Harper v. Virginia Board of Elections, 1410
  Henry v. Mississippi, 1406
  Idaho Sheet Metal Works, Inc. v. Wirtz, 1405
  Jencks v. United States, 1330
  "John Cleland's Memoirs of a Woman of
    Pleasure" v. Massachusetts, 1412
  Jones v. United States, 1412
  Katz v. United States, 1417
  Klopfer v. North Carolina, 1411
  Klor's, Inc. v. Broadway-Hale Stores, Inc.,
    1405
  Labine v. Vincent, 1532
  Lerner v. Casey, 1331, 1355, 1414
  Levy v. Louisiana, 1410
  McGautha v. California, 1532
  Maisenberg v. United States, 1415
  Malloy v. Hogan, 1411
  Mancusi v. DeForte, 1417
  Mapp v. Ohio, 1411

  Marchetti v. United States, 1408
  NAACP v. Alabama (1958), 1406, 1407,
    1416
  NAACP v. Alabama (1959), 1407
  NAACP v. Alabama (1964), 1407
  NAACP v. Button, 1416
  Nelson and Globe v. County of Los Angeles,
    1356
  Noto v. United States, 1413
  Nowak v. United States, 1415
  Oestereich v. Selective Service Board, 1417
  Perez v. Brownell, 1408, 1414
  Poe v. Ullman, 1406, 1412, 1416
  Pointer v. Texas, 1409
  Reapportionment Cases, 1412, 1418
  Reid v. Covert, 1415
  Reitman v. Mulkey, 1411
  Reynolds v. Sims, 1399, 1409, 1410, 1418
  Robinson v. California, 1411
  Rogers v. Missouri Pacific R.R., 1412
  Roth v. United States, 1412
  Rowoldt v. Perfetto, 1415
  Scales v. United States, 1413
  Service v. Dulles, 1415
  Shapiro v. Thompson, 1410
  Shelton v. Tucker, 1553
  Shuttlesworth v. City of Birmingham, 1416
  Simmons v. United States, 1417
  Slochower v. Board of Education, 1329
  Societe Internationale v. Rogers, 1407
  Spencer v. Texas, 1412
  Stamler v. Willis, 1417
  Street v. New York, 1651
  Supreme Court appointment, 1404
  Swift & Co. v. Wickham, 1408
  Talley v. California, 1416
  Townsend v. Sain, 1581
  Trop v. Dulles, 1414
  on trusts, antitrust suits, 1405
  United States v. Archie Brown, 1389
  United States v. Continental Can Co., 1405
  United States v. Dow, 1405
  United States v. Procter & Gamble, supra,
    1405
  United States v. Shotwell Mfg. Co., 1407
  Uphaus v. Wyman, 1355
  Vitarelli v. Seaton, 1415
  Watkins v. United States, 1388
  Wesberry v. Sanders, 1409–10
  Williams v. Illinois, 1773
  Wong Sun v. United States, 1581
  Yates v. United States, 1386, 1413
Harlow v. Fitzgerald
  Powell, Lewis F., Jr., 1656
Harmelin v. Michigan
  Blackmun, Harry A., 1707
  Stevens, John Paul, 1707–8
  Thomas, Clarence, 1840
  White, Byron R., 1591

I

J

Memphis Light Gas & Water v. Craft
Powell, Lewis F., Jr., 1650
Merchants' Loan & Trust Co. v. Smietanka
Clarke, John H., 1042
Merrill v. Sherburne
Woodbury, Levi, 423
Metro Broadcasting, Inc. v. F.C.C.
Kennedy, Anthony M., 1751–52
White, Byron R., 1598
Metromedia, Inc. v. City of San Diego
Burger, Warren E., 1477
White, Byron R., 1595
Metropolitan Life Ins. Co. v. Wood
Powell, Lewis F., Jr., 1657
Metropolitan Washington Airports Authority v. Citizens for the Abatement of Airport Noise, Inc.
White, Byron R., 1603
Meyer v. Nebraska
Holmes, Oliver Wendell, 879–80
McReynolds, James C., 1012
Taft, William, 1012
Miami Herald Publishing Co. v. Tornillo
Burger, Warren E., 1484
Stewart, Potter, 1557
Michael H. v. Gerald D.
Brennan, William J., 1726, 1781
Kennedy, Anthony M., 1726, 1781
O'Connor, Sandra Day, 1726, 1781
Rehnquist, William H., 1781
Scalia, Antonin, 1725–26, 1781
Stevens, John Paul, 1781
Michael M. v. Superior Court
Blackmun, Harry A., 1624
Burger, Warren E., 1624
Powell, Lewis F., Jr., 1624
Rehnquist, William H., 1624
Stewart, Potter, 1624
Michigan v. Clifford
Powell, Lewis F., Jr., 1637
Michigan v. Mosley
Burger, Warren E., 1481–82
Stewart, Potter, 1564
Michigan v. Tyler
Stewart, Potter, 1562
Middlesex County v. Sea Clammers
Powell, Lewis F., Jr., 1656
Milkovich v. Lorrain Journal
White, Byron R., 1594
Milk Wagon Drivers Union v. Meadowmoor Dairies
Frankfurter, Felix F., 957, 1190
Hughes, Charles Evans, 957
Reed, Stanley, 1190
Miller, Samuel, 504–18
Asylum v. New Orleans, 546
bond cases, 513, 514
Chicago, Milwaukee & St. Paul Ry. Co. v. Minnesota, 515

citizen, privileges and immunities, 514, 515
on civil rights, 509, 512, 513, 515, 516
Civil Rights Cases, 512
Crandall v. Nevada, 514
Cummings v. Missouri, 510
Davidson v. New Orleans, 515
on discrimination, 512
Dow v. Johnson, 511
on Due Process Clause, 515
on Fifteenth Amendment, 512–13
on Fourteenth Amendment, 512, 514–15
Garland, Ex parte, 510
Gelpcke v. Dubuque, 513
Georgia v. Stanton, 511
Granger Cases, 516
Hepburn v. Griswold, 511
on interstate commerce, 514
regulations of rates, 516
Juilliard v. Greenman, 511
Kansas-Nebraska Act, 507
Kilbourn v. Thompson, 516
Knox v. Lee, 511
Legal Tender Cases, 510–11
Loan Association v. Topeka, 514
Miller v. United States, 511
Milligan, Ex parte, 524
Mississippi v. Johnson, 511
Munn v. Illinois, 516
Neagle, In re, 710–11
Reconstruction Acts, legality of, 511–12
Siebold, Ex parte, 513
Slaughter-House Cases, 514–15
on slavery issue, 507
Strauder v. West Virginia, 512
Supreme Court appointment, 508
on taxation, 509, 511, 513–14
test oath cases, 510, 558
Tyler v. Defrees, 511
United States v. Cruikshank, 512
United States v. Harris, 512
United States v. Lee, 516
United States v. Reese, 512
Virginia, Ex parte, 512
on voting rights, 512–13
Wabash, St. Louis & Pacific Railway Company v. Illinois, 516
Yarbrough, Ex parte, 512
Miller v. California
Blackmun, Harry A., 1593
Burger, Warren E., 1476, 1593
Powell, Lewis F., Jr., 1593
Rehnquist, William H., 1593
White, Byron R., 1593
Miller v. Standard Nut Margarine Co.
Butler, Pierce, 1086
Miller v. United States
Clifford, Nathan, 485
Field, Stephen J., 485

Powell, Lewis F., Jr. (cont.)
Fiallo v. Bell, 1644
First Nat'l Bank of Boston v. Bellotti, 1653
Florida v. Royer, 1637
Formost-McKesson, Inc. v. Provident Securities
   Co., 1659
Franks v. Bowman Transportation Co., Inc.,
   1647
Frontiero v. Richardson, 1623, 1645
Fullilove v. Klutznick, 1648
Gannett Co. v. DePasquale, 1653
Garcia v. San Antonio Metro. Transit Auth.,
   1632, 1657
Garner v. United States, 1635, 1637
Gateway Coal Co. v. United Mine Workers,
   1660
Georgia v. United States, 1647
Gertz v. Robert Welch, Inc., 1538, 1652
Griffiths, In re, 1643–44
Gulf States Utilities v. Federal Power
   Commission, 1658
Guy Oil Corporation v. Copp Paving Co., 1659
Hampton v. United States, 1641
Harlow v. Fitzgerald, 1656
Harris v. McRae, 1624
Healy v. James, 1651
Heckler v. Day, 1656
Henderson v. United States, 1641–42
H.L. v. Matheson, 1661
Hobbie v. Unemployment Appeals Comm'n,
   1655
Hoover v. Ronwin, 1659
Hughes v. Alexandria Scrap Metal Co., 1657
Hunt v. McNair, 1654
Imbler v. Pachtman, 1656
Industrial Union Dep't v. American Petroleum
   Institute, 1658
Ingraham v. Wright, 1649, 1650, 1658
ILGWU v. Quality Mfg. Co., 1660
Island Trees Board of Education v. Pico, 1651
James v. Strange, 1646
Jefferson County Pharmaceutical Ass'n v.
   Abbott Laboratories, Inc., 1659
Jenkins v. Anderson, 1636
Johnson v. Louisiana, 1642
Johnson v. Transportation Agency, Santa Clara
   County, 1680
Johnson v. Zerbst, 1703
Kahn v. Shevin, 1865
Karcher v. Daggett, 1654
Kassel v. Consolidated Freightways Corp., 1657
Kastigar v. United States, 1634–35, 1643
Keyes v. Denver School District No. 1, 1647
Kirby v. Illinois, 1641
Kleppe v. Sierra, 1661
Kuhlman v. Wilson, 1636, 1641
labor law, 1661
Lemon v. Kurtzman, 1654
Lewis v. City of New Orleans, 1651

Lloyd Corporation v. Tanner, 1650
McCleskey v. Kemp, 1634, 1642, 1646
McDonnell-Douglas Corporation v. Green, 1647
Maher v. Roe, 1645–46, 1661
Martin v. Ohio, 1640
Matthews v. Eldridge, 1649, 1650
Mayor of City of Philadelphia v. Educational
   Equality League, 1646–47
Memphis Light Gas & Water v. Craft, 1650
Metropolitan Life Ins. Co. v. Wood, 1657
Michael M. v. Superior Court, 1624
Michigan v. Clifford, 1637
Middlesex County v. Sea Clammers, 1656
Miller v. California, 1593
Mississipi University for Women v. Hogan,
   1645, 1771
Mitchell v. W. T. Grant, 1648–49
Moore v. City of East Cleveland, 1632, 1661
Moore v. Illinois, 1641
Moorman Mfg. Co. v. Bair, 1657
Morris v. Gressette, 1647
Mourning v. Family Publications Service, 1661
Mullaney v. Wilbur, 1640, 1643
NAACP v. Button, 1653
NAACP v. FPC, 1646
Nebraska Press Ass'n v. Stuart, 1652
Neil v. Biggers, 1639
New Jersey v. Portash, 1635
New York Telephone Co. v. New York State
   Dep't of Labor, 1660, 1661
Nixon v. Fitzgerald, 1656
NLRB v. Bell Aerospace Co., 1660
NLRB v. Weingarten, 1660
NLRB v. Yeshiva University, 1660
North Georgia Finishing, Inc. v. Di-Chem,
   Inc., 1649
Nyquist v. Mauclet, 1644
Ohralik v. Ohio State Bar Ass'n, 1653
Oil Workers v. Mobil Oil Corp., 1660–61
Oliver v. United States, 1637
Pacific Gas & Electric v. PUC, 1650–51
Patterson v. New York, 1640
Pell v. Procunier, 1652
Pennhurst State School & Hospital v.
   Halderman, 1657
Pennzoil Co. v. Texaco, 1658
Phyler v. Doe, 1632
Pillsbury Company v. Conboy, 1635
Pittsburgh Press Co. v. Pittsburgh Commission
   on Human Relations, 1653
Plyler v. Doe, 1644
Primus, In Re, 1653
Procunier v. Martinez, 1652
Pruneyard Shopping Center v. Robbins, 1650
Regents of the University of California v.
   Bakke, 1540–41, 1634, 1647–48
Ristaino v. Ross, 1646
Roberts v. United States, 1636
Rose v. Clark, 1640

Reed, Stanley (*cont.*)
  Milk Wagon Drivers Union v. *Meadowmoor Dairies*, 1190
  Minersville School District v. *Gobitis*, 1192
  Missouri ex rel. Gaines v. *Canada*, 1187
  Morgan v. *Virginia*, 1187
  Murdock v. *Pennsylvania*, 1192, 1193
  National Labor Relations Board v. *Fansteel Metallurgical Corp.*, 1186
  Niemotko v. *Maryland*, 1190–91
  Pennekamp v. *Florida*, 1190
  Pennsylvania v. *Nelson*, 1188
  Peters v. *Hobby*, 1185, 1189
  Pierce v. *United States*, 1273
  Poulos v. *New Hampshire*, 1191
  Prince v. *Massachusetts*, 1193
  Quinn v. *United States*, 1185–86
  Railway Mail Association v. *Corsi*, 1187
  Saia v. *New York*, 1191–92, 1327
  Schechter Poultry Corp. v. *United States*
    as counsel, 1183
  Shuman v. *United States*, 1273
  Slochower v. *Board of Education*, 1189, 1329
  Smith v. *Allwright*, 1188
  Southern Pacific Co. v. *Arizona*, 1187
  Stark v. *Wickard*, 1186
  Stein v. *New York*, 1196
  Summers, In re, 1193
  Supreme Court appointment, 1181, 1183
  Supreme Court retirement, 1183
  Sweatt v. *Painter*, 1187
  Switchmen's Union v. *National Mediation Board*, 1186
  Takahashi v. *Fish and Game Commission*, 1188
  Terminiello v. *Chicago*, 1190
  Thomas v. *Collins*, 1187
  Thornhill v. *Alabama*, 1190
  Times-Mirror v. *California*, 1273, 1276
  Toth v. *Quarles*, 1186
  United Public Workers v. *Mitchell*, 1191
  on United States Civil Rights Commission, 1184
  United States v. *Appalachian Electric Power Co.*, 1184
  United States v. *Butler*
    as counsel, 1183, 1184
  United States v. *California*, 1187
  United States v. *C.I.O.*, 1186
  United States v. *Columbia Steel Co.*, 1187
  United States v. *Darby Lumber Co.*, 1185
  United States v. *du Pont de Nemours & Co.*, 1187
  United States v. *Hutcheson*, 1186–87
  United States v. *Kahriger*, 1186
  United States v. *Line Material Co.*, 1187
  United States v. *Rock Royal Cooperative*, 1184, 1186

  United States v. *Teamsters' Union*, 1273
  United States ex rel. Knauff v. *Shaughnessy*, 1367
  Utah v. *Aldrich*, 1275, 1276
  West Virginia State Board of Educaton v. *Barnette*, 1193
  Winters v. *New York*, 1190
  Wolf v. *Colorado*, 1196
  Youngstown Sheet & Tube Co. v. *Sawyer*, 1185
Reed v. *Reed*
  Burger, Warren E., 1474, 1489, 1624
  Ginsburg, Ruth Bader
    as counsel, 1864–65, 1866
Regents of the University of California v. *Bakke*
  Blackmun, Harry A., 1541, 1617–18
  Brennan, William J., 1540–41
  Burger, Warren E., 1540–41
  Marshall, Thurgood, 1512, 1541
  Powell, Lewis F., Jr., 1540–41, 1634, 1647–48
  Rehnquist, William H., 1540
  Stevens, John Paul, 1540, 1541, 1711
  Stewart, Potter, 1540
  White, Byron R., 1599
Rehnquist, William H., 1663–1689
  abortion cases, 1672, 1674, 1684–85
  affirmative action cases, 1675, 1680, 1684
  Andresen v. *Maryland*, 1700
  Arizona v. *Fulminante*, 1687–88, 1815
  Arizona v. *Roberson*, 1746
  Barnes v. *Glen Theaters*, 1682–83, 1818
  Bob Jones University v. *United States*, 1673
  Brewer v. *Williams*, 1702
  Burns v. *United States*, 1818
  Butler v. *McKellar*, 1686
  Califano v. *Goldfarb*, 1867
  Central Hudson Gas & Electric Co. v. *Public Service Comm'n*, 1673
  Charles D. Bonanno Linen Service v. *NLRB*, 1773
  Chisom v. *Roemer*, 1749
  City of Richmond v. *J. A. Croson*, 1684
  on civil liberties, 1673
  County of Riverside v. *McLaughlin*, 1782, 1820
  criminal law, 1675, 1680–81
  Cruz v. *Beto*, 1673
  Cruzan v. *Director, Missouri Department of Health*, 1686–87, 1803
  Dawson v. *Delaware*, 1847
  Delo v. *Stokes*, 1747
  Doe v. *Bolton*, 1615
  Doggett v. *United States*, 1746, 1844
  Duren v. *Missouri*, 1868
  Eddings v. *Oklahoma*, 1800
  Edmonson v. *Leesville Concrete Company, Inc.*, 1821

S

Stevens, John Paul (*cont.*)
  County of Riverside v. *McLaughlin*, 1704,
    1782, 1820
  criminal law, 1699–1700, 1704, 1706,
    1708–9
  Doyle v. *Ohio*, 1701
  Due Process Clause, 1698, 1703
  *Employment Division, Department of Human
    Resources* v. *Smith*, 1712
  Estelle v. *Gamble*, 1698
  Evans v. *United States*, 1851
  Federal Election Commission v. *Massachusetts
    Citizens for Life, Inc.*, 1679
  Florida v. *Bostick*, 1823, 1704
  Florida v. *Jimeno*, 1705
  Fort Wayne Books v. *Indiana*, 1712
  Frisby v. *Schultz*, 1711–12
  Gardner v. *Florida*, 1703, 1704
  Gerstein v. *Pugh*, 1704
  Graham v. *Collins*, 1801
  Gregg v. *Georgia*, 1565, 1591
  Groppi v. *Leslie*, 1692
  Guardians Association v. *Civil Service
    Commission*, 1710
  Hampton v. *Mow Sun Wong*, 1696
  Hankerson v. *North Carolina*, 1701
  Harmelin v. *Michigan*, 1707–8
  Henderson v. *Morgan*, 1703, 1704
  Hernandez v. *New York*, 1708, 1745
  Honda v. *Oberg*, 1789
  Hudson v. *Palmer*, 1698–1700
  Idaho v. *Wright*, 1781
  I.N.S v. *Cardoza-Fonseca*, 1724
  *International Society for Krishna
    Consciousness, Inc.* v. *Lee*, 1821
  Jeffers v. *United States*, 1701
  Jett v. *Dallas Independent School District*,
    1710
  Johnson v. *Transportation Agency, Santa Clara
    County*, 1680
  Johnson v. *Zerbst*, 1703
  Jones v. *North Carolina Prisoners' Labor
    Union, Inc.*, 1698
  Kadrmas v. *Dickinson Public Schools*, 1697
  Lankford v. *Idaho*, 1816
  Lechmere v. *National Labor Relations Board*,
    1852
  Lee v. *Weisman*, 1823, 1824
  Lewis v. *Jeffers*, 1801
  Ludwig v. *Massachusetts*, 1701
  McCleskey v. *Zant*, 1705
  McNary v. *Haitian Refugee Center*, 1815
  McNeil v. *Wisconsin*, 1703, 1707
  Manson v. *Brathwaite*, 1701
  Maryland v. *Craig*, 1781
  Mathews v. *Lucas*, 1696–97
  Meacham v. *Fano*, 1698
  Members of City Council v. *Taxpayers for
    Vincent*, 1712

  Michael H. v. *Gerald D.*, 1781
  Moody v. *Daggett*, 1698
  Mullaney v. *Wilbur*, 1701
  Mu'Min v. *Virginia*, 1705
  Oklahoma City v. *Tuttle*, 1710–11
  Oregon v. *Mathiason*, 1701
  Parker v. *Dugger*, 1814
  Patterson v. *McLean Credit Union*, 1747
  Patterson v. *New York*, 1700
  Payne v. *Tennessee*, 1706
  Penry v. *Lynaugh*, 1698
  *Planned Parenthood of Southeastern
    Pennsylvania* v. *Casey*, 1802, 1825
  Regents of the University of California v.
    Bakke, 1540, 1541, 1711
  Rosales-Lopez v. *United States*, 1696
  Rose v. *Clark*, 1704
  Rust v. *Sullivan*, 1802
  Schad v. *Arizona*, 1592
  South Dakota v. *Opperman*, 1700
  Stone v. *Powell*, 1700
  Sullivan v. *Everhart*, 1724, 1725
  Supreme Court appointment, 1693
  Tashjian v. *Republican Party of Connecticut*,
    1710
  Texas v. *Johnson*, 1712
  Town of Newton v. *Rummery*, 1711
  United States v. *Agurs*, 1700
  United States v. *Chadwick*, 1701
  United States v. *Donovan*, 1701
  United States v. *Eichman*, 1712
  United States v. *Martinez-Fuerte*, 1700
  United States v. *Martin Linen Supply Co.*,
    1701
  United States v. *Miller*, 1700
  United States v. *Providence Journal Co.*,
    1709–10
  United States v. *Ramsey*, 1701
  United States v. *Sanatana*, 1700–1701
  United States v. *Washington*, 1700
  Wainwright v. *Sykes*, 1701
  Wallace v. *Jaffree*, 1790
  Weatherford v. *Bursey*, 1700
  Will v. *Michigan Department of State Police*,
    1711
  Williams v. *United States*, 1846
  Wygant v. *Jackson Board of Education*, 1711
Stevenson v. United States
  Peckham, Rufus, 848
Steward Machine Co. v. *Davis*
  Cardozo, Benjamin, 965
Stewart, Potter, 1546–73
  Abood v. *Detroit Board of Education*, 1558
  Almeida-Sanchez v. *United States*, 1561
  Amalgamated Food Employees v. *Logan Valley
    Plaza*, 1558
  Ambach v. *Norwick*, 1554
  Ashe v. *Swenson*, 1563
  Baird v. *State Bar of Arizona*, 1558

Swayne, Noah H. (*cont.*)
  Virginia, Ex Parte, 498
  on voting rights, 498
Swearingen v. *United States*
  Brown, Henry Billings, 786
  Gray, Horace, 786
  Harlan, John M. (1833–1911), 786
  Shiras, George, Jr., 786
  White, Edward Douglas, 786
Sweatt v. *Painter*
  Burton, Harold, 1329
  Marshall, Thurgood
    as counsel, 1501
  Minton, Sherman, 1369
  Reed, Stanley, 1187
  Vinson, Fred M., 1339
Sweezy v. *New Hampshire*
  Black, Hugo L., 1354
  Burton, Harold, 1330
  Clark, Tom C., 1330, 1354, 1356
  Frankfurter, Felix F., 1212, 1354
  Warren, Earl, 1388
Swift v. *Tyson*
  Story, Joseph, 268
  Thompson, Smith, 283
Swift and Company v. *United States*
  Holmes, Oliver Wendell, 1064–65
  Moody, William, 914–15
Swift & Co. v. *Wickham*
  Harlan, John M. (1899–1971), 1408
Switchmen's Union v. *National Mediation Board*
  Reed, Stanley, 1186

T

Taft, William, 1050–68
  Adkins v. *Children's Hospital*, 1067, 1075
  Bailey v. *Drexel Furniture Co.*, 1066
  on commerce, 1064, 1067
  on Due Process Clause, 1063–64
  as governor general of the Philippines, 1053
  Grossman, Ex parte, 1065
  on injunction, 1063–64
  on interstate commerce, 1064–65
  on judicial reorganization, 1056–58, 1060, 1067
  Maple Flooring Manufacturers Association v. *United States*, 1096
  on Marshall, John, 1066
  Meyer v. *Nebraska*, 1012
  Myers v. *United States*, 1065, 1183, 1722
  Olmstead v. *United States*, 1033
  as president, 1054–55
  on property rights, 1063–64
  Sonneborn v. *Cureton*, 1061
  Stafford v. *Wallace*, 1064, 1066
  Supreme Court appointment, 1052, 1056

  on taxation, 1066
  Truax v. *Corrigan*, 1063–64
Takahashi v. *Fish and Game Commission*
  Reed, Stanley, 1188
Talbot v. *Jansen*
  Iredell, James, 37–38
  Paterson, William, 113–14
  Rutledge, John, 37
Talbot v. *Seaman*
  Marshall, John, 174–75
Talbot v. *Ship Amelia*
  Paterson, William, 274
Talcott v. *City of Buffalo*
  Peckham, Rufus, 839
Talley v. *California*
  Black, Hugo L., 1169
  Harlan, John M. (1899–1971), 1416
Taney, Roger, 337–358
  Ableman v. *Booth*, 356
  Baltimore Bank riots, 344
  Bank of Augusta v. *Earle*, 270, 349
  Bank of the United States, Second, 340
    attack on, 341–42
  Briscoe v. *Bank of the Commonwealth of Kentucky*, 345
  Bronson v. *Kinzie*, 265, 348–49
  Brown v. *Maryland*, 351
  Charles River Bridge v. *Warren Bridge*, 345–48, 431, 618, 625
  on commerce, 345, 349, 351, 352
  on contracts, 348–49
  Cook v. *Moffat*, 349
  Cooley v. *Board of Wardens*, 352
  on corporations, 345, 347, 349–51
  Dred Scott v. *Sandford*, 338, 354–56, 468, 622, 625, 633, 986
  dual sovereignty, 341, 345, 356, 358
  Groves v. *Slaughter*, 352, 353
  judicial review upheld, 351, 356
  Kendall v. *United States ex rel. Stokes*, 369
  Lane v. *Dick*, 393
  License Cases, 351–52
  Luther v. *Borden*, 430
  Marshall v. *Baltimore & Ohio Railroad Co.*, 465
  Milligan, Ex parte, 357
  nullification question, 341–42
  Ohio v. *Debolt*, 308
  Passenger Cases, 351
  Pennsylvania v. *Wheeling and Belmont Bridge Company* (1851), 402
  Planters' Bank of Mississippi v. *Sharp*, 431
  on police power, 345–46, 352, 354
  Prigg v. *Pennsylvania*, 353
  Prize Cases, 358
  on property rights, 348–49, 353, 354
  Providence Bank v. *Billings*, 347
  Rowan v. *Runnels*, 353
  on slavery issue, 340–41, 352, 353

Thomas, Clarence (*cont.*)
Georgia v. McCollum, 1854–55
Harmelin v. Michigan, 1840
Hudson v. McMillan, 1751, 1826, 1840–43, 1845
International Society for Krishna Consciousness, Inc. v. Lee, 1855
Jacobson v. United States, 1826, 1845–46
Keeney v. Tamayo-Reyes, 1826
Lechmere v. National Labor Relations Board, 1852
Lee v. International Society for Krishna Consciousness, Inc., 1822, 1855
Lee v. Weisman, 1823, 1855–56
Lujan v. Defenders of Wildlife, 1852
Molzof v. United States, 1836–37
Morales v. Trans World Airlines, 1853
Morgan v. Illinois, 1847
National Passenger Corporation v. Boston & Maine Corporation, 1852
New York v. United States, 1850, 1851
obscenity cases, 1846
Planned Parenthood of Southeastern Pennsylvania v. Casey, 1754, 1802, 1855, 1856–57
Price Waterhouse v. Hopkins, 1797
R.A.V. v. St. Paul, 1822, 1855
Riggins v. Nevada, 1849–50, 1851
Sochor v. Florida, 1847
Stringer v. Black, 1851
Supreme Court appointment, 1832–36
Suter v. Artist M, 1852
United States v. Fordice, 1853–54
United States v. Salerno, 1853
White v. Illinois, 1837–38, 1843, 1845, 1846
Williams v. United States, 1845–46
Wright v. West, 1851–52
Wyatt v. Cole, 1852
Wyoming v. Oklahoma, 1852
Thomas v. Arizona
Whittaker, Charles, 1429
Thomas v. Collins
Frankfurter, Felix F., 1112
Reed, Stanley, 1112, 1187
Roberts, Owen J., 1112
Rutledge, Wiley, 1112
Stone, Harlan Fiske, 1111–12
Thomas v. Dakin
Nelson, Samuel, 411
Thomas v. Review Board of Indiana
Rehnquist, William H., 1673
The Thomas Jefferson
Story, Joseph, 259–60
Thompson, Smith, 273–91
Bank of the United States v. Halstead, 282, 289
Beers v. Haughton, 289
Briscoe v. Bank of the Commonwealth of Kentucky, 285
Brown v. Maryland, 282, 285

Carpenter v. Butterfield, 282
Charles River Bridge v. Warren Bridge, 285
Cherokee Nation v. Georgia, 285, 289
City of New York v. Miln, 285, 369
Craig v. Missouri, 284, 285
dual sovereignty, 276, 287–88
The Emily and The Caroline, 289
on equity law, 289
Gaines v. Relf, 289
Groves v. Slaughter, 287
Hallett v. Novion, 276
Hitchcock v. Aicken, 276
Holmes v. Jennison, 370
Inglis v. Sailor's Snug Harbor, 289
Jackson ex dem. St. Joan v. Chew, 283
Jackson ex dem. Sparkman v. Porter, 285
Kendall v. United States ex rel. Stokes, 286
Lee v. Lee, 290
Lewis v. Few, 289
Livingston v. Story, 289
Livingston v. Van Ingen, 276, 282, 285, 287, 288
Martin, In re, 290
Mason v. Haile, 283, 285
Missouri question, 278, 290
Ogden v. Saunders, 282, 285
Osborn v. Bank of the United States, 282
People v. Croswell, 276
presidential aspirations, 278–80
Prigg v. Pennsylvania, 287
Renner v. Bank of Columbia, 282, 288
on slavery issue, 287, 289, 290
on states' rights, 276, 283–85
Supreme Court appointment, 280
Swift v. Tyson, 283
United States v. Arredondo, 289
United States v. The Schooner Amistad, 287
Weston v. City Council of Charleston, 284, 290
Wheaton v. Peters, 289
Thompson v. Oklahoma
O'Connor, Sandra Day, 1798–99
Scalia, Antonin, 1798, 1799
Thorington v. Smith
Chase, Salmon P., 564
Thornburg v. American College of Obstetricians and Gynecologists
Blackmun, Harry A., 1616, 1679
Burger, Warren E., 1483–84
O'Connor, Sandra Day, 1616, 1679
Rehnquist, William H., 1679
White, Byron R., 1601, 1679
Thornburg v. Gingles
Brennan, William J., 1541
Thornhill v. Alabama
Hughes, Charles Evans, 957
McReynolds, James C., 1016
Murphy, Frank, 1260
Reed, Stanley, 1190

U

V

W

White, Byron R. (cont.)

Franklyn v. Gwinett County Public Schools, 1598
Franklyn v. Lynaugh, 1592
Fullilove v. Klutznick, 1598
Furman v. Georgia, 1591
Gaffney v. Cummings, 1596
Garrity v. New Jersey, 1582
Gertz v. Robert Welch, Inc., 1593, 1594
Gibson v. Florida Legislative Investigation Committee, 1581
Goss v. Lopez, 1599
Graham v. Collins, 1592
Gravel v. United States, 1587
Gregg v. Georgia, 1565, 1591
Harmelin v. Michigan, 1591
Harper & Row Publishers, Inc. v. Nation Enterprises, 1596
Harris v. McRae, 1624
Helling v. McKinney, 1600
Hicks v. Miranda, 1600
Hunter v. Erickson, 1583
Idaho v. Wright, 1781
Illinois Brick Co. v. Illinois, 1602
Imbler v. Pachtman, 1601
Ingraham v. Wright, 1599
I.N.S. v. Chadha, 1603
International Society for Krishna Consciousness, Inc. v. Lee, 1855
Island Trees Board of Education v. Pico, 1590–92
Jackson v. Denno, 1583
Jacobson v. United States, 1826
Johnson v. Louisiana, 1590
Johnson v. Transportation Agency, Santa Clara County, 1680, 1795
Johnson v. Zerbst, 1703
Jones v. Hildebrandt, 1601
Keeney v. Tamayo-Reyes, 1826, 1827
Keyes v. Denver School District No. 1, 1582
Kirkpatrick v. Preisler, 1597
Kremer v. Chemical Construction Corp., 1600–1601
Lamb's Chapel v. Center Moriches Union Free School District, 1595
Lankford v. Idaho, 1816
Lechmere v. National Labor Relations Board, 1852
Lee v. International Society for Krishna Consciousness, Inc., 1822, 1855
Lee v. Weisman, 1823, 1855, 1856
Lugar v. Edmondson Oil Co., Inc., 1600
McMann v. Richardson, 1584
Malloy v. Hogan, 1581
Mancuse v. DeForte, 1588
Massiah v. United States, 1581
Masson v. New Yorker Magazine, 1594
Maynard v. Cartwright, 1592
Meacham v. Fano, 1591

Memoirs v. Massachusetts, 1582, 1593
Metro Broadcasting, Inc. v. F.C.C., 1598
Metromedia, Inc. v. City of San Diego, 1595
Metropolitan Washington Airports Authority v. Citizens for the Abatement of Airport Noise, Inc., 1603
Milkovich v. Lorrain Journal, 1594
Miller v. California, 1593
Milliken v. Bradley, 1597
Miranda v. Arizona, 1582
Missouri v. Jenkins, 1598
Minnesota v. Dickerson, 1589
Montanye v. Haymes, 1591
Moore v. City of East Cleveland, 1602
Morgan v. Illinois, 1592, 1826, 1847
Morris v. Board of Estimate, 1597
NAACP v. Button, 1581
New York v. United States, 1602
New York Times v. Sullivan, 1593
New York Times v. United States, 1588, 1594–95
Nixon v. Fitzgerald, 1600
Northern Pipeline Construction Co. v. Marathon Pipeline Co., 1602
obscenity cases, 1592–93
O'Callahan v. Parker, 1583
O'Connor v. Ortega, 1589
Oestereich v. Selective Service System, 1583
O'Shea v. Littleton, 1600
Palmer v. Thompson, 1598
Paris Adult Theatre v. Slaton, 1593
Parker v. North Carolina, 1584
Pennsylvania v. Delaware Valley Citizens' Council for Clean Air, 1601
Penry v. Lynaugh, 1800
Philadelphia Newspapers, Inc. v. Hepps, 1594
Planned Parenthood of Southeastern Pennsylvania v. Casey, 1601, 1754, 1802, 1825, 1855, 1861
Pocunier v. Navarette, 1600
Pulley v. Harris, 1592
reapportionment cases, 1596–97
Regents of the University of California v. Bakke, 1599
Reitman v. Mulkey, 1583
Reynolds v. Sims, 1597
Robinson v. California, 1580–81
Rockefeller v. Wells, 1597
Roe v. Wade, 1483, 1601, 1861
Rogers v. Lodge, 1599
Rosenbloom v. Metromedia, 1593
San Antonio Independent School District v. Rodriguez, 1598
Schad v. Arizona, 1592
Schneider v. Rusk, 1581
See v. City of Seattle, 1583, 1588
Segura v. United States, 1589
Shaw v. Reno, 1599
Soldal v. Cook County, 1589